HUMAN RIGHTS FOR PRAGMATISTS

HUMAN RIGHTS AND CRIMES
AGAINST HUMANITY

Eric D. Weitz, Series Editor

Human Rights for Pragmatists

SOCIAL POWER IN MODERN TIMES

JACK SNYDER

PRINCETON UNIVERSITY PRESS

PRINCETON & OXFORD

Published by Princeton University Press
41 William Street, Princeton, New Jersey 08540
99 Banbury Road, Oxford OX2 6JX

press.princeton.edu

First paperback printing, 2024
Paper ISBN 978-0-691-23155-6
Cloth ISBN 978-0-691-23154-9
ISBN (e-book) 978-0-691-23153-2
LCCN: 2022507171

British Library Cataloging-in-Publication Data is available

Editorial: Bridget Flannery-McCoy and Alena Chekanov
Jacket/Cover Design: Pamela L. Schnitter
Production: Erin Suydam
Publicity: Kate Hensley and James Schneider (US) and Kathryn Stevens (UK)
Copyeditor: Melanie Mallon

Jacket/Cover Art: Thomas Shanahan / iStock

This book has been composed in Arno

CONTENTS

PREFACE AND ACKNOWLEDGMENTS

THE VIRTUES of human rights are commonly seen as self-evident and sacred. But sometimes the exercise of rights, even worthy ones, leads to disastrous outcomes. The constitutionally protected right to unfettered freedom of speech stoked a viral myth that the 2020 US presidential election had been stolen from Donald Trump, inciting an insurrection at the US Capitol. Religious rights are invoked to justify discrimination. Cultural rights are invoked to justify the abuse of women and children. Rights claims need to be evaluated in terms of their consequences.

In this book, I examine how human rights support a whole social system that sustains beneficial outcomes. Over the long haul, societies that generally comply with the principles laid out in the Universal Declaration of Human Rights achieve better outcomes in terms of social peace, political stability, and economic performance than societies that routinely violate those rights. Social systems based on human rights pass the pragmatic test of superior results.

This track record is a justification neither for complacency nor for anxious hand-wringing over occasional setbacks to the liberal rights project. At the end of the Cold War, when I began three decades of research on democratization and rights, it seemed that liberal democracy had decisively defeated the rival social systems of fascist nationalism and totalitarian communism. Triumphalism was in vogue. In that period my research could be called conditionally contrarian.

My coauthors Edward Mansfield, Karen Ballentine, and I warned that the absence of war among mature democracies did not mean that countries just beginning to experiment with competitive elections would necessarily be peaceful and rights respecting, especially if they lacked institutions of accountable government and a constructive marketplace of ideas. Later, my coauthor Dawn Brancati and I wrote about the danger of pushing for early postconflict elections before disarming belligerents and reforming administrative institutions.

A second conditionally contrarian project was a series of articles in the early 2000s on transitional justice with Leslie Vinjamuri. We questioned the untested claims that "ending impunity" by holding trials for perpetrators of atrocities would deter future crimes and strengthen the rule of law and democracy. We found that trade-offs between peace and justice were sometimes acute. In post-conflict and postauthoritarian regimes where spoilers maintained significant power and legal systems were weak, trials almost never produced the outcomes that their proponents hoped for, and amnesty often fared better.

After the rise of illiberal populisms and authoritarian Chinese technocracy, conventional wisdom has flipped from liberal triumphalism to the fear that the liberal system is running out of steam. People have increasingly come to believe that the aspiration to spread democracy and human rights should be scaled back in resignation to a new game based on national interests and expedient deal making.

This swing of the pendulum risks going too far. As conventional wisdom has flipped, what it means to be a conditional contrarian has flipped along with it. Pragmatism should be considered not an alternative to the rights-based order, but rather a tool for evaluating its performance and designing its strategies. In this changed setting, I wrote articles arguing that rights-based liberalism still had a far better track record than any competing model of modern society, notwithstanding the unconsolidated Chinese economic successes that the liberal international order had made possible. Democracy's fixable problem is that unregulated forms of liberalism—libertarian economics and free-speech absolutism—have thrown away the pragmatic steering mechanisms that were designed to keep rights-based societies on a constructive path.

This book is an attempt to integrate these pragmatic arguments in a social power theory of the role of human rights in making modernity work. I emphasize the strategies that can successfully advance the rights project. I am indebted first to these several coauthors who played central roles in shaping my thinking at every step of this evolution. I have drawn on their contributions wherever I discuss institutional capacity and the sequencing of reforms, especially in chapters 4 and 7.

Those efforts left plenty of tasks uncompleted. Ever since Ballentine and I published "Nationalism and the Marketplace of Ideas" in 1996, I have wanted to test in a more ambitious way the liberal assumptions about mechanisms connecting increases in media freedom to consequences for peace, human rights, and democracy. Notwithstanding the stack of classic political theory writing by such luminaries as John Milton, John Stuart Mill, and Jürgen

Habermas, the systematic empirical work on this topic is vanishingly small. After two decades of false starts, my Columbia colleague Tamar Mitts came to the rescue, training and working with our able researcher China Braekman to marshal systematic evidence on those liberal hypotheses and our own arguments about the regulation of the marketplace of ideas through constructive media institutions. This work is in chapter 7 and its appendix. In the course of this effort, I learned a great deal from many conversations with journalism colleagues Nicholas Lemann, Anne Nelson, and Alexander Stille.

I also owe many intellectual and personal debts to the vibrant cohort of international relations scholars who study political psychology, which is the theoretical foundation for chapter 8 on backlash against human rights shaming. I learned the psychology of decision making as an undergraduate from the late, brilliant John Steinbruner. As a grad student my quasi-Talmudic marginal annotations crammed every inch of white space on the pages of Bob Jervis's *Perception and Misperception in International Politics*. Although I often teach this material, I've never used psychology as the focal point for a whole paper until now. I relied on a team of experts to help me with that chapter: Jervis, Rose McDermott, Jon Mercer, and Keren Yarhi-Milo.

Another subject on which I push the limits of my accustomed expertise is China. Thomas Christensen, Andrew Nathan, and Susan Shirk were kind enough to let me know which of my conjectures might be on target and which not. I owe a special debt to Professor Yu Tiejun of Peking University, whose questions while translating *Myths of Empire* into Chinese sometimes probed more deeply into subtle points than had my original text. Tiejun also did me the huge service of connecting me to numerous interview subjects in Beijing. Other learning opportunities about China arose during several trips to Hong Kong, including visits to review the distinguished Government Department of the Chinese University of Hong Kong, which educated countless community activists and introduced generations of students to John Stuart Mill. I am grateful to Michael Davis, Courtney Fung, Enze Han, Victoria Hui, and Kellee Tsai for sharing insights and facilitating those occasions.

Many colleagues at Human Rights Watch, Freedom House, the Open Society Foundations, and PEN—Aryeh Neier, Kenneth Roth, Leonard Benardo, Sandra Coliver, Rachel Denber, Richard Dicker, Karin Karlekar, Suzanne Nossel, Dinah PoKempner, Nate Schenkkan, Sarah Leah Whitson, and others—went above and beyond in inviting me to present chapters at their organizations and accepting my invitations to speak at Columbia. Although I repeatedly fence with Neier's writings in this book, I consider him a world historical figure of penetrating insight and (yes) unique pragmatic impact, contributing immeasurably to the advancement of human rights.

Although this book is a work of synthesis, not of field research, I did travel to some front lines of the struggle for human rights in the Global South and conducted interviews there. Notwithstanding my argument that some places still have much pragmatic work to do in establishing the preconditions for rights, this does not mean that I don't admire the aspirations for rights of the grassroots of civil society there. I marched with cheerful, admirable, banner-carrying Burmese community and labor groups on the one day of the year that the junta allowed them to pay their respects at the mausoleum of General Aung San, father of his country and of Nobel Prize–winner Aung San Suu Kyi. We braved the monsoon and the sheepish army privates, who carried assault rifles and borrowed pink and purple umbrellas while lining our Yangon parade route. As a pragmatist, when I arrived in Jakarta, Indonesia, in July 2001, I also appreciated the differently motivated mass deployment of well-behaved troops enforcing the contested but legitimate election of President Megawati Sukarnoputri. (If only we had had some of them at the Capitol on January 6.) Most unexpectedly, I also admired the smart, feisty, modernizing, Erdogan-supporting, wealthy wives of pious businessmen who had set up a "human rights institute" in conservative Konya, Turkey. They aimed to promote government funding of child care for working women and demanded recompense for lost opportunities for women's education and employment due to discriminatory headscarf bans under former secular regimes.

At Columbia, my colleagues Zori Barkan, Alex Cooley, Yasmine Ergas, Andy Nathan, and Tonya Putnam provided a lively and congenial human rights community. During the long gestation of this book, amazing Columbia PhD students—Fiona Adamson, Hadas Aron, Dana Burde, Bruce Cronin, Kate Cronin-Furman, Shareen Hertel, Sarah Khan, Adrienne LeBas, Summer Lindsey, Sarah Mendelson, Lara Nettelfield, Dafna Hochman Rand, Thania Sanchez, Stephanie Schwartz, Michelle Sieff, Leslie Vinjamuri, and Rachel Wahl (sitting in with us from NYU)—taught me about human rights, transitional justice, humanitarianism, and democratization. These PhDs' job of educating me is never-ending: Cronin-Furman and Vinjamuri organized a globe-spanning virtual book manuscript conference that included penetrating commentary from Adamson, Michael Barnett, Anthony Dworkin, Steve Hopgood, Milli Lake, Sarah Nouwen, Christian Reus-Smit, Ruti Teitel, Lisa Vanhala, and Jennifer Welsh. Jeffry Frieden, a Columbia PhD of an earlier vintage, corrected some of my loose writing about political economy. Columbia's

University Seminar on Human Rights provided opportunities for feedback on several chapters. Just up the street, the CCNY human rights seminar organized by Rajan Menon and Eric Weitz provided feedback on chapter 9. Research assistants Elena Barham, Laetitia Commanay, Dylan Groves, Jenny Jun, Abigail Kleiman, Abigail Melbourne, and Urte Peteris contributed ideas and research, often under difficult pandemic conditions. Another learning experience, hosted by Ingrid Gerstmann and the staff of Columbia's Saltzman Institute, was the authors' conference for *Human Rights Futures*, coedited with Hopgood and Vinjamuri, which included lively debates among such diverse contributors as Geoff Dancy, Hertel, Sam Moyn, Kathryn Sikkink, Beth Simmons, and our commentator Peter Katzenstein. The book in your hands was read in its entirety by Gary Bass, who demonstrated not only his encyclopedic knowledge and deep insight into its subject matter, but also his finely tuned sense of how readers would react to nuances of tone, style, and humor. Because of him, you are spared the "hallelujah" joke. Thomas Lebien, an editorial whiz at Moon & Company, gave presentational advice on the whole book and taught me things about writing and reading that I never knew. Other key input on the chapters and papers that preceded them came from Amitav Acharya, Sheri Berman, Vince Blasi, Agnès Callamard, Allison Carnegie, Sumit Ganguly, Elisabeth Hurd, Sally Engle Merry, David Pozen, Thomas Risse, Bob Shapiro, and Bettina Shell-Duncan. I am grateful for financial support from the Carnegie Corporation of New York and from Columbia University.

A side benefit of my research has been that my wife, Debra Rawlins, got so interested in wars, empires, and German history that she took courses to get a second opinion on those subjects. She read the biography of Carl von Clausewitz's wife, Marie, who she was pleased to learn played a significant role kibitzing on and editing the classic *On War*.

Having benefited from the wisdom of Bob Jervis as my mentor throughout my career, I want to take this opportunity to acknowledge him as the unparalleled role model of both principle and pragmatism in all aspects of scholarship and life.

This book is dedicated to the memory of my mother, Irene Snyder, who practiced pragmatic humanitarianism as a nurse, and whose ancestors were pacifists, honest capitalists, and seekers of religious freedom.

Jack Snyder
New York, NY
July 1, 2021

HUMAN RIGHTS FOR PRAGMATISTS

1

Power Leads, Rights Follow

HISTORICAL ADVANCES of human rights since the Reformation and the Enlightenment have always depended on the rising social power of the people who benefit from those rights. These successes have been based on a new way of organizing society. Boiled down to its essence, the path to human rights is a journey from personalistic social relationships based on favoritism toward the individual right to equal treatment according to impersonal rules. The success of this revolutionary system depends on the power of its core supporters, the pragmatism with which they advance toward their goals, and the persuasiveness of their ideas to those who remain ambivalent. Victories for rights have always fused power, self-interest, and principle.

The battle to establish the social order based on rights is both very old and very new, and remains only half won. The early prehistory of rights gained impetus from the increase of trade among the townspeople of northern Europe, who challenged aristocratic privileges constraining commerce and labor, and whose Protestant Reformation proclaimed the right of all believers to read the Bible in their vernacular languages.[1] The development of commercial society created powerful constituencies for due process of law to protect property, regulate contracts, guarantee the free flow of speech and information (the shipping news vital to their livelihoods), and to protect individuals, including wealthy religious dissenters, against abuses by authorities.[2] The expansion of literacy and commerce gave educated, industrious subjects greater bargaining leverage against their kings. This made plausible the idea of national self-determination of the "chosen people" through sometimes orderly, sometimes revolutionary processes of accountability.[3] Later, industrialization and the organization of trade unions provided clout behind demands for economic, social, and labor rights for the working class.[4]

Setbacks to rights have happened when the underpinnings of the social power of rights beneficiaries have come unglued. The worst historic setback to the world's rights project occurred in the first half of the twentieth century, when structural flaws in the global economy undermined the still-shaky, rights-expanding coalitions of export industry and labor in Weimar Germany and Taisho Japan.[5] This shift in power and interests created an opening for a rights-hostile mass politics of militarized nationalism in these two great powers. After 1945 those flaws in the liberal system were repaired with the help of Keynesian tools of economic management and the Bretton Woods international economic institutions. These pragmatic adjustments helped the liberal rights project get back on track with the Universal Declaration of Human Rights and the consolidation of democratic welfare states in the non-Communist great powers. The eventual collapse of the Soviet Union seemed to put the icing on the liberal cake, the crucial ingredient of which was human rights.

This period of liberal near-hegemony and great ambitions for the global human rights movement turned out to be short-lived. The social power base on which it rested eroded, while its detractors and free riders grew in strength and assertiveness.[6] Mainstream ruling coalitions frayed in the wealthy democracies as some of their key support constituencies decided that liberal business as usual—including the worldwide promotion of human rights, democracy, and free trade—was not in their immediate interest. Liberal failures to solve problems and serve tangible interests piled up: the world financial crisis of 2008, increased economic inequality, deindustrialization in struggling communities, the inability to integrate Muslim immigrants into European society, America's failed nation-building wars abroad, and the mismanagement of the coronavirus pandemic.

These repeated shortcomings convinced critics on the left and the right that the core systems of liberalism—its markets, institutions of representative government, courts, and media—were broken or somehow rigged against the people to whom they were meant to be accountable. Some formerly mainstream progressive constituencies, including the ethnic majority working class, increasingly backed sharp limits on refugees and immigration, suppression of voting by minorities, economic protectionism, torture of suspected terrorists, and populist political candidates, especially those on the nationalist right. Astonishing proportions of young adults, especially in the United States, told pollsters it doesn't matter if their country is a democracy.[7]

Ideological trends within the liberal rights camp have contributed to this crisis. Economic libertarians, who tout the unfettered freedoms of global capital, have relentlessly undermined the regulatory structures that stabilized liberal markets and media, hollowing out the pragmatic class compromise of the welfare state. These were sins of commission, whereas the shortcomings of the liberal human rights movement were mainly sins of omission. Trying to maintain an unconvincingly apolitical façade, rights activists adopted a stance of legalism, moralism, and idealistic universalism that distanced them from an earlier, more successful tradition of pragmatic progressive reform. This wariness toward pragmatism has limited the power of the human rights message at a moment of precarity not only for the rights movement but for the liberal project as a whole.

The Argument of the Book: The Pragmatic Path to Rights in Modern Times

Human rights are central to how the modern social system works. Thinking about them in a narrower way—as just ethics or law, or as an isolated niche endeavor—misses the point and leads practical recommendations astray.[8]

The purpose of this book is to advance a theory of human rights that places them in their broad social, political, and economic context. Chapters explore their historical development, their contemporary manifestation in diverse issue areas, and their tailoring for diverse local settings. The goal is both to understand the rights systems that actually exist and to prescribe how to move the rights project forward. These prescriptions are pragmatic in the sense that they apply outcome-oriented criteria for judging the appropriateness of tactics for advancing human rights, taking into account short-term considerations of power and interest as well as longer term effects on the power of pro-rights coalitions and the institutional entrenchment of a rights-based system. Some prescriptions are directed to the community of human rights activists and to aspiring activists who are training to join that community. Most, however, are directed to anyone in any country—students, scholars, policy makers, reformers in the opposition, journalists, businesspeople, community organizers, citizens—who seeks a pragmatic, results-oriented yet wide-angle view of problems of human rights.

My guiding hypotheses are that rights thrive (1) when the prevailing mode of social organization is no longer based on repression and favoritism but has evolved toward social relations among individuals based on impersonal rules of equal treatment, (2) when rights serve the interest of a dominant coalition, and when they are stabilized by (3) implementing institutions and

(4) a locally persuasive ideology. This book is an attempt to show in general and for specific issues and national contexts how these conditions come about. Thus, a fifth hypothesis: (5) in sequencing the shift to a rights-based society, power and politics lead, and rights follow. In addition to elaborating this argument, I also argue that the mainstream approach to rights activism and scholarship has not adequately taken these points into account and is in trouble because of it.

Each of these five hypotheses stipulates a logic of the emergence and success of the rights project, as well as the corresponding logic of barriers to its success. The first hypothesis proposes that rights provide significant functional advantages for the modern mode of production and governance. I define modernity as a system that sustains economic growth through technological innovation and achieves political stability. I treat as an empirical question what institutions and ideas are used to achieve that stable outcome. The rights-based liberal form of modernity depends on impersonal social relations based on impartial rules and free contracts enforced by accountable political authority. The emergence and success of the rights program corresponds with the development of that modern mode, as it replaces the traditional mode of social order based on personalistic social relations, patronage in economic exchange, and favoritism in the arbitrary exercise of authority.

Struggles between rights-based and favoritism-based systems of social order fill the long periods of transition between tradition and modernity. These struggles destroy the supports of the old order and create the structural preconditions for the modern system to function. While economic development has tended over the long run to create a social constituency for expanding the rights-based order, this trend has by no means been a smoothly linear progression.[9] Ambivalent interests of rising constituencies and shifting alliances between rising and traditional elites have often sent liberal rights down a detour of "two steps forward, one step back." When societies first embark on the process of modern development, illiberal technocratic systems sometimes succeed in building some precursors of modernity, but their internal contradictions have so far prevented them from sustaining economic success and political stability. To succeed, they have had to liberalize, or else they get stuck in the middle-income trap, collapse from their inefficiencies, or flame out from the volatile politics that accompanies illiberal modernization.

The second hypothesis holds that rights prevail when they serve the interests of the dominant political coalition. The core groups of a successful rights-seeking coalition define rights in a way that serves their own interests, advancing their economic power and personal security. To succeed, their rights project must serve the interests of the majority of the society or those that control the preponderance of social resources. To win such preponderance and to gain acquiescence from those who might be indifferent or opposed to rights, bargaining and side payments among diverse interests are necessary. To neutralize potential spoilers, groups that embody the logic of the modern rights-based system normally need to bargain with still-powerful remnants of the old favoritism-based regime. Even when many of the structural facilitating conditions for a rights-based order are in place, a bungled coalition strategy can produce a setback for the rights project. While the particulars of a pro-rights coalition strategy vary with local conditions, a rule of thumb is to avoid alignments based on exclusionary social identities such as ethnicity and aim instead for inclusive groups that draw in middle and working classes that cut across cultural identities. In forging a powerful coalition, rights pragmatism provides a direction-finding compass, not an invariant recipe.

The third hypothesis posits that the emergence and stabilization of the rights-based system and the empowering of its dominant coalition depend on the creation of impartial institutions to carry out its functions and enforce its rules. These must be strong institutions in the sense that their rules shape people's expectations of everyone else's behavior. If rights-supportive institutions are weak, existing only on "parchment," expectations will revert to the habit of coordinating around the personalistic norms of relations based on patronage, discrimination, corruption, and the arbitrary use of coercive power. In the absence of effective rights-based institutions, these traditional default behaviors are locked in place by decentralized routines that sustain all manner of abuses, ranging from child marriage to ethnic cleansing. Creating effective institutions is a step-by-step process in which incentives and performance must align with power and interests at every step along the way. Sometimes effective institutions can be formed by repurposing and making more inclusive the rule-based institutions that had previously stabilized relations among elite groups in premodern or early modern society.[10]

The fourth hypothesis proposes that a successful rights system depends on the promotion of a locally persuasive ideology and culture. The main advocate for rights-based norms is the powerful group that will benefit most from their adoption and from the weakening of traditional favoritism. This advocacy must necessarily begin in an aspirational mode in an attempt to persuade other groups of the benefit of rights. In justifying the new normative approach, advocates must criticize to some degree the unfairness and inefficiency of traditional social practices, but successful advocates also typically try to adapt a usable normative legacy of religion or folk practices to modern purposes. Just as coalition building and institution building require compromise with and adaptation to the remnants of the old order, so too does rights ideology require the integration of modern rights ideas and traditional notions of virtue through a cultural revitalization movement.[11] Failure to adapt rights ideas to the local cultural idiom plays into the hands of traditional cultural elites who can characterize modern rights as the leading edge of an imperialist conspiracy.

The fifth hypothesis, on sequencing, envisions that all four elements—a rights-based mode of production and political relations, groups and coalitions benefiting from rights, institutions based on these practices, and ideologies justifying them—will emerge partially and gradually in the course of the transition out of the traditional system and toward the hegemony of the rights-based system. Just as mainstream human rights theory posits a norms cascade that begins with normative persuasion and culminates in institutionalization and internalization, I posit a pragmatic counterpart that begins with incipient changes in the structural organization of society, proceeds through shifts in social power and coalitions, solidifies rights in the course of struggles to build enabling institutions, and legitimates rights through a locally persuasive ideology.[12] This can be an iterative process, punctuated by resistance from remnants of the old regime and setbacks at the hands of those who exploit a predatory equilibrium of partial reform. Details of sequencing vary with local conditions.

An important question for pragmatic proponents of rights is when to begin treating rights as if they are obligatory for the whole society rather than just aspirational. The general pragmatic guideline for finessing that threshold recommends "power first, rights follow." Jumping the gun increases the likelihood of triggering and institutionalizing backlash that leaves the rights project more distant from its goal.

A related sequencing question is whether the spread of a rights-based order must follow the same sequence and strategies as the original creation of that order. For example, even if one accepts that the background conditions of modern society were essential to the emergence of rights-based societies in Europe and North America, must other national societies likewise undergo the same processes of modernization before rights can take root, or can they skip over the development of those facilitating conditions, climbing directly up the institutional and ideological scaffolding already constructed by the originators? For the most part, the analysis presented here warns against counting on such shortcuts to a rights-based society. The central role of the nation-state in defining and realizing rights cannot be effectively circumvented by transnational or supranational routes.

Alternative Views of Human Rights Futures

In the course of developing these arguments, I engage with important contrary views, some doubting the centrality of rights to successful modernity, others agreeing with the central role of rights but disagreeing about how to bring about their supremacy.

On one hand, some question the notion that liberal systems based on rights have major advantages in producing the benefits of wealth and stability in modern conditions. To them, China's recent successes suggest that a durable modern order can be constructed on the foundation of technocratic competence without any functional need for rights, liberal legality, or democratic accountability. Others question whether any single model of modernity is likely to prevail given the cultural, institutional, and historical diversity of the world's civilizations. In such a world, pragmatism might require a live-and-let-live transactional approach to international relations, not the imposition of universalistic standards. They point to the recurrent contradictions within liberalism and doubt that it has a distinctive advantage in the competition among multiple modernities.

On the other hand, mainstream human rights activists claim that their accustomed methods have been succeeding in spreading human rights norms and improving rights outcomes. Legalism, moralism, and universalism done the right way *are* effective and pragmatic, they say. At the same time, a quite different brand of rights idealists, the libertarians, extol the expansion of human freedom by means of the invisible hand of global market competition and free speech absolutism on global social media. They are skeptical of the need for pragmatically regulating the freedom of economic action and of speech.

These debates appear intermittently throughout the book. Here I introduce my general view of these opposing claims.

Successful Technocratic Modernity without Rights?

Classic social theory posits two images of the fundamental nature of the transition to modern society. The one that I rely on, anchored in the approach of Emile Durkheim and Ferdinand Tönnies, emphasizes the shift from homogeneous communities with little differentiation of individuals' social roles to societies based on a complex division of labor held together by rule-governed contracts in an inclusive state.[13] The other, based on one strand of the work of Max Weber, emphasizes the disenchantment of the world from religion and magic, and its rationalization through science, technology, and rational rules imposed by the "iron cage" of bureaucracy.[14] Following the logic of the first approach, liberal democratic capitalism based on individual rights seems like a plausible destination. Following the logic of the second, Chinese-style authoritarian technocracy captures the essence of its vision of modernity quite well.

While social science can't predict the future, it can draw inferences from the past. As of 1989, Francis Fukuyama argued that the final verdict of history had come in, and it showed that rights-based liberal societies had decisively won the tournament against all authoritarian alternatives.[15] The Soviet experiment had proved that central planning was no match for liberal market economies. German and Japanese militarized, nationalist authoritarianisms—despite their technological and organizational prowess—had proved politically and ideologically self-destructive. Only liberalism was left standing. But the economic rise of China, the apparent cohesiveness of its steely regime, and the chilling efficiency of its suppression of Uyghur Muslims, Hong Kong democrats, and the coronavirus has convinced many that the iron cage of authoritarian modernity is still very much in the game. Can it succeed where other authoritarian modernities have failed so spectacularly?

Setting aside a handful of petrostates and the city-state of Singapore, which are like specialized companies dependent on the liberal international economy, it remains true that no country has ever progressed beyond the middle-income barrier without adopting the full set of liberal civic rights.[16] For countries below one-fourth of US per capita income, democracy per se makes no difference in the likelihood of economic growth. In this cohort, having strong institutions relative to one's per-capita-income peer group helps growth, but these institutions do not need to be liberal. The reason is that authoritarian late developers with reserves of cheap labor and fallow resources can exploit the "advantages of backwardness" to commandeer factors of production in a project of forced-draft accumulation of capital, as Stalin did in the first two Five-Year Plans.[17] In more recent times, analogous strategies of state-led development have been able to accelerate even faster by plugging into the globalized liberal system of trade and finance. But once the backward economy matures, further growth depends on shifting from the marshaling of new factors of production to the more efficient use of factors that are already in use. Experience to date shows that this can occur only when a country adopts liberal-style institutions making for more efficient capital and labor markets, dramatically curtailing corruption, and exposing political authorities to accountability through free speech and democratic political participation.[18]

The question remains whether the technocratic innovations of China, Singapore, or other illiberal or shallowly liberal states are discovering a way out of these contradictions without adopting fully liberal reforms, as Japan, South Korea, and Taiwan did.[19] China stands well below the benchmark of one-fourth US per capita income, measured by the method used for developed economies.[20] As its wealth has risen, its World Bank measure of institutional quality compared to its income peer group has declined. Commentators see signs that the middle-income trap is setting in: slowing growth despite over-investment, dramatic declines in the productivity of capital, and debt bubbles.[21] Even if nonliberal forms of transparency and participatory consultation would be sufficient to sustain efficient growth, China has moved to limit such experiments in the Xi Jinping era.[22] What this portends for human rights and democracy in such regimes, and pragmatic strategies for promoting them, is taken up in chapter 5.

Contradictions within Liberalism and Their Pragmatic Remedy

Even if authoritarian versions of modernity do have fatal flaws, liberalism too has internal contradictions, or at least tensions, which can undermine its stability in transitional states and even in established democracies.[23] Some of these tensions have become acute, producing the sense that liberalism may be unable to manage them.

At the most general level, liberalism's contemporary contradictions are rooted in the tension between individual liberty and the civic cooperation that is needed to make its inclusive, rule-based systems function. In economic policy, communications media, and even public health, libertarian tendencies have promoted the idea that an unfettered invisible hand of rational self-interest will reconcile everyone's sovereign individualism with the public good. A deregulated global economy, absolute freedom of speech on social media, and the God-given right not to wear a mask in a pandemic have pushed that conjecture to the limit. The result has shown that the success of liberalism depends on the *visible* hand of collective, rule-based, democratically accountable regulation of individualistic interactions and a degree of informed deference to the professional expertise of journalists and scientists. Finding a workable balance between individual rights and their public regulation is a main theme of this book, especially chapter 7 on media freedom.

Liberalism's endemic tension between liberty and equality has sharpened with the growth of economic inequality in some liberal capitalist democracies. Individual liberty requires political equality insofar as a liberal system is based on equality before the law and the universal right to equal political participation. And yet exercising the liberty to pursue a personal life plan in which happiness is based on the freedom to accumulate property can produce gross economic inequalities that place liberal democracy under stress.[24]

This tension has heightened liberalism's latent contradiction between free markets and mass democratic participation. Karl Polanyi's 1944 classic, *The Great Transformation*, argued that the rise of populist fascism had stemmed from the incompatibility between free markets regulated by the invisible hand of the gold standard and mass political participation by the losers from cruelly automatic market adjustments.[25] In contemporary times, populist nationalism similarly expresses the demand for national political control over domestic markets and borders in the face of socially disruptive underregulated flows of capital and labor. As in the interwar period, there is a mismatch between the unaccountability of international markets and the fact that institutions of democratic accountability exist only at the national level. This loads the dice in favor of nationalist forms of remedy.[26]

The people of the illiberal great powers in Polanyi's day demanded that their states protect them from the global systemic contradictions of liberal capitalism. To accomplish that, Germany and Japan chose strategies of military expansion to achieve direct autarkic control over resources and markets. This turned out to be a path to unconditional military defeat. In our own era, illiberal great powers likewise face serious challenges in finding a sustainable way to fit into the system of globalized liberal capitalism. Inequality, governance deficiencies, and corruption intensify when illiberal systems have one foot in the political economy of global capitalism and the other in the domestic political economy of traditional patronage relationships. Except for China, the economic boom of the rising BRICS countries (Brazil, Russia, India, China, South Africa) was brief, and even China is tapering off. Those who benefit from autocracy and corruption on the way up often succumb to the temptation to block essential reforms and play the nationalist card when economic complications arise.

This is creating an impasse in two senses: an international equipoise of power between liberal and illiberal states, and the domestic impasse inside unreformed rising powers that are heading into the middle-income trap. In the past, the outcome of such situations has depended heavily on how well the liberal powers have managed them. In the 1920s, the leading liberal states lacked the technical knowledge and the political support to create a system to solidify liberal rights-based regimes in rising illiberal or transitional states. After 1945, they did far better in creating a stable capitalist system with social welfare democracies at its core. The rise of "neoliberal" deregulated markets after 1980 weakened some of the stabilizing practices of the post-1945 system, contributing to the 2008 world financial crisis.[27] In the aftermath of 2008, some commentators still argued that "the system worked," but that conclusion seems more in doubt from a vantage point after the populist electoral surge of 2016–17.[28]

A solution will need to come not from illiberal states that take shortcuts on rule of law and human rights, but from the liberal states themselves. The latter are the states that have created the international order that illiberal powers are exploiting for their rise. The sometimes perverse incentives of this system are shaping many of the illiberal powers' central social, economic, and institutional features. For that reason, the liberal powers need to stabilize their system in a way that creates the right incentives for rising powers to liberalize.

Fortunately, the liberal tool kit already contains the solutions to Polanyi's conundrum. They have been used successfully before: politically regulated markets embedded in democratic social welfare states, using policy tools of Keynesian domestic economic management and Bretton Woods–style adjustment arrangements at the international level.[29] The growing contradictions in liberalism have been caused by the disembedding of markets for capital, goods, and labor from democratic control, and they can be fixed by redesigning the control mechanisms of social welfare democracy for adaptation to current conditions.

Human rights, including civil-political and economic-social rights, are central to the functioning of this system. Its market dimension requires stable and fair rights to property and contract. Its dimension of political accountability requires freedom of speech and assembly, democratic participation, and governance through institutions that regulate domestic and international markets and make them accountable to citizens. Both the market and the political dimensions rest on the impartial rule of law (not Chinese-style politicized rule by law).[30] Rights are not a sideshow to justice in the functional welfare state;

they are the keystone to all the elements that makes liberal modernity work.[31] No rights, no functioning modernity.

In pragmatic efforts to restabilize this system, the human rights movement will be on firm ground theoretically and tactically if it prioritizes the struggle against corruption and inequality. Not only do these issues resonate with the zeitgeist, they are anchored in the modernizing logic of the shift from clientelistic societies based on in-group favoritism to inclusive societies based on impartial rules. Corruption should be considered a human rights issue, as laid out in the 2005 UN Convention against Corruption, which has over 140 state signatories.[32] The nearly universal popularity of the anticorruption issue harbors great potential for human rights mobilization. The human rights movement has been relatively disengaged from these issues, which constitute a major missed opportunity when human rights are under duress. Recently, however, Kenneth Roth, the executive director of Human Rights Watch, has been more vocal in featuring corruption in his criticism of "zombie democracies."[33]

Are Legalism, Shaming, and Universalism Working?

In recent decades, the international human rights movement has played down the central role of political power and self-interest in advancing its cause, emphasizing instead themes of legalism, moralism, altruism, and universalism. I argue that this bias hinders the ability of the movement and its potential constituencies to mobilize effectively in defense of human rights at a critical time when opponents of rights are everywhere on the rise.

The mainstream community of nongovernmental human rights activists has developed a standard strategy that features formulating and publicizing human rights norms, codifying them in human rights treaties, persuading audiences to press states to ratify the treaties, institutionalizing laws and norms in domestic and international practices, and shaming and punishing violators.[34]

The blueprint for this strategy is in the preamble of the UN General Assembly's 1948 Universal Declaration of Human Rights, which claims the status of "a common standard of achievement for all peoples and all nations, to the end that every individual and every organ of society, keeping this Declaration constantly in mind, shall strive by teaching and education to promote respect for these rights and freedoms and by progressive measures, national and international, to secure their universal and effective recognition and observance."[35] Many of the loosely formulated aspirational rights listed in the UDHR were subsequently defined and codified in treaties such as the International Covenants on Civil and Political Rights and on Economic, Social and Cultural Rights.

Once aspirations, norms, and laws begin to take shape, activists seek to persuade more states and nonstate actors to ratify or endorse them, hoping to set off a "norms cascade," leading to a widespread social or legal consensus on a standard of appropriate behavior.[36] Treaty ratifiers who fail to live up to their commitments are "named and shamed" into compliance. In cases where claims for a consensus of right-thinking people can be made with some plausibility, even nonratifiers are shamed and pressured. A crucial second-order tactic is to shame powerful ratifiers, such as the governments of wealthy democratic great powers, into exerting diplomatic, legal, economic, or even military coercion against noncompliant norms outliers and cheap talkers.

Sometimes this approach can work. In an early poster case for this so-called boomerang model, Argentina's aggrieved Mothers of the Disappeared fed information to the New York–based NGO Americas Watch (a precursor of Human Rights Watch), which publicly pressured the US government to impose sanctions on the Argentine military junta and demanded trials of "big fish" generals once the regime fell.[37] This strategy got a lot of help from the fact that the incompetent junta had presided over the collapse of the national economy and lost a war that it started with Great Britain over who owned the Falkland Islands.

Sometimes the unbending, universalistic tactics of legalism and shaming can overreach and provoke sharp resistance. In the Argentina case, trials had to be called off when a tank army threatened a revolt to stop them. Sometimes, however, trials are not called off when threats loom. In the aftermath of ethnic slaughter in Bosnia, when pragmatists criticized Richard Goldstone, the war crimes prosecutor of the International Criminal Tribunal for the former Yugoslavia, for launching trials that risked provoking violent backlash from Serbian nationalists, he replied with the classic dictum, "Let justice be done, though the world perish."[38] Note, however, that while Goldstone gave no quarter to Serb war criminals who were outright spoilers, such as Ratko Mladic and Radovan Karadzic, he was careful to delay indicting Serb President Slobodan Milosevic, who was bargaining seriously with the US peace negotiator Richard Holbrooke.[39]

Human rights activists argue that their strict, unrelenting standards of accountability for violations are valid irrespective of whether they lead to successful results in the short term. Nonetheless, they do typically claim that the tactics of legalism, moralism, and universalism have been successful in improving human rights outcomes. In chapter 2, I examine the normative differences between my pragmatic outlook and the activists' more absolutist stance, but let's first review the empirical track record of mainstream efforts to advance the rights cause.

In the three decades since the collapse of communism, mainstream rights advocacy has enjoyed substantial public and private funding, the backing of all advanced democratic states and major international organizations, massive favorable media publicity, and ideological hegemony in liberal circles. It is a fair question to ask how well they have been doing. Some critics say not well: the mainstream approach is "utopian," having only a shallow impact and possibly heading toward its "endtimes."[40] Defenders of existing methods, in contrast, argue that there have been major successes in establishing norms and creating institutions, as well as steady if partial successes in achieving practical outcomes on the ground. What does the best research say?

Empirical research on human rights has flourished over the past two decades, moving from a productive early phase of empirical theory development into a more recent phase of sophisticated, multimethod research and debate among different theoretical approaches and research strategies.[41] Broad consensus exists among both critics and defenders of mainstream practices about the conditions that promote and hinder positive rights outcomes.

Quantitative studies report that two factors are the most important predictors of the quality of rights outcomes in a country: whether the country is at peace or at war, and how democratic the country is. Some might see the democracy finding as bordering on the circular, since most measures of democracy assume the existence of the civil liberties and legal apparatus that makes democracy possible. And so it is.[42] But many of the other strong findings about the correlates of good rights outcomes are either causes, attributes, or consequences of democracy. This suggests that the link between democracy and rights is not just a tautology but is based on a complex of mutually supporting causal factors that sustain rights outcomes. These include a reasonably high per capita income, which is the single strongest predictor of democracy. Also important is a fairly strong institutional capacity of the state, including an effective, impartial bureaucracy and strong representative and legal institutions. Also conducive to rights is a progressive, socially inclusive ruling coalition that is "on the left."[43]

Risk factors that harm rights also threaten democracy. Economic inequality undermines both rights and democracy.[44] A large population is likewise a risk factor for rights abuse, possibly because of the difficulty of democratically governing culturally diverse peoples in a single state.[45] Some findings suggest that there is "more murder in the middle": democratizing states endure similar levels of rights abuse to authoritarian states as a result of contentious mass mobilization in a context of weakly developed institutions for managing mass political participation. These studies find that any benefit to rights outcomes from democratization accrues only after passing a rather high threshold to nearly complete democracy.[46] Treaty signing and mainstream methods of legal and activist follow-up have their greatest benefit for rights improvement in these successfully democratizing states.[47]

These statistical results correlate fairly closely with the list of conditions that qualitative scholars say hinder typical strategies of rights promotion. They find that mainstream methods work less well in authoritarian regimes, in very weak and very strong states, in issue areas where violations are socially decentralized, and where the rights-abusing state enjoys popular support.[48]

Notwithstanding this consensus on the facilitating conditions for rights, there is much less consensus on the overall success of rights activism in improving rights outcomes. Critics of prevailing human rights strategies argue that most rights outcomes, defined in terms of treaty compliance, have not improved in recent decades despite the intense rhetoric and mobilization of the global rights movement.[49] Defenders of the movement's achievements argue that the apparent lack of progress is an optical illusion: improved data have turned up violations that previously would have gone unreported.[50] They also argue that it is too soon to judge the success of mainstream rights strategies, because strengthening global norms through persuasion and institutionalization is necessarily a gradual process. For example, despite the International Criminal Court's minimal conviction rate and Africa-dominated docket, they emphasize that the institutional base for future success has been established.[51]

There is only partial consensus about the effects of different tactics. Research suggests that mainstream rights approaches work well mainly in what might be called easy cases: countries that are already fairly democratic, have respectable administrative capacity, have somewhat independent courts, and tolerate robust activism by principled civil society groups.[52] There is little agreement, however, on the effects of different tactics in harder cases.

Many studies have attempted to identify the conditions in which shaming works, but with little convergence so far. Some studies find that shaming is often ineffective or even counterproductive, leading to backlash.[53] Emilie

Hafner-Burton, based on statistical findings and numerous brief illustrations, finds that shaming is generally correlated with improvements in political rights but not physical integrity rights. She concludes that denunciations can have a "whack-a-mole" effect, leading the abuser to shift from more visible repression to clandestine measures.[54] Other studies stress more positive findings, many of them trying to identify the conditions under which shaming is effective. Ann Marie Clark, illustrating her statistical study with the example of Indonesia, finds that shaming reduces rights abuse in countries that have ratified rights treaties, even if they are nondemocracies.[55] Another statistical study, by Amanda Murdie and David Davis, finds that shaming by human rights organizations improves rights outcomes if local activists are numerous and if foreign states echo the denunciations of the activists.[56]

This pattern of research findings suggests that there are four key barriers to improving rights using mainstream tactics, which correspond to four main arguments of my book. The first barrier is a set of structural factors that make a social or political situation impervious to solutions based on law, normative persuasion, shaming, and punishment. These techniques are unable to gain traction in conditions of war, anarchy, autocracy, dire poverty, illiteracy, institutional incapacity, and the absence of strong political coalitions that favor or benefit from human rights. The implication is that a preliminary step for rights improvements must be to create stronger facilitating conditions.

The second barrier, typically an outgrowth of such underlying structural problems, is the presence of powerful spoilers that have strategic reasons to resist human rights improvements because their power and their predatory economic methods rely on violence, repression, intimidation, corruption, and discrimination.[57] Insofar as some of these actors, such as warlords and criminal organizations, are purely strategic actors who are impervious to normative leverage, hardly any of the usual tactics of mainstream rights advocates carry much weight. Such spoilers must be forcefully defeated, politically isolated, or bargained with.

The third barrier is a set of decentralized social dilemmas in which established practices lock people into abusive patterns of behavior even when their self-defeating nature is widely understood. For example, situations of lawless anarchy or extreme resource scarcity compel individuals or groups to adopt aggressive and predatory behaviors in struggling for security and subsistence. Related to this, entrenched systems of corruption commonly compel the participation of individuals regardless of personal inclination; when "everybody does it," there is often no other way to accomplish a task.[58] This corresponds to another major argument of the book: human rights prevail when they are stabilized by effective implementing institutions that solve social dilemmas by reshaping incentives and reliably providing public goods.

The fourth barrier is resistance from illiberal, traditionalist, or communitarian norms competitors who can make persuasive appeals to constituencies that are skeptical of or threatened by human rights ideas. Cosmopolitan ideas coming from powerful liberal states, law-based institutions, and market-driven economic actors inherently challenge the worldviews and interests of religious actors, nationalists, tribal leaders, anti-imperialists, and patronage-based economic networks.[59] All such elites have at their disposal deeply embedded ideological tools and mass social constituencies that can be easily activated to resist outsiders' alien ideas that threaten established interests and folkways. Naming and shaming are likely to play directly into the hands of these forces of ideological resistance.

A common thread tying together these points is that insisting that people act based on the fiction that aspirational norms are actually in force misunderstands the problem and can aggravate abuse. Yet the mainstream approach often adopts this counterfactual stance, demanding that "what ought to be" should trump "what is." Instead, I argue that in sequencing the shift to a rights-based society, politics and power must lead, rights follow.

Plan of the Book and Standards of Evidence and Argument

This book is a work of synthesis, pulling together insights and evidence from diverse sources to show how human rights can become a reality in modern societies. The order of the chapters is designed to follow the logic of the five steps of my pragmatic theory: the emergence of favorable conditions for the system of impersonal social relations, bargaining among powerful self-interested coalitions, the institutionalization of rights, persuasion in the vernacular, and throughout the book, pragmatic sequencing of rights initiatives. Within each chapter, I flesh out the mechanisms that come into play in laying the foundation for human rights.

Chapter 2 accomplishes two framing tasks. First, it addresses readers who might think that a pragmatic theory of human rights is a contradiction in terms. When I told one of my research assistants that I wanted her to work with me on a book on a pragmatic approach to human rights, she was perplexed. She said, "I thought that human rights are by definition idealistic, not pragmatic." Activist exhortations could indeed create that impression.

The chapter begins by explaining how pragmatic philosophy applies to human rights.

Second, the chapter explains how rights emerged along with modernity. Drawing on the canon of historically grounded social theory, I argue that one does not need to see liberalism as the teleological end of history to understand the long-term functional advantages of rule-based individualism for modern social organization. I stress the difficulty with which the liberal system emerges, however, and the likelihood of failures and reversals on its path. I argue that a successful trajectory depends on facilitating conditions and advantageous sequences in development. In this contest, the winning system can still have flaws; it just needs to perform better than the menu of alternative models of society with which the system competes and cooperates at any given time.[60] I also argue that the necessary role of national self-determination in the realization of civic rights gives states rather than international bodies priority in the advancement of human rights.

Chapter 3 fleshes out all the building blocks of the social power theory of human rights, including its structural preconditions; the role of power, self-interest, and bargaining in the making of a pro-rights coalition; and its facilitating institutions and ideology. The chapter addresses how these mechanisms build on each other and how to sequence pragmatically the development of these facilitating conditions for rights. It also explains how and why the process proceeds from rights motivated by self-interest to more general conceptions of rights, including human rights. This happens, I argue, because general rules are functional to cooperation in complex systems and because generalized norms help persuade diverse groups to join in a broader, more powerful reform coalition.

Chapters 4 and 5 focus on the fraught process of moving across the threshold from a society based mainly on repression and patronage to one based on impartial rules for rights-based political participation and economic activity. Chapter 4 applies the theory laid out in chapters 2 and 3 to understanding political transitions from authoritarian to liberal regimes, with special attention to pragmatic designs for anticorruption reforms, accountability for the crimes of the old regime, and the first post-transition elections. Chapter 5 deploys the theory to illuminate the crucial role of human rights in shaping the politics of contemporary China's incomplete transition to a market economy.

Chapters 6 and 7 highlight the role of institutions in facilitating the advancement of rights. Chapter 6 argues that the contemporary human rights movement is weakened by its narrow view of civil society. The chapter shows the need for a mutually supportive tripod of complementary institutions to underpin a powerful coalition to push for human rights: not only elite human rights advocacy organizations, but also mass social movements and progressive political parties, all acting in concert. Chapter 7 corrals a sacred cow of the US human rights movement: free speech absolutism based on a widespread but unjustified understanding of the First Amendment. The benefits of free speech depend decisively on the journalistic and regulatory institutions that create forums to organize open discourse in a constructive way. Freedom of the press is the complementary but overlooked ingredient that is needed to produce the magic of the First Amendment.

Chapters 8 and 9 illustrate the need for human rights advocacy to undertake persuasion in the local vernacular. Chapter 8 takes on another sacred cow: the naming and shaming of rights violators. When outsiders denounce routine local practices as violations of universal rights, custodians of sacred values can readily mobilize mass support to protect their culture against imperialist meddling. The chapter draws on social psychology to propose pragmatic steps to promote better practices without triggering counterproductive backlash. Chapter 9 reviews a large body of research on the conditions that sustain female genital cutting, drawing out recommendations for combining more subtle persuasion with the creation of facilitating structural conditions for reform.

The empirical chapters are designed to demonstrate pragmatism's relevance across a broad range of major, contentious rights topics. These include topics most conducive to the view that "power leads, rights follow," such as bargaining with powerful spoilers during democratic transitions, but also cultural identity issues that might not seem like the easiest terrain for a pragmatic approach. The latter include the role of religion in mobilizing mass movements for social justice (chapter 6), community sensitivity over shame and status (chapter 8), and culturally entrenched practices affecting women's reproductive health (chapter 9).

Works like this one that attempt to synthesize arguments across a broad range of periods, locations, and issues are obligated to employ diverse strategies of evidence and inference. My standard for evaluating broad framing theories from the canon of historical sociology is whether they have generated an active empirical research program that demonstrates staying power in rigorous debates.[61] For generalizing applications of these theories across diverse thematic issue areas, the standard is demonstrating empirical reach without having to stretch the meaning of the core concepts.[62] For empirical illustrations of concepts, the standard is depicting the causal mechanism at work and variations in outcomes. For invoking secondhand statistical findings, the standard is the use of well-vetted sources and the acknowledgment of any significant contrary findings. In some places, I employ standard principles of comparative research design, for example, chapter 4's "most similar case" and "hard case" comparison of ethnic politics in democratizing Malaysia and Sri Lanka. In the free-speech and media chapter, I reframe the best available secondary sources to analyze a naturally occurring experiment in which the sudden arrival of satellite TV dramatically increased the availability of information and diversity of opinions in Arab media. Because little existing research directly addressed the main questions of that media chapter, my Columbia colleague Tamar Mitts and I designed and carried out some correlational statistical tests, while not making strong causal claims. In contrast, one of the reasons I chose to study female genital cutting in chapter 9 was the wealth of statistical, survey, comparative, and ethnographic research that allowed a multifaceted exploration of the topic. In several chapters I have also drawn illustrations from my own interviews of human rights activists, humanitarian practitioners, businesspeople, journalists, government officials, and scholars in New York and on research trips to China, Egypt, Hong Kong, Indonesia, Myanmar, Turkey, and Ukraine.

Sometimes the most important methodological question is where to place the bar for an argument to be convincing as a guide to action. In presenting this research to audiences of mainstream human rights professionals, I have found that the most common disagreement hinges not on the facts or the causal interpretation, but on what to do about it. Conversations tend to go like this: "All of us here know that shaming by outsiders is not the preferred approach, so we always try to quote locals who make critical remarks. In any case, how is it possible to push for change without making justified criticisms?" Or like this: "Of course there will be resistance from people who want to continue these abuses, but saying that critical persuasion works only in favorable circumstances is essentially saying we should do nothing."

The part of my presentation that practitioners usually like best comes when I tell them that they may be able to use their current approach more successfully if they adjust their tactics slightly: for example, focus on guilt for the action, not shame for the character flaw that led to it. What doesn't always get through is the more important part of the message: the most effective role for outsiders is to change the incentives and opportunities in the broad environment in which abuses occur. For example, eliminate import tariffs on fair trade products. Import parts only from suppliers that comply with certified labor standards based on routine, transparent inspection. Offer free accounting training and technology upgrades for foreign banks that voluntarily and verifiably implement a standard package of anticorruption measures. Then wait for the targets of persuasion to decide for themselves whether adopting rights-compliant attitudes and behaviors will work for them. At the level of the country or the individual firm, research shows that international trade can produce a "race to the top" when incentives are favorable, not just a race to the bottom for cheaper, more exploited labor.[63] This can be best achieved not with the hard sell, but through the open door.

Far from "doing nothing," the strategy of the open door requires doing a lot. In fact, it takes more effort than sending out a scathing press release. As I explain in chapter 10, it requires patience, and it sometimes requires action by people with skills, resources, and social networks who are different from many human rights activists. Most important, it requires thinking about the big picture and the fundamental drivers of action over the long term.

2

Power and Rights in the Modern State

THE OBJECTIVE of a pragmatic approach to human rights is to prepare the way for the successful establishment of law-based rights. Making headway on human rights requires devising a pragmatic political strategy to enhance the power of constituencies that benefit from an expansion of rights while neutralizing opposition to a pro-rights coalition. This task requires sustained strategic effort to overcome durable forces that are adapted to traditional ways. A strictly normative approach can miss people's practical motivations to accept the status quo, even at the expense of their rights. It can also underrate the likelihood of backlash against rights promotion. Even countries that display many outward features of modern democratic governance and markets actually function by entrenched corruption, which nourishes the power of opponents of human rights.[1] In weighing the risks of moving too fast or too slow, a pragmatic approach to rights promotion needs to analyze the balance of power, anticipate resistance, and strategize politically to minimize or overcome those risks.

America's most effective icons of human rights progress have been ruthlessly pragmatic when they needed to be. Abraham Lincoln rejected abolitionism, which he saw as dividing the antislavery vote and alienating Northern white workers who cared mainly about keeping enslaved labor out of new western states. Franklin Roosevelt saved the country from the Great Depression and undertook a vast expansion of the rights of labor at the expense of tolerating a political coalition with Southern segregationists. Eleanor Roosevelt, in negotiating the Universal Declaration of Human Rights, agreed to exclude mention of racial equality because of that same deal with the devil of Jim Crow. Ultimately the heirs of these pragmatists achieved abolition and major civil rights reform, but only by cultivating a long process of economic and social change, which underpinned a shift in the balance of political power.[2]

The stability of any social order is built on a social equilibrium—a mutually reinforcing constellation of power, interests, institutions, and ideology. Breaking down the old equilibrium based on repression, favoritism, and deference to unaccountable authority cannot be achieved without a sustained assault on all these intertwined arrangements. Establishing a new social equilibrium based on equal rights and accountable government similarly requires the systematic construction of an interlocking structure of all these elements. Mixed social orders that combine contradictory elements of old and new—of practices of arbitrary favoritism and claims of equal rights—are the terrain in which efforts for social reform must operate during a long period of transition. In moving toward a new equilibrium that installs a central role for human rights, bargaining is necessary to create a social and institutional foundation for effective rules. Early in this process, bargaining cannot assume the efficacy of rights-based rules.[3] Rather it must proceed from an objective assessment of the power and interests of key participants who can affect the outcome of the contest.

In laying out this argument, I first discuss the philosophical basis for a pragmatic approach to rights and then examine strategic considerations in advancing a rights-based social order through bargaining and rules, emphasizing the central role of the nation-state.

Legitimacy, Backlash, and the Halo of Success

Rights, by their nature, invoke a claim based on legitimacy—that is, some general principle is invoked to justify the claimed entitlement to a liberty or benefit. Advancing a normative claim should not be seen as an alternative strategy to bargaining but as a complement to successful negotiation. Basing an argument on a convincing normative principle can help persuade the bargaining partner that the proposed deal will be mutually beneficial and reliably implemented.

One such principle bases the claimed entitlement on the binding decision of an authority who has the standing and the capacity to grant and enforce the claim. In some legal doctrines, the claim of a right may be based solely on the will of such an authority without any other principled justification. This is sometimes called rule *by* law, a phrase that Chinese officials and their critics have both adopted to describe the Chinese legal system today. A related justification of an existing right is precedent, the decision of a prior authority.

Human rights advocates, however, are often in the position of arguing to expand the scope of rights or to give effect to rights that have been ignored or routinely violated, including by authorities. Therefore, arguing for the legitimacy of a claim based on authority or precedent often fails to get them to their goal. Instead, they often need to make counterfactual appeals based on speculative ethical or legal arguments claiming that people *should* have a certain right even though authorities have not acted to formulate, recognize, or enforce it. Mainstream human rights proponents expect that these kinds of speculative counterfactual claims will eventually be successful because of their normative force. They believe that rights claims often have a face validity of fairness, decency, sympathy, and empathy that will elicit assent.[4] Many rights proponents also believe that most of the world's normative systems are based on principles that include analogs to the tenets of the Universal Declaration and formal human rights treaties, which most states have ratified.[5] Finally, they expect that most people will understand that their societies will be better off if they adopt these good practices as rights. Consequently, rights activists see little problem in making such counterfactual normative claims for rights.

One difficulty for this assumption is that the success of a rights campaign is affected by several practical motivations in addition to the normative persuasiveness of its claims. One motive is the self-interest of the targets of persuasion. For example, men in societies that legally repress and discriminate against women are likely to resist claims based on the Convention on the Elimination of All Forms of Discrimination Against Women (CEDAW) no matter how cogent the ethical and legal arguments are in its favor, in part because even reformist men anticipate social sanctioning by their self-interested peers. A second motive is fear. Thomas Hobbes famously argued that it makes perfect sense for people to give up almost all their rights to a nearly absolute dictator to escape the dangers of anarchy.[6] Bearing out this insight, a survey found that the vast majority of civilians in war zones in such places as Somalia and Afghanistan endorsed international humanitarian law protecting noncombatants, but few respondents thought that such rules would be followed, so their normative preference had no impact on their practical plans.[7] A third motive is the need to secure reliable access to the means of sustenance. Social systems throughout the world are stabilized, though inefficiently, by routine corruption and patronage whereby people sell their votes and turn their back on fairness and due process just to get by in their system as it exists, for better or worse. Trapped in social systems in which perverse incentives that sustain routine abuses are hard to escape, people are likely to resist normative persuasion that has no apparent material basis for implementation. These practical reservations add to the resistance based on the unfamiliarity of foreign normative systems and their clash with their own traditional ideas about appropriate behavior.[8]

Consequently, a pragmatic proponent of rights must assess the likely consequences of normative campaigns, taking the possibility of backlash into account. Anecdotally, we know that backlash is routine.[9] In Kenya, Uhuru Kenyatta and William Ruto, politicians indicted by the International Criminal Court for organizing election atrocities against members of each other's ethnic groups, found common cause in running together for president and vice president on the same ticket in the next election, winning with the pitch that only they could protect their ethnic constituents against the ICC's "imperialism." Likewise, rights-abusing politicians from Vladimir Putin to Yoweri Museveni have had considerable success in discrediting the human rights movement in their countries through its association with LGBTQ rights campaigns that they successfully portray as decadent, immoral, alien, and arrogantly imperialist. The slim margin of defeat in the first referendum on Colombia's peace settlement with the FARC rebels was reportedly due to an election-eve furor over the inclusion of gay rights provisions in the agreement linking peace and amnesty. Polish President Andrzej Duda's razor-thin 2020 reelection victory rested on the combination of welfare benefits for rural communities and a campaign vilifying gay rights.[10] On the grassroots level, the local director of a small human rights NGO in a town in Moldova told me that her international funders had pressed her to hold a gay pride parade, which corrupt town officials used to discredit her efforts to promote fiscal accountability, due process, and other civic rights.[11] A prominent survey experiment found that framing statements about Black Lives Matter that emphasized feminist and LGBTQ+ goals tended to "demobilize" support for the movement among Black men.[12]

Especially concerning would be backlash leading to the mobilization, institutionalization, and cultural embedding of extreme resistance that would not have otherwise occurred except for the provocation of the rights campaign.[13] "Backlash from the old elites," say political scientists Gerardo Munck and Carol Leff, can "lead to the adoption of institutional rules that are not optimal for democratization" and "leave a legacy that hinders governability and democratic consolidation."[14] V. I. Lenin warned that pushing for revolutionary progress before the correlation of forces was favorable would allow the class enemy to organize a coalition to crush the premature Bolshevik revolution.[15] Counterfactual history is necessarily speculative, but arguably the rise and social embedding of backlash movements such as the mujahideen resistance to Soviet-backed reforms in the Afghan countryside and antisecularist grassroots movements in India, Iran, and Turkey were spurred in part by outsiders' pressure to install civil law, proselytize for secular attitudes, alter gender roles, eliminate caste discrimination, get rid of old corruption, open free markets, or introduce competitive elections.[16]

That said, the fear of backlash may sometimes make well-intentioned pragmatic reformers unnecessarily cautious. Ruth Bader Ginsburg declined to push abortion rights early in her career, and much later as a Supreme Court Justice, she sought to delay the push for gay marriage out of fear of a political and public opinion backlash against a move she considered unripe, but events proved her to be underestimating the pace of change in public attitudes.[17] Some have argued that the actions of the Supreme Court itself were the cause of much of this change in public opinion.[18]

Rights claims that lead to successful outcomes are more likely to be considered legitimate in retrospect, whereas failure and pushback tend to discredit normative claims. This might be called persuasion by social proof: the claim is legitimate because when it succeeds in achieving its aims, it generates the power and resources needed to sustain it, and it appears to work in the way that is claimed for it. Social proof can work for or against human rights. For example, growing economic prosperity allowed the Chinese regime to increase social and economic welfare and maintain high public approval despite its disdain for international human rights standards. This lent credibility to China's illiberal welfare-based approach to what its reports called "human rights." Pragmatists expect citizens and other supporters to grant some normative leeway to authorities that have demonstrated their ability to exercise power effectively, even if they cut corners legally and morally. Targeted killings, harsh interrogations, or civilian collateral casualties are likely to receive less scrutiny if they are seen as contributing successfully to peace, security, regime stability, and national power.[19] The Russian public criticized Yeltsin's brutal war in Chechnya mostly because he lost, whereas they glorified Putin for his brutal replay of the Chechen war because he won. In that sense, the right to grant or compromise rights stems from a kind of social proof. Nothing succeeds like success.[20] Rights activists need to take this into account in designing persuasive strategies for promoting rights.

Why Make Claims through the Rhetoric of Rights?

The discourse of rights provides one of the languages in which claims of justice, fairness, appropriateness, possession, or other legal, ethical, or political grounds for entitlement can be framed. An alternative discourse for advancing claims is the language of bargaining and coercion based on power and interest. Both languages may lead to clashes or to concord. Both may appeal to norms (e.g., you are weaker, so you should accommodate my demand) and to external authorities or concerned third parties (judges, mediators, or power holders) to settle disputes over resources or relationships.

The power of rights claims, as compared to other types of claims for advancing substantively similar demands, can vary widely across different cultural, historical, and institutional settings. Rights language enjoys pride of place in liberal Western social systems, which are highly legalized, well institutionalized, and responsive to the claims of individuals.[21] Although rights talk is deeply embedded in Western cultures, it is not just a cultural bias. There are compelling pragmatic arguments for basing a strategy for achieving global justice goals on rights claims. The West offers, so far, the most successful model of modernity, and rights are central to its operation. Advocates can argue plausibly that the Western rights-based system resonates with globally widespread values of fairness, prosperity, and peace as well as or better than any practical alternatives. And finally, the West has the resources and sometimes the motivation to promote the rights project. Rights advocates have made a reasonable bet on this mode of claim making, despite its pitfalls.

Rights claims advanced as legitimate or authoritative entitlements stipulate both processes and outcomes. Deng Xiaoping's most characteristic and famous quotation is that "it makes no difference whether a cat is black or white, so long as it catches mice." His policies promoting economic development and public education had a dramatic effect in reducing child labor in China, outstripping in practical impact the worldwide efforts of the human rights community to address this kind of abuse of children's rights.[22] The mechanism for accomplishing this, however, had nothing to do with creating, monitoring, or enforcing any child's right not to be working. On this and other issues, the PRC's official reports on human rights have typically emphasized social welfare outcomes achieved rather than any rights-based processes that led to them. China's proposed resolution at the 2017 meeting of the UN Human Rights Council, for example, avoided endorsement of any individual's rights claims or protections, praising only "the indispensable contribution of development to the enjoyment of all human rights by all."[23] This approach leaves international human rights activists unsatisfied, because strengthening the rights process in the right way is as important for them as tangible improvements in substantive outcomes. While this stickler's attitude may seem stubbornly inflexible, it gains support from empirical findings on Chinese anticorruption and government transparency reforms, where the prevailing strategy of one-off campaigns typically leads to rapid backsliding rather than generalized institutionalization.[24] Rights advocates have a point in stressing both process and outcome.

Justifications for Rights Moralism and Rights Pragmatism

One reason for the universalistic, moralizing bent of much mainstream rights advocacy is that commonsense Western ideas often include the unspoken assumption that morality is deontology: that is, the ethical theory that the morality of an action should be based on whether that action itself is right or wrong under a general rule, rather than based on the consequences of the action. Even when a degree of consequentialism is accepted, it often takes the form of rule-utilitarianism (the idea that a good action would lead to good consequences if generalized to all cases) against the backdrop of the Kantian categorical imperative (right actions should be capable of being generalized as a universal law). But viewed from other philosophically respectable approaches to morality, deontological purism is simply one approach among many.

One does not have to be a full-on utilitarian, let alone an expedient opportunist, to agree with the moral dictum that "ought implies can." And one does not have to descend into rudderless moral relativism to endorse the ancient Greek notion that ethics may involve the development of virtues that reflect the highest values of one's community.[25] Barack Obama, early in his first term as president, acknowledged being powerfully influenced in his approach to ethics by the realist theologian Reinhold Niebuhr, who warned that whereas deontology provides a yardstick that citizens could apply to choices in their personal lives, leaders of a community should adopt a consequentialist ethic of responsibility.[26]

Mainstream human rights advocacy implicitly reflects the assumption that human beings constitute their own social reality through discourse about proper social norms.[27] This assumption becomes explicit in the theories of some key academic works on the power of the movement's methods, which highlight norms that constitute, not just regulate, actors and social systems— for example, giving rise to Helsinki Watch, a precursor of Human Rights

Watch, and the office of the prosecutor of the International Criminal Court.[28] But that insight gives both too much and too little credit to the human rights mainstream's understanding of the world. On one hand, it underestimates the extent to which mainstream tactics rely on material coercive power, as in the role of sanctions by powerful states to coerce compliance. It also sells short the consequentialist claims for mainstream tactics: advocates think shaming works, and they undertake statistical analysis to try to prove it.[29] On the other hand, it would give the mainstream far too much credit to say that advocates believe that social reality is created through open normative deliberation in something akin to German philosopher Jürgen Habermas's power-free "ideal speech condition."[30] Mainstream concepts of global human rights discourse typically depict one-sided persuasive mechanisms (issue framing, agenda setting, exploiting informational asymmetries, setting universalist rules of discourse) that take place in the shadow of coercive material and institutional power.[31]

This ontology of mainstream human rights advocacy, whose centerpiece is the social construction of reality through coercive discourse, differs substantially from the assumptions that underpin this book.[32] I proceed from the assumption that social life is constituted through interactions predicated on the power and interest of individuals and the groups they form, and through bargaining and coalitions among those groups. I do, however, accept the point commonly made by social constructivists that ideas are needed to define interest and to generate social power by forming social groups. Discourse about norms and rules is part of this process.

Where I would part company with some social constructivists of human rights—and with the implicit worldview of much mainstream rights activism—is the notion that a global normative community such as the one envisioned by human rights utopians can be created principally through normative persuasion about standards of appropriate behavior for individual actors whose politically relevant social identity is "human." While I think that such a goal is worthy and perhaps ultimately necessary to sustain successful liberal modernity, the processes needed to advance it depend on the creation of social power in the hands of groups that perceive an interest of their own in achieving it. Forging that social power involves, at various stages in the process, the formulation of aspirational norms and deliberations about the role of social rules. It also involves, however, the creation of the material preconditions for such a global society, as well as bargaining and coalition-making processes that are based on expediency as well as principle. Any general rules that emerge in this process will have to be expressed in the cultural vernacular of the diverse corners of the globe. The institutional arrangements that support proto-universal human rights practices will need to be assiduously tailored to local conditions everywhere, whether in Texas or Tanzania. While sequencing will be complex and locally varied, the general rule of thumb will be "social power leads, norms follow."[33]

There is no strong philosophical justification for privileging mainstream human rights ideology over more pragmatic, consequentialist, contextualized alternatives. The UDHR shies away from any coherent philosophical foundation for what is simply a list of rights that the UN General Assembly could agree to in 1948. America's Founding Fathers likewise begged the question of foundations, simply asserting that the rights to "life, liberty, and the pursuit of happiness" were "self-evident." Aryeh Neier, the founder of Human Rights Watch, embraces a "natural law" justification for rights but fails to say what that means or to defend it against contemporary philosophers' skeptical view of that approach.[34] Indeed, justifications of human rights that are taken seriously by philosophers are more likely to be nonfoundationalist, such as Richard Rorty's: "On the pragmatist view I favor, it is a question of efficiency, of how best to grab hold of history—how best to bring about the utopia sketched by the Enlightenment."[35]

Pragmatism as the Philosophy of the Progressive Movement

Various academic theories that take an outcome-oriented view of norms and law may be called pragmatist, realist, or positivist.[36] Pragmatism in law and social policy, as articulated by the likes of Oliver Wendell Holmes and John Dewey, is a hallmark of the Progressive movement in the United States.

According to an approach that is sometimes called legal realism, "judges consider not only abstract rules, but also social interests and public policy when deciding a case."[37] Pragmatism as I use the term accepts this as a description and a prescription. John Austin's theory of legal positivism held that what is legal is whatever the sovereign says is legal, because he has the power to make the claim be accepted. Pragmatism recognizes that rights backed by a powerful sovereign have very different practical implications than speculative claims to rights backed by principled advocates.

Moral realism is the philosophical viewpoint that ethical norms have an objective quality that does not depend on subjective perceptions, feelings, or attitudes.[38] Rather they emerge from the factual patterns of actual social relations. One interpretation is that valid moral norms, such as cooperative reciprocity, are those that are functional for a social group and welfare enhancing for its members. Adding a subjective element to this empirical insight, people may come to think that expected behaviors that benefit an interdependent social group are moral actions.[39] Even if morality cannot be reduced entirely to social science laws of cooperative efficiency, moral arguments often make some empirical assumptions about enabling conditions and causal effects of action.[40] Thus, even Ronald Dworkin, who is not considered a moral realist, notes that "most people's moral convictions embed non-moral assumptions that are hostages to non-moral refutation."[41] My pragmatist approach to human rights shares this general sensibility.

Overall, the pragmatist approach I am proposing for human rights has much in common with the Progressive tradition of American social reform and law, with its emphasis on the development of rules and institutions as effective policy tools to achieve improvements in social welfare.[42] Progressives prided themselves on having solutions to problems that would actually work to make people's lives better. The test of Progressive proposals was not just that they conformed to underlying principles but that they were practical and would ban tainted meat, improve education, and pull the economy out of the Depression.[43]

Social Order Based on Power, Bargaining, and Rules

Any social order, including one that accommodates human rights, is based on configurations of social power and interest that reflect cleavages between groups. While these cleavages are sites of contention, they are also sites for bargaining over rules that can establish an equilibrium based on power and interest, reducing the cost of conflict for all parties. As the legal sociologist Richard Wilson puts it, invoking both Karl Marx and Max Weber: "Human rights are above all the result of historical political struggles between individuals and groups . . . and serve as an indicator of the balance of power."[44]

Bargains based on institutionalized rules operate simultaneously on two dimensions: the efficiency of cooperation and the distribution of its benefits. We often think of institutions as mainly solving problems of collective action, in which opportunistic behavior or the difficulty of coordinating efforts leads to inefficiencies that leave almost everyone worse off. The community as a whole gains if people can coordinate on driving on the right side of the road or if officials can monitor tax payments so that bridges can be paid for. But an equally important function of institutionalized rules is to coordinate the distribution of benefits from social order, even if the resulting equilibrium leaves some better off than others.[45] Rules that sustain an asymmetric distribution of power and benefits might be better than endless costly fighting over distribution, especially if fighting might lead to even less just distributional outcomes. This idea has been applied not only to bargaining over domestic rules but also to the institutionalization of rules by war-winning coalitions in international relations.[46] John Ikenberry has argued that postconflict international settlements forged by democratic victors are more stable because their transparent political systems based on law and rights encourage weaker states to trust the hegemonic democracy to abide by its own rules.[47]

This analytic frame has several important implications for human rights promotion. First, the potential for human rights successes in any social system depends on the relative power of available groups and the feasibility of organizing them through bargaining into coalitions that strengthen peace, democratic participation, rule of law, and other underpinnings of rights progress. Second, as the classic study by Seymour Martin Lipset and Stein Rokkan shows, mobilized social cleavages exhibit a stickiness that can endure over centuries, so divisive strategies that unnecessarily stimulate and institutionalize opposition to a rights agenda could incur lasting costs.[48] Third, where conditions for fully liberal outcomes remain unripe and where spoilers are strong, asymmetric bargains that acknowledge the current power advantages of illiberal groups may be acceptable so long as they create conditions that are conducive to human rights development in the long run. A negotiated order characterized by peace, economic development, law, and potential growth of rights constituencies would create prospects for progressive social evolution in the future.

It is important to contrast this strategic way of thinking about bargaining over institutionalized rules with a more tactically legalistic view of pragmatic bargaining. Legalists typically seek to advance human rights by reducing the scope for political control over the legal process. They fear that state politicians will normally seek to compromise rights in the pursuit of other national interests. For example, legalists have sought to increase the freedom of the International Criminal Court from interference by the UN Security Council in deciding whether to pursue cases against perpetrators of atrocities. And yet tactically pragmatic legalists may realize that pushing for greater legal autonomy could spur opposition that would ruin the chance for effective limited reforms. David Scheffer's account of his diplomacy as the US negotiator for the Rome

Statute establishing the ICC provides an example of such tactical pragmatism in full detail.[49] While personally aiming for the goal of maximum feasible legal autonomy for the ICC design that would emerge from the treaty negotiations, Scheffer demonstrates a subtle and pragmatic understanding of the forces and attitudes pushing European and some developing countries toward an extreme formula of court autonomy that would make US ratification politically impossible, and thus compromise the effectiveness of the court. Scheffer's pragmatism in bargaining was merely tactical, serving a larger antipolitical goal. In contrast, I am proposing a form of pragmatism in which long-term political judgment guides the strategy at all times.

Legalists sometimes offer shallow, pragmatic-sounding arguments that serve mainly to fend off consequentialist criticisms. For example, proponents of war crimes trials have argued that legal accountability puts deterrent pressure on perpetrators. But critics of indicting powerful actors who have already committed war crimes have long pointed out that such indictments give perpetrators an added incentive to fight to the bitter end unless credible guarantees of amnesty can be negotiated. Yet legalists have argued that amnesties for war crimes and crimes against humanity cannot be legally given. Caught in this contradiction, the legalist fallback is that indictments weaken perpetrators by isolating them from crucial supporters who lack the stomach to defy the ICC. This fallback works logically but not empirically. The most commonly invoked case of this mechanism is the abandonment of indicted Liberian war criminal Charles Taylor by his cronies, but this outcome was more a consequence than a cause of the collapse of his armed forces.[50] To avoid tortuous contradictory arguments about bargaining, pragmatists need to consider the whole political and social context, not just superficial tactical moves.

The Logic of Modernity and Human Rights

The most basic anchor for a pragmatic theory of human rights is the insight that sustaining successful modernity has so far been impossible without them. Processes of modernization populate the social landscape with groups and interests, and the logic of modernization affects the range of feasible strategies for creating social order, which all norms entrepreneurs, including human rights activists, need to take into account.

A justly criticized version of liberal modernization theory, associated with American social science and exploited as American Cold War ideology, anticipated that sooner or later all societies would modernize and wind up looking like the trailblazer on that path, liberal England.[51] This teleological claim went too far. Many societies have tried to modernize and wound up looking nothing like liberal England. Indeed, many of the most interesting modernization theorists wrote about the detours that authoritarian modernizing countries such as Germany, Russia, and Japan had taken off the main road.[52] For the most part, however, these scholars saw such illiberal versions of modernity as mere short-term successes that led to disastrous dead ends. If that dismal track record holds up, liberal systems based on individual rights may enjoy distinctive practical advantages under modern conditions if only because of the fatal flaws of their competitors. Recall Winston Churchill's remark that "democracy is the worst form of government except for all those others that have been tried."[53]

The teleological version of modernization ideology also had shortcomings as theory. In its structural-functional form, it was long on taxonomy and short on falsifiable, conditional hypotheses that could explain or predict variations in outcome. As a functional theory, it seemed to imply that efficient outcomes had to happen simply because they were efficient.[54] More useful theories about modern forms of social organization need to specify who has the power and the motive to make an effort to bring about efficient changes.

I define modernity in a minimal way as an enduring social order that produces self-sustaining economic growth based on scientific and technological progress. The question is what institutional or cultural features are needed to bring it about and to sustain it?

Modernization theorists since Ferdinand Tönnies's breakthrough work on "community and society," *Gemeinschaft und Gesellschaft* (1887), have posited that the crucial move in the shift to modernity is from personalistic social relations based on family, lineage, patron-client networks, and cultural in-group favoritism to impersonal social relations based on rules that apply equally to all individuals.[55] Similarly, Emile Durkheim's *Division of Labor in Society* (1893) posited a transition between two distinct forms of social solidarity, from traditional society's group solidarity based on similarity to modern society's solidarity based on complementarity of functional roles in its complex division of labor. Durkheim went so far as to claim that the whole idea of the individual and of individualism emerged from this change in social organization. Other foundational figures of social science made similar points in filling in other pieces of the modernization picture. Karl Marx had already analyzed the breakdown of feudal caste privileges as ushering in capitalist relations of production based on free contracting. Max Weber in turn discussed the shift from organized nepotism to rational, legal, meritocratic, rule-following bureaucracies.

In this framework, culture matters as well as institutions. But the crucial cultural divide is not between civilizations bearing different cultural legacies, as in the theory of "multiple modernities," but rather between the culture of tradition and the culture of modernity.[56] Viewed this way, the list of purported "Asian values" is not about cultural distinctiveness at all but actually expresses values typical of traditional societies everywhere, including the historical West (such as patriarchy, duties rather than rights, priority of society over individuals, rewards due to ascriptive status rather than personal achievements), or typical policy concerns of developing countries (such as the assertion of state sovereignty or the priority of economic development over civil rights).[57]

These ideas animated American modernization theories of the 1950s and 1960s, and they remain central to contemporary social science works on the evolution and efficacy of the modern state. Francis Fukuyama's two-volume, 1,250-page masterwork argues convincingly that the central problem of political order and decay from prehistory to the present has been the struggle to overcome the inefficiencies embedded in lineage-based, clientelistic social systems, supplanting them with modern systems of impersonal rules and accountable government.[58] Premodern organizations, whether empires or churches, tried all manner of institutional innovations devised to overcome the deadweight costs of corruption. Celibacy, eunuchs, and orphan slave armies were just some of their imaginative failed experiments to stamp out nepotism. Finally, liberal societies developed impersonal rule-of-law institutions that removed nepotistic and clientelistic fetters on growth. Ending on a somber note, however, Fukuyama argues that remnants of the old corruption remain endemic in institutional legacies even in the most advanced democracies, not to mention rising state-dominated capitalist powers such as China. In these hangovers from premodern personalistic systems, he foresees dangerous implications not only for economic inefficiency but also social disorder.

How did the miracle of impersonal rules and open institutions finally emerge out of the morass of old corruption? Nobel Prize–winning economist Douglass North and his coauthors John Wallis and Barry Weingast have offered a plausible account that avoids the claim of teleological inevitability.[59] Drawing on a broad range of historical examples from many cultural settings as well as a detailed analysis of the evolution of English property rights, they argue that rule-based relationships and legal adjudication developed in premodern societies as ways to predictably guarantee armed groups' rights to control resources. Having rules reduced the risk that nobles' forces would fight the king or each other to protect or expand their share of the spoils. Over time, these arrangements sometimes became more institutionalized in courts and representative bodies. Crude methods of resource extraction became regularized as complex rules governing ownership, land sales, commercial privileges and monopolies, and taxation. Where the system worked well and made the use of force less relevant to distributional struggles, law and institutions became paramount. Protections for elites' personal safety, property, and liberties were guaranteed. In this way, the institutional and conceptual tools needed for representative democracy, equality before the law, and an open market economy were developed in a way that was functional for broader circles of society, not just for armed elites.

North and his coauthors do not portray the move across the "doorstep" from the law-governed oligarchy to inclusive liberal society as inevitable. Rather the institutions that were needed to make the open society work were available if events and incentivized actors pushed the system in that direction. In an argument that fills in some lacunae in Weingast's model of bargaining between the state and powerful factions in England's Glorious Revolution of 1688, Kevin Narizny contends that the rise of capitalist agriculture during the late seventeenth century gave the Whig reform faction the resource independence and the motive to push the monarchy and the Tories to accept the Bill of Rights and responsible parliamentary government. This victory and the structural change that underpinned it opened the way to "positive feedback" that further entrenched economic and legal reform.[60]

An illiberal variant of this pattern that remains common and rather durable in contemporary times is the one-party regime, which institutionalizes authoritarian rule in a way that tends to outlast military juntas and personalistic dictatorships.[61] Although many of the institutions of one-party regimes adopt similar terminology as counterparts in competitive democratic regimes (such as parties, legislatures, courts), they function according to the basic principles of premodern society, namely personalistic patronage based on loyalty and the implied threat of violent repression of opposition.[62] When they function best, they coopt and train reliable individual functionaries with the prospect of predictable career opportunities rather than buying off more dangerous independent elites that have their own power base.[63] Despite being anchored in premodern principles of rule, these single-party regimes may tentatively incorporate several more modern practices, such as greater regularity and transparency of operations, institutionalized opportunities for intraparty participation and discussion, and rules for succession of leadership. When these conditions hold, single-party regimes are not only more durable on average than other forms of dictatorship, but they are also less reckless in their foreign relations.[64] Because the single or dominant party in an authoritarian system can sometimes compete successfully in elections after a democratic transition, such as Taiwan's KMT, this can provide a route across the "doorstep" to true democracy.[65] Yet, dominant-party regimes can also regress toward a more clientelistic system, as in Putin's Russia, which he governs based on informal rules and personal relationships that play off rival elite networks.[66]

Charles Tilly offers a complementary analysis of how societal pressures effectively exerted that kind of push toward modern democratic arrangements, including civic rights. Tilly's distinctive insight, which parallels the modernization theorists' stress on personalistic versus impersonal relations and Fukuyama's stress on patronage systems, is the importance of governmental policies with respect to "categorical inequalities" and "networks of trust."[67] Categorical inequalities are those between identity groups based on sex, caste, ethnicity, religious sects, or enserfed labor. A person relies on trust networks when undertaking risky long-term enterprises such as marriage, long-distance trade, guild and trade associations, investment of savings, and time-consuming specialized education. In premodern society, governmental authority depends on favoritism within exclusionary trust networks based on categorical inequality. Structures of power and of culture are organized to reinforce hierarchies of authority and boundaries between identity groups.[68] In stable systems of patriarchy and caste, networks of domination control resources and ideas, establishing a social equilibrium that is hard to escape. Tilly studies the social mechanisms whereby these arrangements are broken down and replaced by democracy and civic rights through contestation and bargaining between the excluded and the state.[69]

Some of these mechanisms reduce the impact of categorical inequalities on public life: eliminating legal economic privileges of elites; freeing market forces that equalize returns to economic effort; adopting secret ballot elections; equalizing access to communications media; brokering political coalitions that cut across categorical lines. Others reduce the influence of segregated trust networks on public life: the rise of threats and opportunities that overwhelm traditional trust networks, such as war, famine, disease, and mass migration; the collapse of patronage networks; an increase in the proportion of people who are excluded from trust networks, such as landless peasants; government-guaranteed benefits for military service, old-age pensions, and disaster insurance; bargaining between government and tax resisters to regularize taxpayers' obligations and to institutionalize popular participation in fiscal decisions. Finally, other processes increase the breadth, equality, enforcement, and security of mutual obligations between citizens and officials: forming coalitions between reformist elite factions and groups excluded from power, imposing uniform governmental structures and practices, and centralizing and bureaucratizing irregular militias.[70]

By unpacking these mechanisms and processes, Tilly shows how modern democratic civic rights and practices emerge from the concrete exercise of social power and from pragmatic self-interested bargaining. When they are working properly, these practices and the institutions that support them provide widespread access to public goods, efficient incentives, and equitable distribution of benefits.

The Dangers of Incomplete Liberal Modernity

A crucial question for the debate over multiple modernities is how far a society must go in adopting the full package of liberal social arrangements to achieve self-sustaining economic growth. Virtually all societies that have been highly successful over a long period of economic development have moved quite far in the direction of the fully liberal model, both in formal arrangements and in effective rights for most segments of society. This includes due process of law, nondiscrimination, rule-based protections of property and sanctity of contracts, and widespread rights to political participation through free speech, political organizing, and fair, competitive elections of representatives that are bound by law. Setting aside oil sheikdoms and city-state entrepôts that exist under the protection of their liberal customers, the correlation between high per capita income and stable liberal democracy remains overwhelming.[71]

That said, the rise of China, the dynamism of politicized religion, and the assertiveness of authoritarian regional powers have lent credence to the notion that there might be various ways to be successfully modern, including illiberal ones. Liberalism's recent woes have stoked support for illiberal alternatives even in core liberal states. China's unprecedented run of sustained economic growth raises the question of whether its illiberal formula, based largely on the technocratic skill of its elite, can succeed indefinitely.[72] Modernization theory might pose it this way: is Weberian technical and administrative rationality enough to sustain modern economic performance and political stability if the system's legal rationality is poorly developed and its social practices remain rife with clientelism?

The canonical historical scholarship on illiberal modernization warrants skepticism about its prospects.[73] This research—none of it by naïve or dogmatic liberals—highlights late-development traps leading to political turmoil and regime crisis. Many of these illiberal variants of modernity ran aground because of illiberal nationalism, which provides a tool for authoritarian elites to adopt the pose of rule for the people without actually allowing rule by the people. Karl Polanyi explained how free markets and mass politics clashed in the Great Depression, spurring populist fascist nationalism to assert national political control over domestic and international markets.[74] Alexander Gerschenkron, discussed in chapter 5, showed how nationalism served as a popular ideology legitimizing a centralized, elite-controlled pattern of late development in Germany. Barrington Moore analyzed the authoritarian nationalist alliance between the old aristocratic state and the rising but still weak bourgeoisie against the working class in late-developing states. Samuel Huntington explained how rapid economic development produced illiberal, turbulent politics when the demand for mass political participation outstripped the development of state institutions. Ernest Gellner described the strife produced when national marketization created pressures for cultural homogenization, forced assimilation, ethnic separatism, and ethnic stratification.[75] These dire outcomes were averted only in states that shifted decisively to liberal institutions, ideas, and political coalitions before navigating these development traps. Each of these classic studies seems as current as today's headlines.

The concept of social equilibrium offers a unifying way to think about these myriad dangers of incompletely liberal modernization.[76] As implied by North and by Tilly, any stable governance system has to solve a few basic problems: efficient bargaining between armed elite factions, at least passive consent by the broad mass of the governed, and succession of leadership.[77] In traditional societies at low levels of mass social mobilization, authoritarian governance systems such as monarchy can often establish a fairly durable equilibrium. The king manages elite contestation through repression and stable bargains for distributing rents. Low levels of literacy and economic development make passive consent fairly easy to accomplish through repression, economic hegemony by local elites, and religious ideology. Lineage principles provide a fairly predictable solution to the problem of leadership succession. As a result, dynastic tenures can be enduring. Perturbations from outside the system might disrupt these arrangements temporarily, but the tendency is for the system to snap back into something like the old equilibrium, perhaps staffed by a new dynasty. Consolidated democracy also normally constitutes a stable equilibrium, solving the problems of elite bargaining, mass consent, and succession through the rule-based institutionalization of civil rights principles.

In contrast, mixed regimes, sometimes called "competitive authoritarianism" or "illiberal democracies," embody internal contradictions that leave them in disequilibrium.[78] Semimobilized societies mix volatile, demagogic mass electoral politics with elite factional politics based on threats of force and corrupt practices, making election periods rife with the risk of violence.[79] Weak leaders need to undertake risky elections to maintain their legitimacy but have the motive and the opportunity to use intimidation and unfair practices to win them. Such stolen elections stimulate elite and mass resistance that can lead to coups, "color revolutions," and civil war.[80] Rules for orderly succession are weak or absent, and leaders' fates when they step down are often dire, so they try to hang onto power in the face of term limits, provoking political crisis.[81]

Internally contradictory, such mixed regimes have shorter life spans and are more fraught with violence and rights abuse.[82] Seva Gunitsky finds that different indexes measuring regime type, based on somewhat different components and weighting schemes, are in somewhat closer agreement when measuring highly democratic and highly autocratic regimes than when measuring mixed regimes in the middle of the scale.[83] This suggests that the pure types of democracy and autocracy converge on self-reinforcing, systemic equilibria of mutually supportive components. In contrast, mixed regimes may be composed of different, even mismatched arrangements of attributes. Some mixed regimes might have fairly modern administrative structures yet weak institutions regulating political participation; others might have the opposite combination, yet both could occupy the middle of the regime-type spectrum. One interpretation could be that there is no stable equilibrium in the middle of the range, which could be why mixed regimes are more diverse in their features, less durable, and more conflict prone.

Another possibility, however, is that different forms of mixed regimes and semiautocracies vary in their degree of structural coherence, stability, susceptibility to violence, and governmental performance. In particular, single-party regimes with well-institutionalized mechanisms for bargaining and mobilizing support stand out as lasting longer, suffering few coups, surviving insurgencies more successfully, and sustaining stronger economic growth than other kinds of mixed, oligarchic, or semiautocratic regimes, such as personalistic or military regimes.[84] This may be true of highly authoritarian single-party regimes, like China, especially ones that forged a cohesive regime as a result of a successful social revolution, as well as more oligarchic, law-based, single-party (or dominant-party) regimes, such as Singapore.[85]

The variable durability of mixed regimes has ambiguous implications for strategies of transition from the authoritarian rights-deficient equilibrium to the democratic rights-based equilibrium. On the one hand, relatively stable forms of mixed regime might offer "hand holds" while climbing the cliff of liberalizing modernization. These partially stable intermediate points could provide a blueprint for how to design and sequence steps in building the institutions and political support coalitions that would provide a platform for the next stage of the ascent. On the other hand, there is some evidence that intermediate equilibria can be too stable, running the risk of getting stuck in a low-level equilibrium trap, such as the middle-income trap I discuss in chapter 5. [When single-party regimes do evolve further, changes might lead down a detour rather than serving as a platform from which to democratize.] According to one study, single-party regimes are more likely to transition into military regimes or dominant-party regimes than into democracy. Single-party regimes are less likely to transition to democracy than are military regimes or "anarchies."[86] Chapter 4 on political transitions examines more closely how states may be able to navigate the passage through this zone of partial, low-level equilibria or disequilibria.

Modern States as the Primary Vehicle for Rights

One of the most basic facts about the modern order is that territorial states are the primary vehicle for recognizing and guaranteeing rights. A pragmatic strategy for promoting rights acknowledges this reality, but mainstream human rights approaches are often misaligned with it.

The book that has provoked the most discussion in human rights circles over the past decade is Samuel Moyn's *The Last Utopia*.[87] Among the book's central claims is that human rights in the contemporary sense were an invention of the human rights movement in the late 1970s. Before then, says Moyn, the term *human rights* was rarely used. In his view, the Universal Declaration of Human Rights was a momentary aberration, largely ignored during the era of Cold War realpolitik and the nation-building projects attendant to decolonization.

This claim runs directly counter to most people's common sense and to other prominent scholarship that dates the invention of human rights to the

Enlightenment: Thomas Jefferson's "inalienable rights" in the American Declaration of Independence, the US Bill of Rights, and the French Revolution's
Declaration on the Rights of Man. Lynn Hunt's prominent book *Inventing
Human Rights* places the impetus for this epochal development in readers'
empathetic reaction to injustices suffered by characters in eighteenth-century
Enlightenment novels.[88] This expressed the sensibilities of highly literate,
urban, law-governed, commercial society and its increased expectations for
personal security. Hunt doesn't mention the later text that most obviously
supports her argument, *Uncle Tom's Cabin*, which revolutionized attitudes of
Northern readers about slavery.

One reason that these earlier excursions into the language of rights don't
count for Moyn is that they were mainly national projects of civic rights, not
internationally guaranteed rights for all people in all nations. According to
Moyn, the rights project moved in a transnational and international direction
in the late 1970s because of the widespread disappointment with the repressive, authoritarian turn of the postcolonial states. Since the rights of postcolonial peoples were not being protected by their own regimes, that task fell to
principled transnational activist networks wielding international treaties and
transnational press releases on documented abuses.

Moyn expressed dismay at this development, seeing it as a superficial, utopian effort that made first-world liberals feel good but detracted attention from
more fundamental issues of global social justice. His works show that this is
part of Moyn's larger critique of liberalism as an incoherent set of ideas, some
of which are used to justify an exploitative libertarian understanding of markets.[89] Moyn's distinction between international human rights and national
civic rights is fundamental, and he may be right that the excessive internation-
alization of the rights project has been counterproductive. This is not a sufficient reason, however, to give up on the human rights project. Rather it is a
reason to shift its emphasis back to states and civic rights. States, not international organizations and transnational networks, are the most effective organizations for institutionalizing the rule of law and defending rights. If some
states are falling down on the job, the main solution must be to get them to do
better, not to try to replace them with international providers of rights.

The advantages of states over international actors as instruments for securing rights are pithily captured in Luis Moreno Ocampo's standard stump
speech to reassure states that he would not disregard their concerns as the first
prosecutor of the International Criminal Court. He repeatedly declared that
he needed to persuade states to get them to investigate crimes and arrest

criminals. A prosecutor in the United States, he said, "has a police force at his disposal. I have none of this. In effect, I am a stateless prosecutor."[90]

Though proponents of an all-powerful ICC might not like it, society is organized as states for some good reasons. States monopolize legitimate violence on a given territory, set rules that organize market transactions, establish a system of law and its enforcement, and in modern, high-functioning states, organize a system of accountability to the state's citizens. This brings resources and responsibilities into alignment under a coherent authority with an open-ended time horizon for policymaking. In the words of Mancur Olson, states are like "stationary bandits" that have a long-term stake in governing their fief reasonably well.[91] International functional organizations or transnational lobbying groups may have constructive supporting roles to play in their niches, but they lack the features that make general-purpose territorial states the dominant organizational form of the modern era.

Territorial states are said to have several advantages in efficiency, which on balance may help with the provision and enforcement of rights but may sometimes introduce complications. Citizens of nation-states are more likely to have similar preferences on policies and rights than human beings chosen randomly from the globe.[92] Admittedly, this commonality of preferences might also facilitate agreement to maintain rights-challenging practices such as the death penalty, early marriage, or punishment for homosexuality. Citizens of nation-states are more likely to be densely interconnected in social and economic relationships; therefore, states are well positioned to internalize the social costs and benefits of those relationships through regulation, policy coordination, public goods provision, and taxation.[93] In addition, large territorial organizations like states are the only manageable units that comprise all the elements of an economic division of labor on a functioning scale. While this creates a foundation for economic nationalism, it also makes possible a democratically accountable framework for managing the macroeconomic policies needed by a modern welfare state. Finally, states have the advantage of being survivors of path-dependent evolution. Working to reform existing state structures is likely to cause less chaos than starting over from stateless anarchy. As Huntington argued, and even ardent human rights scholars recognize, weak governance institutions are often more of a threat to social order, peace, and rights than ones that are too powerful. For all these reasons, international organizations and lobby groups work through states; they cannot succeed as a substitute for states.

It is true that some international organizations, such as the World Trade Organization, establish rules that effectively shape the behavior of member

states. The WTO has even set up a working quasi-legal system for dispute resolution that members abide by most of the time. Obligations under human
rights treaties, however, are fundamentally different in kind from the WTO's.[94]
WTO members receive huge benefits from participating in reciprocal relations
and undertaking reciprocal obligations. WTO obligations are clarified by decisions of its Dispute Settlement Bodies, but enforcement depends ultimately
on the threat of reciprocity. Human rights treaties, for the most part, entail
obligations that are not reciprocal with the obligations of other states but are
mainly unilateral, including duties toward the state's own citizens. Even the
laws of war are not reciprocal in the sense that one state's violations, say in
mistreating prisoners of war, do not legally justify retaliation by the victimized
state against prisoners from the violator state.[95] In trade, the incentives for
outsiders to enforce a state's international obligations are nearly automatic, at
least among equals, whereas in human rights, outsiders' incentives to enforce
another state's obligations toward its own citizens are weak. For that reason, a
pragmatic strategy for protecting citizens' rights should look first to their own
state's stable equilibrium than rely on utopian expectations of international
supporters.

The International Context of Successful
Human Rights Mobilization

I argue that the most vital international influence on human rights is the stability of the basic structures of the liberal international system. Intrusive interventions that specifically aim to promote human rights projects in particular
foreign states are less important, and they have a mixed record. What matters
most is whether the great powers are stable democracies and whether those
democracies can sustain liberal international economic and security institutions that incentivize and socialize rising powers to adopt liberal norms and
practices.

Statistical research shows that before 1990, the domestic characteristics of
states were the strongest predictor of their likelihood of being a democracy,
but since the Cold War ended, the liberal character of the international system
and its leading powers has become a stronger predictor of regime type.[96] That
is a key reason many more states are now democracies or semidemocracies
than previously. As Seva Gunitsky has shown, the tide of victory in the World
Wars and the Cold War has spread waves of democratization and liberal social
transformation. He also shows, however, that international democratic waves

recede quickly from superficial transformations of societies that lack the local
facilitating conditions to sustain democracy and rights, which is one reason
that there have been multiple democratic reversals since the high-water mark
in the 1990s.[97]

Strategies for promoting liberal democratic transition, including human
rights, differ between the "open door" and the "high-pressure sales" approaches. The former, exemplified by the European Union's strategy of democratic enlargement, makes available the benefits of membership in the liberal
democratic club to states that ask for admission and meet its membership
criteria, including the rule of law. The high-pressure approach demands that
all states conform to basic liberal standards, especially in human rights, and
employs assertive persuasion, shaming, sanctions, and in extreme cases, military intervention to require compliance.

Neither of these approaches is guaranteed to work. Major EU policy failures in the handling of economic austerity and immigration spurred the rise
of illiberal political movements even in the old democratic core of the EU, let
alone in some of the new democracies that still struggle with corruption and
institutionalization of courts and parties. If even these basics are not done
right at home, there is little wonder that high-pressure sales abroad also
flounders.

As we saw in chapter 1, empirical research comes to ambiguous conclusions
on the effectiveness of assertive human rights promotion. Claims for a rights
"cascade" are more persuasive when they chronicle the elaboration of basic
legal standards at the global level and the institutional development of the
transnational network of activist organizations. Claims for a rights *compliance*
cascade at the grassroots level are more dubious. There is very little evidence
that international norms and institutions have been able to fill the vacuum
where states have failed to fulfill their rights-protecting mandate.

This failure has been evident in several high-profile issue areas. One of the
marquee undertakings of rights activists over the past two decades has been the
codification in a vote of the UN General Assembly of each state's "Responsibility
to Protect" its populations from genocide, war crimes, ethnic cleansing, and
crimes against humanity. Updating the norms of international humanitarian
intervention to prevent atrocities, R2P recognized the responsibility of the international community to take active measures, including the possibility of military intervention, when the state couldn't or wouldn't provide that protection.

R2P has had four major tests since its passage in 2005.[98] The most consequential was the international intervention in Libya in 2011, which toppled

Muammar Ghaddafi's regime and set the stage for an ongoing anarchic civil war, endemic human rights abuse, and the spread of Islamic terrorism to the south. Michael McFaul, former US ambassador to Moscow, argues that Vladimir Putin blamed his puppet president Dmitry Medvedev for failing to veto the UN Security Council vote authorizing the intervention and for the West's broken promise not to use the humanitarian operation as a cover for regime change. He dates Putin's shift to a strategy writing off cooperation with the West to this episode.[99] Another test was the UN-authorized military intervention in Côte d'Ivoire's civil war following a stolen election in 2010, which ended in the military defeat of the usurper but was marred by thousands of casualties, major population displacements, and atrocities perpetrated by the local allies of the international humanitarian force.[100] In late 2020, the elected president forcefully installed by the 2011 international intervention announced his candidacy for an unconstitutional third term, coinciding with violent repression of dissent, according to an "atrocity alert" issued by the Global Centre for the Responsibility to Protect.[101] A third test was the failure of European trial balloons lofted for humanitarian military intervention in the Syrian civil war, which were deterred by anticipated vetoes from Russia and possibly China. In the fourth test, the genocide case before the International Court of Justice against the Myanmar military junta's bloody expulsion of the Muslim Rohingya minority provided the occasion for the cringe-inducing testimony of the country's civilian leader, Nobel Peace Prize–winner Aung San Suu Kyi, fending off international accountability.[102]

This dubious track record might have been anticipated if R2P's proponents had had a clearer understanding of the purportedly successful NATO intervention against Serbia in Kosovo in 1999, which was lionized as a model operation reversing the ethnic cleansing of hundreds of thousands of Kosovar Albanians at the cost of zero NATO casualties. What actually happened was that NATO imposed a ceasefire on Serbian counterinsurgency efforts against the Kosovo Liberation Army in 1998, freeing the KLA to rearm and ramp up a renewed phase of their military campaign. When Serbia reacted brutally against the KLA and some Albanian civilians, the NATO powers issued an unacceptable ultimatum to the Serbian negotiators at Rambouillet, including the demand that NATO could deploy its forces anywhere in Serbia at any time. The breakdown of talks was followed by NATO air attacks on Belgrade and by Serb President Slobodan Milosevic's desperate decision to violently expel nearly the entire Albanian population from Kosovo. Although some defenders of the NATO strategy claim Milosevic had intended this move all along, evidence suggests that his preferred strategy was to reestablish Serb control in Kosovo through more limited repressive measures.[103] With the Kosovo operation as its model, it is not surprising that R2P has failed to protect human rights.

Other high-profile rights-promotion projects in which international actors sought to fill gaps left by domestic shortcomings likewise have a mixed record at best. Chapter 4 recounts the limitations and sometimes counterproductive impact of international criminal tribunals' attempts to "end impunity" for atrocities. Chapter 7 discusses the negative effect of unregulated freedom of speech on the globalized internet when exploited to sow hate and division. Chapter 8 discusses the disadvantages of international out-groups shaming rights-violating members of other cultures. Chapter 9 recounts the tensions between complex local realities and the sometimes blunt strategies of international rights activists in the areas of women's health and children's rights. That chapter cites the research of Shareen Hertel on the effectiveness of local NGOs in the Global South that use localized tactics in solving problems of food access, child labor, and pregnancy discrimination, while struggling to keep unhelpful interventions by international NGOs in check.[104]

Even worse, in some cases, a major source of global rights abuse stems from entrenched practices at the international level. A particularly egregious example is the enabling of global systemic corruption through internationally tolerated practices such as money laundering, opaque shell companies, numbered bank accounts, tax havens, and bribery. Since these international systemic ills sustain domestic rights abuses of all kinds, this is indeed an area where international actors can take the lead, mainly by fixing themselves.[105]

In short, international efforts to guarantee human rights rarely succeed as a direct substitute for inadequate domestic institutions. The aim of international action should be to indirectly strengthen the incentives and capacity of states to institutionalize rights in their own basic social structures. International support works best when it creates a broadly rights-supportive environment conducive to international security, economic development, and voluntary participation in rule-based international organizations and networks. Think "open door," not "high-pressure sales."

In current circumstances, the most vital and enduring measures to strengthen democracy and rights worldwide are efforts to sustain the functioning of democracy in its core of liberal states and to maintain the stability and openness of the liberal international system that they created. Pragmatic efforts to promote democracy and rights in illiberal states may also be worthwhile,

but they should mainly operate through the principle of the open door—
liberal democracy as a club that states and societies can choose to join when
they are ready and willing to take on its rules.

In the piecemeal process of state-by-state attempts to transition to democracy, one of the strongest correlations to the smooth, peaceful consolidation
of a liberal regime is a surrounding neighborhood of peaceful, stable democratic states. Conversely, bad neighbors export their wars, corruption, and
turbulent refugee problems and spoil the whole barrel. These international
neighborhood effects have the consequence of creating what might be called
zones of law and rights and zones of anarchy and repression. An important
question for human rights pragmatism is how to sustain a global aspiration for
universal rights while acting realistically and effectively in a world where zones
of rights and of repression may remain balanced in equipoise for some time to
come.[106] I return to this question in chapter 10.

3

Building Blocks and Sequences

BARGAINING BASED ON POWER and interest is necessary to advance the
cause of human rights. People's conflicted interests about rights make strategizing to assemble a powerful coalition for rights a complicated matter. A principal task of the pragmatic approach is to offer a range of practical strategies that
meet the challenge of these complications.

In thinking through strategies for successfully promoting rights, a necessary first step is to consider the structural conditions that have led to human
rights successes in the past. As I discuss in the first chapter, the most prominent of these are peace, democracy, and a list of factors that correlate with
both rights and democracy, such as high per capita income, a diversified
economy, an educated population, and usable administrative institutions.
Also important are a favorable international environment and a settled national identity. Within the context of those structural features, a strategy for
strengthening human rights in a given setting should consider what kinds of
social interests, configurations of social power, political coalitions, institutional arrangements, and political ideologies can be mobilized to establish a
plausible foundation for rights.

Some oversimplifying modernization theorists wrote in the 1950s and '60s
as if the trajectory of economic development would automatically produce the
whole inventory of constituencies, skills, and capacities needed to underpin
liberal democracy, including human rights. In this view, economic development and the flourishing ethos of enlightened individualism would move forward in lockstep with the growth of literacy, the middle class, and social relationships based on legal equality and fair contracts.[1] Even in the heyday of the
modernization approach, however, the most astute theorists working in this
vein understood that social and economic development could turn onto either
liberal or illiberal paths, depending on varying circumstances in which

development unfolded. For example, these scholars took to heart Barrington Moore's insight that economic and political development would lead to dictatorship, not democracy, when a weak bourgeoisie makes a pact with a reactionary ruling class to resist the demands of the rising working class, a finding that is supported in recent scholarship.[2] Modernization may be necessary for the full development of liberal democracy and rights, but the building blocks that produce this outcome are not automatically constructed and aligned in a smooth, linear, or inevitable fashion.[3] That process involves choices about the goals and the strategies of political development.

This chapter discusses how to think about the role of these building blocks in a successful rights strategy. It considers some basic pragmatic tactics for advancing liberal rights as well as maneuvers that are commonly attempted by opponents of those rights. Since circumstances and pathways of political development vary across societies, the choice of an effective strategy of rights promotion will necessarily vary based on those conditions. Such a diagnosis requires an assessment of the power and interests of key groups, a plan for assembling an effective pro-rights coalition, a realistic appraisal of the institutional capacity to support a rights-based order, and a deft strategy for rhetorically navigating the local discursive terrain.

Where favorable conditions for rights are lacking, the overall strategy must include a plan for sequencing and integrating efforts to bring them into being. Given that societies have somewhat different starting places on that journey and face somewhat different barriers to success, it would be incorrect to look for a one-size-fits-all formula. Nonetheless, general guidelines for how to strategize these particulars can be offered. That is the task of this chapter, culminating in specific recommendations for sequencing reform efforts. Following up on these diagnostic rules of thumb, I discuss how to sequence these tactics in an integrated strategy designed to move the rights project over the "doorstep" to an open society.[4]

Some reformers may be tempted to think of the various building blocks of rights development as substitutes for each other—for example, a British colonial legacy of independent courts as a substitute for a strong middle class. While reformers must work with whatever materials are at hand, it is more plausible to consider available facilitators as means to develop the necessary intermediate tools for reforms rather than as shortcuts that provide a substitute path directly to the final goal. Power, interest, institutions, and ideology are linked elements in the developmental process, not substitutes for each other or competing explanations for rights progress.

In thinking about the timing of efforts to accumulate the necessary ingredients, some macro sequences make progress smoother. For example, luminaries as different as Robert Dahl and Samuel Huntington agreed that the development of basic institutions of state administration and law should precede mass electoral politics.[5] There are also some tactical sequencing choices that reduce the likelihood of mobilizing disadvantageous identity-based coalitions as opposed to preferred class-based coalitions. For example, when possible, institutions should be designed to encourage the formation of cross-identity coalitions before the election rather than waiting to hammer out bargains between identity groups after the election. Nonetheless, pragmatists must "fight with the army they have," as the saying goes. The sequencing of choices often needs to be improvised in light of the possible. Even when this is the case, sequencing strategies must look more than one step ahead. For example, ethnic power-sharing deals often look like the safest way to navigate through short-run instability, but this temptation must be weighed against the risk of locking in divisive identity-based politics. Thus, power-sharing moves should be designed to have built-in sunset mechanisms.

A final puzzle in sequencing is how groups that seek rights to serve their own interests can develop a more general rights consciousness, which is ultimately necessary to consolidate the rights-based order. Luckily, incentives to generalize rights beyond mere privilege are built into two basic mechanisms of pragmatic rights-based politics. First, rational administration is necessarily based on generalized rules through which the sovereign power carries out its organizational tasks. Second, political coalition making is more stable between groups that can find some general interests in common, especially ones based on common principles, than between coalitions that rely entirely on the logrolling of parochial interests. Insofar as pragmatic political entrepreneurs and brokers seek durable political bargains, they will generally look for political formulas that can be articulated in terms of some general public interest, including the institutionalization of general rights.

This chapter proceeds through the entire catalog of pragmatists' building blocks, beginning with interests and culminating in overall conclusions about sequencing and about the evolution of special privileges into equal rights.

Interests for and against Rights

Let's begin by thinking about the role of social interests in a pragmatic approach to rights. Rationalists tend to adopt one of two approaches to studying interests: either they theorize in terms of revealed preferences, in which actors reveal their interests through their behavior in pursuit of specific ends, or else rationalists assume that on average most people have a selfish interest in their own security and wealth, which together can advance many of the other interests, such as status, that people might care about.[6] In the latter approach, the key variables driving analysis are not individuals' preferences but the situational constraints in which people pursue their generic interests. Rationalists assume that people strive to strike bargains and to set up institutions that create favorable circumstances for them to advance their interests.[7]

Social constructivists, in contrast, believe that interests are not analytical primitives at the individual level, but rather that people come to an understanding of what their interests are through interaction in a social context. The factors that shape their subjective understanding of their interests include the social role that they occupy in an institutionalized setting characterized by rules, habits, and standards of appropriate behavior. In addition, interests emerge through social discourse about appropriate behavior, consensual knowledge that coordinates behavior in the group, and ideas, ideologies, and symbols that establish patterns of shared meaning within the social group or subgroup.[8]

Since both ways of thinking about interests make sense at a general level, from a pragmatist standpoint in analyzing a phenomenon like human rights, it may be promising to ask about the elements they have in common.[9] One is that they see the individual as acting within a system that establishes constraints, incentives, and routinized patterns, such as institutionalized rules or social roles. Another is that they understand the individual to be a purposeful agent employing reason to achieve a favorable outcome. A pragmatist, in short, can think in terms of agents reasoning in all these ways to act within social structures of constraint and opportunity.

Although the material and technical arrangements available to society are likely to loom large in a pragmatist account of human rights (what Marx would call the "mode of production"), a pragmatist is unlikely to read an actor's interest directly off a given endowment of material resources. Rather, a pragmatist is more likely to consider actors' interests strategically in terms of the broader setting of institutional rules, available ideas, and possible coalition partners. In a complex system, interests are a matter of contingency, with options to be explored and judgments to be weighed.

Some scholars have argued that certain constituencies—the middle class, the working class, or disadvantaged groups—have a generally favorable inclination toward many rights, since rights are weapons of the weak that protect them from arbitrary domination by ruthless elites.[10] In addition, common sense might suggest that people will favor rights that especially protect people like themselves—for example, women will favor women's rights; racial and ethnic minorities will favor protections against discrimination. If so, a good way to collect a pro-rights coalition would be to target social classes that generally support rights and recruit groups that want rights-based protections for their particular interests.

A problem is that almost all constituencies have conflicted interests to some degree when it comes to rights. Everyone has an interest in preserving their own life and not being tortured, but many people may be ambivalent about the personal integrity rights of terrorists, criminals, distrusted ethnic foes, and revolutionaries who threaten their power, security, or property. Everyone has an interest in personal liberties such as privacy, movement, and information, but many people are willing to let the government monitor their email to track terrorists, complicate even their own travel to some degree to hinder the travel of dangerous people, and restrict even their own access to fake news. Those who have considerable property have an interest in strong protection of property rights, but if these same people obtain property in ways that prey on the weak property rights of others, they may prefer to protect their own by means of gated communities and political connections to corrupt officials rather than beef up property rights protections in general.

If the middle-class and bourgeois property owners are unreliable supporters of rights, what about the working class? One of the most impressive books on democratic consolidation, Rueschemeyer, Stephens, and Stephens's *Capitalist Development and Democracy*, concludes from an exhaustive survey of European and South American history that only when the working class is firmly enfranchised is democracy solidly consolidated. While this is true almost by definition, there are nonetheless reasons to be skeptical about counting on the working class to be the engine of liberal rights. Rueschemeyer's team acknowledges that their hypothesis works far better in Europe than in Latin America. The Peronist regime of Argentina was based on a backscratching alliance between government-subsidized, tariff-protected industrial labor and the military populist authoritarian state. The Tunisian regime under Habib Bourguiba did the same.[11] Seymour Martin Lipset's research on working-class authoritarianism studied cultural orientations that tended to work against the seeming structural incentives for the base of the social pyramid to favor rights protections.[12]

If the historically disadvantaged should favor human rights protections against the strong, women should be a reliable rights constituency. On average they are, but the gender gap in vote preference is modest, complex, and variable, and more white women in the United States voted for Donald Trump than for Hillary Clinton.[13] It turns out that women are cross-pressured by conflicting concerns. Mala Htun notes that religiously conservative women provided a reliable voting constituency against legalizing abortion in post-democratization Chile. Ironically, women's rights to work, health benefits, and birth control had been stronger in South American economic developmentalist regimes run by military dictators who sought to harness the productive power of women in the workforce.[14]

Populists, too, occupy an anomalous position vis-à-vis rights. After the 2008 financial crisis, many progressives put their hopes for human rights in populist movements like Occupy Wall Street, but populists have turned out to be among the chief threats to rights. In the United States, right-wing populists are accused of "weaponizing" rights when they invoke First Amendment protection for defamation and incitement or claim the religious freedom to discriminate against gays who seek to use their business services. Even when populists' core constituency is an oppressed racial group, such as the indigenous Bolivians who elected President Evo Morales, once populists come to power in weakly institutionalized states, they typically rule in a corrupt fashion rather than seeking to end discrimination by institutionalizing law.[15]

Endangered groups often reverse their view of a right once they are in the driver's seat. When French Calvinist Protestants faced discrimination and oppression in Catholic France, John Calvin composed eloquent pleas for religious freedom that closely anticipated the later arguments of Roger Williams in Rhode Island and more generally of Enlightenment rights philosophers. But once in power in Geneva, Calvin burned at the stake for heresy his former coreligionist Michael Servetus, declining his plea for a painless beheading.[16]

In short, though structural interests are relevant to groups' attitudes toward rights, the likely ambivalence or changeability of their interests means that their strategic choices depend on alliance possibilities with other groups, institutional arrangements that shape opportunities, and ideologies that affect interpretations of interest. Understanding how to reinforce the social power of a pro-rights constituency requires thinking in terms of an overall coalition of social groups, an institutional structure that incentivizes and empowers reformists, and an ideology that animates their efforts.

Social Power

Interests can succeed in advancing or blocking rights insofar as they are powerful. Robert Dahl famously pronounced that "A has power over B to the extent that he can get B to do something that B would not otherwise do." This "power over" may work through punishments or inducements.[17] When two parties have the *power over* each other to block or to reward mutually beneficial cooperation, they have an incentive to engage in bargaining, whose outcome will be shaped both by their relative power and by the intensity and compatibility of their interests in agreement. A common way to assess the bargaining power of each is through their evaluation of the alternatives to agreement. This interaction does not necessarily depend on rules, though it could be influenced by rules if they are imposed by a powerful outside party or if the rules have been internalized by the bargainers. An important objective of this book is to show the ways in which bargaining based on power and interest is often necessary to advance the cause of rights.

In addition to *power over*, social power can also be conceptualized as the *power to* achieve outcomes that the actor wants.[18] *Power to* depends on technical knowledge and capacity—science, technology, engineering know-how, available capital, skilled labor—as well as the ability to persuade and organize collective action among the people necessary for the task.[19] The power to mobilize effective collective action can depend on various factors: institutions, which coordinate predictable, usually rule-based patterns of behavior around which expectations converge, solving problems of free riding and opportunism; group ideologies or diffuse cultural norms, which define and motivate contributions to a collective benefit; or the power to coerce or reward contributions to collective action.

Social power can play out in specific interactions with other actors, such as US economic sanctions on the Argentine military junta, but it can also work by shaping the environment within which interactions take place. Social power can work by defining what issues are put on and left off the agenda, or by establishing categories, such as "rights," that shape expectations of how claims should be advanced and processed. Social power can also constitute and empower new actors, such as the power of social movements and states to work together to set up the International Criminal Court and define its rules. The power of a human rights coalition needs to be assessed simultaneously in terms of its power to act within the rules and its power to change the rules.

A pragmatist should realize that *power over* and *power to* can be conceptually distinct, but in action they may be causally intertwined. In the lawless state of nature, for example, a potential Leviathan or Genghis Khan could use purely coercive force to subjugate all opposition, while solving collective action problems within his core group of armed supporters by drawing on any combination of varied tools and tactics: kinship ties, trust ties based on long-standing relations of reciprocity, ethnic myths, religious indoctrination, material side payments, pie-in-the-sky promises, monitoring and punishing free riding and noncompliance with organizational rules, praetorian "coup proofing," charismatic leadership, and fear of backlash from the hatred and resentment of the opponents they had subjugated.[20] In this way, *power to* and *power over* may be entwined even in extreme cases that superficially appear to involve pure coercion.

Power to and *power over* are also entwined in the realm of human rights. The effective instantiation of human rights depends on the *power to* organize collective action through the institutional infrastructure of rights-based governance, including a functioning legal system, a rule-following bureaucratic administration, the apparatus of democratic elections including political parties, and a free press. This creates a mighty apparatus that can wield *power over* not just petty criminals but also corrupt politicians, rogue generals, and predatory oligarchs. Once firmly established, human rights constitute a potent *power to* organize collective action, which is demonstrated by the comparative success of rights-based democracies in sustaining economic growth, generating technological innovation, maintaining internal social peace, avoiding wars against each other, and winning wars against major illiberal great powers.

A pragmatist is not concerned that in full-fledged liberal systems human rights are both a cause and an effect. What matters to the pragmatist is to how to use power to achieve that goal. Of particular interest is how to combine and sequence the use of these different forms of power.

Coalitions for and against Rights

Forming effective coalitions around a programmatic set of issues requires identifying and mobilizing a core base of support and orchestrating bargaining with potential cooperators. Since an individual's interests are rarely obvious, and since people may not automatically know to which political group they should belong, constituting a core group of supporters is a preliminary step. This generally requires exploiting an existing social identity, such as Evangelical Christian, Democrat, or union worker, or promoting a plausible new one, such as Progressive, New Dealer, or Tea Party enthusiast.[21] To be politically effective, a social identity must be packaged with an interrelated set of policy attitudes that has some coherence and can serve as the basis for a plausible narrative. Valuable attributes in target constituencies pose some trade-offs among size, social compactness, and intensity and commonality of preferences. Connections between the political arm of the project, normally a political party, and a popular social movement, such as the civil rights movement or the Tea Party, are valuable for mobilizing a base of support. The movement helps the party understand the attitudes and goals of its core constituency, whereas the party helps the movement accomplish its policy objectives.[22]

Once a base is identified and mobilized, the next task is to form a coalition with other groups. This may involve bargaining with the leadership of those groups as well as targeting appeals to attract their members. Coalitions may be based on proximity of views (such as a progressive middle-class party aligning with a democratic working-class party) or complementarity of views (a socialist party logrolling with an environmentalist party). Coalitions supporting liberalization may even be entirely opportunistic, embodying what seems to be a direct contradiction of principles. In many countries, for example, coalitions supporting trade liberalization include swing factions that are brought in through promises of trade protection for their constituencies' most important economic sector.[23] Positionality can matter a great deal in bargaining: small swing parties that occupy the pivot between alternative plausible majorities can extract more policy concessions than larger factions whose alignment can be taken for granted for lack of alternative partners.[24] In the showdown over repeal of the Corn Laws, for example, Robert Peel's small, progressive Tory faction occupied the pivot between conservative, protectionist Tories and reformist, free-trading Whigs. As a result, Peel became prime minister and passed progressive legislation with votes that straddled factions of the two parties. Likewise, Quakers and Dissenters held a modest number of seats in Parliament, but they were intensely motivated on the antislavery issue and willing to pivot between Whigs and Tories, so they often prevailed on that issue regardless of who was in power. As a result of this "saintly logroll," they got Britain to spend 2 percent of its entire GDP on suppressing the Atlantic slave trade every year over several decades.[25]

In coalition politics based on vote trading, cooperating factions don't need to share the same underlying motives or values. Southern Democrats voted for FDR's policies that strengthened labor rights in the North but in exchange were allowed to maintain Jim Crow and weak, segregated unions in the South. And sometimes factions can favor the same policy, but for different reasons.

Abolitionists voted for Lincoln because he would stand against the moral evils of slavery, whereas bigoted Northern workers and potential westward migrants voted Republican to keep enslaved labor from competing with them for land through the westward expansion of slavery and for work in the North under the Dred Scott ruling.[26]

Straddles that cut across the central partisan cleavage are important in trying to form or to block coalitions. Wedge issue strategies, for example, appeal to groups or individuals who normally would be in the opponent's identity base (say, working-class Catholic Democrats), but who may be intensely motivated to cross party lines as single-issue voters on, say, abortion or trade protectionism. When it is not a single issue that prompts the defection on a single occasion, but rather a set of issues (abortion, trade, immigration, and militant foreign policy), the wedge strategy may give rise to a partisan realignment connected to a new identity narrative.[27]

A variant of the wedge strategy may be called *divide and rule*, wherein a strong political broker with agenda-setting power may split a potential opposition coalition by coopting one wing and portraying the other as a pariah group. Often authoritarian nationalists have used this tactic to prevent the emergence of a mass coalition in favor of liberal civic rights. The quintessential example is Chancellor Otto von Bismarck's use of Protestant nationalist appeals in the 1870s to drive a wedge between the German middle classes and their potential democratic allies in the working class and among Catholics.[28] Even human rights issues can be used to create such divisions. For example, King Mohammed VI of Morocco, like many Middle Eastern monarchs and autocrats, succeeds in dividing the popular opposition by means of fairly superficial women's rights reforms. This heightens the split between the liberal, cosmopolitan, democratic opposition and the Islamist opposition.[29] The women's health initiatives of Suzanne Mubarak, the wife of Egyptian dictator Hosni Mubarak, served the same function. In patronage-based systems, the central cleavage divides cooperative insiders who get paid off from resistant outsiders who don't.[30]

Such tactics play out against the backdrop of the overall structure of social interests in a society, which reflects the legacy of its overall trajectory of modernization. The classic study of the emergence of modern European social cleavages by Seymour Martin Lipset and Stein Rokkan depicts a historically layered process that laid down four enduring, crosscutting axes of contention shaping the party systems of the European states: between supranational centers and national peripheries over language and religious freedom during the

Reformation; between state and church over control of resources and education; between land and industry over economic freedoms and tariffs; and between owners and workers over organizing power and economic rights.[31] In Lipset and Rokkan's account, differences in the social power and historical embeddedness of groups defined by these layered cleavages created different opportunities to form dominant coalitions in different European states and regions. Variations in the distribution of social power across these cleavages led to bargains and rules that were more conducive to democratic party systems and universal rights in some configurations but to authoritarianism and oligarchy elsewhere, with various permutations within and between these types.[32] Following up on this research program, Gregory Luebbert's *Liberalism, Fascism, and Social Democracy* emphasized the role of traditionalist rural groups in illiberal, populist European coalitions in the early twentieth century, a finding that remains resonant in the current period of right-wing populist revival in many of the same countries.[33]

Whatever the specific coalition that might support human rights in a given situation, coalition organizers should keep in mind Charles Tilly's prime directive: work on breaking down discrimination and distrust across social identity categories and on providing broad access to important public goods. In modern circumstances this means preparing the basis for a democratic welfare state.

Knowing that modern rights coalitions are likely to tend in this direction, authoritarian leaders who seek to limit rights may try to coopt some welfare themes of this progressive agenda while playing divide and rule on identity themes. Thus, Bismarck preventively introduced social insurance programs in the 1880s while exploiting religious and class divisions and rallying support around military, colonial, and nationalist themes. In Poland today, the populist ruling party has similarly packaged nationalist themes with traditional religiously inspired social policies and welfare benefits targeted on the rural population.

Working against these divisive tactics, however, are several tendencies that favor inclusiveness in the politics of coalitions driven by self-interest. One of Tilly's core principles for an effective social movement is to demonstrate the group's "worthiness."[34] As chapter 8 elaborates further, identity groups worldwide are obsessed with intergroup comparisons and highly sensitive to stigma portraying them as lazy, slovenly, backward, and untrustworthy, which justifies discrimination against them. A major reason for the success of the movements led by Gandhi and Martin Luther King was that they motivated their followers to demonstrate the qualities of dignity, self-control, and inclusiveness that vividly defy stereotypes.

A typical tactic in appealing to a needed coalition partner is to invoke or invent some shared principle of identity or character than can serve as the basis for inclusion. Lars-Erik Cederman has argued, for example, that Croatians have adopted a narrowly ethnic ideology when facing rival groups of their own size but more inclusive identities such as South Slav or "Illyrian" when facing larger imperial threats requiring a broader alliance to resist them.[35] Similarly, Fotini Christia has shown how warring factions in Afghan civil wars shifted between ethnolinguistic identity appeals in moments of more local struggle to appeals to common religion when threats from foreigners were on a larger scale.[36]

Capable but vulnerable minorities such as the Quakers or Jews have a distinctive motive to generalize self-interest as a rule for universal application. They reason that mobilizing a coalition to block discrimination against the most vulnerable groups in society, such as the enslaved or victims of segregation, will empower a principle that will apply in their own case as well. Liah Greenfeld pushes this reasoning even further, arguing that it applies even to hegemonic cultural majorities in weakly consolidated democracies. Her historical case study of the collapse of rights and democracy in Germany, for example, describes a slippery slope that starts with denial of equal citizenship rights to Catholics and Jews as "enemies of the Reich" and ends with even Prussian Protestants being branded as enemies without any meaningful rights.[37] Martha Finnemore shows how the slippery slope can also work in a progressive direction: principles of humanitarian intervention and restraint in war that originally made appeals to a common Christian identity were later generalized for application to intervention to prevent atrocities against non-coreligionists as well.[38]

Interest configurations and cleavages are a good starting place for analysis of the social power of a pro-rights coalition. An important next step in the analysis is the effect of institutions on how those interests are aggregated.

Institutionally Induced Equilibria in Their Social Context

How coalitions form and which prevail depends not only on the interests of groups and the individuals that they comprise but also on the institutional rules that aggregate those interests. Some institutional arrangements might facilitate a strong pro-rights coalition, and others may undermine its

prospects. Sometimes institutions are endogenous to interests: powerful coalitions pick rules that solidify their domination.[39] Sometimes institutions are
exogenous to local interests, however: new or reforming nations simply follow
the rules of their former colonial power or the prevailing model offered by
powerful or nearby states. Either way, rights promoters need to think about
the effects of different institutions in structuring opportunities to empower a
favorable coalition.

To strengthen the rights coalition, these should normally be institutions
that move coalitions and policy outcomes in the direction of reducing categorical inequality and increasing trust in inclusive forms of public goods provision. Exactly which institutions will advance the rights cause may depend on
the specific features of the social context in which they operate, such as the
degree of economic inequality between social classes and the degree of ethnic
polarization in the society. That said, the general rule of thumb is to move
institutions in the direction of democracy, to reduce institutional incentives
to coalesce around ethnic difference, and instead to organize politics around
social class differences.

Recent theoretical work by John Huber, backed up by his suggestive empirical research, helps to explain the logic behind these strategies.[40] In a way
that echoes Tilly, Huber argues that moving toward more just social outcomes
in democratic systems involves shifting the political equilibrium from one
based on inequality and ethnic favoritism to one based on equality and class
politics. He argues that the feasibility of this move depends on the preexisting
levels of economic inequality and ethnic demographic polarization. Whether
the potential for change can be fulfilled also depends in part on the institutional setting. In working out this argument, he is assuming that the country's
political competition is carried out in accord with some kind of democratic
rules and that voters are generally rational and strategic in serving their material interests.

To keep the analysis simple, Huber begins by assuming that parties can
appeal to voters on the basis of either class or ethnicity. Institutionally, he
begins by assuming a plurality electoral rule: the candidate with the most votes
in each district wins. Since every voter has an ethnicity and a class position,
the voter must decide which alignment offers the greatest benefit. In line with
typical theories of representative democracy, Huber reasons that voters will
flock to the party that can offer them the biggest slice of the distributional pie,
which will be the smallest group that can still win a majority (a minimum
winning coalition).[41] Consequently, class politics is unlikely to prevail if the

rich are a tiny minority, and ethnic politics is unlikely if the majority identity group constitutes the overwhelming bulk of the population. Conversely, class parties will do well if the relatively rich and relatively poor are close to 50-50, and ethnic parties will do well if the demography is close to a 50-50 split. In the latter case, the rich will do much better by seeking a coalition with poor co-ethnics than by trying to buy off the middle class of both ethnicities. Crucially, even those poor co-ethnics will be better off banking on the targeted payoffs from a deal with rich co-ethnics than by sharing the more diffuse payoffs from a deal with the overlarge coalition of all the poor from both ethnic groups.[42]

Ethnic polarization tends to be self-perpetuating in this situation, with dire consequences for civil liberties and socioeconomic rights. The winning ethnic party can be expected to deliver policies of ethnic favoritism, including legalized discrimination, and to redistribute wealth and provide public services selectively only to its own co-ethnics. Whenever possible, the ethnic winners will try to lock in their gains by changing laws, electoral districting, and other institutional arrangements to guarantee the continuation of these advantages. This outcome works against the Tilly criterion of reducing categorical inequalities and increasing trust in state public goods provision, and the irony is that it can occur even in electoral democracies.

Huber then asks how institutional variations across democracies might affect the chances of rights-compatible class politics emerging instead of rights-endangering ethnic politics. In electoral politics, for example, a basic institutional distinction lies between legislative systems that elect representatives by a plurality of the vote in single-member districts, as in the United States and the UK, as opposed to electing them by the party's proportion of the overall vote, as in many European countries. Mature, stable plurality systems normally tend toward competition between two parties that each try to forge a minimum winning coalition before the winner-take-all election. In contrast, parties in proportional representation (PR) systems can target a base constituency in the election and then try to negotiate participation in a multiparty minimum winning coalition after the election.

Often it is claimed that PR favors "minority rights" because ethnic parties can gain seats in the legislature even if they are a demographic minority. Power-sharing approaches to multiethnic governance often count on this possibility. Based on deductive logic and empirical findings, Huber argues that the opposite is more likely: PR favors class politics, or at any rate, broadly inclusive politics. He argues that it is hard to form parties based on hybrids of ethnicity and class that are cohesive enough to contest elections with a clear platform. PR makes this unnecessary, since hybrid coalitions comprising class and ethnic parties can form after the election, based on expedient bargaining and logrolling.[43] If so, PR should normally be conducive to the development of inclusive rights protections.

Huber's argument is a good first cut in favor of proportional representation when strategizing the empowerment of rights-supportive coalitions. Rights advocates, however, are not concerned only with what usually happens statistically or what should happen if voters are strategic. They also need to consider the perhaps nonstandard effects of institutions on coalitions in whatever country they seek to strategize for. Sometimes these deviations from the expected equilibrium path may be perverse. For example, US and UK catchall parties have sometimes been able to forge improbable hybrid coalitions of economic redistribution to the poor and regional white supremacy (the New Deal) or coalitions of the rich and uneducated nativists (Trump and Brexit). Sometimes, however, deviations from the normal equilibrium may create unexpected opportunities for inclusive politics, which rights advocates might exploit. One of Huber's main examples, Malaysia, is illustrative.

Huber argues that plurality systems create an incentive for the politics of ethnic favoritism when the size of the ethnic majority is not too much above half, as in Malaysia.[44] But plurality systems can also create distinctive opportunities for ethnic moderation depending on specific geographic patterns of ethnic residence. Malaysia illustrates the potential for vote trading in single-member districts to facilitate an inclusive form of cross-cultural power sharing.[45] Malays, the "sons of the soil," resented the very large Chinese minority who had been imported as laborers and merchants under British colonial administration. Malays had grievances against the comparatively well-off Chinese business class and also against rural Chinese in northern Malaya who had fomented a Communist insurgency in the early Cold War. After defeating the insurgency, the British orchestrated the Alliance coalition between the moderate Chinese business-oriented party and the moderate, traditional, elite-dominated Malay party. The British hoped this coalition would survive in the face of militantly hostile ethnic parties based respectively in the Chinese working classes and in Malay rural and lower classes. The British made maintenance of the power-sharing coalition a condition of national independence.

After independence, however, Malay populists challenged the moderate power-sharing deal. Malay militants sought to outbid the moderate Malay elitist party in attracting rank-and-file Malay voters with proposals to strip citizenship from Chinese immigrants, even those who had been in Malaya for generations under the British. For some time, though, the Westminster-style system of parliamentary representation by single-member districts helped the moderate power-sharing Alliance win electoral victories by vote trading. In ethnically mixed districts, the moderate Malay and Chinese parties agreed to run a joint candidate of the ethnicity of whichever group held a local majority. Since their militant Malay and Chinese rivals could not benefit from a similar vote-trading deal, the moderates would typically win a plurality even in constituencies where the militant parties won more votes overall than the moderates.

This Malaysian moderate logroll was a consequence not only of the single-member district representation rule but also of the fact that Malaysia had numerous multiethnic urban districts where vote trading could work to isolate both Chinese and Malay extremist parties. In the 1950s, Sri Lanka had similarly inherited a Westminster electoral system and the legacy of a British-required power-sharing system, but it lacked demographically mixed Singhalese/Tamil electoral districts, so vote trading could not work in the same way. Instead of empowering moderates, the monoethnic districts in Sri Lanka rewarded parties that outbid each other in clamoring respectively for government jobs for Singhalese only or for Tamil ethnofederal autonomy. Voters were mobilized by polarizing appeals, and when politicians tried to negotiate necessary post-election compromises with swing-vote factions in Parliament, they were assassinated or stymied by the militant constituencies they had unleashed.

Even in Malaysia, the moderate vote-trading coalition eventually needed the strong-arm power of the state to survive in the face of populist polarization. Arguably, this eventual collapse of cross-ethnic party cooperation supports Huber's expectations for cases with polarized demographics. With each election after independence, the vote share of the militants increased, and during the 1968 currency crisis, militants resorted to violence in the streets. Rather than face elections, the Alliance suspended democracy for a few years while it rewrote the constitution to ban ethnically divisive speech, reorganized patronage to ensure support for Alliance rule, and deployed tough Sarawak ranger police units, who were from Borneo and ethnically neither Chinese nor Malay, to impartially enforce strict discipline in the streets. It doesn't matter if elections are PR or plurality if everyone expects political issues to be settled by militias fighting in the streets rather than parties in the legislature. Affirmative action for Malays in governmental employment, education, and rural development funding was balanced by advantageous rules for Chinese internationalized businesses. Ironically, many of the original policy goals of the democratic power-sharing Alliance and its British sponsors could be accomplished only by limiting civic rights and legislating constructive forms of ethnic discrimination.

This case illustrates not only the effects of institutionally induced equilibria and the strategic control of the political agenda on rights outcomes, but also the necessary pragmatic trade-offs between means and ends when the facilitating conditions for liberal rights are only partially present. Malaysia routinely receives fairly poor rankings on indices of democracy and civic freedoms, and its insufficiently accountable officials are routinely subjected to naming and shaming by NGOs for corruption. Even so, compared to Sri Lanka and Indonesia, Malaysia has kept ethnic strife to a minimum and laid down some foundations for the eventual achievement of ethnic peace and rule of law. Malaysia's democratic election in 2018 brought down the corrupt government of Najib Razak and replaced it with a multiethnic ruling coalition of opposition parties.[46]

A few general points emerge from this discussion of the role of institutions in influencing rights outcomes. Those who seek to promote rights-enhancing outcomes should keep in view a general strategy of how institutions can help empower a pro-rights coalition. The Tilly criteria and the Huber framework of strategic choice could be good starting points. Institutional strategies need to consider the circumstances in which institutions will be operating, such as the degree of economic inequality and demographic polarization. Often these conditions will not be ideal, so strategies need to include "second-best" options. Such expedients may require inventing adaptations, such as the moderate Malaysian vote-trading alliance, that find potential for inclusive cooperation even when institutions (such as plurality elections) and demographics (such as extreme polarization) seem on first inspection to be unfavorable.

Ideologies for and against Rights

For rights promotion, as for any other political project, an effective ideology is indispensable to help people understand their interests in the desired way, to bind together a sufficiently broad and powerful coalition, and to tell a motivating narrative. Notwithstanding Samuel Moyn's arguments about the conceptual incoherence and contradictions in liberalism's evolving ideology, liberalism has a record of success in various settings that stands up well in comparison to its rights-abusing competitors, such as authoritarian versions of nationalism, militarism, socialism, theocracy, populism, monarchism, mafia or warlord rule, and personalistic dictatorship. It attracts support in most of the world's powerful states. Elsewhere its basic concept of democratic national self-determination typically gains lip service even from authoritarians who go through the motions of unfair elections and some simulacrum of legal procedure. In settings that lack the facilitating conditions for democracy and rule of law, liberalism struggles to compete for legitimacy with illiberal forms of nationalism, but because national self-determination is an inherent part of the liberal model, it remains a latent contender in the nationalist game.[47] Overall, liberalism provides mainstream human rights advocacy with a promising ideological foundation.

One problem, however, is that mainstream human rights advocacy has chosen to emphasize a variant of liberalism that relies on moralism, legalism, and universalism. These themes often play poorly in societies that are still in the process of emerging from traditional society and patronage-based political economy. Universalism in particular creates difficulties where elites are nationalist, anti-imperialist, non-Western, and non-Christian.

A related problem, which is no fault of the human rights mainstream, is that since the 1980s liberalism has become associated with *neoliberalism*, free-market fundamentalism, and the corruption that is often a side effect when economic globalization comes to societies with weak legal institutions. Probably the only way to extricate itself from this branding disaster is for the human rights mainstream to shift its ideological priorities to increase emphasis on social welfare and economic justice as central to its mission. Given that the second half of the Universal Declaration of Human Rights deals with social and economic rights, which has been developed and codified in international law as the International Covenant on Social, Economic, and Cultural Rights since 1976, this should be a natural move for human rights advocacy.

Complicating this move, however, is the libertarian dimension of the liberal rights project, which reaches out in a progressive direction as free-speech absolutism and in a conservative direction as antiregulation free-market fundamentalist economics. Adding to the libertarian image problem of the rights movement, the two major figures at Human Rights Watch since its founding, Aryeh Neier and Kenneth Roth, have been slow in moving away from prioritizing civil and political rights over economic and social rights.[48] Combined with their emphasis on universalistic naming and shaming of the many countries that don't measure up, this presents ideological challenges for mobilizing mass social movements around mainstream human rights themes in the developing world.

The most important issue facing the ideological development of the human rights movement is how to adapt to the reality that normative persuasion is a competitive game. Much recent human rights practice has developed in a post–Cold War context, where it was assumed that cosmopolitan liberalism had become the only game in town. That assumption is no longer tenable given the assertive pushback from authoritarian great powers and illiberal social movements. Accepting that rights promotion is not just a matter of teaching the unenlightened or mobilizing an inexorable rights "cascade" means accepting the notion of back-and-forth normative discussion. It also means avoiding gratuitous provocation of likely resisters, bargaining with a sense of long-term strategy, thinking in terms of timing and sequences, and accepting some long-term compromises of principle at the margins.

Within those broad parameters, pragmatic rights strategy faces choices on several dimensions, some of which pose trade-offs whose solution is not simple. These trade-offs involve basic philosophical choices about objectives as well as choices of how to relate means to ends.

Idealism, Self-Interest, and Expediency in Pragmatic Ideology

Neier argues that the antislavery movement was the world's first true human rights movement because it was the first to work for the rights of people outside the activists' own religion or national group.[49] He argues that altruism is the hallmark of human rights. The historical record of successful human rights movements, however, suggests that this is an ideological mistake. An effective ideology combines idealistic and self-interested attributes. It motivates core constituencies to do what is right as a generalizable principle and to see it as beneficial for themselves. An ideological model that combines these elements is Adam Smith's doctrine of the invisible hand of the market, which portrays self-interested liberty as a win-win proposition for everyone. Even more basic is the Golden Rule: do unto others as you would have them do unto you, which is both a moral precept and an appeal to the mutual benefits of reciprocity.

Successful rights idealists do not ignore selective incentives for their followers. The pious American abolitionists of the Second Great Awakening in the 1830s, arguably a least likely case for selfish motivation, included many Perfectionists, who believed that the Second Coming of Christ would be delayed until the sinful world had been perfected. They saw it as in their interest to hasten that day by ending slavery and promoting strict Sabbath observance, temperance, prison reform, and women's equality.[50] In another example, constituency self-interest in tax reduction and decolonization was central to the project of the self-abnegating ascetic Gandhi.[51]

Acknowledging a core of self-interest may help targets of persuasion understand why the advocate is trying so hard to convince or reform them. Mennonites who engage in humanitarian service abroad among people of a different faith explain that their motivation to help all others is what their God expects of them.

Principled idealists raise their eyebrows not only at self-interest, but also at tactical expediency in the means of achieving human rights goals. A convincing pragmatist ideology of rights promotion needs to have rules about when bending the rules is warranted. Expedient compromise can be justified within a liberal human rights ideology when it is necessary to empower a pro-rights coalition over the long term, when rights are not yet enforceable, when their deterrent effect remains weak, and when actors have not converged on the expectation that others' behavior will conform to human rights norms.

Universal versus Community Standards and Language

Most human rights activists accept in principle that some rights can and should be defined locally as long as their rationale makes some reference to general rights principles that are shared globally. This kind of localization is a matter of the content of the rights as well as how rights concepts are articulated.[52]

Proponents of vernacularizing rights discourse argue that many of the world's normative systems contain ideas that are similar to those of liberal, transnational rights advocates. They recommend using local terminology to promote human rights practices. Even they admit, however, that this can come at a cost. Some cultures are deeply embedded with concepts that justify discrimination and oppression of women, cultural and religious minorities, and outcast groups. Local audiences may see vernacular norms talk as part of the problem they want to escape. When the most modern and successful societies in the world use universalistic language to talk about human rights to the powerless, it can send a compelling message of liberation.[53]

A major barrier to successful vernacularization of rights talk is that ideas about specific rights are embedded in a comprehensive liberal worldview that is typically at odds with the worldview of the local vernacular. Anthropologists Peggy Levitt and Sally Merry, leading exponents of the concept of vernacularization, note that human rights are part of what they call a "neo-liberal package" that also promotes democracy, capitalism, rule of law, transparency, accountability, and gender equity. This constitutes a "global values package" that competes and coexists with a "fundamentalist religious package" based on tradition, conservatism, authority, and gender complementarity. They also argue that the framing of issues such as gender tends to be path dependent. Once a culture settles into a secular or a religious mode of discourse about an issue, it tends to stay on that track.[54]

Arguably it is not just cultural inertia and institutional vested interest that pushes toward continuity of practice and discourse, but also the functional coherence of the packages of issues and the conceptual coherence of their frames. The liberal package hangs together because its elements share the taproot of individualism and rule-based social relations, whereas the traditional package makes sense for societies that are organized around patron-client relations in an identity-based community.[55] It is no wonder that Levitt and Merry see "more friction than flows" in attempts at vernacularized persuasion across the gulf between systems that have been coherently structured around antithetical logics.[56]

Unpacking the gender component further in their empirical research, however, Levitt and Merry observe some variants and hybrids that integrate elements of each global package. Examples include "Chinese social work ideology," a professional ethos that seeks many of the same practical outcomes as liberal gender advocacy while operating in an authoritarian setting; liberation theology in Peru, which adapts religion to the pursuit of typically liberal social justice aims; Gandhian thought and socialism in India, which draw on religious or nonliberal concepts to advance progressive objectives in a democratic state; and LGBT and "people of color" activism in the United States, which adopts a liberal formula for identity politics.[57] It is worth noting that these hybrids, though drawing on strands of liberal modernity in circulation in global discourse and practice, were all forged locally by actors native to a particular culture. They were not crafted as pedagogical performances of vernacular persuasion by outsiders.

Still, there are pitfalls in using both vernacular and universalistic language. Localizing human rights talk risks watering down the concept, while appropriating universalist talk risks turning it into its opposite—for example, rhetoric claiming that police torture of suspects is protecting the "human rights" of people in the community on whom criminals prey.[58] Developing a rights ideology that captures the best features of both universalism and vernacularism—and avoids their worst features—is a priority that may require deft political skills as well as cross-cultural rhetorical abilities.[59]

Understanding the Ideological Competition with Nationalist Populism

A first step in winning the ideological competition is to understand better the nature of the nationalist populist ideology that has emerged as liberalism's fiercest competitor. Populist ideology often reflects elites' efforts to shift the main axis of political cleavage from class to identity politics.

One tried and true method that elites use to escape confiscatory taxation in democracies is to play up the political salience of group identity, nationalism, and culture.[60] In the United States, this dynamic was colorfully captured in the 2004 book *What's the Matter with Kansas?*, where the journalist Thomas Frank argued that wealthy Republicans were duping low-income, small-town, white citizens into voting against their own economic interests by hyping cultural "wedge issues" such as abortion, gay rights, racism, and threat-inflating militaristic patriotism. The best antidote to this framing is usually class politics. Nationwide surveys show that Americans overall tend to be more favorable to progressive arguments when they are couched in terms of class than racial equality.[61]

Variants of the cultural wedge tactic are widespread across time and space, including seminal cases of late development. In the wake of Germany's rapid industrialization, the aristocratic monarchist Bismarck responded to middle-class demands for constitutional government and limited parliamentary democracy by going them one better: universal manhood suffrage including the working class and the peasantry. He gambled that the peasants would vote the way conservative landlords told them to, and that appeals to true German national identity could split up a hypothetical progressive coalition among labor, Catholics, and middle-class Protestant nationalists. He was right. In nine national parliamentary elections between 1870 and 1914, the conservative coalition did much better in the five that were fought on so-called national or cultural issues defined by the Kulturkampf against the Catholics, colonial expansion, and military budgets to defend Germany against "hostile encirclement" by the Entente powers, which German diplomacy had largely provoked in the first place.[62] Bismarck and his successors used nationalism and cultural conservatism to divide and conquer the potential progressive coalition of organized labor and free-trade interests, which came to power only after Germany's defeat in World War I.

The all-purpose logic of shifting the axis of electoral politics from economics to identity politics also explains urban rioting in India. Steven Wilkinson's definitive research shows that riots occur when municipal elections are expected to be close between an elite-dominated identity-based party, such as the Hindu nationalist BJP, and a lower-class-based party attempting to appeal across identities such as Hindu and Muslim.[63] Using thugs and rumors to foment rioting polarizes politics on the identity axis on the eve of the election, inducing lower-class Hindus, for example, to vote their cultural ties rather than their pocketbook.

Often elites play the nationalist card in response to earlier efforts to mobilize mass support for progressive change. Bismarck's strategy was a response to the revolutionary upheavals of 1848 and the initial successes of Germany's "national liberals." The BJP's strategy was shaped by the political landscape that had been created earlier by the populist tactics of the Congress Party, including the foundational efforts of Mahatma Gandhi and the later populist authoritarianism of Indira Gandhi's emergency rule period. Similarly, the Chinese government's flirtation with mass nationalism since the mid-1990s was a direct response to the threat from the 1989 mass "liberty" protests in Tiananmen Square, arising at a time when orthodox Communist legitimations of authority fit poorly with Deng Xiaoping's turn to market economics.

A typical danger is that nationalist gambits from above and below feed on each other in a contest of outbidding. Before 1914, for example, German middle-class mass nationalist and colonialist groups exploited the ruling elite's embrace of nationalist threat mongering, arguing that if Germany really was encircled by the hostile Entente powers, then the army should be increased in size, the aristocracy should be taxed for it, and middle-class officers should be allowed into the aristocratic preserve of the General Staff. The discourse of nationalism and identity politics that Bismarck and his successors fueled played into the hands of mass nationalist groups. This ultimately set the stage for the quintessential right-wing populist group, the National Socialists, to emerge from the collapse of global markets that ended the Weimar Republic.

To win the ideological battle against nationalist populism, human rights liberals need to keep the axis of struggle focused on equal rights and public goods instead of cultural identity and patronage favoritism. Doing this means not only adopting the right rhetoric, but also organizing ideologically conscious social movements that can attract swing constituencies in a pro-rights coalition. Chapter 6 discusses how to organize for this.

Sequencing Rights-Promoting Efforts

No less an authority than Robert Dahl argues that Britain followed an ideal trajectory in the development of its liberalism.[64] Nearly all the institutions needed to support democratic, rule-of-law, rights-based politics were in place before mass suffrage. These included a well-developed legal system based increasingly on due process and equality before the law, freedom of the press, a largely rule-based civil service, and a system of representative government in which party factions stepped down from power when they failed to win a majority in popular elections. Also important was the development of a capitalist economy with a flexible financial system that allowed traditional privileged elites to shift their assets into the same kinds of mobile investments as the rising bourgeois classes. All of this dampened social conflict and facilitated the adjustment of ruling coalitions as first the middle classes, then the working classes, and finally women were given the franchise between 1832 and 1918.

Dahl went on to argue, however, from his vantage point in 1971 that this institutions-first sequence of liberal democratization had become a thing of the past. In the era of decolonization, nations would refuse to wait until institutions were built to embark on the politics of mass democratic participation. As a result, there had been a surge in the prevalence of "illiberal democracies," holding mass elections but lacking strong institutions to guarantee free and fair contestation, the rule of law, rule-based constraints on officials, nondiscrimination, and basic civic rights.[65] The result has been a surge of semidemocratic regimes suffering from ethnic strife, corruption, instability, poor governance, and endemic rights violations.

While Dahl may be right that future transitions to a liberal rights-based order are unlikely to follow the advantageous British sequence, the poor outcomes from the out-of-sequence transitions of many third-wave semidemocracies suggest that there may be room for improvement. Even if countries and activists cannot choose any sequence of rights development that they want, they should try to make thoughtful choices about sequencing at the margins.

Sequencing structural preconditions. Structural facilitating conditions still matter. Among the Arab Spring regime changers, Tunisia had the best outcome for human rights as well as the most favorable pretransition circumstances in terms of its per capita income, its World Bank rating of governmental administrative capacity (the other states were even worse), and its ethnic homogeneity.[66] Not all facilitating background conditions need to be in place, however, to have a good chance at inculcating a liberal rights-based order. After the Second World War, Japan's economy lay in ruins, South Korea was one of the poorest countries on earth, and Taiwan was ruled by the rump of the alien, brutal, authoritarian Chinese nationalist regime. Japan had an imposed constitution, and the latter two were divided nations. Yet each had a disciplined population with the capacity to work productively in modern economic firms and state bureaucracies. The sequencing of their evolution toward democracy, though interrupted in South Korea by a military coup, allowed time for economic development to produce the middle-class, educated public that could support it. In contrast, South Africa had a different mix of facilitators and disadvantages: elements of a first-world economy and British institutions for the white ruling class, but a legacy of extreme racial discrimination that affected the social capital needed to support a society-wide rights-based order. Different challenges require different strategies to build on whatever usable preconditions may be available.

Finally, circumstances barren of almost any favorable conditions beg for strategies of political stabilization that do not count on the rapid emergence of a self-sustaining liberal rights-based order. Elections in Burundi in 1993 were forced by democratic international donor states and predictably led to disaster. Likewise, an academic article that evaluated Iraq's readiness for democracy, written at the very moment of the US 2003 invasion, gave nothing but black marks on a checklist that included its oil-based economy, sectarian and ethnic divisions, and lack of usable institutions.[67] The *Washington Post*'s December 2019 disclosure of internal US government studies revealing the confusion and pessimism about US counterinsurgency and nation-building efforts during the Afghan war showed once again the cost of assuming that liberal rule-following systems will thrive in unprepared soil. Sometimes the lack of preconditions should be decisive in choices of strategy.

The same logic applies to the sequencing of peace and justice. War is such a strong predictor of human rights abuse that peace can be considered a virtual precondition for rights and justice. While in the long run, peace and justice are mutually supportive in a working rights-based system, whenever there is a short-run tradeoff between peace and justice, the tactical priority of peace is usually overwhelming.[68]

Sequencing the state and the nation. An even more basic dictum than "no bourgeoisie, no democracy" is "no state, no democracy." Setting up an

administrative apparatus that governs territory by some semblance of legitimate rules is the most basic precondition for civic rights and indeed any kind
of rights. Establishing a state that has some congruence with a nation is on the
short list of preconditions for coherent statehood, democracy, and therefore
rights.[69] Co-ethnicity is a common basis for nationhood, defined by the sense
of constituting a distinctive people that seeks to rule itself in its own state.[70]
The difficulty has been that ethnic groups have traditionally resided intermingled inside the territories of multinational or colonial empires. When these
old empires or colonial territories gave way to successor nation-states, which
sought legitimacy from the idea of popular sovereignty, intermingled ethnic
groups often struggled with each other to seize exclusive control of the state,
to expel ethnic rivals from it, or to secede in a new territorial state of their own.
Mostly this has been accomplished by war. It took a bloody shakedown cruise
in the century between the Balkan Wars of 1912–13 and the completion of the
breakup of Yugoslavia in 2000 before Europe established nation-states that
were more homogeneous with respect to long-residing peoples.[71]

A better way to arrange congruence between the state and its nation is to
create an effective state well before its people are politically mobilized. As in
the process of turning linguistically diverse peasants into Frenchmen over the
course of the nineteenth century, the state socializes its citizens to a predominant ethnic identity or to an inclusive identity based on civic principles, using
the tools of standardized education, compulsory military service, common
laws, and integrated systems of communication and transportation.[72] In most
cases, however, state and nation builders are not completely free to choose
whether to emphasize ethnic or civic principles of belonging. Still less can they
choose a sequence of building the state or the nation first. But on those occasions where a choice remains open, it can have huge implications for rights
outcomes.

Whenever possible, following Tilly's framework, state builders should be
persistent but realistic in promoting inclusive civic nationalism. Success in
this, however, depends on the institutional tools at their disposal. Dawn
Brancati's research shows that the stability of ethnic federalism has depended on the existence of nonethnic statewide parties like the Socialists in
Spain or the Congress Party in India that remain competitive in autonomous
ethnic subunits.[73] Sometimes, however, such parties are unavailable, and the
best that can be done is to retain some fluidity in the politicization of ethnic
or tribal identities. For example, in Zambia, voters have switched back and
forth between linguistic loyalties and smaller-scale tribal loyalties, the

former prevailing when the three large language groups were the most relevant blocs to contest for national-level power in multiparty elections, the latter prevailing when local contests were most relevant for gaining patronage in times of single-party rule.[74] This gives political entrepreneurs some latitude in the types of loyalties they want to encourage through institutional or rhetorical means.

Even when ethnic or sectarian identities are already entrenched, liberal multiculturalism, which organizes ethnic contestation under an umbrella of rights-based rules, is to be preferred. That said, sometimes avoiding outright warfare will require illiberal forms of power sharing or armed stalemate in which peace must temporarily trump liberal state building. When institutions are extremely weak, liberal rights-based systems are usually less feasible than repression and patronage-based systems, which can piggyback on traditional ethnic or religious networks.[75] One of the most important questions for sequencing is how to move from power-sharing expedients, which may be needed to achieve a peace settlement despite the risk of locking in invidious ethnic politics, toward a preferable long-term system based more on liberal civic rules. In postconflict settings, the likelihood of an early return to fighting can be reduced by delaying elections until after institutions can be improved, rebels disarmed, and rule-based power sharing negotiated. I discuss this in chapter 4.

Sequencing in coalition making. In crafting a rights-advancing coalition strategy, reformers will normally engage the old regime on disadvantageous terrain and with tools that need to be forged in the course of the struggle. Rights advocates will need to begin by proposing aspirational norms and goals that will resonate with the concerns and interests of the most likely core group of supporters, yet they will need to articulate those principles in ways that are not off-putting to potential tactical allies or gratuitously provocative to powerful spoilers. At the same time, advocates will need to avoid acting and talking as if their aspirational norms are already in force, which risks discrediting them as ineffective.

Following John Huber's logic of minimum winning coalitions, rights-based reformers should normally try to mobilize a core constituency based on the middle and lower classes. In societies where class distinctions are not salient or institutionalized, however, liberal reformers face trade-offs. Anchoring support for rights in a core constituency of the ethnic majority fits with the goal of democracy and has the practical advantage of appealing to a powerful base. Yet, mobilizing for the rights of the ethnic majority has the double danger of creating too big a winning coalition, by Huber's logic, and degenerating into a tyranny of the majority. Reformers who have no practical alternative to an ethnic majoritarian strategy may need to highlight the inclusive potential of religious ideas and networks that offer a bridge of common identity across ethnic differences.[76] Alternatively, an encompassing linguistic identity, say Swahili or Arabic, could in principle provide an inclusive civic umbrella under which to organize a religious sectarian multiculturalism. Some reformers have argued for this approach in Lebanon. Different raw materials and historical legacies will require different tactical choices, while nonetheless keeping in view the basic guidelines, as laid out by Tilly and Huber.

Once the outlines of a support constituency are in view, options for alliance tactics need to be assessed based on calculations of power, interest, and ideological proximity. Which rights-tolerant or rights-neutral actors can plausibly control the swing-voter pivot in the political system? How can they be coopted to support the rights cause? What are possible inducements for them to compete for benefits that would come with a prominent place in the pro-rights coalition? Who are the veto groups, such as the military, who must be appeased or somehow neutralized, lest rights policies be blocked or crushed?

Playing this coalition game well or badly can be decisive. One key to Turkish President Recep Tayyip Erdogan's success in monopolizing power and overturning liberalizing reforms has been to position his AK Party as the most natural coalition partner of most of Turkey's other factional constituencies. Starting from his base among the near-majority core group of pious, historically "left behind" Anatolian Turks, he has been able to shift into and out of alliances with pious traditionalist Kurds, pious modernizers in the Gülenist faction, secular Turkish nationalists, and pragmatic entrepreneurs, while isolating Westernized secular liberals, who face severe alliance handicaps with other opposition groups. In recent elections, however, strategic voting coordinated among secular liberals, modernized Kurds, and the numerous, wealthy, dispersed, persecuted Alevi religious minority has shown some potential to become a pro-rights minimum winning coalition.

To succeed simultaneously in mobilizing core supporters and attracting opportunistic coalition partners, rights-oriented reformers need to sit firmly on all three legs of the stool described in chapter 6: a mass social movement, a politically astute progressive party, and principled rights activist organizations. In Turkey, secular liberals were saddled with a secular Westernizing political party inherited from the Ataturk system, which had conspired in military coups, corrupted state support of industrial enterprises, and banned headscarves to block professional advancement of pious women. Secular rights activist organizations were too easily dismissed as tools of the liberal West, unlike the more religiously based rights NGO Mazlumder, which doesn't take foreign money. The liberals' mass movement made a temporary splash protesting Erdogan's neo-Ottoman development plan for Istanbul's beloved Gezi Park, but the movement has yet to demonstrate institutionalized staying power.

In Egypt, liberal rights-supporting factions have likewise been outorganized and outmaneuvered. In the waning days of the Mubarak regime, Egypt's secular pro-rights faction had some professional NGOs to protest abuses but no sustained rights movement, no coherent labor movement, no crosscutting elite networks to forge compromises with other moderate factions, and no pragmatic reform party. The potential constituencies for reform, though constituting 49 percent of the voters in the first round of the presidential election, remained divided and disorganized. Individual reform-minded citizens shared the antiregime protest space of Tahrir Square with the Muslim Brotherhood, but unlike the more secular moderates, the Brotherhood commanded a strong social movement that could get out the vote and a leadership that prevented rival Brotherhood candidates from competing in the same district. This won them the elections for president and Parliament, but the Brotherhood lacked a pragmatic governing party and had no interest in coopting reformists in an alliance to neutralize the common threat from the military.

While the sequencing of tactics must vary with the opportunities that circumstances present, in general an effective strategy should work over the long term to strengthen all three mutually supporting legs of the organizational triad of social movement, activists, and reform party.

Sequencing voting and coalition making. One of the longest running debates about governing deeply divided democratic and semidemocratic societies is whether to try to forge cross-ethnic cooperative alliances before or after elections. The orthodox *power-sharing* view expounded by Arend Lijphart holds that each cultural group should be granted generous group rights to internal, local self-government and a guaranteed share of representation in electoral and administrative governmental organs at the national level. In his view, each group should organize for elections independently to choose its own representatives, and then engage in group-based bargaining and compromise after the elections.[77] The alternative view expounded by Donald Horowitz, illustrated in this chapter by the Malaysia example, holds that the cultural groups should forge *vote-trading* alliances before the elections, running for office on a platform that appeals to moderate voters of more than one cultural group. Proponents of the Horowitz approach argue that mobilizing in separate groups to contest the election does the damage of needlessly locking in identity politics and mobilizing mass support in a way that leads to intraethnic outbidding: candidates compete to be the most militant in fighting for the group's interests, signaling that they will never sell out to the enemy.[78] Horowitz's example of Sri Lankan ethnic politics shows that once electoral campaigns have been mobilized in this way, stable postelection compromise is nearly impossible.[79] For this reason, a pragmatist approach to forging an effective rights coalition should always consider the Horowitzian solution first and opt for the Lijphart approach as a last resort.

Sequencing the package of civic and economic rights. Historically, the emergence of civil liberties in the liberal state preceded the emergence of economic and social rights guaranteed in the welfare state. This sometimes creates the impression that civic rights are logically prior to and a political precondition for economic and social rights. The strong correlation between liberal democracy and the protection of rights of all kinds suggests that this is the case. That said, the reason that liberal civic rights emerged first is historically due to the timing of the development of bourgeois capitalism, which is a precondition in most places for the development of industrial society. The working class and its concern for economic, labor, and social welfare rights normally came later.

A distinctive path led to single-party or dominant-party regimes. Societies with a large peasantry, a weak bourgeoisie, and a repressive alliance between the state and industrial elites were more likely to buy the support of favored workers and managers with targeted economic benefits than they were to offer universal political rights. Under those conditions, patronage benefits for favored sectors and skilled labor—a system that had much in common with traditional arrangements—took priority over demands for political liberalization. Examples include socialist regimes and bureaucratic authoritarian regimes in the later developing world.[80]

In strategizing for rights promotion, these considerations suggest that neither civil liberties nor economic and social rights should have absolute priority in all cases. Touting only bourgeois rights to a society that lacks a powerful middle class will not add political clout to the rights message. Yet harping only on wealth disparities and elite corruption in such a society is likely to play into the hands of illiberal demagogues who will use those issues to target political rivals rather than pursue systemic reform. Civic and economic rights need to be brought together in a narrative stressing that economic fairness and social

equality can be achieved only if the broad mass of the people enjoys institutionalized political power and equality before the law. This is the take-home
lesson from the discussion of Tilly's analysis of historical social movements in
chapter 6. This narrative may be a hard sell, however, when some liberal democracies display inequalities and corruption that look similar to those in
illiberal societies.

Lenin famously criticized some of his Bolshevik comrades for indulging in
the "left wing disorder" of advocating ideologically purist policies, which were
not yet ripe for implementation in backward Russia.[81] In light of the extensive
research on the social background conditions for democracy and rights,
human rights ideology should consider how to sequence its arguments and its
remedies to fit the different stages and contexts in the evolution of rights.[82]
Chapter 4 discusses rights sequencing in political transitions.

Conclusions

This chapter has considered the building blocks from which a rights-based
order must be built, including its basis in social power and interests, the coalition that supports it, and the institutions and ideas that enable it. General
guidelines for sequencing strategies should keep in view the overall goal of
moving from a social system based on repression and patronage to one based
on governmental accountability, impersonal social relations, and equality before the law. Since societies depart from different starting points and embody
different mixes of facilitating conditions, however, tactics must also be tailored
to fit these varied circumstances. How these building blocks and sequences
come together in societies as they cross the threshold to a rights-based system
is the subject of the next chapter.

4

Crossing the Political Threshold

THE TRANSITION to a liberal rights-based social order, one country at a time, is crucial to the long-term success of human rights as a global project. By definition, any country that enacts the full panoply of human rights is a liberal democracy. By empirical observation, the countries that perform best on almost all rights are in fact liberal democracies.

A change of this kind requires a monumental shift over a long period from the traditional social order, based on coercion and favoritism, to the liberal modern one, based on rights, law, and democratic accountability. How to bring about such a change has been a central preoccupation of practitioners of democracy promotion, civil and human rights advocates, experts on economic development, and every kind of progressive reformer. This chapter proposes a way to think strategically about this process by putting pragmatic politics first.

Although the culmination of shifts from authoritarian to liberal political systems can sometimes happen quickly, the preparation for such shifts, if they are to be durable, requires local actors' step-by-step efforts to put in place the indispensable supports for a liberal order. These include the social underpinnings for the constituencies, citizen skills, institutions, and ideas that make liberal society possible.

These constituencies and capacities of the rights-based system are nurtured in the womb of the illiberal order that precedes it. Many of them are created without full-blown rights-based liberalism as the directly intended result. Instead, they result from immediate incentives to advance actors' power, security, wealth, and status within the constraints of the existing system, taking advantage of opportunities for feasible change at the margins. This process requires using tools and resources that are at hand, strategizing to mobilize support, and bargaining to strengthen the coalition for reform against its opponents. Success means establishing positions of strength that will serve as a platform from which to press for further progressive change. These changes must be functional not only in the hypothetical future, after the rights-based system is fully constructed, but also sustainable in the short run, or else the platform will collapse. For this reason, the sequencing of changes matters, although which sequence is workable may vary depending on circumstances. The general rule is that politics leads, rights follow.

In this chapter, I consider how this process unfolds when it is successful and when it is not. I begin with a historically grounded general model of how societies move across the threshold from a partially ruled-governed but exclusionary social order to an open, inclusive society. I then discuss some empirical findings illustrating how democratic rights and anticorruption reforms have actually been achieved through the step-by-step accretion of political, institutional, and ideological supports.

Since moving across the threshold does not guarantee consolidating democracy, I finish by discussing two practices that affect whether a transitional rights-based democracy will survive: transitional justice accountability for past atrocities and the timing of postconflict elections. I focus on these as hard cases that engage life and death interests of local actors, while also being issues where international activists are at their most legalistic and moralistic. These are issues where pragmatic politics is most intense, yet rights-based activism is especially begrudging of compromise. All four of these issues—preparation for democratic transition, anticorruption reform, transitional justice, and postconflict elections—shed light on how to sequence reforms pragmatically to achieve a rights-supportive outcome.

Transitioning from a System of Coercion and Corruption to One of Rights

Premodern systems of authority are typically based on coercion and patronage, ideologically legitimated through religion, custom, and family lineage. These methods are an inefficient, often disruptive, unreliable way to maintain social order, but societies with limited literacy, governance institutions, and productive technology lack the capacity to do better. In this kind of low-level equilibrium, the system's weaknesses are also its strengths insofar as people's habits are adapted to function within the society's entrenched limitations. A key question for strategy is how to move the system out of its rut of coercion and favoritism without winding up at a less stable, even bleaker outcome.

Historically, small-scale, face-to-face communities were largely organized along kinship lines as extended families, local clans, and episodically cooperating tribes.[1] With the arrival of settled agriculture, accumulated wealth, and permanent towns, kinship organization was overlaid with a layer of political authority based on armed coercive power, arrogation of material resources, the power to adjudicate disputes, and some culturally grounded basis of legitimation. Such so-called natural states relied heavily on coercion of labor, repression of armed opposition, and patronage networks to maintain their authority and to sustain the resource base of armed elites.[2]

Central authorities struggled to achieve a monopoly of violence over localized armed groups. An endemic principal-agent problem for the natural state was its limited ability to control violence among armed factions, local power centers, distinct cultural groups, and the central state's own subordinate agents. This was a global pattern, as kingdoms and empires periodically succumbed to internecine conflict—the Chinese warring states, the Japanese warring barons, England's War of the Roses, and the like. To limit endemic warfare, the authorities punished rebellion, bargained with potential rebels, and sought to agree with rivals on rules, privileges, and rights to regularize resource distribution.[3] In some cases, law, courts, rights to representation, property rights, sanctity of contracts, guarantees of monopolies and charters, and personal protections of nobles and notables became better institutionalized over time. In Britain, this not only stabilized relations among elites, but many of these rules and institutions strengthened the state by making it a more efficient tax collector and reliable borrower in financial markets, especially during wartime.[4]

These efforts to stabilize and regularize rule in the natural state created many of the institutional preconditions making possible a passage across the threshold into an *open order*, which happened when more and more citizens were given access to legal equality, privileges, and protections that had initially been established for elites only. Nobel Prize–winner Douglass North and his collaborators contend that the existence of these facilitating conditions made it possible, but not inevitable, for this transition to occur.[5] In some ways, however, legally institutionalized elite privilege also hindered the transition to an open order, leading law and politics down a path that was hidebound by rural overrepresentation, "rotten boroughs," and radically unequal educational opportunity and inherited wealth.

Like North, Francis Fukuyama issues warnings about the politics of transition and post-transition to open order. Fukuyama stresses that the equal-opportunity rules of the open order are overlaid on societies that maintain or re-create network structures and habits of patronage, kinship, and identity-group favoritism. These well-endowed networks may try to exploit the open order to extract rents through monopoly and political favoritism rather than seeking profit through efficient competition in free markets. Throwbacks to the old order block social mobility in liberal democracies, including the United States, and sustain corruption in supposedly "meritocratic" authoritarian states, most notably China. They also confound efforts for liberalization in transitional states. In interviews in Ukraine in May 2015, ostensibly progressive local activists repeatedly told me that their bold ideas for reform had to await support from their oligarchic backers, without whom they could not buy the TV time to persuade voters, who were themselves wary of losing access to their meager trickle-down of patronage.[6]

Rule-based institutions may look superficially similar in the mature natural state and in the open order, but they often regulate politics differently. Their form is similar, but they may serve opposite functions in these different systems. For example, free and fair elections between contending political parties are supposed to stabilize and maintain the openness of a liberal democratic order, ensuring the accountability of government to the presumably reasonable median voter. In that context, clean elections are an unalloyed benefit. In a mature natural state that is approaching the threshold to an open order, however, scrupulously free and fair elections are likely to upset delicately calibrated power sharing and distributional bargains among elite factions. Each of these factions may wield the economic, coercive, and discursive resources to disrupt the social system and derail a liberalizing transition. Power-sharing agreements between ethnic communities or other kinds of armed factions exist in part to take the risk out of democratization for elites whose position is threatened by opening up. When outsiders don't understand this finely balanced system, their interventions based on their imported assumptions of what an election should be may disrupt the fragile consolidation of a nascent open order.[7]

Step-by-Step Transition

Two recent systematic studies have directly addressed the question of how to move a society out of a low-level traditional equilibrium toward a more functional, modern, liberal one while minimizing the risk of unintentionally producing an even less functional outcome. Working independently, Kurt

Weyland's study of democratic transitions and Alicia Mungiu-Pippidi's study of the control of corruption have come to remarkably similar conclusions about the risks of regression as a result of ill-prepared moves for change. They offer similar prescriptions of layered, multidimensional preparation for step-by-step advances.[8]

Weyland's motivating puzzle is why the liberal revolutions of 1848 were a flash in the pan that culminated in an updated form of authoritarian retrenchment, whereas the "third wave" of democratization in Southern Europe and South America led to a more successful advance of liberal politics. His answer is that European liberalism in 1848 was a disembodied idea that spread like wildfire among the atomized newspaper-reading public from the example of the overthrow of the French monarchy. People in Europe's capital cities were inspired to rally in the streets, but they lacked organizational structures in civil society or in the institutions of government to sustain a liberal politics against the old order.

After the defeat of Napoleon in 1815, the victorious monarchs agreed to cooperate in a concert of Europe's great powers with the aim of containing any resurgence of the twin dangers of social revolution and mass nationalism. The following decades brought the acceleration of the industrial revolution, especially in Britain, and the flourishing of commerce. Cities and large towns grew along with politically engaged middle and working classes. Literacy in vernacular languages and cultural self-awareness of ethnic peoples trapped inside the "prison-house" of multiethnic empires began to grow. These burgeoning social forces shared an antipathy toward the old regimes and rose up against them in 1848. These diverse social classes and ethnolinguistic peoples had few positive interests in common, however, and they were not well organized to bargain and coordinate on a new structure to put in place of the old regimes. The armies and elites of the old regimes were better organized than the forces of change and reestablished their authority.[9]

Not only did the liberal revolutions fail, but nationalist and imperialist counterrevolutionary power structures were built on top of the old regimes by conservative modernizing elites such as Bismarck and Napoleon III. They constructed illiberal systems that married a popular nationalist following and capitalist development to updated forms of authoritarian governance and status privilege with the trappings of mass politics. "German political liberalism never fully recovered from the failure of 1848," Weyland remarks. "The inability of the mid-nineteenth century revolutionaries to forge Germany's unification left the national question unresolved and allowed conservative forces,

especially Otto von Bismarck, to use it as a wedge issue, divide political liberals, and further strengthen the Prussian military machine and royal house."[10]
Backlash against 1848 radicalism remained a reactionary rallying cry for the
next fifty years through the reign of Kaiser Wilhelm and World War I.[11]

In contrast, Britain's 1832 Reform movement had taken place in a setting
that was already thickly populated with principled civil society movements,
electorally accountable representative institutions, a free press, and independent courts with an individual rights tradition. As a result, effective aristocratic
and conservative pushback from the likes of Benjamin Disraeli took the form
not of reactionary nationalism but of extending the franchise to workers who
could be counted on to join a coalition to contain the self-interest of liberal
capitalists.[12]

Weyland argues that the third-wave democratic revolutions in Southern
Europe and South America in the 1970s and '80s were more successful than
the revolutions of 1848 because they built on a legacy of pragmatic organizational development, especially in civil society. Labor unions, peasant
organizations, and progressive political parties, though intermittently sup-
pressed or coopted by authoritarian regimes, had nonetheless been able to
strengthen their leadership cadres and sustain long-standing grassroots networks. In the most successful cases, particularly Chile, institutions needed for
liberal governance had an established track record despite their periodic overthrow by military regimes.

These well-established organizations and movements preferred to advance
their progressive agenda gradually through bargaining for incremental adjustments to the system. While the international environment created opportunities, whether by opening doors for reform, as in Vatican II, or by destabilizing
the autocracy, as in the Latin American debt crisis, successful reform movements didn't simply import foreign models. Rather, they developed domestic
progressive reforms rooted in established local practices and vetted through
local negotiations.[13]

Even then, inexperienced reformers could sometimes provoke setbacks by
pushing too hard for rapid change. Weyland offers the example of Chilean "up-
start" activists' unsuccessful plan for a general strike to force dictator Augusto
Pinochet's resignation after a 15 percent contraction in the national economy in
1983. The overeager activists did not realize that the regime's middle-class backers remained more fearful of an abrupt return to the leftist politics that Pinochet
had overthrown than of authoritarian military rule.[14] This, combined with the
Pinochet regime's fear of the human rights movement seeking retribution for

its crimes, explains why Pinochet was able to hang onto power despite the public's preference for more competent democratic government.[15]

Weyland wraps up his study by showing that African regime changes at the end of the third wave, the post-Communist "color revolutions," and the Arab Spring movements generally failed to fulfill progressive hopes in part because of the lack of sustained civic organization and pragmatic strategy among their pro-rights participants.[16] In Egypt the Muslim Brotherhood was able to sustain a mass popular movement and win an election, though it was not able to craft a pragmatic coalition to govern with the support of the military or more secular urban constituencies. These secular enthusiasts for reform lacked pragmatic skills of coalition making. They could show up en masse at Tahrir Square but not coordinate among themselves on any electoral strategy. Similarly, even in Hong Kong, where the social preconditions for a sophisticated civic rights movement were all in place, the virtually leaderless Umbrella Revolution of 2014 was able to mobilize youth in the streets but not plan a realistic strategy or sustain the routine activities of a grassroots movement. The rerun of the Umbrella Revolution in 2019–20 struggled with the same shortcomings of strategy and sustainable off-street organization, though its activists did manage to coordinate for symbolic success in local elections. As in many recent demonstrations, even in the United States, peaceful protesters had no strategy for dissociating themselves from violent protesters, which confirmed the authorities' narrative and helped to justify repression.[17]

Mungiu-Pippidi's argument about sequencing anticorruption efforts, which are a crucial element in the package of democratic rights reforms, closely parallels Weyland's more general account. Corruption, she says, must be analyzed in the context of a systemic shift from a social equilibrium based on patronage and clientelism to an equilibrium based on impersonal social relations and equality before the law. She calls this "ethical universalism," a system that is upheld by the "integrity pillars" of an impersonal judiciary and civil service, elections, free media, and a supportive civic society.[18] Integrity (or the lack of it) in this case must be understood as a property not so much of the individual, she insists, but of the system that entraps the individual in its self-reinforcing vicious or virtuous circles. Participation in petty bribery should be seen as a weapon of resistance by the weak who are shut out of the system of entrenched favoritism, where the real action is.[19] For this reason, she stresses that the goal of anticorruption efforts must be systemic changes such as routinely transparent accounting practices, not illusory "eradication" of corruption by punishing individuals.[20]

Mungiu-Pippidi begins her historical analysis by asking how those states that successfully control corruption achieved that outcome. She finds that "modernization theory" accounts for a lot of this. More affluent, urbanized, secularized, rationalized societies with large middle classes, high literacy, and extensive economic and political individual autonomy are more successful in controlling corruption.[21] And yet her statistical analysis reveals many outliers: fairly modern societies such as Russia experiencing corruption at similar levels to Congo. If structural factors associated with modernity explain a lot, there is still considerable variation in corruption that needs to be explained by agency and strategic choice.

The transition to a working anticorruption system must not be seen as marching through a static checklist of components to be ticked off in random order. Rather, the strategy of reform must be guided by a theory of the "dynamic of change."[22] As Samuel Huntington argued, the early stages of modernization typically lead to an increase in corruption because there is more to steal, and strong institutions for transparent, impersonal dealings have not yet been constructed.[23] In moving toward stronger institutions, Mungiu-Pippidi argues that incentives and power come first: "The adoption of institutions currently considered to be quintessential in the control of corruption followed changes in a power equilibrium—or threats to an existing one—that generated strong demands for better governance."[24] Anticorruption efforts, spearheaded by consequential actors "who lose out under power inequality and corruption," succeed by "empowering the losers under current institutions."[25]

Mungiu-Pippidi shows that successful reforms unfold in a "succession of equilibria."[26] This gradual, layered process reflects the mutually supportive nature of the plethora of institutional and normative "pillars" of the reformed system. It also reflects the iterative process by which partial reforms increase the power of the reform constituency in graduated stages.[27]

As in Weyland's study, Chile stands out as a success case, in part because of its relatively high stage of democratic and legal institutional development before the Pinochet coup. Another factor was the market-based policies that Pinochet introduced under military rule. Although his University of Chicago style of economic management failed to prevent a steep downturn during the Latin American debt crisis, its lasting legacy was to decentralize economic structures that hindered concentrations of economic power and rent-seeking ties to governmental authorities. For that reason, the conservative bloc of social and economic interests, which remained strong after Pinochet's fall, was not keen to lobby for corrupt practices. With redemocratization in 1990, the liberal bloc consolidated this favorable situation by introducing administrative reforms such as an Office for Transparency and E-Government.[28]

The success of these general strategies for sustained, multidimensional, multistage efforts to prepare the way for a transition to a rights-based system often hinges on finding well-aimed tactics to forge a strong pro-rights coalition.

Interests and Coalitions at Equipoise

The mid-nineteenth-century Victorian era was sometimes called the *age of equipoise*, balanced evenly between an industrializing and an agricultural society, between an enfranchised middle class and an unenfranchised working class, and between the world of aristocratic privilege and equality before the law. Our own world is also perched precariously at a kind of equipoise. The third wave of democratization increased the number of democracies but even more dramatically increased the proportion of countries that ranked as only "partly free." In the era of populist strongman Narendra Modi, the renowned historian Ramachandra Guha has described India as a "50-50 democracy."[29] With the rise of authoritarian China, not only are many individual countries 50-50, but the world as a whole is poised at 50-50, wavering at the threshold to expanding rights and democracy or backsliding into repression. Masses demonstrated for democracy in Hong Kong, while the illiberal nativist AfD became a significant opposition party in Germany.

Systemic equipoise is a situation with distinctive properties from the standpoint of political interests and coalition bargaining. To even begin to formulate a strategy for promoting rights in this situation, reformers need to be able to analyze which groups might have an interest in joining the reform coalition and how they can be attracted to support it. In the previous chapter, I argued that it is not a simple matter to read off the rights interests of a group from its sociological position, as in the arguments that the middle class or the working class is the key constituency for democracy. The interests of groups are likely to be mixed with respect to different rights or even ambivalent with respect to a given right. The property-owning middle classes in Germany after 1848, for example, typically voted for the National Liberal Party, which had one foot in a liberal stance in favor of constitutional rights and the other marching in a nationalist alliance with traditional elites.

In such a situation, the ruling group tries to use its agenda-setting power to formulate a package of rights, privileges, or abuses that defines the system and sustains its supporters.[30] Once this formula is institutionalized, the equipoise of 50-50 defines interests in a way that removes ambiguity: the *ins* whose sustenance and position depend on the maintenance of the existing system oppose the *outs* whose advance depends on changing it. Formerly ambivalent groups now have sunk costs that lock in their choice of coalition partners—for example, Bismarck's "marriage of iron and rye" among German heavy industry, protectionist aristocratic agriculture, the military, and the Protestant middle class against German industrial workers. This creates a provisional "partial-reform equilibrium" that benefits those who obtain rights in a political transition at the expense of those who are excluded from the deal.[31]

At equipoise, the choice of coalition tactics of *ins* and *outs* hinges on assessments of the trend of the balance of power between them. If trends in military power, economic dynamism, or ideological momentum are running against those in power, insider factions with a potential for outsider alliances may provoke a split in the ruling group. Powerful swing groups who can credibly align with either insiders or outsiders may be in a position to define the terms of reform or repression of reform. Groups whose economic or organizational assets are mobile—that is, retain their value whether or not the system undergoes fundamental change—are likely to occupy the pivot in any realignment. For example, German export industry realigned after World War I to forge a democratic coalition with industrial labor in the Weimar Republic and then reversed their alignment once again in support of fascism.[32] Groups whose assets are more fixed—that is, tied to the privileges and rules of the prevailing system—are likely to play the game of coopting potential defectors from the regime with side payments for continued loyalty. In addition, they may try to divide and rule potential systemic opponents by playing on their group identity differences, which cut across class interests. Examples are the personal rights concessions to German Catholics in exchange for their vote for the 1898 battlefleet budget, and the use of nationalism and colonial policy to divide Protestant German middle classes from trade union workers.[33] Groups with a fixed base of support may also invest in mobilizing their core constituency. The German regime before World War I, for example, promoted mass-membership naval, army, and colonial leagues among status-hungry local dignitaries.[34]

Weyland brings this kind of analysis to his discussion of the struggle to promote democracy in the third wave in South America. He argues that the "bureaucratic authoritarian" military regimes with their strategies of import-substituting industrial protectionism were far too solid to be directly confronted by pro-democracy and pro-rights activism. These regimes combined the military capacity for repression with support from protected industrial sectors, including the government-aligned labor unions. Opposition parties, workers and peasants organizations, and civic groups sustained their networks by mounting local protests and strikes with limited aims, leading when possible to negotiations with officials.[35] This allowed them to be ready for coordinated action when circumstances produced splits in the regime—for example, the Argentine military junta's economic mismanagement and the backlash against its brutal campaign of "disappearances," culminating in defeat in its reckless Falklands War.

All the bureaucratic authoritarian regimes of South America were rocked by the systemic debt crisis of the early 1980s, which produced divergent preferences between the fixed-asset industrial and mobile-asset financial interests, splitting the regime coalitions.[36] As a result, the third-wave regime changes in South America, following the recent Spanish model, were *pacted transitions* whose terms were generally negotiated between elements of the outgoing dictatorship and the democratic opposition groups. The democratic coalitions and systems that emerged from this process included unalloyed proponents of democratic rights as well as fence-sitters, economic opportunists who could profit from the move out of protectionism, and potential military spoilers whose neutrality was bought by reassurances about limited criminal accountability. Weyland attributes the relative success of these transitions to their moderate, bargained character and the organizational coherence of the opposition partners.[37]

Tailoring Rights Ideas to Local Circumstances

When a country has accumulated many of the social preconditions for human rights, including a dynamic pro-rights coalition, it should be well prepared to make use of the standard persuasive rhetoric of the transnational human rights movement. For example, Vaclav Havel's Civic Union social movement was already in the ideological vanguard of the global human rights movement by the time of the collapse of communism and Czechoslovakia's democratic transition.[38] Quantitative studies find that transitional countries that enjoy favorable legal or civic conditions are likely to improve their human rights outcomes when they sign international human rights treaties and when their governments are criticized for falling short of their obligations.[39]

Nonetheless, some successful transitional states chose not to copy the exact template of international rights standards. Weyland argues that societies prepared with well-established social movements, mature political parties, and well-organized interest groups tend to "turn inward" as they approach the threshold to rights-based democracy.[40] This reflects the reformist opposition's tendency to bargain with the old regime and within the reform movement's own constituent factions, tailoring acceptable compromises based on home-grown adaptations of basic rights principles. This is in sharp contrast, he argues, to less established reform movements' tendency to copy the international fad of the day, as in the Europe-wide aping of the French Revolution in 1848. More established progressive movements sometimes resent international meddling, naming, and shaming as unhelpful in navigating the political complexities of the transition.

To sum up this approach to advancing rights in the course of a political transition, politics leads, rights follow. An effective strategy must systematically knock down the barriers that block the threshold to a rights-supportive system. This means creating the social preconditions to sustain the rule-of-law system, strengthening the political coalition that might benefit from an inclusive rights system, investing in the institutions needed to implement such a system, and offering a locally persuasive ideology of rights. Success in these tasks requires bargaining with supporters, fence-sitters, opportunists, and potential spoilers of rights. It is a process that unfolds over the long haul, requiring evolving tactics and objectives at different stages. Progressive political parties, mass social movements, and principled advocacy organizations each have roles to play in moving reform efforts through a series of strategically designed, organizationally grounded, mutually supportive, multidimensional steps toward and across the threshold.

Once this juncture is reached, many transitional states must still deal with two dangerous legacies of the past: first, accountability for atrocities perpetrated by still-powerful remnants of the old regime, and second, choosing a time to hold the first post-transition elections that include illiberal contestants. Pragmatism about power balances and sequencing of reforms is the watchword for navigating these transitional threats.

Principle and Pragmatism in Transitional Justice

When the International Criminal Court became operational in 2002, at the height of optimism about ending impunity, Leslie Vinjamuri and I wrote about the underlying mindset of this enterprise, which we characterized as the "logic of appropriateness," which differed from our own emphasis on the "logic of consequences."[41] We argued that human rights advocates of criminal trials for past abuses were motivated by their commitment to what they saw as right principles, and then they added unwarranted assertions about causal outcomes to convince pragmatists to support criminal trials. Since then, the debate about trials and amnesties as tools of peace and justice has progressed through several stages and methodological iterations.[42] This subsequent debate provides an opportunity to elaborate the role of both principle and pragmatism in the social power approach, in which politics leads and justice follows.

Advocates of legal accountability claimed then—and still do claim—that trials contribute to ending atrocities and consolidating peace and democracy in transitional societies. These proponents argue that trials send a strong signal that perpetrators will be held individually accountable for their actions. Human Rights Watch contends, for example, that "justice for yesterday's crimes supplies the legal foundation needed to deter atrocities tomorrow."[43] Proponents also claim that trials strengthen the rule of law by teaching both elites and masses that the appropriate means of resolving conflict is through impartial justice. Typically, they further contend that the demonstration effect of procedural justice and the consolidation of democracy are mutually reinforcing in postconflict or postauthoritarian societies.[44]

Proponents argue that both domestic and international trials can promote these positive ends. International trials, they believe, have the distinctive effect of underscoring the universality of these crimes, focusing world public opinion on the violence committed, and ensuring that international standards govern trials. Some argue, however, that domestic trials are likely to have a greater impact on attitudes in the country where the abuses took place.[45] Mixed tribunals, held under the joint aegis of international and local judges in the country where abuses occurred, aim to capture the best of both worlds by bringing justice to local communities in a tangible way, while maintaining international standards and oversight. Mixed tribunals, as in Sierra Leone, are also intended to help build the institutional capacity of local judiciaries and thereby strengthen the rule of law.

At the same time as human rights activists were advocating trials for perpetrators of major human rights violations, they also successfully argued for banning amnesties for the crimes specified in the mandate of the ICC: war crimes, genocide, and crimes against humanity. This introduced a major qualification to prior international law, which had encouraged amnesties in the course of civil war settlements.

According to the logic of consequences, amnesties may sometimes be an expedient tool to reach a peace agreement and end the fighting that is the cause of the worst rights abuses. Trials or indictments may provoke violent resistance from still-powerful perpetrators as well as their hard-core supporters.[46] Intense, widespread backlash in the face of attempts to impose justice can make legal rules seem ineffectual and thus undermine respect for human rights. The stronger the parties who might be prosecuted, the greater the danger that backlash will occur. Only a decisive military victory over the criminal parties removes this danger entirely. Therefore, in the absence of a decisive victory, amnesty may be a necessary first step in the process of consolidating peace, the rule of law, and democracy. Sometimes a de facto amnesty—doing nothing or deferring action on justice—may serve the same purpose. An effective institutional apparatus—above all, a strong, competent state—is needed to enforce norms of justice in a predictable manner that carries deterrent force. Some proponents have therefore argued that trials should be delayed until the reforming state is stronger, and perpetrators lose strength in the wake of a transition.

Vinjamuri and I argued that both amnesties and trials require effective state institutions and political coalitions to enforce them. Without those conditions, neither approach is likely to succeed.[47] A key question is therefore whether trials or amnesties offer the better chance in a given situation to strengthen the hand of a pro-justice coalition.

To assess the effects of these different strategies of justice (international tribunals, domestic trials, mixed tribunals, amnesties, de facto amnesties, truth commissions, and combinations of them), we began by considering all cases of civil wars since 1989. In this period following the Cold War, calls for post-conflict justice became more common and more politically efficacious. We used Freedom House and Polity rankings of democracy and civil liberties to establish a rough measure of democracy, the rule of law, and human rights standards in our cases. To assess more subtle issues of causality, we discussed several cases in more detail.

We found that the holding of trials tends to contribute to the ending of abuses only when spoiler groups are weak and when the infrastructure of justice worked predictably and effectively. In other words, trials work best when they are needed least. When trials take place in venues that lack such advantages, there is little evidence that they have a positive effect.

Similarly, we found that the capacity of truth commissions to promote reconciliation is far more limited than proponents suggest. Truth commissions contributed to democratic consolidation only when a pro-democracy coalition held power and enjoyed an adequate institutional base. When those conditions were absent, truth commissions could have the perverse effects of rubbing salt into wounds or of providing a veneer of legitimacy for a rights-abusing regime.[48] Truth commissions, we found, are most likely to be useful when they provide political cover for amnesties.

We found that explicit or de facto amnesty could be an effective tool in paving the way for peace. Amnesties, like tribunals, however, require effective political backing and strong institutions to enforce their terms. Indeed, the point of giving an amnesty should be to create the political preconditions for strengthening and reforming state institutions.

In examining each strategy of justice that was adopted in our set of cases of recent international and civil wars, our first goal was to trace the impact of the strategy of justice, for good or ill, on social peace and subsequent abuses. Our additional goal was to consider the conditions under which each strategy is likely to be necessary and successful.

International Tribunals

Evidence from post–Cold War cases tends to cast doubt on the claims that international trials deter future atrocities, contribute to consolidating the rule of law or democracy, or pave the way for peace. In the 1990s, there were two cases of international criminal tribunals, the ICTY (Yugoslavia) and the ICTR (Rwanda). In neither case did trials deter subsequent atrocities nor contribute to bringing peace in the region. Subsequent democratization and pacification of the Yugoslav successor states came despite the tensions provoked by the tribunal and not because of it. In the context of this chapter on transitions toward democracy, the Yugoslavia case is particularly relevant.

Two years after the 1993 UN resolution creating the International Criminal Tribunal for the former Yugoslavia, Serbian forces massacred thousands of civilians at Srebrenica, Bosnia. Even after the tribunal began to convict war criminals, the Serbian regime committed new mass war crimes in Kosovo. The tribunal's case against President Slobodan Milosevic stressed that he ignored face-to-face warnings that he would be prosecuted if he failed to stop Serbian abuses in Kosovo.[49]

After the Kosovo fighting spilled over into adjacent Macedonia, NATO countries negotiated a peace settlement between the Macedonian government and ethnic Albanian former guerrillas, who were granted an amnesty except for crimes indictable by the international tribunal. The tribunal's head prosecutor, Carla Del Ponte, decided to investigate, leading the guerrillas to destroy evidence of mass graves. This created a pretext for hardline Slavic Macedonian nationalists to renew fighting in late November 2001 and to seize Albanian-held terrain.[50] In such circumstances, legalists need to exercise prosecutorial discretion: a crime is a crime, but not all crimes must be prosecuted. Such choices risk putting judges and lawyers in charge of decisions that political leaders are better suited to make.[51]

The tribunal did not lead Bosnia's major ethnic groups to attribute guilt to individuals rather than to ethnic groups. Many Serbs have complained that the tribunal unfairly targeted Serbs, while many Croats have argued that the tribunal indicted and arrested an unwarrantedly high number of Croats. Rather than individualizing guilt, the tribunal seems to have reinforced ethnic cleavages.[52] Once ethnic groups are polarized by intergroup violence, it normally takes a decisive change of strategic circumstances and political institutions, not just the invocation of legal norms, to get people to think in terms of individual rather than group responsibility.[53]

Survey results suggest that there was a public relations backlash in Serbian areas against the tribunal. In Bosnia's Republika Srpska, individual respondents to a survey conducted by the National Democratic Institute for International Affairs registered only a 22 percent approval rating for the Republika Srpska's adoption of a law on cooperation with The Hague.[54] In Serbia itself, the public's acquiescence to the ICTY was based on expediency, not conviction. In April 2002, 44 percent of Serbs said they found the argument for cooperation with the ICTY to help a move to EU membership to be highly convincing, while another 22 percent found it somewhat convincing; 36 percent felt that cooperation with the ICTY to get US aid was also very convincing, and 22 percent found this somewhat convincing. In contrast, only 20 percent were convinced that cooperation with the ICTY was "morally right," and only 10 percent saw the ICTY as the best way to serve justice.[55]

Subsequent book-length studies have confirmed the main thrust of our skeptical interpretation.[56] Some scholars, however, have argued that such efforts to measure the impact of international transitional justice have set the bar for success too high. Lara Nettelfield, for example, shows that the legal proceedings in The Hague constructively shaped grassroots Bosnian attitudes toward justice and the rule of law by provoking fruitful debates, even if not everyone immediately drew the conclusion that the justice process had been fair.[57] Attitudes may evolve through discourse and contestation over time.

Paola Cesarini argues convincingly that Portugal's successful democratic consolidation was facilitated by its reformed national narrative of transitional justice, whereas unresolved legacies of injustice have contributed to problems of democratic consolidation in Italy and Argentina.[58]

Domestic Trials

We found that the effect of domestic trials on the deterrence of future abuses and the consolidation of peaceful democracy was marginal and sometimes even counterproductive. Where legal institutions were weak, as was the case in many states that had recently experienced atrocities, domestic trials typically lacked integrity, failed to dispense justice, and sometimes even failed to protect the security of those participating in trials. In states where the post-atrocity regime retained autocratic features, elites sometimes used trials to legitimate their rule vis-à-vis domestic opponents or gain international legitimacy through the veneer of legality (as in Cambodia and Indonesia). In other states with weak rule-of-law institutions, trials languished for years from sheer bureaucratic incapacity (as in Ethiopia). In contrast, trials were most effective in cases where legal institutions were already fairly well established, and therefore where the demonstration effect of trials is least needed. In many cases, for example, domestic trials took place after rights-respecting democratic regimes were firmly installed (as in Germany and Poland in the 1990s, or in Greece after the fall of the junta in 1974).

Complications from domestic trials are especially problematic when the new regime is based on a negotiated settlement with still-powerful perpetrators of atrocities. The case of Argentina shows that spoilers can remain a problem even where reformers have gained the upper hand. Following the collapse of the military junta after defeat in the Falklands War, five leaders of the former military junta were convicted for their crimes during the "dirty war" against the regime's domestic political opponents. Activists pressed for more extensive prosecutions. Arguably, these trials were unnecessary to deter future abuses, because the junta's practices were already thoroughly discredited by the failure of the Falklands War, their disastrous stewardship of the economy, and the widespread publicity about disappearances and rights abuses. Pressure for these trials provoked unrest in some military units and threats to use force by unreconciled elements of the officer corps. Even sympathetic analysts admit that human rights groups' demands to expand the scope of the trials played into the military's hand and created a backlash among moderate opinion in favor of curtailing the trials.[59] Ultimately, President Carlos Menem pardoned even the five convicted "big fish" in 1989.

Amnesty

Amnesties were negotiated following eleven of the civil wars that ended between 1989 and the appearance of our article in 2002. Some of these were combined with truth commissions, as in South Africa, El Salvador, and the original plan for Sierra Leone in 1999. In other cases, such as Namibia and Afghanistan, no official amnesty was granted, but a decision was made not to hold war crimes trials.

Many of these amnesties or de facto amnesties helped shore up peace and an improved human rights situation. In Mozambique, for example, peace was sustained for decades after the signing of a 1992 accord mediated by the St. Egidio Catholic Church organization, which provided that neither party to the civil war was obliged to take public responsibility for its crimes. The Mozambican Parliament subsequently granted a general amnesty for "crimes against state" in the belief that a focus on past crimes would impede reconciliation.[60] Likewise, Namibia's durable peace settlement was not disturbed by the failure to prosecute crimes. In Macedonia, an amnesty for some crimes of the ethnic Albanian rebels was an essential component of the peace settlement that dampened conflict after the post-Kosovo fighting.

In El Salvador, too, an amnesty helped to gain the cooperation of key actors in implementing a successful peace accord. The conservative government granted the amnesty as a defensive move following the release of reports by a truth commission and an ad hoc commission on crimes committed during the civil war, which called for the discharge of several military officers and the resignation of a number of judges. Contrary to proponents' claim that truth commissions shore up peace by reconciling former enemies, the Salvadoran government viewed the release of these reports as a dangerous provocation. The military, the defense minister, and the Supreme Court all denounced the reports as biased. Three days after the truth commission report was released, the president proclaimed the amnesty, and two officers convicted of murdering Jesuit priests were freed. Although 55 percent of the public opposed the amnesty, and 77 percent favored punishing those who had committed crimes, the decision for amnesty and against punishment was crucial in gaining the cooperation of the military, the judiciary and, more generally, the government in subsequent stages of the peace process. ARENA, the governing party, argued for the amnesty on the grounds that forgetting was critical to reconciliation.[61]

Nonetheless, amnesties are likely to succeed only if they are accompanied by political reforms that curtail the power of rights abusers. In both Sierra Leone and Ivory Coast, rebels were offered both amnesty and key posts in the new government. Neither situation proved to be stable. In Sierra Leone, the Lomé Accords gave amnesty to the still-powerful RUF leader, Foday Sankoh, and installed him as the minister in charge of diamond mining in the new government. Far from being reconciled to peace and the rule of law, the RUF saw the accord as a step toward entrenching their practices of domination and plunder. When this view of the settlement was challenged, Sankoh's rebels renewed their violence against the government and civilians. In Ivory Coast, the decision to offer rebels key posts in the government brought protesters to the streets, and sporadic fighting continued. In July 2003, the government of Ivory Coast announced plans for a new amnesty.

As these instances show, amnesties, like tribunals, require effective political backing and strong institutions to enforce their terms. Indeed, the point of giving an amnesty should be to create the political preconditions for strengthening and rationalizing state institutions. For example, to end the civil war in El Salvador, moderate conservatives in the business community eagerly supported the provisions of a UN-brokered agreement to completely reconstruct the country's army, police, and other governmental institutions. These economic elites had realized during the course of the war that they could no longer make money through coffee production with repressive control of labor. Instead, they sought to take advantage of the trend toward economic globalization by expanding maquiladora light manufacturing exports. This meant turning their back on their former allies in the right-wing death squads and making peace with the leftist rebels.[62] An amnesty for crimes committed during the war helped to seal this deal for institutional transformation, which was grounded in an ironclad political and economic logic, whatever its shortcomings from the standpoint of backward-looking justice.

In some cases, doing nothing has been a viable strategy for consolidating peace. In Namibia, the terms of the postconflict transition were negotiated before the international human rights movement began to emphasize war crimes trials. As a result, the question of accountability for atrocities was left off the agenda, with no apparent ill effects.

In Afghanistan, efforts to press forward with war crimes trials were rebuffed. UN Human Rights Commissioner Mary Robinson pressed Afghanistan's interim government to set up a truth commission with no amnesty powers to investigate crimes not only of the Taliban, but also of the earlier regimes whose members had once again secured high positions in Hamid Karzai's interim government. Lakhdar Brahimi, UN special representative for Afghanistan, was successful in persuading the international community that pressing for war crimes investigations would undermine his efforts to institute peace.

Despite the political utility of amnesty, recent international legal developments call into question the credibility of offers of amnesty or de facto amnesty.[63] The International Criminal Court lacks any provisions that explicitly guarantee the sanctity of domestic amnesties. This assault on the granting of amnesty and asylum coincided with several prominent attempts to use such measures to induce rights-abusing leaders to step down from power. For example, just days before the United States began its military campaign in Iraq, President Bush suggested that Saddam Hussein could avert war by leaving Iraq. Bush also indicated that the treatment of Iraqi Army officers would be contingent on their behavior during the war, emphasizing that the use of chemical or biological weapons would make them subject to war crimes trials.[64] At the same time, Arab leaders spoke out in favor of amnesty for Saddam as a means to forestall US military action.

To sum up, horrifying human rights abuses have been rampant in many parts of the world in recent decades. Averting such disasters is one of the most important issues on the international agenda. Legalism, focusing on the universal enforcement of international humanitarian law and persuasion campaigns to spread benign human rights norms, offers one strategy for accomplishing this. We found little support for the central empirical assumptions that underpin this approach. Trials did little to deter further violence or consolidate democracy.

In contrast, the empirical hypotheses underpinning pragmatism and the logic of consequences fared better. Amnesties or other minimal efforts to address the problem of past abuses were sometimes the basis for durable peaceful settlements in difficult cases. We concluded that the international criminal justice regime should permit the use of amnesties when needed to secure reforms. Deciding what approach to adopt in a particular case requires political judgment. Consequently, decisions to prosecute should be overseen by political authorities, such as the UN Security Council or the governments of affected states.

Evaluating Transitional Justice Controversies

Debates over the effectiveness of trials, amnesties, and truth commissions intensified as a result of disappointments with the International Criminal Court. Convictions were few and slow in coming, with only African cases on the docket, and prosecutions were expensive. African presidents used the forum of the African Union to denounce the ICC, and Burundi withdrew its membership to evade prosecution.[65] The indictment of Sudanese dictator Omar al-Bashir triggered the expulsion of Western aid organizations, while the indictment of Libyan dictator Muammar Ghaddafi squelched any chance for a war-ending asylum deal. In this context, even former Yugoslavia tribunal prosecutor Louise Arbour warned that "criminal prosecutions can complicate if not impede peace processes."[66] The ICC had to drop its case against Kenyan President Uhuru Kenyatta and Vice President William Ruto when crucial witnesses were murdered. Meanwhile, great power support ebbed. The United States "unsigned" the treaty to protect its officials from prosecution. Russian opposition headed off a French initiative for ICC action in the egregious case of Syria.

Amid these ongoing controversies, statistical and comparative case studies have tried to evaluate the consequences of trials and amnesties for peace, law, rights, and democracy. The most influential study of the ICC's effectiveness in deterring atrocities, praised by Kenneth Roth, the executive director of Human Rights Watch, is by Hyeran Jo and Beth Simmons, who is also the author of a prize-winning, gold-standard book on the impact of human rights treaty accession on rights compliance.[67] Jo and Simmons argue that a state's ratification of the ICC's Rome treaty reduces, on average by 60 percent, the number of its intentional killings of civilians in military confrontations. Unfortunately, their ICC study's methods failed to distinguish between states that are "deterred" from atrocities and states that sign the treaty because they are already committed to ending atrocities. Repressive regimes that thought they might need to resort to atrocities to survive would have had an incentive not to sign the treaty, while states that ratified the Rome Statute might logically be those that had no intention to commit atrocities. In fact, Jo and Simmons acknowledge that in many of the ratifying cases included in their sample, civilian killings declined in the year or so *before* ICC ratification. It is doubtful that the ICC deterred these signers.

Another significant reason that some authoritarian regimes might sign the Rome Statute is to use the ICC as leverage against rebel groups that might be accused of atrocities. Governments have more resources to hide evidence of their own crimes so may gamble that the risk of opening themselves to prosecution is less than the deterrent effect on rebels.[68] Uganda's referral to the ICC of the crimes of Joseph Kony's Lord's Resistance Army is an example.

Contrary to Jo and Simmons's research design, it is the nonsigners that most need to be deterred. Most of the states that perpetrated large-scale atrocities in the relevant period (such as Libya, Sri Lanka, Sudan, and Syria) have not joined the ICC. Even so, under the Rome Statute, these states can be referred to the ICC by the UN Security Council, which means that even in non-member states, the ICC still has a deterrent potential. After all, Libya and Sudan did come under the ICC's jurisdiction as the result of a referral, but in both cases, deterrence failed.

In Kenya, which Jo and Simmons claim as a case of successful deterrence, election-related mass killings shortly followed the country's joining the ICC. Domestic investigations were slowly suffocated. When the ICC made good on its implied threat to prosecute Kenya's sitting president Uhuru Kenyatta, the bribing and murder of key witnesses left the ICC with no recourse but to halt proceedings. Kenyatta gained political leverage by running against the "imperialism" of the ICC, a platform that united former enemies. As Jo and Simmons note, this unity may explain the subsequent reduction in electoral violence. If this is a success case, it is not one that illustrates the mechanisms they highlight.

In another significant study, Geoff Dancy uses an extensive database to assess the effect of amnesties on peace. Alert to the need to theorize the offer of amnesty as a bargaining situation, Dancy conjectures that amnesty proposals in wartime are likely to be seen as a trick, while amnesty as part of a post-conflict comprehensive peace deal has more credibility. His statistical results indicate that "(1) only amnesties passed following conflict termination help resolve civil wars, (2) amnesties are more effective when they are embedded in peace agreements, and (3) amnesties that grant immunity for serious rights violations have no observable pacifying effects."[69] A follow-up study by Lesley-Ann Daniels, however, finds that formal amnesties for less serious crimes during conflict can incentivize peace.[70] While these findings seem plausible, they remain hard to interpret because of the lack of a contextually sensitive measure of the power of spoilers. To try to compare similar cases, Dancy uses a statistical matching method that takes into account "rebel strength" at arms and "rebel capacity" to mobilize resources, which are significantly associated with the likelihood of agreement and of amnesty.[71] To unpack what this means more concretely for bargaining, it is necessary to look at case studies that delve into the context, process, and calculations of the battling, negotiating parties.

Priscilla Hayner, an experienced human rights advocate and investigator of atrocities, has written a more fully contextualized book on the trade-off between peace and justice.[72] In myriad detailed examples, Hayner makes the case that both sides in the peace versus justice debate have valid concerns. On one hand, she gives full credit to the peace negotiators who say that efforts to bring combatants to justice are "an impediment to our work."[73] For example, she says ICC prosecutor Luis Moreno Ocampo's statement against amnesty for Ivoirian dictator Laurent Gbagbo ensured that he would "fight to the end."[74] Citing the additional examples of "Bashir in Sudan, Kony in Uganda, [Ntaganda] Bosco in Congo, [Charles] Taylor in Liberia, Kenyatta and Ruto in Kenya, and Gaddafi in Libya," Hayner finds that "the public release of arrest warrants or direct threats against targeted individuals only reduced the possibility of a negotiated settlement, and in some cases led to further violence."[75] On the other hand, she says that militias in eastern Congo and in Guinea "quickly rid their forces of child soldiers" in the face of credible, specific threats to prosecute by the local police and by the ICC prosecutor. She concludes from this that "if the threat of consequences is real and effectively delivered, and the person targeted can do something to avoid the threat, then the likelihood of a positive result is greatest."[76] In other words, threats should be delivered at the stage of investigation, before indictments are handed down, tying the hands of prosecutors and negotiators.

She finds no evidence, however, for the idea that the mere existence of the ICC has a general deterrent effect. Quite the reverse: she attributes perpetrators' puzzling indifference to accountability clauses in negotiation documents to the widespread assumption that no one will try to enforce them. For the same reason, she argues that amnesties are not the main barrier to prosecution; the bigger problems are "political and other immoveable realities . . . including weak or compromised judicial institutions."[77] Over time, however, she acknowledges that demands for meaningful amnesty guarantees are looming larger in negotiators' thinking, as perpetrators have learned that international players are serious about prosecuting major ICC crimes. Likewise, Kony became untrusting of peace negotiations once he learned that Nigeria had reneged on its grant of asylum to Taylor.[78]

Hayner's culminating case study is Colombia's 2016 transitional justice law, which was negotiated along with the peace treaty that sought to end the fifty-year war between the government and the drug-dealing Marxist FARC rebel group.[79] Although the FARC at one point in the 1990s commanded 40 percent of the national territory and twenty thousand fighters, twenty years later government military offensives backed by a US-aided war on rebel drug production left the FARC ready for a deal. In the waning years of the conflict, perhaps the major issue delaying a settlement was accountability for the huge number of atrocity crimes perpetrated by the FARC, the government military, and government-aligned paramilitaries. A series of proposals and laws considered every imaginable transitional justice mechanism—trials in government courts leading to long prison sentences, special tribunals based on confessions and more limited punishments, truth commissions, historical commissions, and reparations for victims.[80] Obstacles included the sheer scale of the offenses by tens of thousands of perpetrators on all sides, the weakness and corruption of biased judicial institutions, and the complicity of the state in the crimes of the regional paramilitaries, who backed the ruling conservative political parties.

The FARC refused to lay down its weapons without the equivalent of an amnesty. But domestic and international opinion resisted any peace deal based on anything like a Mozambique-style exchange of amnesties for all crimes by all parties. Human Rights Watch denounced the December 2015 peace plan whose sentences without prison terms were not "meaningful punishment," and Amnesty International complained that penalties did "not appear to be proportionate to the severity of the crimes."[81] The ICC and local Colombian human rights organizations, however, supported the plan. When the government and the FARC signed a peace accord based on these concepts in September 2016, voters in a referendum the following week narrowly rejected the deal because of its weak punishment of atrocity crimes, complicated by a conspiracy campaign trying to link the deal to the gay rights movement.[82] Voters in the regions most affected by the conflict heavily favored the peace agreement whereas those less affected by the war rejected it. A few months later, a somewhat tightened up version of the agreement was approved by the national Congress. The denouement to the story is that serious armed violence soon broke out again as demobilized fighters of various descriptions struggled for control of land and the drug trade in the vacuum created by FARC's demise and the state's corrupt incapacity.

Superficially, Colombia's tragedy shows that people care about punishing past atrocities, especially the other side's, in a way that drags out bargaining over the terms of peace. At a deeper level, it shows that any backward-looking justice modality is unlikely to solve the problem of social order unless it is part of a comprehensive effort backed by a strong progressive coalition to reform and strengthen state institutions. As always, power and politics lead, justice follows—sometimes very far behind.

This pattern has important lessons for bargaining strategy. Bargainers with blood on their hands and a public relations problem on their minds increasingly resort to ambiguous declarations and toothless agreements that promise to give "consideration" to justice while also including implicit amnesty clauses.[83] Hayner argues that this is simply the political reality that peace negotiators and prosecutors must understand and deal with. Along those lines, she argues for a flexible interpretation of the ICC statute clause taking into account the "interests of justice." In many situations, she contends that this permits rather long delays in seeking legal accountability for crimes on the assumption that spoilers will become weaker as time passes.[84] The incentives for ambiguity in making commitments to justice and to amnesty have implications for research strategies on the trade-off between peace and justice. Databases built on binary coding of commitments may produce invalid results if actors' expectations of what will happen diverge from the language of the text.[85]

In the rough-and-tumble world where mass atrocities are likely to occur, regimes and rebels often have blood on their hands. Spoilers often have the motive and the opportunity to use their clout to wreck political and legal reform, and thus evade legal accountability. In strategizing effective ways to contain such menaces, the role of law must be placed realistically in its political context.[86] As I have been arguing, reducing atrocities and advancing accountability depends first on the construction of a powerful coalition based on bargaining among legal reformers, opportunists, and fence-sitters. In this, law does not lead, it follows.

How this bargaining unfolds, and whether it must include explicit or implicit amnesties, depends crucially on the power of spoilers and whether they can be reconciled to a reformed political order. An amnesty that includes no strategy for containing spoilers will be as ineffective as a threat of trial that provokes rather than constrains. Processes of political bargaining and coalition making, more than processes of law, are crucial to understanding the long-unfolding cases in Kenya, Sri Lanka, and Uganda, just as they were central to earlier success cases based on amnesties in South Africa, El Salvador, and Mozambique.

Dangers of Early Post-Conflict Elections

The path across the threshold from conflict and autocracy to democratic elections remains fraught with danger even after a peace settlement. To minimize the risk of a return to war and rights abuse, the social power approach focuses on first establishing the political and institutional preconditions for a rights-based order.

Democracy advocates have long favored early elections in countries emerging from authoritarianism and violent conflict. Since democracies do not fight each other and tend to settle internal disagreements peacefully, these advocates have reasoned that the sooner elections are held, the better. In their view, pushing autocratic war-prone regimes along the fast track toward democracy should break the power of violent authoritarian elites, accustom people to the habits of democratic participation, provide legitimacy for new leaders, and in cases of international peacekeeping or military occupation, hasten the withdrawal of foreign forces. "It is the practice of democracy that makes a nation ready for democracy," opined President George W. Bush, "and every nation can start on this path."[87]

Recent troubled transitions to democracy have raised doubts, however, even among some staunch democracy advocates, about whether early elections are beneficial for peace and democracy. As in Bosnia after the 1995 Dayton Accord, early elections may lock in the power of former combatants, who remain the best organized groups in the immediate aftermath of conflict, whereas progressive, programmatic political parties have typically not had time to organize to overcome communal barriers. Moreover, early elections typically take place when the rule of law is weak, making it more likely that elections will suffer from irregularities and that losers will refuse to accept the results peacefully. For these reasons, the short-run chance of peace and the long-run prospect for democratic consolidation might both be improved by postponing fully competitive elections until some progress has been made in strengthening the institutions needed to make democracy work. These include competent state bureaucracies, independent courts, professionalized media, integrative political parties, and functioning market economies.

This issue is taking on greater urgency because postconflict elections are being held much more quickly than in the past. The average time between the end of a civil war and the first postconflict election has been cut in half since the end of the Cold War. Prior to 1989, an average of 5.6 years passed before countries held their first postconflict election. After 1989, this figure fell to 2.7 years.[88]

Much of this is due to international urging. In Bosnia, for example, the early timing of elections was to justify an early exit of US occupation troops. Since the end of the Cold War, foreign countries have increasingly pressured civil war–ridden countries to end their conflicts with negotiated agreements and to hold elections in the expectation that democracy will promote peace and stability.[89] As Séverine Autesserre shows in her research on eastern Congo, prioritizing electoral politics—instead of directly addressing local security problems and building the institutional capacity of the state—often fails to achieve these goals.[90]

Based on an original dataset of all post–civil war elections that occurred between 1945 and 2008, Dawn Brancati and I found that holding elections too soon after a civil war raises the risk of war occurring again.[91] On average, waiting five years to hold the first election reduces the chance of war recurring by one-third. Yet, the study also found that early elections do not necessarily increase the risk of war under all circumstances. Decisive victories, demobilization of rebel armies, and international peacekeeping diminish the fighting capacity of former combatants who might otherwise be tempted to return to war when faced with unfavorable election results. Effective institutional reforms can help new pro-reform actors come to power. But if elections are held before adequate administrative and legal institutions are put in place or before former rebels are demobilized, the risk of going back through the revolving door into civil war increases.

Liberia's experience with elections in 1997 illustrates the danger of holding elections when institutions remain weak, whereas its 2005 election illustrates the stabilizing role of elections in an improved institutional setting. Liberia held presidential and legislative elections, supervised by a West African peacekeeping force, two years after signing the 1995 Abuja Accords. Former warlord Charles Taylor wielded enormous advantages over his opponents, as a result of his pervasive organizational network, his monopoly over the media, as well as his extensive military and financial resources. Preelection disarmament efforts were marred by bloody resistance from bands of local warlords. Many voters supported Taylor because they expected him to devastate the country in renewed fighting if he lost. Nonetheless, Taylor's exploitative, arbitrary rule after his election soon provoked resistance and a renewed civil war in 1999.[92]

In contrast, Liberia's 2005 elections took place in a more highly institutionalized setting, overseen by fifteen thousand United Nations peacekeepers. These elections achieved much better results, although they too were held only two years after signing a peace treaty. With Taylor having fled the country, the 2005 elections were not dominated by a single candidate or party. Demobilization occurred prior to the election and more smoothly than it had before. Prior to the election, Liberia's media was liberalized, and some media outlets, such as Star Radio, offered reasonably balanced coverage of the election. An independent electoral commission, despite shortcomings, maintained neutrality, and unlike in previous elections, political groupings were genuine parties, not just unreformed rebel groups. Ultimately, disputes about the electoral process were settled in court, not on the battlefield.

Power-sharing agreements between rival factions in postconflict settings offer another method for reducing the risk of early elections.[93] An agreement to share power regardless of the outcome of the election can reassure both sides that they will have a place in government, reducing the chances of them rejecting the election results and returning to war. Examples include the power-sharing deals in South Africa following violence at the end of the apartheid regime, in Mozambique after the long civil war between FRELIMO and RENAMO, and in Sudan at the end of the civil war between North and South. Power sharing, however, can sometimes cause instability in the short or long run if it is not combined with other favorable conditions, such as peacekeeping or strong governmental institutions.

In the short term, powerful groups that are accustomed to ruling outright may resist the implementation of agreements that require them to share power. In Burundi in 1993, for example, international aid donors insisted that the military dictatorship led by the Tutsi minority hold elections. The elections were won by the majority ethnic Hutu candidate, Melchior Ndadaye. When the new president moved to institute power-sharing arrangements that would have integrated Hutus into the formerly all-Tutsi officer corps, the military assassinated him, plunging Burundi into another, even more intense civil war. Power sharing imposed by international donors also contributed to the onset of the Rwanda genocide by excluding from power the militant Hutu government faction that controlled armed security forces and machete-wielding militias.

Power sharing can also increase the odds of a return to war in the long term by allowing leaders to govern in an arbitrary and exploitative manner with little risk of losing office. By locking former combatants into positions of authority, power-sharing institutions provide group leaders with little incentive to broaden their support bases beyond old cleavage lines and tend to reduce democratic accountability to a process of outbidding appeals to narrow constituencies. Power-sharing arrangements tended to freeze and deepen lines of conflict for this reason in Lebanon and Yugoslavia.[94]

International actors have been part of the problem of premature elections, but they have sometimes also been part of the solution. Internationals have often pushed for early elections in risky conditions, when recently warring factions remain well armed and able to use violence to contend for power. Indeed, international actors have helped create these conditions in the first place by pressing warring factions to reach settlements before one side has defeated the other.[95] Nonetheless, international actors can sometimes create conditions that mitigate the risk posed by early elections when they provide robust peacekeeping, facilitate the demobilization of armed forces, back power-sharing agreements, and help build robust political institutions. Thus, international pressure in favor of early elections strengthens peace when it provides these stabilizing instruments, but it undermines peace when it is not backed by effective means to achieve stable democracy.

Conclusion

Moving a society across the threshold to a liberal rights-based order requires creating the social preconditions for empowering the core constituencies that benefit from and strengthen inclusive institutions and ideologies. The work of sequencing from a less liberal equilibrium to a more liberal one is best done through a pragmatic approach. It must craft a strategy to harness the power of mass social movements, anticorruption reforms, expedient transitional justice initiatives, and well-timed elections. Democratic transitions are necessarily complicated, often volatile. In navigating this perilous terrain, politics leads and rights follow. Pragmatism guides expediency and allows for patience, recognizing that these are not violations of rights principles but progressive tools toward making those ideals a reality.

5

Crossing the Economic
Threshold in China

IN FULLY SUCCESSFUL FORMS of modernity, both states and markets are organized around impersonal rules—for states, rules of administration; for markets, rules governing economic production and exchange. These rules do not emerge overnight. Most societies pass through an extended transition from patronage-based orders to fully modern ones.[1] For late developers, the trajectory of this transition often detours into a dead end that has dire consequences for human rights. When the country is a great power like China, those consequences can be fateful for the whole world. A pragmatic approach to human rights is needed to safely navigate this perilous passage.

Especially now, the pattern of late, authoritarian, "catch-up" development poses challenges to the liberal project of modernity and human rights. Over the past two decades, several large states in the developing and postcommunist worlds have experienced significant economic growth as they introduced liberalizing reforms in their domestic markets and international economic relations. Impressive improvements in mass living standards, along with spikes in economic inequality and corruption, have often accompanied this growth. The emergence of illiberal nationalism with populist overtones reflects a growing contradiction between economic development and illiberal governance institutions, which is leading these states into the so-called middle-income trap and its attendant syndrome of human rights abuses.

During the Cold War, large developing states were able for a time to pursue strategies of state-led economic development and import-substituting industrialization (ISI) under "bureaucratic authoritarian" regimes.[2] This relied on what the economic historian Alexander Gerschenkron called the "advantages of backwardness": mobilizing underutilized labor and resource inputs, copying well-known industrial processes, and exerting state power to accumulate capital and protect infant industries from foreign competition.[3] Subsidies and protectionism were a drag on productivity growth, however, so the system gradually stalled out. As ISI was losing momentum, global policies of easier capital mobility and deregulation of markets, increasingly favored by advanced capitalist states and international financial institutions, offered opportunities for more dynamic, export-led growth. China, India, Brazil, Turkey, and other large developing states signed up for market liberalization, and as a result each for a time experienced an acceleration of economic growth.

In many of these states, the initial phase of liberalization remained based on many of the same advantages of backwardness as in ISI, only the market now became global. Cheap labor, easily extracted natural resources, copycat technology, and development-pushing state policies were now harnessed to foreign direct investment and integration into internationally managed production processes. A crucial benefit of plugging into the world economy was exposure to market signals of supply, demand, and price, tethering state-influenced investment decisions to economic reality. Late-developing states selectively cherry-picked from the liberal institutional package of modernity, assimilating features needed narrowly for liberalized trade and finance, but approaching broader rule of law, freedom of speech, and open democratic political competition with varying degrees of wariness. Clientelistic economic and political arrangements more commonly associated with traditional societies and state-run economies continued. Neoliberal in many such states became an epithet meaning crony capitalism.

There are strong signs that this model of globalized market development is leading rising states into a transition trap. Extensive growth has been based largely on adding more inputs: more labor coming off the farm, more land foreclosures, higher rates of capital investment, exploiting already-known technologies on a wider market scale. Knowing in advance the outcome they are aiming to achieve, the state and centralized financial institutions have requisitioned and deployed resources by command authority, a model that is compatible with authoritarian rule and administrative control of labor but also accommodates partial democratization.

The very success of this phase undermines its formula for growth. Wage rates rise once most of the useful labor force is employed. New land for commercial enterprises is harder to come by, and requisitioning it creates more resistance from a better-resourced populace. The levers of state power ratchet the rates of savings and investment higher and higher, but force-feeding growth in this way demands more and more capital inputs to generate less and less incremental output. This syndrome constitutes exactly the impasse that China now faces.

The solution is to shift from the strategy of extensive growth to that of intensive growth driven by increases in the combined productivity of all factors of production. This depends not on ever-increasing inputs but on the application of more efficient techniques to existing factors of production and improved allocation of inputs through responsiveness to market incentives. In countries in China's situation, this would require the development of its vast internal consumer market, which is stunted by the strategy of enforced savings. To make this work, the crucial underlying requirement would be the strengthening of liberal institutions of rule of law and governmental accountability to reduce the inefficient drag of corruption, insecure rights of property and contracting, and inequality—an adjustment that China has thus far chosen not to undertake.

While slower-than-average growth can happen at every level and stage of development, a study by Brookings economist David Dollar finds that improving institutional quality is especially important for sustaining economic growth in middle-income countries because of its role in supporting the shift from extensive to intensive growth.[4] China and Vietnam were able to develop relatively good institutions for their lower level of income and stage of development, and they sustained a good rate of growth for a time without developing the whole panoply of civil liberties. For high-income countries, however, he finds a tight connection between good economic institutions—including well-defined property rights, rule of law, effective government, and limits on corruption—and a broader set of liberal rights as measured by Freedom House's civil liberties index. Not counting oil states, Singapore is the only exception to this rule in being wealthy and rule following but not liberal. In the 1990–2010 period, for countries at low levels of per capita income, authoritarian countries grew faster than democratic ones, but democracies above one-fourth of US per capita income grew faster.

By some measures, China is taking a number of positive steps to avoid getting stuck in the middle-income trap. Compared to other large developmental states, China looks more like success cases—Japan, South Korea, and Taiwan—in prioritizing education, investing in research and development, limiting foreign direct investment, and avoiding the expansion of the informal, untaxed, unregulated sector of the economy.[5] On the other hand, its economic inequality and systemic corruption remain warning signs. As China inches up the scale of per capita income, Dollar finds its growth slowing as its institutional quality score declines relative to its GDP per capita peers.

If Dollar is right about the need to continually liberalize institutions and expand civic rights as a country moves up the per capita income food chain, why don't more countries, especially large ones, follow the example of South Korea and Taiwan? A touchstone reason is that the ruling elite, state apparatus, patronage networks, ethnic or religious majorities, and rising middle classes of these emerging powers have vested interests in keeping the incompletely liberalized system going.

To avoid reforms that would endanger their power and privileges, the ruling elite and their key support constituencies have a few options. One is outright repression. Another, trickle-down economics, can also be used to justify wealth inequality. When trickle-down patronage wears thin, however, nationalism is a tested tool for shifting the main axis of politics away from economic grievances to concerns about culture and identity.

A less drastic solution to the problem of the partial-reform equilibrium is to continue to shift the predominant coalition in the direction of gradual reform. An example is the strategy of Vietnamese market reformers in the mid-1990s. Despite opportunities for foreign direct investment and challenges from Chinese economic competition, reform was blocked by the market monopoly position of Vietnam's dominant coalition of state-owned enterprises. But a coalition of underrepresented regions seeking to host private firms bought off some of the better represented regions through financial side payments to support reform. This coalition succeeded in shifting the balance of institutional power by creating new provinces in 1996, which gave them a majority of votes in the Central Committee. Corrupt construction contracts helped to grease the wheels of this power shift. This allowed the reform coalition to push through economic initiatives at the expense of the winners from Vietnam's earlier phase of partial market reform.[6] Still, this new round of reform stopped well short of the introduction of liberal, democratic, rule-of-law political institutions, setting the stage for yet another phase of the partial-reform dilemma.

In short, detours that divert late developers from the path toward liberal modernity limit the social power of constituencies favoring human rights and hinder efforts to push aside illiberal elites. This allows illiberal coalitions to consolidate their power, often deploying nationalist ideologies to gain popular support in the context of disruptive economic growth.[7] Gradualist reform strategies that are compatible with incumbent elite interests are not impossible, but they face entrenched resistance. This creates distinctive and difficult conditions for promoting human rights, which must be the point of departure for devising pragmatic strategies.

China's Illiberal Model of Modernity

In *How China Escaped the Poverty Trap*, political scientist Yuen Yuen Ang argues that China's economic rise under Deng Xiaoping and his successors has required bureaucratic improvisation to overcome institutional shortcomings that would otherwise have led to market failures. Lacking even the rudiments of a legal system to support property rights and contracting, and lacking a banking system to capitalize promising entrepreneurial endeavors, China resorted to many of the same expedients that fueled proto-capitalism in the early modern period in Europe: the selling of offices, the granting of monopolies, and state subsidies for insiders' private enterprise.[8] While such practices conflating public service and private interest created market distortions and inefficiencies, they helped to overcome barriers to the mobilization of land, labor, and resources for the primitive accumulation of capital.

Similar arguments in favor of "second-best" institutions are made by the influential progressive economist Dani Rodrik.[9] He points out that practices that would be considered corrupt dealings in developed market economies may in a patronage system be a rational adaptation to its legal system's unreliability as an enforcer of contracts. The development of ties of mutual dependence and trust based on an iterated track record of quids pro quo may be indispensable when liberal market institutions are absent, weak, or corrupt. Ostensibly liberal reforms that bar such arrangements and push economic transactions into a corrupt legal system, Rodrik says, could lead to outcomes that are worse for the public as well as for private actors.

Second-best strategies of development are a hybrid of the social organization of traditional societies, based on coercive authoritarian rule and particularistic economic and social relationships, and of technologically modern societies with rationalized administration and a deepening division of labor. At the most general level, these strategies emerged because they are an easier adaptation from traditional arrangements than is full-blown liberalism, for which most late-developing states lack the social preconditions.

Rodrik's examples are from Vietnam and Mali; Ang makes the same point about China. She notes that Xi Jinping's anticorruption campaign, which is not aimed at reforming the system but at removing political opponents, is predictably producing a dysfunctional "paralysis within the bureaucracy." Since "the most lucrative stream of corruption comes not from brute extraction of private wealth but from greasing access to emerging and booming markets," she argues that "cozy state-business ties and collusive deals are often what it takes to assure entrepreneurs of their property rights and to entice investments."[10] For this reason, "the crackdown on corruption as it is currently done indirectly stifles bureaucratic risk taking, innovation, and state-led growth."[11]

In China as elsewhere, appeals to national pride in wealth and state power have caulked the gaps in legitimacy opened up by all-too-visible corrupt practices. Facing outward, nationalism mobilized the people for competition with the cosmopolitan ideologies of liberal and socialist foreign powers. Facing inward, nationalism shifted the main axis of domestic politics away from class and individual rights toward identity politics and in-group unity, which served the needs of the ruling coalition.[12]

This syndrome of late, illiberal modernization is being replicated in today's rising powers, but China is the state best poised to make a success of it. The half-decade before the 2008 global financial crisis was a period of strong economic growth for many of the world's illiberal or partially liberal major powers. The American bubble economy fueled by tax cuts, deceptive investment lures, and military deficit spending coincided with economic opportunities in "emerging markets" that had not yet exhausted the potential for rapid growth from cheap labor, resource windfalls, or moderate improvements in institutions and business climate.[13] Chinese growth surged after being admitted to the WTO on the strength of vague promises of rule-based economic reform and an irresistible chance for global supply-chain partners to cash in.

After the global financial bubble burst in 2008, the trajectory of China—along with India, Brazil, and Turkey—looked quite different. As the unusually favorable international setting turned sour, these rising powers' internal weaknesses became more apparent. In every case, the setbacks involved a failure to complete the liberalization that was needed to move past a partial-reform trap, which risked slipping back into traditional patterns of corruption, repression, and playing the nationalist card to legitimate this regression. Brazil's oil windfall turned into an oil curse as the political repercussions of its orgy of corruption brought down a series of governments and left every party discredited. India's bungled currency reforms and stalled liberalization of a political economy built on corruption and discrimination slowed Indian growth. When Turkey's ruling regime turned out to be too corrupt, too abusive of human rights, and too un-European to qualify for full EU membership, its president

Recep Tayyip Erdogan fell back on budget-busting patronage for his support base. This he combined with repression of the restive Kurdish minority and of the pious Gülenist technocrats, the insufficiently loyal allies of convenience who became his rivals for power and patronage. In every case, these backward moves amid economic failures coincided with a surge in the regimes' nationalist rhetoric.

But what about China? This is by far the most important case, both because of its size and because it is the closest to having a serious model of alternative illiberal modernity.

It is not difficult to make the case that China checks off all the boxes of the late-development trap. Despite its rapid catch-up growth, taking advantage of access to foreign markets and technology, and its successful use of economic stimulus to navigate the global financial crisis of 2008, China shows the classic signs of being snared in a middle-income trap.[14] Its economic growth rate has been tapering off, despite (or because of) a policy of trying to suppress wages and devoting a nearly Stalinist level of its revenue to investment, which has been yielding an ever-declining marginal rate of return.[15] In recent years, state-owned-enterprises have increased as a proportion of the economy because they have been favored in central investment decisions despite lagging in productivity.[16]

Xi Jinping has attached his prestige to the centrally promoted Belt and Road Initiative, which reflects the typical Chinese infrastructure-based growth model. Now that China's internal infrastructure has largely been built, it has huge excess capacity in construction-related matériel and labor, which it is deploying abroad in building ports, roads, and railroads. State financing of the projects has touched off a pork barrel feeding frenzy. The economic soundness of these investments is speculative at best, but they create opportunities to shovel patronage to Chinese supporters and in some cases buy off corrupt officials in the receiving states.[17] Under the weak leadership of Hu Jintao, the Chinese complained that the "hundred families" that dominated the corrupt economy could not be reined in. Under the strong leadership of Xi Jinping, the same interests are fed through the centralized rationale of the Belt and Road and the China 2025 high-tech drive.[18] Meanwhile, China bridles at the suggestion that it should be treated as a nonmarket economy under WTO rules.

The political dimension of the late-development syndrome also conforms to China's recent pattern. Its formerly routinized process for selecting a successor to the top leader has been abandoned, granting Xi an opportunity to remain dictator for life.[19] Local administrative reform experiments that were encouraged under Hu Jintao have been abandoned, replaced by an anticorruption campaign aimed at Xi's enemies in rival patronage networks.[20] The surveillance state keeps track of average citizens as well as low-level officials.[21]

Despite this system of information gathering and control, censorship of nationalist opinion on China's internal social media sometimes seems to slip out of control, which is a feature rather than a bug in the governance system.[22] Nationalism and repression of rights go hand in hand in Xi's policy of sending Muslim Uyghurs to reeducation camps and suppressing Hong Kongers who demonstrated to retain their accustomed legal rights adjudicated by independent, professional courts. The self-absorbed and self-defeating quality of Beijing's nationalist rhetoric showed up also in Xi's untimely reiteration of Beijing's intention to apply the Hong Kong formula of "one state, two systems" to Taiwan. The Taiwanese people's backlash against PRC policy in Hong Kong turned around the waning political fortunes of the resolutely independent Taiwanese President Tsai Ing-Wen, propelling her to a second term. Xi topped this series of self-inflicted diplomatic wounds by initiating a border skirmish with India in the same spot as their 1962 war—a Wilhelmine-style move seemingly designed to complete China's gratuitous self-encirclement.[23] Amid economic slowdown and endemic corruption, the Xi regime completes the pattern of a late-development crisis with heightened authoritarianism, rights abuse, and nationalist excess.

But how does China's adaptability stack up when evaluated in terms of the logic of its own model rather than a liberal ideal type that many liberal societies fall short of? One yardstick is how well China is succeeding in solving a problem that its own leadership and citizens identify as an endemic shortcoming—the arbitrariness, corruption, and inefficiency of local officials. Scholars distinguish between two methods of monitoring agents' compliance with rules and with the wishes of the principals to whom agents are accountable: the "fire alarm" and the "police patrol."[24] In Hu Jintao's first term as general secretary before 2007, China experimented with the fire alarm model, in which a popular outcry, sometimes supported by investigative media reports, elicited a harsh reaction from higher authorities who were "shocked, shocked to find that gambling has been going on" in the casino. Efforts were undertaken to clean up local corruption in targeted cities, but without lasting effect. Typically, an energetic outsider was designated to rein in corrupt practices, increase transparency, and expose self-dealing. Yet, transparency of land transactions and declaration of assets, for example, was selective; the empowered guardians of rectitude would police the small fry, but no one would police the guardians.[25] After a couple of years, the outside troubleshooter would move on to clean up a new city, and the city he had just cleaned up would quickly slip back into the old pattern.[26]

Under Xi Jinping's intensive surveillance regime, the approach to local corruption is more of a police patrol system. The problem is that they round up not the guilty, and not even "the usual suspects," but rivals from outside their own patronage network, forcing them to engage in Leninist "self-criticism."[27] They characterize the problem in terms of bad people rather than a flawed system. In contrast, when South Korea and Taiwan faced similar problems, they shored up their "police patrol" *and* "fire alarm" capacities, strengthening local institutions of the rule of law and enhancing routine processes of local citizen participation.[28]

The last thing that the Xi regime wants is to strengthen the routine, independent capacity of courts and police to investigate and punish illegality, which would challenge the basic system under which law is merely a passive tool for implementing the policy of the leadership.[29] Nor will the regime strengthen the institution that is most needed to implement the "fire alarm" model—namely, an unfettered, independent investigative local media.[30]

But perhaps none of this matters if China can adapt its late-developer playbook to continue to foster growth of its domestic economy, lift families out of poverty, and gradually improve public health and education. What is the evidence that China would do better on these dimensions of social development with a liberal rights-based approach to modernity?

Let's look at an area that is widely seen as a major success for the Chinese path to development: improvements in public education and opportunities for upward mobility through meritocratic educational testing. Shanghai schools are famous for producing students with high math scores, but half of the country's future workforce will come from rural areas where few students currently go beyond middle school. According to recent studies, a third of rural students are cognitively impaired because of early childhood malnutrition and public health shortcomings.[31] Even middle-income families, which constitute only 12 percent of China's population, face hurdles in using education as a springboard to success. Access to higher education requires significant expenditure on tutoring and cram courses outside the regular school curriculum. A recent study based on panel data shows that China's astronomical, corruption-fueled level of income inequality is leaving middle-income families behind in this race for access to higher education. Because this goal is increasingly looking out of reach for many families, more are deciding to cut investment in their children's education. The study concludes, "China is struggling to avoid the middle-income trap and hoping to enlarge the share of middle-income families. If inequality is more driven by factors beyond people's control, then these middle-income families may lose confidence and invest less in human capital accumulation, which might become a serious obstacle for China's future economic development."[32]

Because the regime understands that it cannot rely only on economic performance for its legitimacy with still-struggling constituencies, it relies also on nationalism, which has the potential to rally otherwise divided interests in support of the state.[33] Yet, this has the potential to open a particularly awkward avenue of criticism of the regime's foreign policy when it fails to assert national interests. Analysts have offered varying interpretations of the nature and causes of Chinese nationalist mass opinion. I see these not necessarily as competing accounts but as an interacting set of forces that makes the resulting assemblage all the more unstable.

Close to the regime's own narrative, some Western scholars have emphasized China's century and a half of humiliations at the hands of imperialists, from the Opium Wars through Japan's atrocities in Nanjing to US protection of the remnant of the Chinese nationalist regime on Taiwan.[34] This is seen as an ingrained psychological obsession, which makes Chinese patriots inordinately focused on questions of status, insatiable in their demands for Japanese apologies, and reflexively assertive over issues of territorial integrity and Japanese efforts to gain a permanent seat on the UN Security Council.[35] Others point out that the connection between individual self-esteem and group status is not especially Chinese, but rather is a well-established finding of research on group psychology in general.[36] Still others, however, argue that the impact of such humiliations tends to wane over time, and in the Chinese case, high dudgeon was brought back to prominence in the popular consciousness only because of the regime's decision to feature these humiliations in the patriotic education campaign of the 1990s.[37] After the Tiananmen showdown, the regime's decision to promote Chinese nationalism reflected the waning relevance of Marxism-Leninism in the era of market reforms and the danger of Western ideological and cultural influences as international economic relations expanded. Chinese commentators were fascinated by Samuel Huntington's idea of a "clash of civilizations," which they endorsed. Even intellectuals who challenged the regime in organizing the Tiananmen demonstrations jumped on this bandwagon, realizing that by publishing an anti-Western book,

China Can Say No, they could safely give voice to popular views at a time when liberal forms of expression were prohibited.[38]

Primed in this way, Chinese citizens on social media have vigorously expressed nationalist attitudes in a series of incidents since the inadvertent bombing of the Chinese embassy in Belgrade during the Kosovo War, the pogroms directed at ethnic Chinese in Indonesia after the fall of the Suharto dictatorship, the downing of the US spy plane at the beginning of the Bush administration, the denunciation of Japan's lobbying for a Security Council seat, and a series of squabbles over islands and oil rigs in the South China Sea.[39] This mass commentary is sometimes aimed only at the foreign foe who is imposing yet another humiliation on China, but often criticism is explicitly or implicitly aimed at the Chinese government for not acting forcefully enough in defense of the national interest and reputation.[40]

Several interpretations vie to explain this. Some say that this simply reflects the sincere views of many in the Chinese public, which many government officials share to a considerable degree. Others argue that the government allows and even encourages this form of militant self-expression even when netizens push for harder line policies, because it sends a signal to China's foreign competitor that the Chinese government has domestic backing to stand firm. Some even suggest that in the 2012 Diaoyu/Senkaku Islands showdown with Japan, the Chinese government reached a point at which it sought to end the crisis with a compromise but felt that it needed nonetheless to allow a final flurry of militant criticism of Japan, which implicitly criticized the government's own insufficiently resolute policy. Some argue further that this and other antiregime nationalist discourse is a stalking horse for a broader set of domestic political complaints, which cannot be as safely voiced.[41] Offline, the regime has quickly moved to stifle unruly street demonstrations at the Japanese embassy. They did not, however, silence an inexplicably counterproductive squabble launched by Chinese academics over the geographical dimensions and ethnic character of the ancient kingdom of proto-Korea, which gratuitously alienated a broad swath of public opinion in South Korea.[42] This would hardly be the first time that nationalism has been found a convenient popular discourse for criticizing demagogic authoritarian regimes, who themselves play the nationalist card.

China's illiberal model of modernity increasingly bears many of the defects that tripped up the progress of several late developers that trod a similar path before it. And yet the fairly recent success of several gradually liberalizing modern East Asian states with technocratic bureaucracies and state-led

economic strategies suggests that the door is not entirely closed to a less disruptive result. As recently as the Hu Jintao period, China still gave a plausible
performance in the role of peacefully rising power and constructive stake-
holder in the international order. Even if a rights-friendly outcome seems unlikely anytime soon, it is worth considering how to avoid an outcome that is
extremely destructive of the rights-supporting liberal international order and
of China itself.

Pragmatic Strategies for Protecting the Rights-Based Order during China's Rise

It is clear by now that a strategy of rights promotion based on decrying the
Chinese regime's oppression of rights activists and violations of legal rights is
an empty, performative exercise. Not long ago China was willing to play the
game, but by its own standards, issuing "human rights" pronouncements that
listed its successes in such areas as education, public health, and economic
opportunity. Now it still has those programs but generally declines to label
them human rights achievements, just as it declines to label the mass incarceration of ordinary young Uyghur men and the forced sterilization of Uyghur
women human rights violations. There is nothing to be lost by rethinking a
human rights strategy toward China from the ground up in pragmatic terms.

One possible strategy is to wait for long-term economic structural evolution to turn China into a rule-of-law democracy, just as it has authoritarian
South Korea and Taiwan. When China was invited into the WTO in 2001,
many people assumed that a rich China with a growing middle class embedded in lucrative trading relations with the world's democracies would gradually
evolve in some kind of liberalizing direction, though not necessarily a competitive party democracy.[43] Although by then political scientists were well
aware that per capita wealth didn't automatically turn states democratic, we
knew that once states above middle income had become democratic, they
never regressed. The only wealthy autocracies were oil sheikhdoms and mi-
crostates. Thus, fostering Chinese social evolution through international trade
seemed a reasonable bet. But the crucial decade for socializing China to its
peaceful rise as a liberalizing trading state was lost, as the United States got
distracted in its fruitless foreign wars and its domestic polarization. The role
played by the United States as the blunderer that authored the world financial
crisis convinced the Chinese leadership and even the Chinese people that
they would be better off figuring out their own route to power, wealth, and

modernity.[44] The proportionately tiny Chinese middle class liked a lot of what it saw in American popular culture and consumerism, but like most weak bourgeoisies in history, it has accepted the protection of the ruling authoritarian elite, which is in any case not offering the alternative of strict rule of law and mass democracy.[45]

The evolutionary strategy that worked for South Korea and Taiwan depended on their relationships with the United States, but the PRC isn't dependent on cooperation with the United States, so all the work must be done by the allure of bourgeois culture and not just its superficial aspects, which China can have without the human rights part. This might eventually work, but only if the United States dramatically refurbishes its allure while China gets mired in stagflation, gerontocracy, and a fed-up youth culture. It could happen, and it could lead to dramatic rights reforms in the long term, but it's not something to count on.

A second type of strategy is to work more actively to create incentives and preconditions for a more rights-based social order through processes of international economic exchange. This takes advantage of the motivations of Chinese leaders, technocrats, and entrepreneurs as they actually exist to create institutional capacity and self-interested constituencies for a more law-based form of modernity. Chinese elites want to continue to move China up the value-added product curve. Research shows that firms in the postcommunist single-party state of Vietnam are willing to improve labor standards if market incentives will reward this.[46] Export-oriented firms want to maintain stable relations with foreign partners and markets. China's foreign business partners and their states have legal and practical standing to require an adequate standard of transparency and legality in their relationships. Chinese localities that take in greater foreign direct investment spend more money improving their courts and have succeeded in raising their independence and efficiency when dealing with commercial cases.[47]

This strategy of luring China into strengthening its legal institutions as a functional spillover from its participation in international markets cuts against the grain of Chinese legal tradition, which is based on administrative law and hardly differentiated from administrative policy. Even proponents of the idea of evolutionary legalization of Chinese practices in the economic realm make very modest claims about the extent and pace of reform. Linda Yueh envisions a causal sequence in which the formation of a constituency of private business property owners precedes and pushes for stronger legal protections.[48] Functional arguments about the need for security, predictability, and regularity to

smooth business activity support this constituency's self-interested arguments. She invokes the example of Property Law 2007, which for the first time
stipulated "equal protection" for private and public property in China.

Western leverage on behalf of a rule-based business climate in China should
have been exerted more systematically and insistently over the past two decades.[49] The weakening of labor unions in the major democracies has limited
the political leverage behind such efforts. But now the rise of nativist protectionism in the United States has mobilized a new constituency that gives employers and politicians incentives to insist that trading partners meet these
standards. If China does not respond cooperatively to these changed incentives, multinational companies could gradually walk away and invest to
strengthen potential partners elsewhere if they are not satisfied, but developing China-sized alternatives will present a challenge.[50] This was a central goal
of the Trans-Pacific Partnership trade deal between the United States and
partners other than China in East Asia. This plan foundered amid the US domestic political wreckage of the "embedded liberal compromise," which had
previously reconciled trade liberalization with domestic labor protections.[51]

It will be harder to exert such leverage now that China has made considerable progress in creating an internal market. The international sector now accounts for only 19.5 percent of Chinese GDP, whereas at its peak in 2006 it
accounted for 36 percent.[52] Hard bargaining alone might now accomplish only
a little.

Another strategy is to wait for China's innovative, small- and medium-sized
private entrepreneurs to push back against the growing deadweight costs of
corruption and politicized investment in inefficient state-owned enterprises,
making common cause with politicians in their regions. In the meantime, improving the functioning of the liberal economic order would provide a model
of how to break through the middle-income trap. This is an influence model
based on *social proof* and persuasion of the merits of liberal social order, where
the persuaders are not activists complaining about political prisoners but
Western CEOs, finance ministers, and central bankers who insist on best practices in business relations. The many Chinese business and technical experts
trained in the West know perfectly well what international standards are. They
just need to have an incentive and an opportunity to push internally for compliance with them.

This includes status incentives as well as material ones. Chinese universities
are obsessed with their international ranking, possibly as a result of the century
of humiliations. They want to teach in English and use the most rigorous,

formalized methodologies not only because they produce results but also because they have global cachet. Insidiously, the Chinese academic hierarchy also invokes international standards of rigor and objectivity to put pressure on liberal, philosophical scholarship as "soft" and unworthy. This status concern gives Western universities status leverage to insist on world standards of academic freedom as a nonnegotiable yardstick for assessing quality. This does not mean overt shaming, which only embarrasses those Chinese who are already suffering from Beijing's transgressions against their academic freedom. Rather it mainly requires relentless reminders of what the standards are and insistence on their being observed as a foundation for any relationship with Western academic institutions beyond the most superficial. Exactly how to tailor this standard setting and implicit sanctioning would have to depend on the lay of the land in different fields, but the general principle behind it should be recognized, and should include the sciences. Blind international peer review of publications is a good anchor.

Two areas in which China might be potentially vulnerable to human rights persuasion over the long run are its systemic corruption and its sugarcoating of its regime history. Both are the equivalent of the proverbial hand grenade on the seminar table.[53] You don't want to pull the pin unless you have a good plan to duck and cover.

Because the Chinese regime has a semimonopoly over information on these topics and a credible threat to ruin the life of any Chinese citizen who tries to break it, it is hardly a simple matter to use—or threaten to use—this weapon to induce systemic change. For the corruption issue, the initial steps could begin with indirect leverage from the outside. This would need to start with organizing an anticorruption campaign aimed not only at China but at all states and societies including our own. Led by all the established democracies, this campaign could use the by now well-honed tools of the international banking system to root out bribery, tax evasion, money laundering, offshoring, shell companies, labor exploitation, shipping registration opacity, and other corrupt practices, many of which remain tolerated or exploited by major law-abiding states and large multinational corporations. Efforts to shore up US legislation on this front are already under way.[54] Even the Trump administration moved to impose Securities and Exchange Commission standards on Chinese stock offerings on the New York Stock Exchange.

Legitimating anticorruption reforms as a campaign for fundamental human rights and economic development would help in getting widespread compliance of the advanced democracies and their trading partners among the middle-income states. Given the mass appeal of anticorruption pretty much everywhere, this would finally give the contemporary human rights movement the basis for leading a mass global social movement.[55] No doubt, Xi would claim that China was already vigorously rooting out corruption, while deflecting attention from the violations of due process that the Chinese approach to "anticorruption" exacerbates. A big part of the battle would be to highlight the difference between law-based anticorruption efforts as opposed to vendettas against domestic political opponents. That objective is an important reason to start the campaign with a series of international-level systemic reforms to publicize the role of law-based transparency and procedural accountability in the effort. This would set up a contest for public support worldwide in which the democratic states and the human rights movement would occupy the high ground, including support among an only partially silenced fifth column inside Russia and China.

The history of PRC mass atrocities against the Han people could be an even more explosive issue. The Xi Jinping regime has recklessly set itself up for the exploitation of this profound vulnerability. Few Chinese have any idea how many millions died in Mao's Great Leap Forward, which far outstripped Chinese deaths at the hands of Japanese invaders. This makes Xi potentially vulnerable when he praises Mao, showing propaganda documentaries that sugarcoat PRC history and justifying his own absolute power based on Mao as his role model. Threats aimed at the intelligentsia to bring back Mao's rural reeducation system from the Cultural Revolution could backfire if people learn the truth of what actually happened then. Likewise, not many understand what happened in Tiananmen Square or Deng Xiaoping's ruthless statements to the Politburo about it.[56] Xi is placing a big bet that the Great Firewall will remain intact and that the coopted elite who are educated abroad will hold their tongues indefinitely. In the Soviet case, a split in the Politburo created an incentive for Nikita Khrushchev to give his not-so-secret "secret speech" about "the crimes of the Stalin era," which led to the replacement of most of Stalin's top henchmen.[57]

Eventually the Chinese middle class, once it gets bigger and more self-confident, may realize it was a mistake to jump on the Xi bandwagon, and they may look for a chance to jump off. The most likely catalyst would be a leadership succession struggle or economic crisis in which a reform faction reaches out to a wider circle of support. Among the demands that could arise in the struggle could be the right to free speech, the right to information, the right to the consent of the governed, and the right to due process before the law.

Probably other factions would try to rally mass support through appeals to nationalism or class-based populism to legitimate various forms of clientelistic rule. Like most successful human rights campaigns, this would require a battle of stages based on a core interest group, the attraction of a powerful coalition, the organization of a mass movement, and the ratcheting up of pressures that shift the balance of power and nudge toward reforms without provoking a premature showdown. Most likely the process would not be linear and would lead to the rights setbacks that always accompany struggle. International actors would not be in a position to play a direct, constructive role in this, but creating a global climate in which human rights anchor a viable liberal model of progressive change would be an important, indirect factor. In that sense, China's long-term human rights prospects would be enhanced by a pragmatic, general global strategy, which I discuss in chapter 10.

6

Aligning with Mass Movements, Reform Parties, and Religion

WHEN ASKED to explain where the contemporary human rights movement gets its power, its advocates typically credit the rise of "global civil society."[1] Human Rights Watch has said that "its strength lies in its partnerships with local human rights groups, further extending its reach to the ground level and across the globe."[2]

The lore of the movement portrays popular social mobilization as foundational to rights advocacy. Aryeh Neier, the founder of Human Rights Watch, describes the British and American abolitionists as heroes whose relentless energy against the injustice of slavery should serve as the model for today's struggles for human rights.[3] Scholars sympathetic to the movement agree: the abolitionists prefigured contemporary rights activists in their uncompromisingly principled stance, their mobilization of civil society through moral rhetoric, and their tireless use of publicity to shame perpetrators and those who abetted them.[4] Likewise, Gandhi and Martin Luther King are iconic for their ability to make rights messages resonate with their mass constituencies.

But compared to these illustrious forebears, the contemporary human rights movement's vision of global civil society got small. Human Rights Watch executive director Kenneth Roth acknowledges "our relative weakness at mobilizing large numbers of people at this stage of our evolution."[5] Critics charge that the movement has become the secular church of a professionalized liberal elite, whose rhetoric fails to mesh with the idiom of its global clientele.[6] Misunderstanding its own inspirational history, the movement learned to be moralistic, uncompromising, and above politics, but the true lesson is that it pays to be pragmatic.

The human rights movement can make substantial progress toward achieving its goals if and only if it does a better job of tapping into the latent power of mass civil society. Successful rights activism depends on the mobilization of a grassroots social movement, backed by the plurality group in society and aligned with a pragmatic progressive political party. It can do this only if it embeds legalistic, professionalized advocacy work in a broad-based movement animated by religious or other locally resonant themes.[7] Success comes together through the mutually supportive efforts of an organizational tripod: principled activists provide an aspirational compass; a mass social movement provides numbers, commitment, and sustainability; a pragmatic progressive party assembles an institutionally powerful, tactically attuned coalition that gets results. This argument, which captures the book's broadest and most urgent prescriptive claim, is anchored in the central themes of its theoretical chapters, including the emergence of rights in modern times; the central role of power, self-interest, and expedient coalitions in successful mobilization for rights; and the value of vernacular normative discourse in rights activism.

Rights Movements: Political Contexts and Organizational Strategies

Historically, the key to the development of civil and human rights has been the evolution of effective organizational forms of collective action to push for and sustain rights. Where reformist social movements and political parties lacked sustainable mass organization, efforts to broaden rights were ephemeral. In early modern Europe, contentious popular collective actions began as one-off outbursts demanding the alleviation of some specific immediate grievance—food shortages, onerous taxation, or arbitrary justice procedures. They flared up and then were over, leaving no institutionalized trace. But by the late eighteenth century in Britain and France, Charles Tilly's research shows that people began to organize not just for immediate redress, but with an eye toward sustained action to reform basic social and political institutions.

As the modern state increasingly imposed costs of war and taxation on its subjects, they came to understand that their welfare depended on gaining influence in the organs of state power through pressure on ruling elites, alliances of convenience with capitalists and wealthy landowners, and changes in the rules of political representation. Popular groups developed ideologies to justify the worthiness of their claims and rituals of mass collective action to demonstrate their unity, numbers, and commitment to bear sustained costs. In this way, modern social movements were born making general claims to civil rights and political power.[8] But legal-sounding pronouncements guaranteeing "the rights of man," as in the French Revolution, were not enough. What really counted was sustained mass organization.

Sometimes the mass organization that has spearheaded democratic advances has been a mass political party, such as the Jacksonian Democrats who expanded direct election of officials and reduced property qualifications for voting. Sometimes, though, reform parties in democratizing circumstances have remained fairly elitist for a time but have aligned with mass social movements of voters. An example is the alliance between Britain's Whig Party and its mass movements demanding parliamentary reform, opposing slavery, and advocating diverse social reforms that swept into power the political coalition that passed the Great Reform Bill of 1832.[9] In 1846 a similar coalition of reform-minded political elites, capitalist employers, and urban workers mobilized in the streets and in Parliament to repeal tariffs on imported grain, simultaneously advancing their economic interests and addressing the humanitarian crisis caused by the failure of the Irish potato crop.[10]

Comparing Britain and France in the nineteenth century, Tilly emphasizes that the British were far ahead in institutionalizing parliamentary politics and in developing the full panoply of social movement repertoires, including demonstrations, public meetings, petition drives, press statements, symbols of personal affiliation, and the emergence of specialized associations sustaining activism around particular social causes. The French, in contrast, remained stuck in a more primitive phase of contentious politics, featuring mass demonstrations but few institutionalized activities tied to parliamentary or other sustained political processes. As an underlying factor, Tilly notes France's slower pace of industrialization making for weaker constituencies for democratic reform and popular rights.[11]

In a similar vein, Daniel Schlozman shows how parties and social movements have worked together inextricably to shape rights outcomes in the United States, for example, in the early Republican Party and the antislavery movement. While some movements remain at arm's length from parties, those that align with a party shape its ideological development and over the long term nudge it away from policies aimed at the median voter. At the same time, movements entering into a long-term alliance with a party "lose their early zeal, radicalism, and *naïveté,* instead accepting the strategies and compromises of ordinary politics."[12] Working through brokers with deep ties to both the party and the social movement, these parties and movements entered into "multilevel bargains that sprawled across campaigns, appointments, and policies."[13] These ties are especially valuable in giving party politicians access to better information about the attitudes of their crucial vote bases. In return, "when constitutional claims of social movements are presented before courts, it matters a great deal whether the movement's representatives have friends in high places."[14] Schlozman applies this model to both progressive and conservative movements and parties.

In modern democratic transitions, the insulation of reforming elites from mass politics cannot last long.[15] If progressive mass coalitions do not form quickly, populist coalitions based on traditional, exclusionary social identities will coalesce around illiberal elites. During the era of decolonization, for example, Britain often tried to hand power to a multiethnic elite power-sharing coalition, as in Sri Lanka and in Malaysia, but more populist parties quickly moved to mobilize the grassroots along ethnically exclusionary lines.[16] For democracy to prevail, inclusionary liberal parties and mass movements need to outstrip illiberal ones in size, cohesiveness, and motivation. Any rights-promotion strategy needs to plan around this elementary fact.

Forms of Organization for Progressive Politics

Popular movements for rights exist in various organizational forms that include political reform parties, various kinds of mass and elite pressure groups, and violent popular insurgencies. Each of these forms of organization tends to have its distinctive modes of strategic operation, which brings with it characteristic advantages and disadvantages. These diverse organizational forms work best to advance rights when they converge on compatible conceptual frames and coordinate their efforts in complementary ways. Their different inclinations with respect to principles, expedient compromise, and support coalitions, however, sometimes create stumbling blocks for rights promotion. Tilly speculated, for example, that the increasingly professionalized rights movement led by elite-run NGOs might tame and narrow the scope of mobilization for social reform.[17]

These differences across progressive organizational forms affect even the definition of civil society used by rights advocates. Some definitions rule out political parties as "political (hence not civil) society" and exclude reformist labor unions or business lobbies as self-interested (hence not principled) economic organizations. Neier makes much of the fact that Quaker antislavery activists of the late eighteenth century constituted the first altruistic rights movement that concerned itself with the rights of others.[18] Keck and Sikkink stress the role of *principled* transnational activist groups, and other commentators on civil society distinguish it from "uncivil society," that is, social movements whose principles the authors do not like.[19]

These definitional efforts come at the cost of diverting attention from the historically necessary connections between rights activism and the group's striving for political power and economic self-interest. Tilly includes the legitimation of a movement's "worthiness" as one of its four generic tasks, but he shows that claims of worthiness do not require forsaking power or self-interest. Indeed, any basic textbook on the history of rights will include chapters showing that the expansion of rights from aristocratic privileges through the protection of bourgeois property rights and personal liberties to labor rights tracked closely the rise in social clout and the self-interest of these social strata.[20] Understanding how rights get established requires studying their relation to power and self-interest, not defining that relationship away. One intriguing theoretical path is offered by Miguel Carter's study of the Brazilian peasant rights movement that was fostered by Catholic liberation theology. Drawing on Max Weber's concept of "value rationality," Carter demonstrates the importance to the rights project of social movements that are grounded in justifiable group self-interest but that focus on normatively internalized long-term goals rather than short-term, instrumental strategies.[21]

Parties, mass and elite pressure groups, and revolutionary insurgencies are each tools that have strengths and limitations that make them appropriate to particular tasks and circumstances (or as they say in the social movements literature, "opportunity structures").[22] Sometimes the prominence of each organizational tool varies over time in the evolution of a rights struggle. Sometimes multiple tools come into play simultaneously in complementary ways, yet they may also work at cross-purposes if their goals, discursive styles, and strategies are misaligned.

Reformist Parties: Tactical Compromisers, Not Sellouts

Ultimately, the goal of any successful, across-the-board rights-promoting movement must be the creation of a strong reform party that is capable of ruling through democratic control of the state apparatus. Without that, rights rest on a shaky foundation. How to accomplish that over the long run is the basic strategic task of a rights movement in countries wherever a strong reform party is lacking.

When conditions allow, the most direct strategy—forming a mass-based reform party to contend for power through elections—is best. For example, when the rather elitist US Whig Party collapsed in the face of the Democrats' pro-slavery Jacksonian populism, Northern ex-Whigs such as Abraham Lincoln constituted a catchall Northern antislavery party. They took advantage of the favorable opportunities provided by demographic and economic growth of the Northern states, democratic constitutional rules, historic Jeffersonian libertarian discursive themes, and widespread Northern dismay over what was seen as the arrogance of "the Slave Power" in the wake of "bleeding Kansas" and the Dred Scott decision. In this situation, the Republican Party functioned as a mass social movement for rights reform as well as a conventional political party.

But often the opportunity to create a dominant reform party is lacking and needs to be created. This is the case when democratic rules of the game are entirely absent or, as in Tory Britain in the eighteenth and early nineteenth century, when restrictions on the franchise, rules of representation, or electoral competition allow a reform-resisting oligarchy to rule. This also occurs when the majority rejects the claims of a rights-deprived minority, as in the Jim Crow system. Indeed, one of the criticisms of taking the political party route to reform is that some principled objectives, such as protection of the rights of the weak and of minorities, may be jettisoned in the process of making the expedient compromises that are needed to forge a ruling coalition. Among scholars, Frances Fox Piven has argued forcefully, if not always convincingly, that elites always sell out "poor people's movements" in the end, and the movements' leaders get coopted and professionalized.[23]

It is important, however, to distinguish sellouts from tactical compromises that in the long run strengthen rights. For example, the uncompromising rhetoric and counterproductive tactics of hard-core abolitionists often frustrated Lincoln. "Slavery is founded on both injustice and bad policy," he said, "but the promulgation of abolition doctrines tends rather to increase than to abate its evils."[24] Abolitionist talk scared off moderates, and Lincoln wanted to avoid alienating the Northern Democrats and border states.[25] The most uncompromising forms of abolitionism were impatient with constitutional niceties, and Lincoln explicitly disavowed William Lloyd Garrison's "higher law" doctrine, which he saw as undercutting the legal basis for antislavery.[26] Lincoln believed that even the more moderate political abolitionists harmed their own cause by splitting the antislavery vote. He argued that the defection to the Liberty Party of antislavery "conscience Whigs" in the religiously obsessed "burned-over district" of upstate New York had cost Henry Clay and the Whigs the election of 1844, having the unintended consequence of electing the pro-slavery expansionist Democrat James K. Polk as president and thus setting the stage for the Mexican War and the destruction of the Missouri Compromise. "By the fruit the tree is to be known," Lincoln said.[27]

A key task for reform parties is to press for institutional changes that will help guarantee effective representation for groups whose rights are at risk. Sometimes this requires pressure from outside the formal political system to overcome resistance to change within it.

Mass Social Movements and Professionalized Civil Society Organizations

When access to power through political parties is blocked or rights issues are stalemated in the party system, the mobilization of mass social movements in civil society may be needed to break the stalemate. These groups may use tactics such as mass protests, strikes, boycotts, picketing, and sit-ins to demand general changes in the rules for the allocation of political power and the freedom of public discourse, or to demand recognition of specific rights to nondiscrimination, union organization, marriage equality, and the like. Mass social movements may also provide organizational means for direct action on the issues of concern to its support community, providing social services and economic support networks, "crowdsourcing" information on abuses, and facilitating decentralized discussion and recruitment of participants. Depending on the context, they can also provide an organized basis for group self-defense or the coercive use of force. Unlike episodic protests and riots, social movements capable of sustained effort require a centralized leadership cadre to develop an ideology, articulate a common framing discourse, formulate strategy, recruit existing groups and individuals to join the movement, and organize coordinated sequences of action.[28]

Professionalized organizations, such as NGOs, provide another way of organizing civil society to promote rights.[29] Typically, they have a professional staff funded by foundations, private donors, governments, or international organizations, and occasionally also have a public membership that plays a limited role in core organizational activities. Rather than organizing mass protests or coercive actions such as civil disobedience, rights NGOs advocate for the adoption of rights norms, collect information about the violation of existing rights norms and laws, demand compliance, comment on or occasionally participate in legal actions to enforce rights, and lobby governments and other powerful actors to sanction or shun rights violators. Allied organizations may deliver services to rights-deprived populations, as in the rights-based approach to development or humanitarian assistance. They may mount grassroots efforts to persuade local communities to abandon abusive cultural practices such as female genital cutting. Thus, they do some of the same tasks as mass social movements, especially framing issues and formulating strategies for publicity, but the most prominent human rights NGOs mainly lobby others to take direct action rather than organizing it themselves.

Parties, Movements, and NGOs Working Together—or Not

Since it is possible to have mass social movements, NGOs, and political parties pressing simultaneously for rights, asking which gets better results is not necessarily the right question. They can be complementary—good at distinctive but additive tasks. That said, it is worth considering what their distinctive tendencies, strengths, weaknesses, and points of mutual friction might be.

A key task for social movements, NGOs, and reform parties is to define rights objectives and strategies, which must be framed in ways that resonate for key audiences. While it is possible that in a given instance these different kinds of organizations might converge on the same priorities, they nonetheless tend to have characteristic biases that stem from differences in the constituencies to which they are accountable and the inclinations and skills of their professional staffs. Social movements are likely to prioritize goals that make life tangibly better for the grassroots participants that they seek to mobilize. Often these will have an economic dimension. In contrast, elite, professionalized NGOs, often staffed with lawyers and other experts, are more likely to prioritize legal objectives. Finally, party politicians are likely to prioritize whatever rights goals can be achieved through the coalition partnerships that might be available.

A telling example is the arc of the US civil rights movement from the 1940s to the late 1960s. As Risa Goluboff recounts the story, grassroots protest by African Americans during World War II and the immediate postwar period were substantially focused on economic issues, especially "the right to work without discrimination."[30] This issue posed problems for the elite lawyers who dominated strategic planning at the NAACP, which at the time was attempting to forge an alliance with the US labor movement, which included segregated unions. Their legal strategy targeted not employment issues but state-mandated discrimination, as in *Plessy v. Ferguson*. They feared that venturing a broad "right to work" interpretation of the equal protection clause of the Fourteenth Amendment would alienate organized labor and endanger the narrower interpretation that eventually led to the *Brown v. Board of Education* decision.[31] Party politicians were even keener to compromise, for example, allowing Southern Senators to water down Lyndon Johnson's 1958 civil rights bill, cutting out the voting rights provisions. With the party system and thus also legal remedies for Jim Crow largely stalemated, a mass social movement was needed to overwhelm opposition in Southern states and to mobilize the potentially sympathetic Northern electorate. Martin Luther King and especially the grassroots Student Non-Violent Coordinating Committee mobilized existing church networks in the North and South to engage in directly coercive action, framing issues around integration and civic equality.[32] As Piven notes, President Kennedy's decisive speech announcing his support for a far-reaching civil rights bill was triggered when nonviolent confrontation using methods of civil disobedience was fast degenerating into violent repression and rioting.[33] The passage of the bill, however, took some of the steam out of the movement and diverted its cadres to implementing the Voting Rights Act, never to return to a full-bore mass effort centered on economic rights.[34]

One of the key tasks for any of these organizational types is framing the issue under contention. Sidney Tarrow, the dean of social movements theory, stresses that resonant frames reflect or create a common identity among participants. They tap into emotion, especially by making a connection between the personal and the political through symbols, practices, and rituals.[35] Thus, social movements work in much the same way that religious movements do, so it is not surprising that many social movements for rights and economic justice, such as the liberation theology movement in Latin America, recruit from religious organizations and are animated by religious ideas. In contrast, insofar as political coalitions are contingent and instrumental, except under sustained polarization, their legitimating frames are less likely to produce a personal sense of belonging and a common future.[36]

Frames selected by professional NGOs often strive to connect the personal to the political for their target audience, especially donors, and for their own cadres.[37] The heavily legal framing of much NGO work, however, can sometimes limit resonance.[38] Reminiscent of Shareen Hertel's study of framing maneuvers over pregnancy testing in Mexico, Catherine MacKinnon's framing of workplace sexual harassment as an economic discrimination issue

did not work in Europe, where the strong labor movement framed the problem as a "violation of worker's dignity." In France, where less social stigma was
attached to on-the-job flirting, the issue of a "hostile work environment" was
dropped, instead framing the problem as arising mainly in the case of a demand for a sexual quid pro quo.[39] Indeed, sometimes framing as rights per se
is considered a barrier to progressive collective action: "rights discourse in-
dividualizes the struggle at work" and thus undermines the preferred labor
solidarity frame.[40]

Another criticism of rights NGO framing habits is the "silent victim advocacy model."[41] In its harshest variant, critics charge that rights NGOs' overall
discourse features first-world saviors of third-world victims who suffer at the
hands of savage third-world abusers.[42] If so, that imagery might resonate extremely well with self-congratulatory, privileged, progressive audiences, as
best-seller fiction and Hollywood have repeatedly demonstrated with narratives such as *To Kill a Mockingbird* and *The Help*. Yet, if Lynn Hunt's theory of
Inventing Human Rights through narrative is correct, victims need to show
pluck, not passive victimhood, to elicit empathy and outrage at rights depriva-
tion rather than mere pity and charity from readers.[43]

Different forms of civil society organization might have different substantive consequences, which might not be intended, and trade-offs among them
might not be explicitly considered. For example, the Czech gay rights movement initially comprised a legislation-oriented lobbying wing as well as a
grassroots component. The lobbying effort proved so successful that the country soon boasted of an internationally cutting-edge set of legal protections of
gay liberty and equality. As an unintended consequence, the steam went out
of the grassroots social movement, and public discourse about gay life evapo-
rated, leaving the change in Czech cultural attitudes incomplete, in the view
of some.[44]

Various scholars portray a mixed bag of tendencies, strengths, and weaknesses associated with different organizational forms. Measured against armed
insurgencies, nonviolent social movements attract more participants, according to the research of Erica Chenoweth.[45] Measured against political parties,
Herbert Kitschelt argues, social movements are constitutionally set up to extract unilateral concessions, not to bargain (the same might be said of NGOs),
which might be good or bad at different moments.[46] Partly for that reason,
protest activity around a rights issue has been found to matter most in agenda
setting, as measured, for example, by spurring congressional hearings, while
having little effect on the endgame of policy change.[47] Kitschelt also argues

that social movements are better than more transitory political coalitions at sustaining the organizational development that is needed for ongoing struggle for social change.[48] Neier makes a similar point about rights NGOs, noting that one-shot mobilizations in response to historical events like "the Bulgarian atrocities" failed to sustain a rights movement, which happened only after the movement began to make its claims in universalistic terms, such that there would *always* be a burning rights issue to keep the movement in perpetual motion.[49] The National Organization for Women, a legally oriented elite organization without a mass component, is held to be very good at getting publicity, but not good at getting policy results.[50] Mary Kaldor argues that "NGOization" erodes traditional grassroots "mutual benefit" organizations in local communities.[51] Judged in terms of Tilly's effectiveness criteria for social movements, NGOs are good at establishing *worthiness*, sometimes good at achieving *unity* among NGOs, weak in demonstrating *numbers* of popular supporters, and extremely good at demonstrating *commitment*, but only their own.

A final tactical trade-off is whether human rights advocacy should hold itself at arm's length from democracy promotion. On the one hand, human rights organizations like to present themselves as apolitical, pressing for legal accountability to universal civic norms but usually not actively promoting democratic regime change per se. In part, this reflects a pragmatic calculation of what is required to maintain the NGO's operations in a nondemocratic country. It also reflects a rhetorical strategy of holding all countries accountable for rights violations whether or not they are democracies. NGOs that explicitly engage in democracy promotion are distinct from human rights NGO in mounting programs that seek to strengthen institutions of democratic participation, such as training the staffs of political parties.[52] On the other hand, human rights NGOs do acknowledge that democracy and rights are mutually reinforcing.[53] The aspirational Universal Declaration of Human Rights says that "the will of the people shall be the basis of the authority of government; this will shall be expressed in periodic and genuine elections which shall be by universal and equal suffrage."[54] Rights NGOs' somewhat coy, arms-length treatment of democracy makes some tactical sense, but this rhetorical positioning may inadvertently create a mindset that hinders developing long-term strategies that fully integrate the necessarily linked goals of democracy and rights.

Overall, it seems reasonable to conclude that the best results come when strategists of rights-based progressive change prepare a full menu of complementary organizational tools, including reform parties as well as social movements and elite civil society organizations. These organizations work best when they converge on a common (or at least complementary) frame that resonates with mass audiences and allows for legal follow-through and the political flexibility to close deals within a capacious reform coalition.

Conditions for Success of Mass Religious Movements for Rights

Framing an appeal in a way that resonates with a mass audience is often easiest when invoking traditional religious or other local cultural themes. The Sermon on the Mount or its local equivalent is likely to sell better in devout communities than CEDAW. One of the reasons that human rights activists have tended to be wary of mass movements, however, is the risk that vernacular themes and populist agendas can lead to unintended consequences. Neier worries that "partisans of social justice," which he equates with the redistribution of wealth and resources, "violate human rights when they have the power to do so." "As for mass mobilization," he continues, "it is often one of the means whereby proponents of social justice seek power. Of course, it does not necessarily follow that such power will be used abusively. Yet it sometimes happens. The methods traditionally used by HRW are less susceptible to abuses."[55]

Pragmatic approaches, too, need to consider the unintended outcomes of mass appeals, especially those to religion and other forms of identity politics, which may cut against the preferred strategy of inclusive appeals based on equal rights for all. Under what conditions will religious mass movements addressed in the vernacular be a safe, reliable partner of liberal rights advocacy? Based on Christian and Islamic examples, I argue that religious movements can sometimes play a positive role in advancing the rights agenda when they can draw on an inclusive narrative of equality and nascent institutional supports for democratic processes.

A superficial look at three canonical mass rights movements—antislavery, the US civil rights movement, and Gandhi's civil disobedience movement—reveals that each took place in a liberal Christian country or empire. Thus, they seem like easy cases that may not generalize. Even worse, the January 6, 2021, assault on the US Capitol by Evangelical white nationalists seeking to reclaim "constitutional rights" for the "true people" suggests that the Molotov cocktail of populist democracy and identity-based grievance can be explosive even in a supposedly easy case.

The pragmatic approach, being designed for application to difficult cases, is not daunted when conditions are unfavorable or when groups are mostly

concerned about their own rights. The question is whether imperfect conditions can be used to advance toward a more perfect goal. Neier's example of
British activism against Ottoman atrocities is imperfect by contemporary universalist standards not only because it was episodic but also because its empathy was directed toward Christian coreligionist victims. The poet and public
intellectual Lord Byron fired up the British public over Turkish massacres of
the Christian Greeks in 1825. Later the highly religious liberal politician William
Gladstone successfully featured the issue of the Turks' "Bulgarian atrocities" in
the first truly modern political campaign in his Midlothian district in 1879–80.
Gary Bass notes, however, that the Christian themes of Gladstone's campaign
were supplemented with more general appeals to "humanity," providing a rhetoric and a conceptual bridge to later ideas of humanitarian intervention.[56]

Pragmatists should note not only the coexistence of parochial religion and
universal humanitarian concerns but also the British government's geopoliti-
cal balancing act to protect the incipiently liberalizing Ottoman regime in the
face of autocratic Russia's military invasion in support of the Bulgarians. The
ubiquitous role of international power politics in humanitarian intervention
is another bridge that connects the nineteenth century to more recent examples. Although Martha Finnemore argues for an evolution from parochial to
universalistic norms of humanitarian intervention over this span, a closer inspection of her cases, starting with India's amputation of Bangladesh from
West Pakistan in the 1971 humanitarian invasion, suggests that every instance
featured some degree of motivating national or military bureaucratic self-
interest without which the humanitarian mission might not have seemed
worth the trouble.[57]

Christian religion, even though tinged with self-serving identity politics
and realpolitik, fostered the cultural environment of the societies and the main
support bases within which the human rights movement has operated. Religious idealism played a central role in early calls for religious freedom, the
antislavery movements in Britain and the United States, the founding of the
International Committee of the Red Cross, and the US civil rights movement.[58] The secular culture of liberty supported these efforts, too. Antislavery
movements in both Britain and the United States developed in an environment where free whites saw their own historic individual liberties as threatened by the same kinds of powerful oppressors as the slave owners and their
abettors. Antislavery activists in Britain were concerned about their own parallel problems of legal and political discrimination against Quakers, Dissenters,
and urban voters. Likewise, the threat of importing enslaved workers to Britain

in the Somerset case of 1772 and to the American North and West through the Dred Scott decision of 1857 generalized concern about the rights of minorities to the historical liberties of the white majority. In this cultural setting, generalizing rights concerns made religious and political sense.[59] The universalizing human rights movement of the late 1970s thrived in this inherited Anglo-American culture. Reinforcing this was the strong role of legal professionals in the human rights movement as well as the majority's commonsense assumptions about equality before the law as the unquestioned natural order in these societies.

But can this positive dynamic between inclusive religion and inclusive politics generalize outside the Christian West? Pragmatists should answer this question on a case-by-case basis, looking not only at the cultural endowments of the society but also at the institutional capacities that it has developed in the course of its transition toward modernity. A look at the hard case of Indonesia—with its authoritarian legacy, Muslim majority, history of mass atrocity, communal violence, and modest per capita income—suggests that religion could play a constructive role in movement along the arc of history toward improved human rights. The collapse of the Suharto dictatorship as a result of the Asian financial crisis in 1998 brought separatist violence in the Islamist Aceh province, riots between Christians and Muslims in the outer islands, and urban pogroms targeting ethnic Chinese. Despite these challenging circumstances, a transitional regime presided over largely free elections that installed pro-democracy religious parties, including Abdurrahman Wahid, the veteran head of a Muslim mass organization, as president, and Amien Rais, the moderate reformist leader of the largest Muslim party, as the Speaker of the Parliament.[60]

Over the subsequent two decades, Indonesia has sustained regular multi-party elections, devolved power through decentralizing reforms, contained threats from religious terrorists and separatists, and consistently elected pro-democracy leaders. To be sure, illiberal Islamic factions get about 20 percent of the vote, corruption remains widespread, parliamentary cartels have insulated themselves from electoral accountability, and both the left-leaning president and his right-wing blood-stained perennial opponent are populists who cut corners on legality. Still, Indonesia remains a fairly successful hard case of a transitional democracy with politicized Islamic religion despite adverse global trends.

What made this possible? Dan Slater points to the egalitarian legacy of the nationalist independence struggle and institutional developments under the authoritarian Suharto regime.[61] Japanese occupation during World War II swept away the traditional elites that had collaborated with the Dutch colonial masters, bringing into power an eclectic generation of nationalists with modest social origins. After the war, these nationalists, such as President Sukarno, convinced Marxists, Islamists, and nationalists to work together in the struggle to expel the Dutch, leaving as a legacy the concept of national unity and political equality. Though honored in the breach, the sentiment survived and underpinned the election of Sukarno's daughter Megawati Sukarnoputri as prime minister after Suharto's fall.

Perhaps counterintuitively, the second facilitator of democratic transition amid religious moderation was the Suharto dictatorship's strengthening of government bureaucracy and semi-independent political parties under the coordinating umbrella of the Golkar organization, which functioned like a dominant party. Muslim political figures such as Wahid and Rais operated with some independence as heads of Muslim parties and mass-membership Muslim organizations. Until the deinstitutionalization preceding the collapse of the Suharto regime, this system of managed representation gave moderate reformist Muslim politicians ties to a social base, elite trust networks, and habits of mutual accommodation in response to both central authority and public accountability. The lesson for pragmatists is that this good-enough outcome for democracy amid politicized Muslim religion did not have to be created by Western rights activists. It exploited local facilitating conditions in which rights advances could gain some traction and create the possibility for further improvement.

A Tall Order?

Asking rights advocates to strategize simultaneously in conjunction with political parties, mass movements, and religious audiences sounds like a tall order, and it is. Some claim that the mainstream human rights movement's more modest vision is better in part because it is more feasible. The problem is that this claim is mostly untrue outside societies that already have relatively favorable facilitating conditions for the promotion of rights through legal remedies and universalistic shaming tactics. Elsewhere those scope conditions need to be created through economic development, peacemaking, and the gradual, expedient strengthening of reform coalitions and social movements. There are no magic shortcuts that get directly to rights through law and moralism by taking a detour around politics.[62]

A second criticism of the mass politics approach is better founded: as Aryeh Neier says, there is no guarantee that mass social movements will respect rights rather than abuse them. The Nazis and the Italian Fascists were after all social movement regimes that emerged from electoral competition.[63] But this is not a reason to set aside mass politics and stay focused on principled legalism and moralism, especially when nationalists, anti-imperialists, and cultural nativists can exploit universalistic rhetoric on rights to mobilize resistance to liberal rights ideas. Instead, the danger of illiberal social movements is a reason to take the effect of advocacy tactics on mass politics into account when crafting human rights strategies.[64]

A third objection might be that my analysis of reform parties and progressive social movements is based just as much on easy cases as is the mainstream rights approach. It is true that the favorably aligned British case provides a starting point for my thinking about the components of an effective rights strategy, but it also provides a basis for identifying what is missing in harder cases.

Human rights activists and scholars look to the antislavery movement in Britain as the earliest model—and a highly effective one—of a true human rights movement. Often this is taken to be a model that validates the contemporary NGOs' operational style of mobilizing civil society through moral rhetoric and the uncompromising use of publicity to shame perpetrators and those who fail to sanction them.[65] The very first book explaining the success of the British campaign to ban the slave trade, written by one of its main protagonists, Thomas Clarkson, makes this kind of argument. Clarkson claimed that the self-evidently true teachings of prominent Christian authorities—Methodists, Quakers, Anglicans, and others—gradually persuaded Englishmen over the last third of the eighteenth century that slavery was sinfully incompatible with the basic precepts of Christian charity and love.[66]

This is a superficial view. A better-rounded interpretation of the case should also highlight the embedding of the antislavery issue in a broader movement for democratization, rights, and social reform. This was a mass social movement in which religion played a central role in motivating participants and legitimating their demands.[67] Its success stemmed from the development of a unified frame for reform that joined together the twin themes of Christian ethics and English liberties.[68] The movement arose in a facilitating context of dynamic economic and social change that empowered the constituencies that favored reform. The antislavery effort made methodical progress through politically pragmatic bargaining between the leaders of the wider reform movement and elites who dominated political parties.[69]

It was not only Britain that followed this pattern. Many of the success cases of the "third wave" of democratization were given their impetus by inclusive mass movements, often with religious dimensions, and reformist political parties. In Poland, the key actors were Solidarity, at first a labor-based social movement and later a political party, and the Catholic Church.[70] In the Czech Velvet Revolution, human rights groups mobilizing around the Helsinki agreement's standards constituted the kernel around which a mass social movement and progressive party formed.[71] Spain, whose transition was stabilized by well-organized business, labor, and religious groups, provided a template for "pacted" transitions led by reform parties in South America.[72] In Brazil, social movements based on Catholic liberation theology and labor provided a push; slow-moving elite negotiations provided a stable political framework.[73] In Chile, the unions and the church played key roles, as did the institutional legacy of Chile's earlier democratic period. In South Africa, the United Democratic Front unified a well-organized movement of four hundred nonprofit civic organizations in the 1980s, even before Nelson Mandela's African National Congress provided the final push to end apartheid.[74] The end of the Cold War removed some of apartheid's ideological cover, and the legacy of British political and legal institutions facilitated an orderly transition to majority rule. The cleric Desmond Tutu presided over the Truth and Reconciliation Commission that made the politically expedient amnesty seem ethical. Indonesia—in what many would consider a hard case because of its ethnically and religiously diverse makeup and history of a politicized military—negotiated a surprisingly smooth transition to democratic party politics in part because of the central parliamentary role played by Amin Rais's moderate, mass-based Islamic party.[75] All of these progressive transitions improved rights outcomes, but only in a few of them were elite-based, legalistic rights NGOs at the center of the action.

True, social movements pushing for political change have not always provided reliable backing for rights-promoting reform parties. The People Power movement that overthrew Ferdinand Marcos did too little to uproot the corrupt system that continues to trouble Philippine political life. Movement-based populist regimes in Venezuela, Bolivia, and Ecuador generally failed to institutionalize liberal rights.[76] Islamic popular movements in Iran, Egypt, and Turkey have not brought liberal rule of law. A theory of rights promotion based on popular social movements allied to reform parties needs to specify its scope conditions and state what strategies are recommended when those conditions are not met. In general, the preferred strategy in that case is two-fold: (1) the painstaking building of a progressive movement, and (2) expedient action to help put in place social and economic conditions that will facilitate progressive change in the long run.

Finally, it must be acknowledged that rights principles were compromised even in relatively successful cases of movement-driven democratic change. In Argentina, the Alfonsín regime decided it had to disappoint the maximalist demands for criminal accountability put forward by the Mothers of the Disappeared to stabilize the newly democratic regime in the face of threats from military.[77] Principles were also compromised in unsuccessful cases. In Myanmar, Aun Sang Suu Kyi's National League for Democracy, a reform party with a strong base in ethnic Burmese Buddhist civil society, impressively coopted elected support from all of Burma's rebellious ethnic religious minorities, though she failed to act against Myanmar's greatest human rights disaster, the subjugation and expulsion of the unjustly reviled Rohingya Muslim minority. As critics point out, party politics is inescapably the politics of expediency, and social movements are inescapably shaped by the prejudices of their constituencies as well as the tactical choices of their leaders. Yet social movements are also shaped by the determination of their committed grassroots supporters, which has been on impressive display in their tenacious resistance against the military junta that overturned the NLD's 2020 electoral victory and jailed Suu Kyi. Thinking back to July 2017 when I marched in the rain to General Aun Sang's mausoleum with banner-wielding representatives of NLD community groups, labor union locals, and dedicated extended families under the eyes of gun-and-umbrella-toting conscripts lining our march route, their principled but costly resistance doesn't surprise me.

These examples suggest that progressive rights reform can draw support from mass social movements, including religious ones, and can make common cause with the pragmatic political strategies of a reform party seeking to form a national ruling coalition. This does not mean that human rights NGOs' accustomed style of work cannot contribute to the overall reform goal, but rather means that its angle of vision is far too narrow to be the central engine of progressive change, even in its own arena of human rights. Rights progress depends on far broader trends of socioeconomic context, political coalition possibilities, and cultural modes of discourse about norms that govern social relations. Human rights activists and the scholars who study them should approach their work with that wider view.

7

Regulating the
Marketplace of Ideas

WITH TAMAR MITTS

FREEDOM OF SPEECH and of the press, jointly protected in the United States by the First Amendment to the Constitution and globally endorsed by international human rights law, are at the center of any successful democratic system.[1] Pragmatists need to assign the highest priority to fostering a well-functioning marketplace of ideas. The social power approach to human rights of all kinds emphasizes the importance of strong institutions that undergird rights-based social relations, and this is no less vital for media that provide news and enable political discussion. These institutions serve as the conduits for persuasion and pragmatic bargaining that allow citizens to understand their world, gain insight into their fellow citizens' attitudes, formulate their interests, recruit supporters, form alliances, and agree on rules for civic cooperation. If the media for news and communication are weakly or perversely institutionalized, the operating system for human rights breaks down.

Americans, even more than other democratic peoples, have inclined toward free-speech absolutism, believing that unfettered competition in the marketplace of ideas automatically increases the chance that truth and wisdom will prevail in public debate.[2] As Thomas Jefferson said, if forced to choose between "a government without newspapers or newspapers without a government, I should not hesitate a moment to prefer the latter."[3]

These absolutist assumptions face an unprecedented challenge. US-led social media have created vast opportunities for free-wheeling speech on a global scale. At the same time, established journalistic standards have collapsed in some politicized broadcast news media. The result has been not the flourishing of truth and wise deliberation but the dissemination of false information, defamation, and the polarization of political attitudes.[4] The insurrection of the far-right extremists that invaded the US Capitol on January 6, 2021, was stoked by wild conspiracy theories nurtured on social media and endorsed by right-wing broadcasters. Globally, new and old media have been exploited to denounce science-based public health measures to deal with the coronavirus pandemic and to instigate attacks on cultural minorities and other vulnerable people.

In response, the instinct of many free-speech and free-media absolutists has been to fall back on the 1922 dictum of Supreme Court Justice Louis Brandeis: "If there be time to expose through discussion the falsehood and fallacies, to avert the evil by the processes of education, the remedy to be applied is more speech, not enforced silence."[5] The problem is that more speech alone is insufficient. Logical rebuttal and fact checking have proved inadequate to correct the ills that mass-scale misinformation sows. When segments of the public become sorted into polarized opinion communities that are captured by self-reinforcing media, cultural identity and slanted information combine to inoculate groups against the force of the better argument.[6] As a result, many progressives have swung away from free-speech absolutism to the opposite pole, advocating censorship of alarming speech and praising the "deplatforming" of Donald Trump from social media.[7]

The remedy proposed by the pragmatic approach is not simply more speech, nor censorship, but speech in a well-structured public forum that enables free expression to produce socially beneficial consequences. This requires a leading role for professional journalism, which has been weakened by technological change and a perverse reorganization of the marketplace of ideas. Freedom of speech has become hypertrophied, while freedom of the press has suffered from economic and political assaults.[8] The First Amendment guarantees not just the freedom of speech, but also the freedom of the press, because the two must be inextricably linked if discourse is to be both free and constructive. To enhance the value of free speech, journalists need to be empowered to exercise professional judgment about newsworthiness, standards for verifying information, and practices governing debate among diverse views. The aim is not to censor the content of free speech but to present speech in a form that serves its democratic function.

Designing a well-ordered, up-to-date media system will require a better understanding of the mechanisms that connect media freedom to favorable outcomes for human rights. How does press freedom work its magic when it is working well? To identify those mechanisms, we draw on the canon of liberal political philosophy, rights-based activist rhetoric, and the Freedom House rating system to specify more explicitly liberals' scattered, often idealized assumptions about how free speech and media are expected to enhance governance, rights, and social order. We see this as a parallel exercise to Christopher Achen and Larry Bartels's attempt to restate what they call the "folk theory" of democracy.[9]

Liberal conceptions of the benefits of free speech feature two general approaches, which both contribute useful insights. A libertarian approach holds that factually true, well-reasoned, constructive ideas will succeed in persuading individual participants in open competition in a free marketplace of ideas, improving the results of public debate.[10] A second approach, the theory of deliberative democracy, holds that open conversation in a common public sphere of discourse will lead to mutual understanding and a degree of social consensus.[11] Sometimes proponents of these perspectives talk as if they expect beneficial outcomes to emerge as a nearly automatic consequence of free speech and open dialogue, requiring only the most permissive, lightly institutionalized support from constitutional principles of freedom of expression. We argue, in contrast, that the historical record shows that the benefits of free speech and common dialogue emerge most reliably when they are enabled by a more active system of strong institutional supports. Most important is the role of independent, well-resourced, professional journalism, supported by arms-length government regulation.

To study these mechanisms and their outcomes, we compare the liberal folk theory of free media to a complementary theory of the "responsible press" that specifies the institutional conditions that enable free speech to yield its expected beneficial results.[12] We call this institutionalized media theory. We make two main empirical claims.

First, diverse evidence supports our reconstruction of how the mechanisms of the liberal folk theory link extensive freedom of speech and news media to desired public policy outcomes. Drawing on cross-national data from multiple sources on 180 countries between 1972 and 2018, we find positive correlations between free media and democracy, respect for human rights, good governance, and social peace. We also find that media freedom positively correlates with a sequence of mechanisms that liberals invoke as the expected pathway from free speech to these outcomes: the quality of media content, robust civil society, citizen mobilization and political participation, and convergence and moderation of political attitudes. Among liberal democratic states, those with the freest media perform better on all these dimensions. The liberal folk theory of free speech and free media passes this basic test.

Second, we show that the positive link between media freedom and these outcomes is not absolute; it depends on a supporting cast of facilitating conditions as well as strong enabling institutions and norms that constructively shape debate in the marketplace of ideas. Absent these supports, increases in media freedom can backfire, fostering misinformation, political polarization, and the hijacking of discourse by hate speech. Beneficial supportive conditions include not only features of the media outlets themselves, such as professionalism and independence, but also features of the broader political system. High levels of media freedom are much less likely to correlate with other outcomes that liberals desire in partial democracies than in full democracies. Highly dysfunctional free media environments have occurred in transitional political systems with strong demand for mass political participation but weakly developed democratic institutions, including those of the media.[13]

We do not make claims about the independent causal effects of increases in media freedom. Although the level of democracy does not perfectly correlate with the level of media freedom in all cases, reciprocal causality pervades the relationship between them. As argued in chapter 2, the mutually supportive, functionally interdependent elements of the liberal package of institutions make this convergence the expected pattern in consolidated liberal systems. In contrast, transitional states, neither fully liberal nor fully authoritarian, are less stable in part because of the internally contradictory features of their components, including their media systems. That said, we do have an analytical interest in studying the effects of largely exogenous technological shocks that increase media freedom in a given institutional setting. For that reason, we examine the introduction of satellite television to the authoritarian media systems of the Arab world, which supports the institutional theory.

In laying out the logic of the liberal folk theory, its institutional counterpart, and their anticipated causal mechanisms, we locate these ideas in the context of their historical development. Liberal ideas of freedom of speech and the press are deeply embedded in history, and their disappointments are similarly long-standing. The development of effective institutional solutions to those problems forms part of that history, which retains its relevance today. Although globalized social media are new, the dependence of healthy free expression on a supporting scaffolding of norms and institutions is not. Ever since the invention of the printing press, mass media and mass politics have come together to produce a combustible mixture. From the French

Revolution to the present, unprofessional, politicized, and poorly regulated media have been vulnerable to polarizing misinformation and hijacking by demagogues. Contemporary pathologies of social media are a new form of an old problem. Historical experience provides the basic outlines of tried and true solutions to these recurrent problems. In the conclusion to this chapter, we discuss the implications of our arguments for policy debates on the regulation of free speech and media, especially with respect to the role of professional journalism.

The Liberal Theory of Media Freedom

The main empirical claim of the liberal folk theory is that increasing freedom of speech, expression, and news media and increasing availability of information through communications media strengthens democracy, good governance, human rights, social order, and peace. Activists for freedom of the press routinely make these claims.[14] The main intuition behind this theory is the assumption, widespread in Anglo-Saxon culture and philosophy, that society is composed of rational, self-interested, reasonably far-sighted individuals who are able to use information to cooperate and compete in ways that make everyone in society better off in the long run. Just as the invisible hand of the free market in perfect competition is expected to improve general social welfare, the free market for ideas scrutinizes and discredits false ideas through publicity.[15] Except for extremely limited, traditional exceptions for libel, fraud, and public safety, any limitations on absolute freedom of speech, especially in the realm of political deliberation, are expected to degrade the quality of information and debate. Maximum freedom of speech and the press is expected to foster widely shared knowledge that will facilitate cooperation and bargaining throughout society.

Already in 1644, the English poet and public intellectual John Milton presented many of the central arguments of the liberal theory. Milton gave absolute priority to the freedom of public debate: "Give me the liberty to know, to utter, and to argue freely according to conscience, above all liberties." "Let [Truth] and Falsehood grapple; who ever knew Truth put to the worse in a free and open encounter," he asserted.[16] In open debate, a participant is "industrious," "informed," "confers with his judicious friends," and "summons up all his reason and deliberation."[17] Even if some readers among the "common people" might be "giddy, vicious, and ungrounded," this is no cause for censorship, because the "licensers" of printing, being "ignorant, imperious, and remiss, or basely pecuniary," will mislead the public more than will open debate. Given the motives of these censors, Milton argued that "there is aught more likely to be prohibited than truth itself."[18]

Liberal folk theory places very few scope limitations on the claim that totally free speech is better than constrained or regulated speech. Libertarians contend that rich people and even corporations should have no limits placed on their right to engage in massively funded political speech. Liberal Democrats also resist limits on speech. The Clinton administration led the way in defining the internet as a zone of laissez-faire in the Telecommunications Act of 1996, which exempted "information services" from common carrier regulations and later provided one of the justifications for tech platforms such as Facebook to disclaim legal or ethical responsibility for their content.

Institutionalized Media Freedom Theory

Institutionalized media theory qualifies the liberal folk theory rather than refuting it. Its main empirical claim is that increases in media freedom will lead to improved results for democracy, human rights, social order, and governance only if they take place in a reasonably well-institutionalized setting with some or all of these key attributes: (1) professionalized journalists are empowered to exercise editorial judgment in financially independent major media organizations; (2) media standards are effectively self-policed by media organizations and journalistic professional norms; (3) an arm's-length government regulatory environment encourages public service journalism and may support it financially; (4) the products of quality journalism are more readily accessible than degraded political speech; and (5) democratic political institutions allow the people to act on the ideas that emerge from public discourse. Otherwise, there is considerable likelihood that a nominally free but weakly institutionalized media market will be hijacked on the supply side by elite propaganda, hate speech, self-serving narratives of identity groups and parochial interest groups, demagogic populism, and "bread and circus" media distractions, and distorted on the demand side by the narrow preferences of consumers for opinion-confirming news and pure entertainment.

Thomas Jefferson was acutely aware that the reality of early American journalism diverged far from any ideal: "A suppression of the press could not more completely deprive the nation of its benefits, than is done by its abandoned prostitution to falsehood. Nothing can now be believed which is seen in a newspaper. Truth itself becomes suspicious by being put into that polluted vehicle."[19] Nonetheless, Jefferson believed that the people "may be led astray for a moment, but will soon correct themselves." If hoodwinked into electing bad leaders, the people will eventually come to their senses and rein them in.[20]

Walter Lippmann, a co-founder of the Progressive *New Republic*, grappled with the same unresolved questions in his 1922 landmark work, *Public Opinion*. Contrary to democratic folk tales, he argued, the people lack a meaningful understanding of public affairs. They are easily swayed because the truth is inaccessible to them, misrepresented by those in the know, myopically perceived through self-serving biases and "tribal" stereotypes, and lacking entertainment value.[21]

After the Second World War, newspapers continued to face widespread criticism for their elitism, commercialization, and oligopolistic control by moneyed interests. To address these concerns, Robert Hutchins, the visionary president of the University of Chicago, convened the Commission on Freedom of the Press at the behest of Henry Luce, the publisher of *Time* magazine. Commission members included such luminaries as Harold Lasswell, Reinhold Niebuhr, and Arthur Schlesinger. The commission argued that journalism's role should be to serve the public interest by providing accurate information and a rich debate among diverse opinions to serve a democratic, deliberative citizenry. Facts should be contextualized, distinguished from opinions, and their sources fully explained. Reporting should probe below the surface of events. Journalists should be impeccably professional: trained in specialized skills, independent, and committed to the vocation to serve the public. Although "the right of free public expression does include the right to be in error" because "liberty is experimental," the media have no "right to be deliberately or irresponsibly in error."[22]

The commission report built on many of the basic ideas of the libertarian theory of the marketplace of ideas, wherein rational citizens could be counted on to extract the truth from the contention of facts and opinion in unfettered debate, but the commission had shown how the market also needed regulation to function effectively. Because many readers are only casually attentive and gullible, the commission argued, they need guidance from professional journalists to sort through information, evaluate its quality, grasp its meaning, and ask probing questions. A follow-up study labeled this "the Social Responsibility Theory" of the press, qualifying and subsuming but not replacing the main arguments of free-speech libertarianism.[23]

Adopting this concept, the US Federal Communications Commission established the Fairness Doctrine, which from 1949 until 1987 required broadcast media companies to provide thorough, balanced, and honest coverage of the most important public issues, or else risk losing their licenses. In the era dominated by radio and television, the scarcity of the broadcast spectrum helped to justify such regulation, but the development of the FCC licensing system also owed a great deal to the acceptance of the responsible press concept by media professionals as well as officials.[24]

Just as behavioral economics recommends nudging lax, inattentive, or impulsive people to increase their retirement savings by requiring them to opt out rather than opt in to employer savings plans, so too institutional media theory seeks to make reliable, factually correct information and reasonable opinions easier to come across than fabrications and hate speech.[25] Markus Prior's prize-winning book, *Post-Broadcast Democracy*, showed how the era of the three network news broadcasts forced all Americans to get common exposure to reasonable news coverage. People were nudged to listen to Walter Cronkite or simultaneous, comparable news shows on the other networks or else turn off the TV. Extremist groups like the John Birch Society could say whatever they wanted in books and pamphlets, but it took more effort to track down their contributions to the debate. Truth did not always prevail, but there was no retreat into hermetic discourse bubbles and no partisan polarization. The later rise of cable television not only enabled the partisan alternative of Fox News, it also allowed viewers to switch channels and avoid substantive news altogether.[26] The end of the Fairness Doctrine in 1987 gave free rein to axe-grinding right-wing talk radio.[27] Institutional theory explains the degradation of the US marketplace of ideas as the result of the dismantling of the institutionalized order that empowered a responsible press and limited partisan media bias.

The same principles apply on the internet. The saga of Wikipedia shows the dangers of anarchical crowdsourcing but also the institutionalized practices that can turn voluntary speech in a productive direction. In its early days, Wikipedia experienced chaotic partisan battles to rewrite versions of controversial topics such as the Armenian genocide. Over time, the nonprofit, largely volunteer online encyclopedia established elaborate rules for contributing content to the site. Volunteers gained more authority to post and edit as they established longer records of responsible judgment. With increased resources and institutional stability, Wikipedia increased the number of employees that exercised oversight of the editorial process, using the voluntary contributions more efficiently to produce a reliable product.[28] Now when content on YouTube is challenged as likely to be inaccurate or misleading, links to Wikipedia are embedded so that users can readily access a reliable second opinion.

Evidence Evaluating the Liberal and Institutionalized
Media Freedom Theories

The central conceptual and practical debates about media freedom remain focused on the tension between the unconditional libertarian model of free speech and the institutionalized media theory of the responsible press. These are both derived from foundational liberal assumptions, but they diverge on the crucial issues of the regulatory role of the state and the centrality of journalistic professionalism in structuring a healthy marketplace of ideas. Free-speech absolutists on the left and the right worry that an anointed "responsible," professionalized press, backed by state power wielding regulatory threats, will recreate the cozy, conformist elite cartels of the "Cold War consensus," shutting out minority voices or hamstringing advocates of dynamic innovation.[29] Institutionalized media theory, however, offers an alternative to unfettered free speech that is not based on censorship but on free speech in a context that allows professional journalists, knowledgeable experts, and responsible officials to impose a modicum of structure so that free discourse can be more constructive.[30]

The liberal folk theory envisions a sequence in which media freedom improves the quality of media content, enhances political knowledge, facilitates the organization of civil society and mobilization of political participation, creates an integrated public sphere, leads to convergence and moderation of political attitudes, reduces partisan polarization, and through these mechanisms strengthens democracy, human rights, social order and peace, and the quality of governance. Higher levels of media freedom are expected to produce better outcomes on these dimensions. Any increase in media freedom is expected to lead to improvements in intermediate mechanisms and outcomes, notwithstanding the inevitability of contentious debate. In the institutionalized theory, these preferred outcomes are expected to occur when a professionalized, independent media operates in a supportive regulatory environment in a fully democratic state. Without these supports, the institutional theory expects that a high level of media freedom will derail these mechanisms and lead to unwanted outcomes.

To evaluate this debate empirically, we next explain how we define and measure media freedom and its component dimensions. After that, for both theories we specify key hypothesized variables, scope conditions, mechanisms through which variables exert their effects, and predicted outcomes.

Because we consider the liberal theory of freedom of speech and the press as historically rooted folk theory, we follow the lead of Freedom House in defining these freedoms through historically grounded legal texts. Freedom House introduces its list of measurement criteria by quoting Article 19 of the Universal Declaration of Human Rights: "Everyone has the right to freedom of opinion and expression; this right includes freedom to hold opinions without interference and to seek, receive and impart information and ideas through any media and regardless of frontiers."[31] A US touchstone for the folk theory is the First Amendment to the Constitution: "Congress shall make no law . . . abridging the freedom of speech, or of the press; or the right of the people peaceably to assemble, and to petition the Government for a redress of grievances." The linking of speech, media, assembly, and petition for redress shows that these rights were seen as part of an integrated, mutually supporting, functional system of self-government designed to achieve public objectives, not just a list of intrinsically desirable rights.

Freedom House's operational definition of media freedom is embedded in its coding template for individual states, which is divided into the legal, political, and economic "environments." Each of these is divided into seven or eight questions, fleshed out by several subquestions. A country's overall press freedom score is calculated by an arbitrarily weighted, additive points system. This mingles factors that focus on state policy (e.g., "Are outlets forcibly closed or taken off the air as a result of what they publish or broadcast?") with situational factors that the state cannot effectively influence (e.g., "Are people able to access a range of local and international news sources despite efforts to restrict the flow of information?").

This list of criteria might be seen as embedding internal contradictions. Because of the strategic interaction of the state with opposition public factions, for example, increases of freedom on one dimension might trigger decreases on another. Jenifer Whitten-Woodring has shown that when authoritarian political systems have uncharacteristically open media systems, increases in press freedom tend to incite popular protests, which lead to an increase of government repression of both the press and civil society groups.[32]

More theoretically coherent criteria should guide the use of kitchen-sink indicators such as Freedom House's press index. For some of our empirical analysis, we separate Freedom House's press freedom subscores into three categories of journalism's functions: watchdog of government and elites, source of public information, and forum for free public expression.[33] These may vary independently, with different consequences for political processes and outcomes. For example, media in Singapore, Qatar, and even China may be broadly and reliably informative on many topics, but they do not provide a free and reliable forum for criticism of their own states.[34] Conversely, when international donors forced Burundi's minority ethnic dictatorship to open up to free elections in 1993, there was a dramatic increase in the diversity of media voices, which provided plentiful forums for hate speech but little reliable information.

Criticism of US media is aimed at all three of these dimensions. Fox News was said to be a lapdog of the Trump administration, not a watchdog. Almost every component of the US media ecosystem is accused of purveying false or biased information. Social media forums are accused simultaneously of allowing hate speech that has incited genocide and vigilantism and of censoring protected political speech of former president Trump and other US citizens. To diagnose problems and design well-aimed remedies, disaggregating speech into its watchdog, informational, and forum components is a worthwhile first step.

In our statistical analysis, we find that these three media functions vary similarly with most outcomes that liberal theory expects, such as level of democracy and quality of government (see figure 1).[35] For other outcomes, however, notably human rights, we find that high scores only on the watchdog and informational functions show statistically significant correlations with the expected positive outcomes, but a high score on the forum function does not. Our interpretation is that when hate speakers have unregulated access to broadcast their views to a wide audience alongside constructive rights advocates, the net effect does not enhance rights outcomes or the marketplace of ideas. If so, this finding counts against the libertarian theory, whereas the overall pattern is consistent with the institutional theory.

One reason there is hardly any systematic empirical research assessing the liberal folk theory of free media and its institutional offshoot is that their causal mechanisms are dauntingly hard to test. In principle, this predicted causal chain could be tested in rare natural experiments based on exogenous increases in media openness, such as the sudden arrival of foreign satellite television or internet-based social media, which would be expected to have knock-on effects cascading through the list of mechanisms and outcomes. That said, in the normal course of events, even if these processes are positively correlated with each other, it is highly likely that any causation will be reciprocal, mutually facilitating, and recursive, which is to say endogenous.

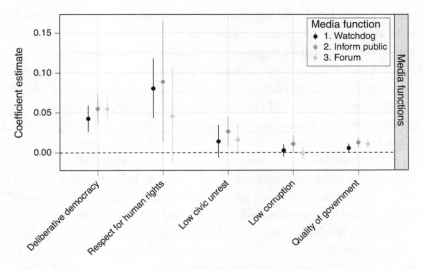

FIGURE 1. Variation by media function.
Note: The figure presents coefficients estimated from a regression of various political outcomes on three measures of media function: watchdog of government behavior, source of information, and forum for public expression. All dependent variables are standardized and coded such that higher values reflect "better" outcomes. The data comes from the Varieties of Democracy Project and Freedom House. Regressions control for country fixed effects, the level of democracy, GDP per capital, and population size.

Although the diverse range of hypotheses about the conditions and mechanisms connecting increases in media freedom to political outcomes cannot be definitively tested here, we have compiled substantial data from existing sources that allow us to probe the plausibility of the liberal folk theory as well as its institutionalized media offshoot. These theories survive this initial plausibility probe.[36] The empirical patterns presented below provide insights into the correlates of media freedom, but our analysis is purely descriptive, and we do not make any causal claims about our findings.

To quantitatively measure media freedom, we draw on Freedom House's press freedom score. This measure evaluates the freedom of print, broadcast, and digital media globally on the basis of a range of parameters capturing the legal, political, and economic media environment in each country.[37] To examine the relationship between media freedom and the political outcomes expected by the theories, we combine the Freedom House score with data from various sources, including the Varieties of Democracy project,[38] the CIRI Human Rights Data Project,[39] the Major Episodes of Political Violence and Conflict Regions

(MEVP) project,[40] the Quality of Government Standard Dataset,[41] and the Polity IV Project.[42] Our integrated dataset includes observations for 180 countries from 1972 to 2018 across a large number of politically relevant outcomes.

We measure various political outcomes as follows. For *democracy*, we use the Polity IV score. For *respect for human rights*, we use the Physical Integrity Rights Index from the CIRI Human Rights Data Project, which measures the extent to which governments engage in torture, extrajudicial killings, political imprisonment, and disappearances.[43] For *social order and peace*, we use data on the magnitude of civic unrest, which capture episodes of civil violence, civil warfare, ethnic violence, and ethnic war in each country and year.[44] Finally, we use data on the level of *corruption*[45] and the *quality of government*[46] to evaluate the link between media freedom and governance quality.

To examine whether media freedom is positively linked to the *quality of media content*, we use an expert-based measure on whether major print and broadcast media in each country represent a wide range of political perspectives.[47] To examine whether *civil society organization and political participation* increase with greater levels of media freedom, we use a variable measuring the freedom of civil society organizations and citizen participation in them, as well as the overall political engagement by the public.[48]

Finally, we examine how media freedom relates to political outcomes in recent years—after the rise of the internet and social media—by drawing on data from the Digital Society Project.[49] We first study whether online media shows patterns of *integration or fragmentation* in countries with greater levels of media show freedom. Using a measure of the extent to which major domestic online media outlets give opposing or similar presentations of major events, we evaluate whether online fragmentation is more likely to exist in country-years with more free media.[50] In addition, we evaluate the relationship between *attitude polarization* and media freedom with a new measure of the level of public disagreement on a range of political issues.[51] Summary statistics are provided in the appendix.

Figure 2 shows average values of these variables in countries with free, partially free, and unfree media systems. Consistent with the liberal folk theory, we find that countries with free media tend to have the highest scores for democracy, human rights, social order and peace, quality of government, and an active, engaged citizenry. They also have the lowest levels of corruption and social polarization. Countries with partially free media have more mixed outcomes—sometimes showing patterns similar to countries with free media, and sometimes looking more like countries with unfree media. Partially free media, for example, tend to correlate more strongly with respect for human

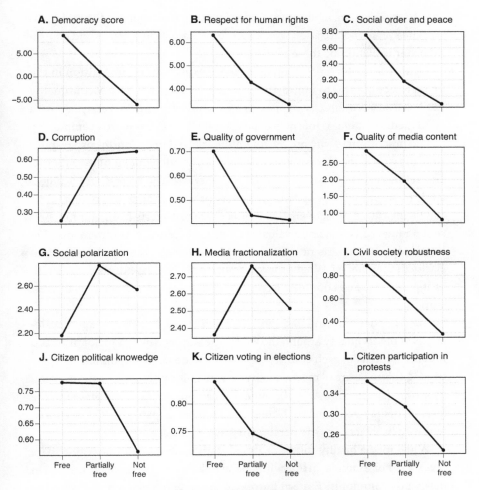

FIGURE 2. Political outcomes in different media environments.
Note: The figure presents average values of various political outcomes in countries with free, partially free, and unfree media.

Mechanisms of Liberal Media Theories

rights, social order and peace, and civil society robustness but fares worse in levels of polarization and media fractionalization.

Drawing on our rich data, as well as on several illustrative cases, we lay out the expectations of liberal theory and institutionalized media theory regarding their chain of mechanisms: quality of media content, political knowledge, civil society organization, media integration versus segmentation, and attitude convergence versus polarization. We report some simple correlations and empirical patterns that probe these expectations.

Quality of media content. Liberal theory expects free competition in the marketplace of ideas to improve the quality of media content. Media quality can be assessed indirectly by measuring features that liberals associate with good media content. Is journalism professionalized in the sense of employing skilled practitioners who are thoroughly socialized to the norms of a responsible press? Are media organizations financially independent of the interests and actors that they report on? Media quality can also be measured subjectively by surveys: Do people think media quality is good or improving? Or it can be measured objectively: Do media distinguish facts from opinion, present a range of views, and evaluate the factual accuracy of statements? Do knowledgeable experts rate the media highly for objectivity, coverage, and clarity in their fields? What proportion of media coverage deals with significant public issues, as opposed to celebrity gossip, sports, or personal interest stories?

The Varieties of Democracy project, for example, aggregates expert evaluations of media quality around the world, measuring whether major print and broadcast media in each country represent a wide range of political perspectives.[52] This measure of media quality varies significantly across countries and over time (see in table A1 in the appendix) and positively correlates with the level of media freedom in each country (see figure 2, panel F). This is consistent with both versions of liberal theory that we discuss.

While media quality can be analyzed statistically, case studies can also be revealing. For example, in line with liberal folk theory, US media assistance in newly postcommunist Eastern Europe in the early 1990s assumed that aid to any opposition media would improve the marketplace of ideas without being fussy about the quality of the media organization, on the grounds that the citizens would be able to sort out the wheat from the chaff. Thomas Carothers studied US funding for independent, critical voices in Romania with little regard to journalistic professionalism and commitment to accuracy.[53] USAID got what it paid for: libelous claims and what would now be called fake news, contributing to a shaky democratic transition and an endemic pattern of official corruption. In contrast, West Europeans invested in media training and professionalization, focusing on the quality of media content. This account supports the institutional media theory and raises questions about the unconditional liberal theory in cases where journalistic norms are weak.

Political knowledge. Freer speech, freer media, financially more independent media, and denser media coverage are predicted to increase the accuracy of factual and causal knowledge about politics and public issues. A statistical study of European cases finds support for this view.[54]

Our own effort to measure political knowledge draws on a large number of nationally representative surveys asking citizens about their knowledge of political leaders and institutions in their country.[55] We created a binary measure that captured when respondents correctly answered political knowledge questions and matched it with their country's press freedom score in the year in which the survey was conducted.[56] We found that political knowledge was higher in countries with free media and almost as high in countries with partially free media. In contrast, political knowledge was much lower in countries without free media (figure 2, panel J). This outcome differs from the pattern of most of our mechanism and outcome variables, where societies with partially free media behave more like societies with unfree media than like ones with free media (see figure 2). A possible interpretation is that this counts against the libertarian theory and in favor of the institutional theory. Partially free media seem to succeed in informing the public, but without a well-institutionalized environment, the public is unable to act on that information in a way that produces the favorable outcomes that liberal theory expects. If libertarians and other free-speech absolutists were right, the mere fact of being better informed should more reliably produce the anticipated beneficial effects on mechanisms such as moderation of attitudes and of outcomes. Our case study of partial media freedom in the Middle East and its mismatch with that region's authoritarian politics illustrates these points.

Civil society organization and political participation. Greater freedom of speech and media is expected to facilitate organizing civil society and mobilizing groups to participate in politics. This is especially important for the *deliberative democracy* dimension of liberal folk theory, which anticipates that an active civil society with political space to organize and deliberate will be a force for human rights and democracy.[57] The most acclaimed empirical studies of effective mobilizing for human rights, most notably that of Beth Simmons, feature the civil society mechanism.[58]

Other studies argue, however, that civil society is a two-edged sword. Sheri Berman found that Weimar Germany had more choral societies and newspaper readers per capita (standard indicators of civil society's vibrancy) than any country before or since, yet it also spawned the right-wing drinking societies of disgruntled World War I veterans that populated Hitler's networks.[59]

Likewise, a high score on civil society mobilization is also consistent with theories that predict the use of media propaganda to activate illiberal identity-based politics.[60] In contrast, a robust civil society is less important for the libertarian variant, in which increased freedom of speech and media can have positive effects even apart from collective action mechanisms by improving the information available to individual voters who may not be active in civic groups.

The institutional theory would expect civil society to function differently in settings with different political institutions. Consistent with this view, Carew Boulding's survey research in South America finds that contact with nongovernmental civil society organizations correlates with a person's likelihood of voting in better institutionalized democracies, whereas it correlates with a person's participation in protests, including violent ones, in less institutionalized electoral regimes.[61]

In our cross-national analysis, media freedom positively correlates with citizen political engagement and the freedom of civil society organizations (see figure 2).[62] This is consistent with the strand of liberal theory that emphasizes the role of deliberation in a well-functioning democracy.

Media integration versus segmentation. Liberal folk theory assumes that free media produce common knowledge that circulates throughout the political community, establishing shared facts and a general awareness of the causal and normative arguments being advanced by fellow citizens. At least the attentive part of the public will seek out facts and arguments from diverse sources, if only to anticipate the claims of other actors to know how to refute or persuade them. Jürgen Habermas's historical argument about the emergence of the common public sphere in the coffee houses of seventeenth-century Britain provides the classic example. Benedict Anderson's *Imagined Communities* makes a similar claim that widely marketed literature printed in the French vernacular created a common political discourse that underpinned the development of a common national identity.[63] Still, it took more than another century after the press boom during the French Revolution for France to evolve into a functioning liberal democracy.

Media sometimes become more segmented when media freedom increases, especially when moving from authoritarian to partially open systems. Partially free media systems tend to have more fractionalized media than free and unfree media do (figure 2, panel H). This can be due in some cases to structural circumstances, such as linguistic barriers between communities, which are exogenous to the theory, or to a preference to consume media that confirms in-group biases, an outcome that is at odds with the logic of the liberal folk theory.[64] When increasing media freedom coincides with democratization or increasing popular demand for mass participation in politics, it is common that identity groups want "their own" media to affirm their cultural distinctiveness and to advocate for national self-determination. These balkanized discourse bubbles create an incentive for *outbidding*, in which factions compete to present themselves as the most militant voices promoting the narrow interests of the group.[65]

Whether an integrated or segmented public sphere emerges when media freedom expands may depend on linguistic demography, institutional and political factors, or communications technology—for example, the three US TV networks of the 1950s and '60s versus the subsequent infinity of cable TV options and specialized internet discussion communities.[66] The case study below of satellite TV shows how the combination of demographic diversity and national politics culminated in the balkanization of the public sphere in the Middle East despite the unifying potential of a single source of Arabic broadcast news for the entire region. This shows that institutional settings can have negative effects, not just beneficial ones.

Attitude convergence versus polarization. The liberal folk theory expects that the attitudes of better-informed citizens, armed with fuller, more accurate information, will tend to converge on more fact-based, logically coherent ideas. Fringe ideas based on myths, conspiracy theories, and flimsy reasoning will fail to withstand scrutiny in an open marketplace of ideas.[67] Even if many citizens remain sloppy in their reasoning and knowledge, plenty of citizens will be paying attention to the facts, and well-grounded ideas will on average prevail in the long run.[68] Attitudes will tend to converge on fact-based propositions rather than polarize around dogmatically held beliefs. In that sense, there will be not only convergence of opinions, but convergence on moderate opinions.[69] This expectation is central to the deliberative aspect of liberal folk theory, though it is not inconsistent with its libertarian strand.

A canonical account of the moderation of democratic politics is Anthony Downs's *An Economic Theory of Democracy*, based like liberal folk theory on a market analogy. He argues that in two-party plurality-vote systems, parties' dominant strategy will be to compete for the favor of the voter who occupies the median position on the continuum of policy preferences. Sadly for the liberal folk theory, Downs's argument depends on the effects of institutional structure more than on rational common knowledge driving converging voter preferences. To the contrary, Downs argues, "Apathy among citizens toward elections, ignorance of the issues, the tendency of parties in a two-party system to resemble each other, and the anticonsumer bias of government action can all be explained logically as efficient reactions to imperfect information in a large democracy."[70]

Some subsequent theorists have argued that even relatively poorly informed citizens can make reasonable political judgments by taking their cues from experts whose biases are well known and can be taken into account. Thus, John Zaller argues, people follow advice from informed authorities who are known to share their general value orientation.[71] While Zaller's formulation salvages the idea that ignorant citizens can act reasonably, it does not generate the expectation of convergence on moderation. In an opposite approach, poorly informed people can draw strong, valid inferences when knowledgeable experts express views on an issue that go against what would have been expected from their usual bias. For example, when the cold-warrior Richard Nixon entered into agreements with Red China, hawkish Americans figured it must be okay.[72] Arthur Lupia and Matthew McCubbins argue that people with quite limited information can make well-grounded decisions as long as institutions such as courts, legislative committees, or political parties structure contestation and deliberation to guarantee a thorough vetting of arguments and evidence.[73] None of these approaches, however, helps save a moderate, rational voter hypothesis in conditions of extreme polarization, when elites on one or both sides are engaging in pure propaganda, when institutions are weak, or when populist voters distrust information from established institutions.[74]

The liberal theory's expectation of moderation depends not only on the emergence of common knowledge through free discourse but also on the assumption that greater media freedom will lead to a more integrated public sphere. But even in Habermas's and Anderson's historical cases, where the population was literate in the same vernacular, the public sphere split into warring ideological camps. Within each camp, if there was a convergence of opinion, it was based on militant outbidding, not moderation. In the harder cases where the polity encompasses different language communities, rare and special facilitating conditions, such as social ties that cut across linguistic groups, as in Switzerland, are needed to forge a common, moderate public sphere.[75]

Our statistical results show that free media correlate with low polarization of attitudes, which is consistent with all the theories we discuss. States with partially free media, however, tend to be highly polarized—indeed more polarized than unfree media systems (see figure 2, panel G). Among states with

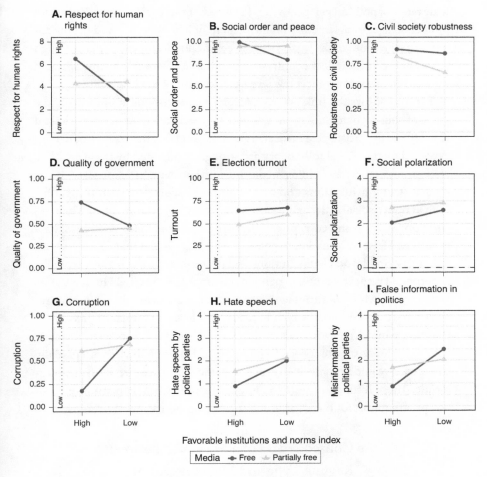

FIGURE 3. The correlates of favorable institutions and norms.
Note: The figure presents average values of various political outcomes in countries with free and partially free media and different levels of favorable institutions and norms.

partially free media, those with strong institutions and norms regulating the media are less polarized than those with weaker institutions and norms (figure 3, panel F). This pattern supports the institutional theory.[76]

In support for institutionalized media theory, our data also show that the correlations are strongly conditional on enabling institutions and norms. We created an index variable capturing contexts where institutions and norms are more likely to constructively shape debate in the marketplace of ideas. This index includes (1) the extent to which major print and broadcast media represent a wide range of political perspectives,[77] (2) whether the legal framework provides protection against defamatory online content or hate speech,[78] and (3) the absence of elite abuse of the legal system to censor political speech online.[79] High values of the index reflect country-years with more favorable institutions and norms, and low values reflect low levels of such norms and institutions.

Figure 3 shows the link between favorable institutions and norms and a range of political outcomes for countries with free media systems (in black) and countries with partially free media (in gray). We find that the positive outcomes expected by the liberal folk theory are strongly moderated by these enabling institutions even when holding media freedom constant. In countries with free media, strong institutions and norms positively correlate with respect for human rights, social order and peace, high quality of government, and low levels of polarization and corruption. They are also linked to lower levels of hate speech and false information in political rhetoric. We find that countries with free media and favorable institutions and norms receive the highest score for government respect for human rights, as measured by the CIRI Human Rights Data Project, while countries with free media and no favorable institutions receive a much lower score, which indicate high levels of human rights abuses (figure 3, panel A). Favorable institutions and norms also correlate strongly with lower levels of hate speech (figure 3, panel H). In countries with partially free media we find similar patterns, although the differences are of smaller magnitude. These results illustrate the importance of favorable institutions and norms, in support for the institutionalized media theory.

The Consequences of a Mismatch between Regime Type and Media Freedom

To test another aspect of institutionalized media theory, we examine in figure 4 additional outcomes that are expected to take place in mixed regimes with freer media: the dissemination of false information by political actors and the use of hate speech by political parties. Drawing on the Digital Social Survey to measure these variables, we examine how their relationship with media freedom varies with regime type, by regressing these variables on an interaction of media freedom with the Polity IV index.[80] In the Polity IV index, countries with scores greater than 5 are democracies, countries with scores lower than -5 are considered autocracies, while countries in the middle are defined as mixed regimes.

Consistent with institutionalized media theory's predictions, we find that in almost all cases, greater levels of media freedom are associated with higher

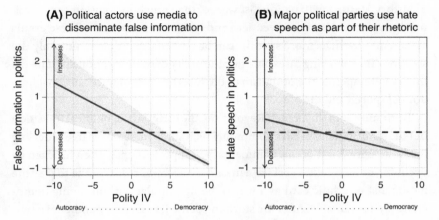

FIGURE 4. Consequences of a mismatch between regime type and media freedom.
Note: The figure presents predicted values estimated from regressions of the dissemination
of false information by political actors (A) and the use of hate speech by political parties (B)
on an interaction of media freedom with regime type. The estimated coefficient on media
freedom is shown on the y-axis, and the x-axis shows different levels of the Polity IV index.

levels of false information dissemination and hate speech by political actors,
except for the most democratic countries. This evidence supports the idea that
media freedom without democratic institutions is likely to result in undesirable outcomes.[81]

Weakly Institutionalized Media and Turbulent Politics in Mixed Regimes

Prominent scholars as different as Robert Dahl and Samuel Huntington have
observed that states in early stages of modernization, democratization, and postcolonial state building typically face a gap between high demand for mass political participation and weak institutions to channel this clamor constructively.[82]
The institutional and professional weakness of the media contributes to this gap
in many regimes that embody a mixture of liberal and illiberal characteristics. In
this setting, mass media are often hijacked by purveyors of divisive forms of
identity politics. Our statistical findings based on contemporary cases discov-
ered a correlation between poorly regulated media in partially democratic regimes and the abuse of human rights as well as a host of other social ills.

This is a problem that is as old as the first printing press and as new as satellite TV and social media. It is associated with some of the marquee calamities

of history, starting with nationalist wars of the French Revolution and culminating in genocides of the twentieth and twenty-first centuries. These events are a reminder that "more speech" can be part of the problem, not only the solution. The following cases illustrate the utility of the institutionalized media theory in tempering the optimism of the folk theorists of unconditional freedom of speech and the press.

Beginning with the French Revolution, the early days of political transition out of authoritarianism have commonly seen sharp increases of free-wheeling media activity. Most of this commentary is unprofessional, often hijacked by declining or rising elites seeking a mass base of support and prone to play the nationalist or ethnic card as a way of being popular without being democratically accountable. After the storming of the Bastille, the number of newspapers in highly literate Paris quickly jumped from sixty censored lapdogs to five hundred contentious factional outlets. Though the revolutionaries initially expected that French national self-determination would serve as a model of pacific coexistence among Europe's peoples, their newspapers quickly descended into nationalist outbidding against the revolution's foreign and domestic foes. The leader of the anti-Austrian war party in the assembly was Jacques-Pierre Brissot, a former "hack writer and police spy" whose editorship of a particularly belligerent newspaper propelled him to leadership of the dominant Girondin faction in the National Assembly.[83] This very first case set the subsequent pattern for turbulent politics and volatile media in mixed regimes, which have been found disproportionately prone to civil wars, international conflicts, and violent human rights violations.[84]

The flawed marketplace of ideas also played a role in the development of extremist nationalism in Weimar Germany, which appeared superficially to enjoy lively, diverse, print news media with large readerships. Forces of supply and demand, however, limited many readers to what we would now call "opinion bubbles." Workers stuck to the Social Democratic newspaper *Vorwärts* or Communist counterparts. Urban liberals read more professional newspapers, often under Jewish ownership. Alfred von Hugenberg, the head of Weimar's main bourgeois nationalist political party and a director of the Krupp Steel armaments firm, held a monopoly on the wire service that fed news to Germany's smaller cities and towns. Its newsfeed regularly featured denunciations of the Versailles Treaty and propagation of the anti-Semitic and antisocialist "stab in the back" myth to explain Germany's defeat in the World War. In the populist wave following the collapse of the German economy in 1929, these constituencies steeped in nationalist myths turned against elite nationalists and voted instead for the Nazis.[85] After World War II, US Occupation authorities effectively reconstructed German news media along the lines of the responsible press model, encouraging a moderate, integrated public sphere by requiring licensed newspapers to have politically diverse but centrist editorial teams.[86]

Notwithstanding Article 19 of the Universal Declaration of Human Rights, American enthusiasm for spreading liberal media took a back seat during the Cold War, but after the fall of the Soviet Union, promoting democracy and free media around the world again came into vogue. Indeed, the opening up of mass media happened spontaneously in Eastern Europe, although not always in accord with the expectations of the liberal folk theory. The Communist Party boss of Yugoslavia's Serbian region, Slobodan Milosevic, realized by the mid-1980s that the political wind was blowing toward competitive elections. He prepared for it by packing the Belgrade TV service with his loyalists and using televised ethnic nationalist speeches to spread falsehoods about rape and "genocide" against Serbs inflicted by Muslim Albanians in the subregion of Kosovo.[87] Having captured the main source of news for the majority of Serbs, Milosevic could burnish his nationalist image without eliminating the partially independent remnants of print and radio media. Seizing only the commanding heights of the media gave him the aura of a democrat and allowed him to prevail in competitive elections without submitting to true democratic accountability. When his ethnically divisive policies hastened the breakup of multiethnic Yugoslavia, Milosevic found himself mired in the ethnic nationalist bloodletting that was the unwanted, unintended byproduct of his opportunistic strategy of media-based dictatorship.[88] Among the take-home lessons of this episode, an exceptionally important one is that establishing a partial monopoly position in the national media environment may be sufficient—there is no need to exercise complete monopoly over public discourse to keep power intact. Freedom House actually increased Yugoslavia's media freedom score while all this was happening. Liberals seeking to constructively regulate mass media can take advantage of this insight, too.

In places where dictatorial regimes did not spontaneously democratize at the end of the Cold War, liberal donor states often gave them a push, sometimes with dire results. The ethnic dictatorships of both Rwanda and Burundi were compelled to accept power-sharing agreements, which included requirements to increase the pluralism of their civil society organizations, allow more open media, and in Burundi's case, prepare for competitive national elections on a short timetable. Freedom House boosted their media freedom scores at this time, too. The problem was that almost all these new voices were spouting ethnic hate speech, some of them consciously preparing their own segment of the public to slaughter the ethnic foe as an alternative to the unacceptable power-sharing deal.[89]

More recently the media used for hate speech in ethnically polarized illiberal democracies has received a technological upgrade, but the situation of incomplete democracy and weak, exploitable media institutions presents the same perverse incentives to play the ethnic card. Social media have been a common medium for deadly trolling of stigmatized minorities in states undergoing stalled democratic transitions, such as the Burmese campaign of hate and expulsion against the Muslim Rohingya on Facebook, and in illiberal democracies like India, using Facebook once again to demonize and target Rohingya refugees and other Muslims. As a result of the outcry against this in the American public, Facebook tightened its rules against these hate campaigns.[90] This pattern underscores that the unconditional liberal media freedom theory needs strong qualifications and that the institutional media regulation theory is key to understanding human rights outcomes in this domain.

As our statistical results showed, however, not every partial democracy has perversely institutionalized media. When mixed regimes have well-functioning media, rights outcomes are better. Beth Simmons similarly finds that having a truly free press stands out as the most significant variable predicting better than expected performance in complying with the antitorture convention, and more generally that independent courts and an active civil society improve rights outcomes in transitional states.[91]

An Exogenous Increase in Media Openness: Satellite TV and the Arab Spring

Because of the likelihood of reciprocal causal relations among the variables of the liberal folk theory, we have been exceedingly cautious about making causal claims about the effects of increases in media freedom. Nonetheless, we are interested in probing opportunities for causal insights. One possible way to assess the impact of an increase of media freedom is to study cases in which there was an increase in media openness as the result of an exogenous technological shock. To explore causal relationships, we draw on studies of the effects of the transnational satellite television revolution on media integration and segmentation and on polarization and violence in Middle East politics.

The liberal folk theory expects increases in information and opportunities for freedom of expression to universally promote democracy and other desirable outcomes. The abrupt introduction of far more open transnational television news media to the Arab world in the few years following 1998 casts doubt on this simplistic expectation of the folk theory. Instead, it supports the more qualified insights of institutionalized media theory. This new medium interacted in explosive ways with the particular political and institutional environments in which it emerged. Arab satellite TV at first stimulated the development of an integrated Arab public sphere, but the subsequent reaction of Arab states and identity groups contributed to segmenting Arab media markets. Rather than leading to social peace and improved governance, these breakthroughs in media freedom sowed division between citizens and their states and between rival identity groups in the Arab world.

Marc Lynch argues that transnational satellite television transformed and unified the Arab public sphere in the years following 1998, when Al Jazeera introduced vibrant, fact-filled, controversial political reporting and debate to take over audience share from tedious, controlled state media. This disruptive news onslaught was outside the control of the Arab states. The Arab nationalist content and hot-button style of Al Jazeera was driven by the desire to reach a big audience, not political motivation.[92]

Based on surveys of broadcast viewership and political attitudes in several Arab countries, studies by Lynch and Shibley Telhami show that the initial effect of these broadcasts was to reignite Arab nationalism. As in the late 1940s and 1950s, Arabs felt justified in expressing views on political developments in Arab states other than their own.[93] Primed by Al Jazeera's programming, public opinion viewed events in the region through the lens of pan-Arab identity, often seeing the Arab nation as the victim of the Arab states and intrusive international forces. This effect was clearest in the years between 1998 and 2002, when Al Jazeera was the only major Arab transnational satellite broadcaster. In 2003 Saudi-funded Al Arabiya launched a fairly successful competitor to Al Jazeera, offering a more conservative version of satellite news.

Arab public attitudes and viewership responded both to political events in the region and to the supply of broadcast TV options. Telhami's surveys show a spike in identification as Arab and Muslim, versus a decline of nation-state identity, between 2003 and 2008, at the time of the US invasion of Iraq, the Israeli-Hezbollah war, and Israel's invasion of Gaza. Arab identity crashed in 2011, notwithstanding the apparent diffusion of revolutionary fervor in that year of the Arab Spring.[94]

On the supply side, by the middle 2000s, more than five hundred television stations were broadcasting in Arabic to the region and accessible to nearly ubiquitous satellite dishes. Much of this proliferation was a response by states and local factions trying to compete with Al Jazeera's framing of events for local audiences. As a result, many viewers watched both Al Jazeera and a local identity-based channel, whether national or sectarian. Thus, Erik Nisbet's team notes, "the dramatic growth in media choice" was "paired with ideological polarization in Arab countries during the last two decades."[95]

The Middle East's experience with a dramatic change in media openness has sobering implications for liberal folk theory. Increased availability of more open, higher quality, more informative media provided a wider forum for speech among better-informed citizens, but it also contributed to polarization and strife. Al Jazeera provided a great deal of information, but in a frame that conformed to the timeless journalistic dictum: "If it bleeds, it leads." Increasingly informed citizens of these authoritarian regimes reacted with frustration that they had no way to act on their newly enlightened insights.[96] Programming and viewers' responses were emotional in terms of their heated style of discourse and "us versus them" interpretation of events. Transnational broadcasts that framed analysis in terms of a pan-Arab identity created a more integrated public sphere, but in a way that drove a wedge between authoritarian regimes and the increasingly radicalized "Arab street." More local or sectarian broadcasts that arose in response to Al Jazeera and Al Arabiya stimulated what Lynch calls "enclave deliberation," or what institutionalized media theory would call a segmented media market.[97] Lynch's subsequent research on social media in Egypt in the wake of the Arab Spring and Syria during the civil war shows a strong tendency toward segmentation of discourse.[98]

The satellite TV case study shows that increases in media freedom and media quality can spur illiberal, destructive consequences in political environments that lack institutions capable of channeling political action in liberal, moderating directions. In particular, the mismatch between the Middle East's state boundaries and its identity-group cultural boundaries was aggravated by the opening of the public sphere to mass deliberation, which lacked an orderly institutional mechanism to accommodate the desire for national self-determination. Only Tunisia emerged more liberal from the experiment with satellite TV and the Arab Spring. It was the Arab state with the most conducive fundamentals in terms of GDP per capita, administrative capacity, a significant constituency for secular politics, and no significant ethnic divisions. An increase in media freedom matters for political outcomes, but its consequences depend on contextual factors including general governance structures and the structure of supply and demand in the media market.

Conclusion: Regulating the Marketplace of Ideas

While recognizing the intrinsic value of the liberties of speech and the press, we also stress their instrumental value for achieving the whole set of human values that liberals prize, including the full inventory of human rights, good governance, and social peace. This pragmatic orientation sheds light on the mechanisms that allow free speech and media to produce these benefits, and to avoid the unanticipated trouble that unfettered speech can sometimes cause.

Many free-speech absolutists, lacking a well-grounded practical guide for dealing with such dilemmas, have ironically been too quick to resort to censorship when speech on social media has become harmful.[99] Libertarians like Twitter magnate Jack Dorsey initially took an "anything goes" approach to problematic speech but then bowed to pressure from idealistic liberals, usually the most adamant proponents of free speech, to "deplatform" conspiracy mongers and hate speakers in ways that went beyond normal legal restraints on incitement and libel.[100] This rudderless approach to regulation of speech and media, swinging wildly from advocacy of unfettered speech to bans on speech content, is standing in the way of proven measures that can enhance both the moderation and the freedom of speech.

The First Amendment guarantees not just the freedom of speech, but also the freedom of the press, because the two are inextricably linked. To enhance speech, professional journalists and editors should be empowered not to censor speech, but to shape the forums in which speech is conducted. Instead of banning routine false information, a better remedy is to take advantage of journalistic discretion to stock the market of ideas so that higher quality goods receive favored placement. This means putting a diverse mix of highly professional journalists and editors in charge of the dissemination of news and opinion on each of the major internet platforms and backing them up with arms-length regulatory oversight. This can be accomplished by a symbiotic combination of self-regulation by platforms, such as Facebook's Oversight Board, and general standard setting by an updated version of the FCC's Fairness Doctrine.[101]

For this solution to be practical and effective, it is important to distinguish between regulation of media's commanding heights and the policing of routine speech to small audiences. Many Americans talk as if the First Amendment guarantees their right not only to voice their opinions in public but to have instant, unfiltered, global access to an audience of millions, regardless of how ill-founded, incoherent, and misleading those opinions might be. In fact, for the first two centuries of the First Amendment, people whose opinions did get widespread exposure achieved this only through the facilitation of the press, whose freedom is likewise guaranteed by the First Amendment. By tradition and common sense, if not by explicit constitutional stipulation, one of those press freedoms is the right to make editorial judgments about the newsworthiness of content.

Although major internet platforms such as Facebook and Twitter have tried to evade responsibility for content by pretending to renounce this right, their business models depend on the algorithms and terms of service through which they shape access to speech on their forums. Because anyone can go on Facebook and say almost anything they want, to the user it feels like freedom, but considered as a whole, this system of discourse is institutionalized by the hidden hand of the platform's hegemonic secret algorithm to generate a profitable equilibrium. The question is not whether speech is to be regulated, but whether it is to be regulated well or badly.

It should be feasible for journalists to exercise editorial judgment on the content of newsfeeds and the social media content of figures of major public interest based on normal journalistic criteria of newsworthiness. Yet, individual or localized problems of defamation, incitement, fraud, personal harassment, and public health and safety will presumably have to be managed by more transparent algorithms, supplemented by staff vetting of routine complaints, and overseen by independent third parties. Established law limiting defamatory speech can provide guidelines for much of this. Fact checking and flagging dubious content can also help, but there is little evidence that this in itself can be an effective antidote to false information. Many people classify statements that they agree with as facts and statements they disagree with as opinions.[102]

Some people fear that more rigorous standards for discourse on mainstream social media could spur substantial flight away from well-regulated media. Our findings suggest, however, that firmly institutionalized mainstream media systems can coexist with peripheral enclaves of contrarian speech and information. This assumes that many ordinary users of social media might be influenced by conspiracy theories that they run across by happenstance on mainstream platforms, but not being mainly motivated by politics, they will not seek out obscure extremist sites.

More problematic is whether a common standard of professional regula-tion is possible in a highly polarized setting where a tendentious broadcaster such as Fox News has already established an influential position in a media market segment. Fox has indeed presided over a race to the bottom in its mar-ket segment. A data-intensive Harvard study contends that the *New York Times* and NPR are the informational anchors that dampen unfounded rumors in the liberal media system, whereas the conservative media system, anchored on the less fact-based Fox News, amplifies rather than dampens conspiracy myths.[103] Defamation lawsuits stemming from Fox's commentary on Georgia's voting machines might conceivably lead Fox to self-regulate to avoid onerous penalties.

Some skeptics worry that media regulation in the wrong hands could go down a slippery slope toward oppression. This fear may be warranted in the context of semidemocratic regimes with weak rule-of-law institutions. In such mixed regimes, bans on "fake news" can easily become tools to suppress op-position to the regime.[104] This provides yet another reason to have profes-sional journalists in charge of exercising judgments about newsworthiness rather than heavy-handed state regulators.

Others worry that distrust of elite professional journalists has led the public even in established democracies to seek out populist "alternative facts," or as QAnon adherents put it, to "do your own research." But this applies only to a part of the public. According to a January 2020 US survey by the gold-standard Pew Research Center, distrust of mainstream professional news media is mainly a phenomenon of the right. Two-thirds of Democrats, people who lean Democratic, and self-described liberals say they trust the news on CNN, and more than half trust the three broadcast networks, the *New York Times*, and PBS. Majorities distrust only Fox, Breitbart, and the radio shows of right-wing commentators Rush Limbaugh and Sean Hannity. Two-thirds of Republicans, Republican leaners, and self-described conservatives trust Fox, but no other mainstream media.[105]

In May 2018, at a moment of intense debate about false news on Facebook, we surveyed twenty-five thousand Google users on their preferred options for the Facebook newsfeed: 43 percent supported letting each user have complete control over which news sources to see and how to display them; 40 percent said Facebook should hire a very diverse staff of experienced, knowledgeable, professional journalists to manage its newsfeed; 21 percent liked the newsfeed as is; 21 percent favored government regulation; and 34 percent said Facebook should eliminate the newsfeed and stick to social interactions.[106] This mix of individual freedom actively facilitated by professional journalists, with a very light role for government regulation, seems a pragmatic and constructive formula in light of our findings about liberal folk theory and the supportive role of a well-institutionalized media system.

Overall, our findings on the conditions that enable constructive freedom of speech and media underscore a broader point about the pragmatic approach to human rights. Pragmatic steps that may look to some like compromises of absolute principles, such as regulatory limits on unfettered freedom of speech, can instead be the indispensable expedients that make human rights a reality.

Regulating the Marketplace of Ideas

Data Sources

For our empirical analysis, we draw on various cross-national datasets, including the Varieties of Democracy project, the CIRI Human Rights Data Project, the Major Episodes of Political Violence and Conflict Regions (MEVP) Project, the Quality of Government Standard Dataset, and the Polity IV Project. The list below explains the source of each variable used in the analysis presented in the chapter.

1. **Media freedom.** We use Freedom House's press freedom score. This measure ranges from 1 to 3 and evaluates the freedom of print, broadcast, and digital media globally on the basis of a range of parameters capturing the legal, political, and economic media environment in each country. In our analysis, we reverse-coded this variable such that higher values reflect freer media systems.[1]

2. **Media freedom subscores.** To examine the role of different types of media function, we also created categories from the questions that underlie Freedom House's press freedom score.[2]

    • The **watchdog of government behavior** variable is generated from the following questions:

---

1. Freedom House, "Freedom of the Press 2017 Methodology" (2017), https://freedomhouse .org/report/freedom-press-2017-methodology.
2. Freedom House, "Freedom of the Press 2017 Methodology."

- (A1) Do the constitution or other basic laws contain provisions designed to protect freedom of the press and of expression, and are they enforced?
- (A2) Do the penal code, security laws, or any other laws restrict reporting and are journalists or bloggers punished under these laws?
- (A3) Are there penalties for libeling officials or the state and are they enforced?
- (A4) Is the judiciary independent and do courts judge cases concerning the media impartially?
- (A5) Is Freedom of Information legislation in place, and are journalists able to make use of it?
- (B3) Is there official or unofficial censorship?
- (B4) Do journalists practice self-censorship?

• The **source of information** variable is generated from the following questions:
- (B1) To what extent are media outlets' news and information content determined by the government or a particular partisan interest?
- (B2) Is access to official or unofficial sources generally controlled?
- (B5) Do people have access to media coverage and a range of news and information that is robust and reflects a diversity of viewpoints?
- (B6) Are both local and foreign journalists able to cover the news freely and safely in terms of physical access and on-the-ground reporting?

• The **forum for public expression** variable is generated from the following questions:
- (A6) Can individuals or business entities legally establish and operate private media outlets without undue interference?
- (A8) Is there freedom to become a journalist and to practice journalism, and can professional groups freely support journalists' rights and interests?
- (B7) Are journalists, bloggers, or media outlets subject to extralegal intimidation or physical violence by state authorities or any other actor as a result of their reporting?
- (C1) To what extent are media owned or controlled by the government and does this influence their diversity of views?

- (C3) Is media ownership highly concentrated and does this influ-ence diversity of content?
- (C7) Do journalists, bloggers, or media outlets receive payment from private or public sources whose design is to influence their journalistic content?

3. **Democracy**. We use two country-year measures of democracy to examine whether greater media freedom is associated with stronger democracy. First, we use Polity IV data, which range from −10 (complete autocracy) to 10 (complete democracy).[3] Second, we use data from Varieties of De-mocracy (V-Dem) on the extent to which a country has deliberative de-mocracy. The index ranges from 0 to 1. The definition of deliberative democracy, according to V-Dem is: "The deliberative principle of democ-racy focuses on the process by which decisions are reached in a polity. A deliberative process is one in which public reasoning focused on the com-mon good motivates political decisions—as contrasted with emotional appeals, solidarity attachments, parochial interests, or coercion. According to this principle, democracy requires more than an aggregation of existing preferences. There should also be respectful dialogue at all levels—from preference formation to final decision—among informed and competent participants who are open to persuasion. To make it a measure of not only the deliberative principle but also of democracy, the index also takes the level of electoral democracy into account."[4] The variable is an index con-structed from a variable capturing the extent of an electoral democracy in a country and "the extent to which political elites give public justifications for their positions on matters of public policy, justify their positions in terms of the public good, acknowledge and respect counter-arguments; and how wide the range of consultation is at elite levels."[5]

4. **Human rights**. The human rights variable comes from CIRI Human Rights Data Project. We use the variable Physical Integrity Rights Index, which is an index ranging from 0 to 8, constructed from variables on

3. Monty G. Marshall, Ted Robert Gurr, and Keith Jaggers, "Polity IV Project: Political Regime Characteristics and Transitions, 1800–2013," Center for Systemic Peace (2016), http://www.systemicpeace.org/polity/polity4.htm.

4. Michael Coppedge et al., *V-Dem Codebook v9*, April 2019, https://www.v-dem.net/media/filer_public/e6/d2/e6d27595-9d69-4312-b09f-63d2a0a65df2/v-dem_codebook_v9.pdf.

5. Coppedge et al., *V-Dem Codebook v9*, 49.

Torture, Extrajudicial Killing, Political Imprisonment, and Disappearance. 0 reflects no government respect for these four rights and 8 reflects full government respect for these four rights.[6]

5. **Social order and peace.** We use data on the magnitude of civic unrest from the Major Episodes of Political Violence and Conflict Regions (MEVP) dataset. This is an index ranging from 0 to 10 capturing the episodes of civil violence, civil warfare, ethnic violence, and ethnic war.[7]

6. **Political corruption index.** We use the Political Corruption Index from the Varieties of Democracy project. The index ranges from 0 to 1, where higher values reflect more corrupt countries. According to the V-Dem Codebook, "The corruption index includes measures of six distinct types of corruption that cover both different areas and levels of the polity realm, distinguishing between executive, legislative and judicial corruption. Within the executive realm, the measures also distinguish between corruption mostly pertaining to bribery and corruption due to embezzlement. Finally, they differentiate between corruption in the highest echelons of the executive at the level of the rulers/cabinet on the one hand, and in the public sector at large on the other. The measures thus tap into several distinguished types of corruption: both 'petty' and 'grand'; both bribery and theft; both corruption aimed and influencing law making and that affecting implementation." In our analysis, we reverse-code this variable so that higher values reflect less corrupt countries.[8]

7. **Quality of government.** We use data on the quality of government from the Quality of Government Standard Dataset, which averages variables on corruption, law and order, and bureaucracy quality. It ranges from 0 to 1, where higher values indicate higher quality of government.[9]

6. David Cingranelli, David Richards, and K. Chad Clay, "The CIRI Human Rights Dataset," Version 2014.04.14. (2014), http://www.humanrightsdata.com.

7. Monty G. Marshall, "Major Episodes of Political Violence (MEPV) and Conflict Regions, 1946–2015," Center for Systemic Peace 25 (2016).

8. Coppedge et al., *V-Dem Codebook v9*, 266.

9. Jan Teorell, Stefan Dahlberg, Sören Holmberg, Bo Rothstein, Anna Khomenko, and Richard Svensson, "The Quality of Government Standard Dataset, Version Jan17," University of

8. **Quality of media content.** We use an expert-based measure from V-Dem on whether major print and broadcast media in each country represent a wide range of political perspectives. The variable is measured as follows:[10]

> *Question*: Do the major print and broadcast media represent a wide range of political perspectives?
>
> *Responses*:
>
> > 0: The major media represent only the government's perspective.
> > 1: The major media represent only the perspectives of the government and a government-approved, semi-official opposition party.
> > 2: The major media represent a variety of political perspectives but they systematically ignore at least one political perspective that is important in this society.
> > 3: All perspectives that are important in this society are represented in at least one of the major media.

9. **Civil society robustness.** We use a measure for civil society robustness from the Varieties of Democracy (V-Dem) dataset v6. The civil society robustness variable is an index ranging from 0 to 1 that includes three measures of civil society activities in a country. The questions that are included in the index are:[11]

   - To what extent does the government achieve control over entry and exit by civil society organizations (CSOs) into public life?

   - Does the government attempt to repress civil society organizations (CSOs)?

   - To what extent are people involved in civil society organizations, and how many diverse, independent CSOs are in a country-year?

10. **Online media fractionalization.** We use an expert-based measure from V-Dem on whether major domestic online media present news in similar or opposite manners. The variable is measured as follows:[12]

Gothenburg: The Quality of Government Institute, April 30, 2020, http://www.qog.pol.gu.se, doi:10.18157/QoGStdJan17.

10. Coppedge et al., *V-Dem Codebook v9*, 187.

11. Coppedge et al., *V-Dem Codebook v9*, 179.

12. V. Mechkova, D. Pemstein, B. Seim, and S. Wilson, "Measuring Internet Politics: Introducing the Digital Society Project," Digital Society Project Working Paper no. 1, May 2019,

Question: Do the major domestic online media outlets give a similar presentation of major (political) news?

Responses:

> 0: No. The major domestic online media outlets give opposing presentation of major events.
>
> 1: Not really. The major domestic online media outlets differ greatly in the presentation of major events.
>
> 2: Sometimes. The major domestic online media outlets give a similar presentation of major events about half the time.
>
> 3: Mostly. The major domestic online media outlets mostly give a similar presentation of major events.
>
> 4: Yes. Although there are small differences in representation, the major domestic online media outlets give a similar presentation of major events.

11. **Election turnout.** We use data from V-Dem on the level of public disagreement on a range of political issues. The variable is measured as follows:[13]

    Question: In this national election, what percentage (%) of the adult voting-age population cast a vote according to official results?

12. **Polarization of society**. We use an expert-based measure from V-Dem on the level of public disagreement on a range of political issues. The variable is measured as follows:[14]

    Question: How would you characterize the differences of opinions on major political issues in this society?

    Responses:

    > 0: Serious polarization. There are serious differences in opinions in society on almost all key political issues, which result in major clashes of views.
    >
    > 1: Moderate polarization. There are differences in opinions in society on many key political issues, which result in moderate clashes of views.

---

http://digitalsocietyproject.org/wp-content/uploads/2019/05/DSP_WP_01-Introducing-the
-Digital-Society-Project.pdf.

13. Michael Coppedge et al., *V-Dem Codebook v10*, March 2020, 70, https://www.v-dem.net/media
/filer_public/28/14/28140582-43d6-4940-948f-a2df84a31893/v-dem_codebook_v10.pdf.

14. Mechkova et al., "Measuring Internet Politics," 26.

2: Medium polarization. Differences in opinions are noticeable on about half of the key political issues, resulting in some clashes of views.

3: Limited polarization. There are differences in opinions on only a few key political issues, resulting in few clashes of views.

4: No polarization. There are differences in opinions but there is a general agreement on the direction for key political issues.

13. **Political parties hate speech**. We use an expert-based measure from V-Dem on whether major political parties use hate speech as part of their rhetoric. The variable is measured as follows:[15]

    Question: How often do major political parties use hate speech as part of their rhetoric?

    Responses:

    0: Extremely often.
    1: Often.
    2: Sometimes.
    3: Rarely.
    4: Never, or almost never.

14. **Party dissemination of false information.** We use data from the Digital Society Project. The variable is measured as follows:[16]

    Question: How often do major political parties and candidates for office use social media to disseminate misleading viewpoints or false information to influence their own population?

    Responses:

    0: Extremely often. Major political parties and candidates disseminate false information on all key political issues.

    1: Often. Major political parties and candidates disseminate false information on many key political issues.

    2: About half the time. Major political parties and candidates disseminate false information on some key political issues, but not others.

    3: Rarely. Major political parties and candidates disseminate false information on only a few key political issues.

15. Mechkova et al., "Measuring Internet Politics," 26.
16. Mechkova et al., "Measuring Internet Politics," 12–13.

4: Never, or almost never. Major political parties and candidates never disseminate false information on key political issues.

15. **Favorable institutions and norms index.** We created an index variable capturing favorable institutions and norms that includes: (i) the extent to which major print and broadcast media represent a wide range of political perspectives,[17] (ii) whether the legal framework provides protection against defamatory online content or hate speech,[18] and (iii) the absence of elite abuse of the legal system to censor political speech online.[19] The index ranges from 0 to 1, where values closer to 1 reflect country-years with institutions and norms that are more likely to constructively shape debate in the marketplace of ideas, and values closer to 0 the absence of such norms and institutions.

To quantitatively measure the relationship between media freedom and these variables, we merged these data sources into one integrated dataset. The dataset includes observations for 180 countries from 1972 to 2018 across a large number of politically relevant outcomes. Table A1 presents summary statistics for the variables used in the study.

Model Specifications and Statistical Results

In order to examine the relationship between media freedom and some of the outcomes and mechanisms expected by the liberal folk theory and institutionalized media theory, we regress our dependent variables on the Freedom House measure of media freedom, while accounting for country fixed effects and the level of democracy, GDP per capita, and population size, as shown in model (1). Table A2 shows the results. Table A3 reports the results by media function: watchdog of government behavior, source of information, and forum for public expression.

$$\text{Outcome}_{it} = \beta_1 \text{Media Freedom}_{it} + \beta_2 \text{Polity IV}_{it} + \beta_3 \text{GDP pc}_{it}$$
$$+ \beta_4 \text{Population}_{it} + a_i + \varepsilon_{it} \tag{1}$$

17. Coppedge et al., *V-Dem Codebook v9*, 187.
18. Mechkova et al., "Measuring Internet Politics," 20.
19. Mechkova et al., "Measuring Internet Politics," 21.

TABLE A1. Summary Statistics

	N	Mean	Std. Dev.	Min	Max
Year (*V-Dem*)	7,837	1996	13.358	1972	2018
Press freedom score (*Freedom House*)	7,837	2.039	0.819	1	3
Media function: watchdog (*Freedom House*)	1,448	20.306	7.566	7	34
Media function: inform public (*Freedom House*)	1,448	14.378	5.047	4	24
Media function: forum (*Freedom House*)	1,448	22.441	7.088	6	34
Polity IV	7,084	1.750	7.390	−10	10
Deliberative democracy (*V-Dem*)	6,141	0.346	0.296	0.001	0.929
Respect for human rights (*CIRI*)	4,513	4.814	2.317	0	8
Social order and peace (*MEVP*)	6,572	9.299	1.680	0	10
Political corruption index (*V-Dem*)	7,803	0.501	0.300	0.005	0.974
Quality of government (*QoG Project*)	4,139	0.545	0.224	0.042	1
Quality of media content (*V-Dem*)	7,837	1.915	1.177	0	3
Civil society robustness (*V-Dem*)	6,358	0.610	0.314	0.009	0.984
Online media fractionalization (*V-Dem*)	3,514	2.432	0.920	0	4
Election turnout (*V-Dem*)*	1,733	64.366	18.609	2.140	223.700
Polarization of society (*V-Dem*)	3,514	2.478	1.137	0	4
Political parties hate speech (*V-Dem*)	3,514	1.522	0.967	0	4
Party dissemination of false information (*V-Dem*)	3,514	1.628	0.986	0	4
Citizen political knowledge (*Surveys*)	205	0.760	0.215	0.131	0.999
Citizen voting in elections (*Surveys*)	461	0.799	0.129	0.283	1
Citizen participation in protests (*Surveys*)	443	0.331	0.236	0.004	0.855
Favorable institutions and norms index	3,514	0.632	0.196	0.000	0.994

*Taken verbatim from V-Dem: "The VAP (voting age population) can reflect irregularities such as problems with the voters' register or registration system. VAP numbers are estimates since they do not take into account legal or systemic barriers to the exercise of the franchise or account for non-eligible members of the population. Thus, it can occur that VAP values surpass 100 which is not an error but reflects such conditions" (V-Dem v10 codebook, p. 70–71).

TABLE A2. Regression Results

	Respect for human rights (1)	Social order and peace (2)	Civil society robustness (3)	Media quality (4)	Media fraction. (5)	Quality of government (6)	Turnout (7)	Corruption (8)	Polarization (9)	Hate speech (10)	False info in politics (11)
Press freedom score	0.734*** (0.175)	0.295** (0.148)	0.040* (0.023)	0.190** (0.077)	0.084 (0.059)	−0.004 (0.018)	1.240 (2.433)	−0.003 (0.015)	−0.349 (0.230)	−0.353* (0.187)	−0.532*** (0.175)
GDP pc	0.00000 (0.00001)	0.00000 (0.00000)	0.00000 (0.00000)	−0.00000 (0.00000)	0.00000 (0.00000)	0.00000** (0.00000)	−0.0003*** (0.0001)	−0.00000 (0.00000)	−0.00002*** (0.00001)	−0.00002*** (0.00000)	−0.00001* (0.00000)
Population	−0.00001*** (0.00000)	−0.00000 (0.00001)	0.00000*** (0.00000)	0.00000** (0.00000)	−0.00000 (0.00000)	0.00000** (0.00000)	0.00001 (0.00001)	0.00000*** (0.00000)	−0.00000 (0.00000)	0.00000 (0.00000)	0.00000*** (0.00000)
Polity IV	−0.003 (0.021)	−0.012 (0.016)	0.035*** (0.003)	0.118*** (0.010)	0.0003 (0.011)	0.006** (0.002)	−0.192 (0.225)	0.001 (0.002)	0.046 (0.028)	−0.003 (0.023)	−0.011 (0.021)
Constant									3.139*** (0.403)	2.388*** (0.352)	2.595*** (0.332)
Country fixed effects	✓	✓	✓	✓	✓	✓	✓	✓	✗	✗	✗
Clustered S.E.	✓	✓	✓	✓	✓	✓	✓	✓	✓	✓	✓
Observations	2,368	3,560	3,440	3,723	500	1,851	706	3,695	155	155	155
R^2	0.728	0.675	0.896	0.878	0.947	0.868	0.726	0.913	0.112	0.252	0.327

Note: *p < 0.1; **p < 0.05; ***p < 0.01

TABLE A3. Variation by Media Function

	Estimate	Std. Err	Dependent Variable	Independent Variable	P-Value	R²	N
1	0.04	0.01	Deliberative democracy	1. Watchdog	0.00	0.98	958
2	0.08	0.02	Respect for human rights	1. Watchdog	0.00	0.91	615
3	0.01	0.01	Low civic unrest	1. Watchdog	0.18	0.91	1227
4	0.00	0.00	Low corruption	1. Watchdog	0.53	0.97	1174
5	0.01	0.00	Quality of government	1. Watchdog	0.05	0.99	1024
6	0.06	0.01	Deliberative democracy	2. Inform public	0.00	0.98	958
7	0.09	0.04	Respect for human rights	2. Inform public	0.02	0.91	615
8	0.03	0.01	Low civic unrest	2. Inform public	0.00	0.91	1227
9	0.01	0.01	Low corruption	2. Inform public	0.06	0.97	1174
10	0.01	0.00	Quality of government	2. Inform public	0.00	0.99	1024
11	0.05	0.01	Deliberative democracy	3. Forum	0.00	0.98	958
12	0.05	0.03	Respect for human rights	3. Forum	0.13	0.91	615
13	0.02	0.01	Low civic unrest	3. Forum	0.09	0.91	1227
14	−0.00	0.00	Low corruption	3. Forum	0.81	0.97	1174
15	0.01	0.00	Quality of government	3. Forum	0.00	0.99	1024

To examine the mismatch between regime type and media freedom, we regress (i) dissemination of false information by political actors and (ii) the use of hate speech by political parties on an interaction of media freedom and regime type, as shown in equation (2). Table A4 shows the results.

$$\text{Outcome}_{it} = \beta_1 \text{Free Media}_{it} + \beta_2 \text{Polity IV}_{it} + \beta_3 \left(\text{Free Media}_{it} \right.$$
$$\left. \times \text{Polity IV}_{it} \right) + \lambda X_{it} + \varepsilon_{it} \qquad (2)$$

TABLE A4. Consequences of a Mismatch between Regime Type and Media Freedom

	Political actors use media to disseminate false information	Major political parties use hate speech as part of their rhetoric
Free media	0.256	−0.145
	(0.253)	(0.253)
Polity IV	−0.034***	−0.015***
	(0.003)	(0.003)
Free media × Polity IV	−0.115***	−0.052*
	(0.027)	(0.027)
Constant	1.961***	1.885***
	(0.023)	(0.023)
Controls	✓	✓
Observations	2,575	2,575
R²	0.345	0.345

*p < 0.1; **p < 0.05; ***p < 0.01

Note: The table presents coefficients estimated from regressions of the dissemination of false information by political actors and the use of hate speech by political parties on an interaction of media freedom with regime type.

Google Survey on Preferences for Facebook Newsfeed

Below are results from a survey we ran with Google Surveys on May 27, 2018. The survey includes 25,097 American respondents recruited by Google when browsing the internet. The sample is representative of American internet users on the basis of age, gender, and region.[20] We asked respondents about their opinion on various proposed changes to Facebook's newsfeed. Each respondent was randomly shown one of five proposed changes and was asked to indicate his or her level of support for it. The proposed changes included:

1. Let each user have complete control over which news sources to see and how they are displayed
2. Facebook should hire a very diverse staff of experienced, knowledgeable professional journalists to manage its newsfeed

20. A white paper on how Google Surveys works can be found here: https://services.google.com/fh/files/misc/white_paper_how_google_surveys_works.pdf

TABLE A5. Public Support for Various Options for Facebook's Newsfeed

Option	Average Support
Let each user have complete control over which news sources to see and how they are displayed	0.43
Facebook should hire a very diverse staff of experienced, knowledgeable professional journalists to manage its newsfeed	0.40
Facebook's newsfeed is fine the way it is	0.21
The government should regulate Facebook's news policy	0.21
Facebook should eliminate its newsfeed and serve only as a platform for social connections between individuals	0.34

Note: The table presents the average support for each proposed change to Facebook's newsfeed, based on a survey of 25,097 American internet users. The averages sum to more than 100 because respondents could express support for more than one option.

3. Facebook's newsfeed is fine the way it is
4. The government should regulate Facebook's news policy
5. Facebook should eliminate its newsfeed and serve only as a platform for social connections between individuals

Table A5 shows the average level of support for each option, which we report in the conclusion to the article. We arrived at these numbers by creating a binary variable called "support" that is coded 1 when a response was 4 and 5 on the response scale, and 0 otherwise.

Figure A1 shows the distributions of the answers for each proposed change. It can be seen, for example, that letting people have complete control over their newsfeed is strongly supported (Panel A), but letting the government regulate Facebook's news policy is strongly opposed (Panel D). We find that many respondents are supportive of having professional journalists manage Facebook's newsfeed (Panel B).

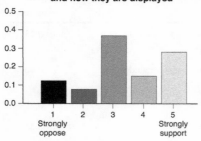

(A) Let each user have complete control over which news sources to see and how they are displayed

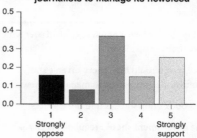

(B) Facebook should hire a very diverse staff of experienced, knowledgeable professional journalists to manage its newsfeed

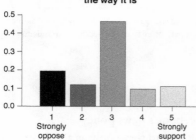

(C) Facebook's newsfeed is fine the way it is

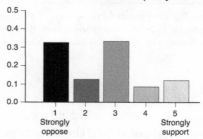

(D) The government should regulate Facebook's news policy

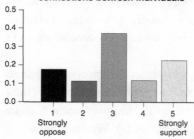

(E) Facebook should eliminate its newsfeed and serve only as a platform for social connections between individuals

FIGURE A1. Preferences for Facebook's newsfeed.

8

Backlash against Human Rights Shaming

"BY NOW," says Human Rights Watch founder Aryeh Neier, "it is widely accepted in the international human rights movement that one of the purposes that was served by 'naming and shaming' during the past four decades has declined in significance. That is, persuading Western governments to exert pressure on governments in other parts of the world to curb abuses of rights is increasingly ineffective."[1] The acknowledgment of this is good news, because shaming is the tool pragmatic advocates of human rights should reach for last. Not only is its effectiveness highly uncertain, but it entails considerable risk of blowback, especially in an era when shameless populist politicians score points with their base by naming and shaming liberals.[2]

Nonetheless, many activists and scholars have been doubling down on shaming as a strategy for advancing the rights cause in the face of this fierce backlash. Alison Brysk's recent survey says "shaming" remains a key element in the "conventional" strategy of the rights movement.[3] Reports and declarations that use the language of shaming continue to be central to the work of Human Rights Watch, many rights advocacy organizations, and the broad mainstream of progressive discourse, with questionable impact. Across the political spectrum, shaming the Chinese government for the "Uyghur genocide" intensified despite widespread popular support in China for counterboycotting companies that boycott Chinese "slave labor" cotton.[4] Prominent US scholars, too, continue to highlight the benefits of shame-inducing indicators that rate and rank state performance on rights obligations.[5]

Social science offers at best tenuous support for pressing ahead with an agenda based on shaming. Empirical findings on the impact of shaming on rights outcomes are mixed, with conditional effects and causal relationships not easy to sort out.[6] Theoretical foundations of shaming are even shakier. Arguments based on the irresistible power of liberal normative persuasion, progressive transnational social movements, and the material leverage of leading liberal states seemed more compelling as conceptual anchors for a policy of shaming when *The Power of Human Rights* was published in 1999 than they do two decades later.[7] Newer efforts to justify shaming through theories of status in international relations suffer from the difficulty of explaining why status incentives should necessarily work in favor of liberal cosmopolitanism.[8]

Advocates of shaming to promote rights have succeeded in identifying one of the most potent levers of social influence, the continuum of emotions between pride and shame, which are crucial motivators of individuals and groups. The problem is that the most relevant and compelling literatures imply that shaming is likely to be counterproductive for promoting rights.[9] Emotional pressures for conformity and other socialization mechanisms typically work far more strongly in favor of traditional authority, which justifies accustomed violations of rights, than in favor of alien progressive norms. Especially when wielded by cultural outsiders in ways that appear to condemn local social practices, shaming is likely to produce anger, resistance, backlash, and the glorification of deviance from hegemonic outsiders' norms, or it may lead to denial and evasion.

Shaming can easily be interpreted as a show of contempt, which risks triggering fears for the autonomy and security of the group. In these circumstances, established religious and elite networks can employ traditional normative counter-narratives to recruit a popular base for resistance. Uhuru Kenyatta, indicted by the International Criminal Court for plotting ethnic massacres, ran for president of Kenya and won on a platform promising to protect his co-ethnics from the "imperialism" of the court. If such countermobilization becomes entrenched in mass social movements, popular ideology, and enduring institutions, the unintended consequences of shaming may leave human rights advocates farther from their goal.

At the group level, theorists of social influence have argued that persuasion and attitude change cannot be understood apart from processes of collective social identity. Much of this literature has grown out of Henri Tajfel's social identity theory, which demonstrated all too convincingly the tendency of people to be biased in favor of members of even the most trivial, arbitrarily established in-groups, whose status they appear to associate with their individual self-esteem. Explicitly grounded in this theory, Donald Horowitz's monumental study *Ethnic Groups in Conflict* invokes the near-universal tendency of cultural groups to obsess over comparative assessments of each other's stereotypical virtues, shortcomings, and especially their relative back-wardness, which are seen as having emotionally charged implications for their worthiness to thrive or even exist.[10] If these well-vetted theories are correct, shaming would seem more likely to persuade insiders to rally around their endangered group than to promote reform of their biased and repressive prac-tices. Later developments in social identity theory have offered less bleak in-terpretations based on groups each achieving high status in different arenas, individuals having multiple normative reference groups, and in-group bias resulting from local "reality testing" rather than self-esteem-boosting.[11] What-ever their merits theoretically, none of these offshoots provides a conceptual foundation for shaming.

I begin by discussing the prominent place of shame and shaming in emo-tional and social psychological theories. I then illustrate the ways in which shaming remains central to human rights advocacy and scholarship. Subse-quent sections explore the difficulty of shaming elites without simultaneously shaming masses and of shaming from outside the group. Finally, I discuss the danger of entrenching the backlash to shaming, and I offer prescriptions for promoting rights while minimizing the adverse consequences of shaming.

Psychological and Sociological Theories of the Emotion of Shame

Some social psychological theorizing and empirical research makes big claims for shame as the central social emotion, the crucial glue that holds social rela-tions together.[12] If so, this would suggest that human rights shamers may be on the right track in their quest for a powerful lever to change attitudes and behavior. Precisely because of shame's apparent power, however, many social psychologists focus on shame's destructive potential and the likelihood that shaming, if carried out ineptly, will produce effects that are the opposite of those intended.

A prominent theme of this literature is that shame and shaming play a nec-essary role in deterring violations of social norms and in the formation of an individual's conscience, yet shaming can also backfire. Depending on the cir-cumstances, the target, and the technique, shaming can lead to a self-reinforcing cycle of humiliation, anger, hatred, social withdrawal, and attachment to a coun-terculture of proud deviance. An alternative undesirable path may lead from shame to despondency and evasion rather than compliance. Shaming is least likely to misfire when it targets discrete behaviors that can be altered rather than inherent character traits, when it comes from inside a social identity group rather than from outsiders, when it avoids denouncing mass cultural attitudes and practices, and when it deftly pressures the abettors and associates of norm violators, not just perpetrators themselves.[13]

Most scholars agree that shame and shaming need to be understood at the individual and the social levels simultaneously. Psychologists tend to emphasize the internal psychological state associated with the emotion of shame, highlighting the perceived "discrepancy between ideal and actual self." Sociologists and some social psychologists tend to emphasize the external social implications of shame, saying for example that "in common parlance, shame is a negative, crisis emotion closely connected with disgrace" which gives rise to "the feeling of a threat to the social bond."[14] Even social psychologists, however, acknowledge that shame is a psychological emotion, not just a social situation. Comparable to other emotional states, shame produces involuntary stereotypical physiological effects such as slumped shoulders, an evasive gaze, and sometimes blushing. It makes sense to begin at the individual level, in part because a predominant group-level theory, social identity theory, is anchored to a substantial degree in individual-level issues of self-esteem.

Some early psychological theories, including offshoots from orthodox Freudianism, placed shame-related concepts at the center of their theories. Alfred Adler based his theory of the "inferiority complex" on prestige and self-esteem, with long-term low self-esteem being tantamount to "chronic shame."[15] Karen Horney, in a move that is closely echoed by several contemporary scholars, posited a "pride system" featuring sequences of shame and anger that when sustained lead to a "vindictive personality."[16] More positively, Abraham Kardiner argued that shame was central to the workings of the "superego," or conscience. Erik Erikson saw shame and guilt as one of the developmental stages characteristic of youth. Charles Cooley wrote about "the looking glass self," implying that the dimension of pride and shame constituted the basic social emotions.[17] An updated version of this theory, recast as "self-monitoring," posited a stable personality trait that captures the individual's level of concern with the impression being made on others. This characteristic has recently been shown to successfully predict which US presidents have been willing to fight for reputation.[18]

Contemporary social psychologists agree that a productive turn came with Helen Lewis's *Shame and Guilt in Neurosis* (1971), which simultaneously addressed the social context of shame, the feeling of shame, and people's cognitive understanding of those feelings.[19] She wrote about "feeling traps" in which people not only feel shame for their shortcomings but may also feel shame for feeling ashamed and for feeling angry about being shamed by others, leading to a self-perpetuating cycle. Her empirical work with transcripts of therapeutic interviews fleshed out earlier theorists' conjectures about shame/anger sequences and placed them in a social context.[20] She argued that either shame can provoke anger toward the source of the shaming, leading to resentment, or anger can turn back on the self, leading to feelings of guilt. In both variants, Lewis highlighted the pathologies that result when the feeling of shame is unacknowledged, repressed, and redirected into festering guilt, "resentment," "hostility," "righteous indignation," and "humiliated fury."[21]

Later, a distinctive line of research based on evolutionary theory came to conclusions similar to Lewis's. It proceeded from the assumption that "rank" and "status" are crucial for the ability to attract material investments and sexual partners. In this context, shame and stigma are attached to failures in performing four key social roles: sexual behavior (based on deviance, exploitation, and unattractiveness), prosocial behavior (based on fulfilling obligations), conformity (to rules, fashion, and tradition), and resource competition.[22] According to this theory, "external" manifestations of shame and shaming are important for status competition, and this can also lead to "internal shame." Although in this view the feeling of shame may have net evolutionary benefits, specific manifestations of shame can be highly dysfunctional.[23] Shame and shaming may lead to destructive defensive emotions, debilitating anxiety, concealment, stifling conformity, and malicious accusations to take competitors down a peg in the status order. Thus, "in a shame system people can behave very immorally."[24]

In short, social psychologists, whether devotees of harmonious social integration or partisans of Darwinian cutthroat social competition, have converged on the finding that shame and shaming can easily degenerate into dysfunction. These conclusions imply that shaming is likely to be counterproductive for promoting rights. But does contemporary human rights activism and progressive rights rhetoric really deploy the language of shame in this social psychological sense?

Shame, Shaming, and Their Role in Advocacy

Adapting a definition from the current international relations literature, I define shaming in the context of human rights advocacy as emotionally charged public criticism that denounces or humiliates human rights violators and their abettors "in a way that targets the essence of an individual's identity."[25] This narrow definition is consistent with the social psychological literature that distinguishes between guilt, which focuses on responsibility for a bad action, and shame, which implies a defective personal trait that may be difficult to remediate. The parallel distinction at the group level distinguishes between routine social practices with low cultural salience as opposed to expressions of culture that are salient to the group's fundamental identity.[26]

Shaming normally involves verbal characterizations of behavior as "shameful" or "inhumane," but simply naming violations for which amnesty is legally forbidden (genocide, war crimes, and crimes against humanity) can be considered inherently shaming. Some human rights advocates and scholars routinely apply the term "naming and shaming" to a much broader spectrum of sins and peccadilloes, ranging from mass killing to the failure to purchase fair trade coffee, but here I am not referring to the more mundane applications of this terminology. While Neier and Brysk are correct about the centrality of shaming to much rights advocacy, contemporary human rights work includes activities that may not include shaming of any kind, such as the provision of health, humanitarian, or economic development services using a method that conforms to the standards of the "human rights approach."[27]

Shaming, in my narrow definition, exists on the harsh end of a rhetorical continuum that includes, on the less harsh end, factual reporting, recommending constructive remedies, and numerical rating and ranking. The middle of the spectrum is occupied by pointedly criticizing policy, identifying legal and normative violations (naming), and pressuring states and other actors to impose punishment for specific misbehavior (ending impunity). To illustrate the various kinds of naming, shaming, and other criticism that characterize contemporary human rights discourse and to assess the prevalence of shaming in that litany, I "randomly sampled" Human Rights Watch's list of its ten most recent reports as of March 2019.[28] Their topics addressed (1) Japan's recent "regressive," "harmful" legislation on transgender status, quoting an interviewee who accused the law of "wrecking people's dignity as a human being"; (2) "segregation" and "discrimination" against disabled children in Kazakhstan notwithstanding reforms that were "too slow"; (3) torture, stigmatization, and forced confessions of children of ISIS fighters held in Iraq; (4) governmental "valorization" of "shameful" "vigilante groups" of "cow protectors" in India whose "cruelty and loathing," according to a quoted local activist, "has penetrated the souls of young people"; (5) Polish "government raids" of pro-abortion women's organizations and associated policies of the Catholic

Church that "demonize women" in a way that "fosters a climate of fear"; (6) unprosecuted acid attacks to disfigure Cambodian women; (7) "abusive laws" passed by Myanmar's elected Parliament targeting free speech and journalism; (8) "abusive" labor practices leading to "tragic" deaths in the context of Pakistan's "conservative society"; (9) a European Union antimigration policy leading to "cruel, inhuman, degrading treatment" of detainees in Libya; and (10) UK government cost-cutting pressures that led to a failure to fund legal entitlements to health care for the elderly.

All these reports reflected a high level of professionalism, and there is no reason to doubt their accuracy. All ten featured factual reporting; naming of violations of law, ethical norms, or professional standards of best practice; criticism of government actions or of the failure of government to take steps against abuses; statements clearly intended to exert pressure on responsible parties; and concrete recommendations for remediation. They interviewed locals and whenever possible expressed the harshest criticism in the words of local sources. They tried not to lead with international law and global moral standards, but these were sometimes invoked.

Criticism was aimed at top-level policy makers in every case. In seven instances, criticism also targeted private actors, religious authorities, or working-level government functionaries. In two or three instances, the targets were ordinary private individuals engaging in abnormal but socially tolerated and generally unpunished abusive behavior, such as acid attacks on women, vigilante attacks on minorities, and neglect of the disabled. In six to eight of these reports, criticism of the government rose to the level of shaming. These included attempts to humiliate explicitly ("shameful," "inhuman") or implicitly given the nature of the charge (ordering or condoning torture). In two cases private individuals or mass groups were targeted for denunciation and humiliation (the acid attackers and the vigilantes).

Especially noteworthy is that in all ten cases, the abusive policies or negligence of the government reflected underlying widespread mass attitudes (gender-based bias, neglect of the disabled, prejudice toward an out-group, religion-based opposition to women's health rights, toleration of child labor practices, opposition to immigration, and popular support for policies enacted by elected legislators). Although it is the policy of Human Rights Watch to name and shame state authorities and individual violators rather than entire nations, peoples, religions, or cultures, in these cases, individuals who see their self-esteem and status as linked to that of their national culture may have reason to react as if they themselves were shamed. The strict definitional standard of shaming that targets culturally salient features of a group's fundamental identity is arguably met in the reports on "soul-penetrating cruelty" of Indian cow vigilantes, Polish Catholic Church policies that demonize women, and inhuman behavior of European opponents of immigration, as well as possibly the reports on Japanese transgender law and labor abuses in conservative Pakistan.

Tracing the degree of backlash to these specific reports was complicated by the fact that many were late entrants into ongoing debates, often including intense disputes among local partisans. The implicated states often did not respond at all or else ducked punches using the rope-a-dope strategy of the boxer Muhammad Ali, saying we oppose all violence, or we have already passed a law banning this abuse. In the cow vigilantes case, the task of back-lashing was tacitly delegated to partisan commentators who argued that the offenses did not happen or that the targets of vigilantism deserved it or both simultaneously.[29] Another diversionary maneuver was the whack-a-mole game: Myanmar released two detained Pulitzer Prize–winning journalists who had reported on the military's massacre of Rohingya minority, but then the government ratcheted up repression, announcing that criminal charges would henceforth be brought against objectionable journalists, since the media law was "not harsh enough."[30]

An increasingly prominent form of human rights criticism is the numerical rating and ranking of government performance, such as Freedom House's rat-ings of media freedom and civil liberties or Transparency International's rat-ings of corruption.[31] While numerical ratings and rankings may be seen as less emotionally charged than verbally shaming reports, and therefore less likely to trigger defensive backlash, political scientists Judith Kelley and Beth Sim-mons note that these indicators are not mainly intended for diagnostic pur-poses: "Recent GPIs are relentlessly comparative, suggesting an intention to pressure, shame or provoke competition among states."[32] Compressing com-plex causality to create simple category labels that have shaming power, rank-ings produce leverage through invidious comparisons with low-status or rival states. The empirical chapters of their volume find strong evidence that state actors are successfully shamed or at least highly annoyed by being called out. Their evidence is less clear that rankings per se succeed in stimulating strong social pressure on the noncompliant state.[33] When improved compliance is observed, ranking interacts with necessary facilitating conditions—for ex-ample, the country is a democracy, the message resonates with the values of the country's citizens, and the state has the resources to comply.[34]

These qualifications echo the well-established finding in mainstream human rights scholarship acknowledging that a long list of structural scope conditions constrains the effectiveness of standard advocacy tactics, including shaming.[35] Many studies in the human rights and democracy promotion fields present evidence that shaming works best in easy cases where civil society resistance to the repressive state is already strong,[36] where the state is less able to hide compensatory repressive moves,[37] where the state has signed a treaty consenting to an obligation,[38] or where the state has fewer opportunities to engage in "counter-norming"—for example, invoking sovereignty and illiberal cultural traditions or denouncing the decadence of liberal sex and gender norms.[39] A major shortcoming of the theoretical anchors of shaming tactics, especially evident in the present climate of illiberal backlash, is the lack of a mechanism explaining why liberal human rights advocacy should prevail in shaming contests with illiberal social movements that oppose abortion, refugees, international criminal accountability, rights for women and gays, and the principle of universalism. These illiberal movements argue with considerable impact that it is the liberal view that is shameful when assessed from the standpoint of religious, communal, or national values.

In short, there is ample evidence that human rights advocacy and other progressive discourse employ some forms of shaming, notwithstanding the well-established risk that backlash to shaming can produce outcomes that are counterproductive for rights. In the following sections, I explore the possibility that some highly adept forms of shaming might reduce these risks, for example by relying on guilt rather than shame or by choosing more tolerable shamers or better targets. While some of these tactics may be useful, I conclude that their feasibility is quite limited and does not redeem the idea of shaming as a standard tool of human rights advocacy.

Effects of Shame and Guilt

Whereas early academic writing on shame was, like vernacular discourse, loose in distinguishing it from guilt, more recent social psychological literature typically sees guilt as focused on a bad action, whereas shame is focused on a flaw in the person.[40] This literature (as well as a big stack of self-help books) argues that feeling or instilling guilt is better for the person and for social relationships than feeling or instilling shame. With guilt, you fix your behavior, pay your debt for past mistakes, and you are good to go. With shame, you (and observers) may feel there is something inherently wrong with you, something that may be impossible to fix.[41] For that reason, shaming can easily degenerate into stigmatization by society and lead either to demoralization or backlash on the part of the shamed.[42] The pragmatic prescription for the activist seems clear: when possible, instill a sense of remediable guilt for the behavior, not irremediable shame.

What can be done when the problem isn't just an isolated bad action, and thus amenable to management in the less volatile guilt frame, but an embedded practice, outlook, or character trait, which gives rise to feelings of shame? In principle, good outcomes from shaming can result either from external deterrent constraints, as when authorities or collaborators are shamed into imposing costs on those who misbehave, or from internalized socialization to a prevailing norm, as when a young person or new group member is shamed into conforming appropriately to an established social role.[43] But much social psychological research confirms Lewis's findings about shame mechanisms that produce negative effects. Since "what counts as shameful is . . . contestable," shaming can become a focal point for indignant resistance that justifies counter-normative behavior.[44] Psychologically suppressing or evading acknowledgment of shame may "displace" shame into such forms of hostility as "bullying."[45] Even when shame and shaming do not provoke violent backlash or scapegoating, they still might not induce conformity with desirable norms. Instead, acceptance and internalization of the legitimacy of the shaming can lead to feelings of hopelessness. For example, interviews report that undereducated, impoverished, rural Wisconsin voters realize that Trump won't really help them, but at least he acknowledges their frustrations with declining status and their resentment toward privileged Madison urbanites who they believe hold them in contempt.[46]

Feeling ashamed and being targeted for shaming have been found to correlate with low empathy, social isolation, nonconstructive violence, and self-destructive behaviors.[47] Indeed, sometimes all these pathologies may emerge and feed on each other. As a result, shaming can be a powerful tool of oppression, as in the shaming of gays and of women whose bodies fail to meet ideal standards, yet also a goad to destructive backlash.[48]

So how can the potentially beneficial effects of shame and shaming be tapped without triggering these negative consequences? An important strand of the literature emphasizes the possibility of "shame management," avoiding unintended outcomes from shaming through practices that lead to the reintegration of the shamed person into society.[49] This school of thought, pioneered by John Braithwaite, argues that shaming should be "respectful," distinguish the person from the person's behavior (as with guilt), and culminate in a ceremony that reintegrates the person or group into society. When possible, he argues, shaming should consist of generic reminders of behavioral standards, which often can be more effective if the violators are not singled out for humiliation.[50] At all costs, shaming should avoid the kind of stigmatization that makes "deviance" a "master status trait" of the shamed, which leads to "greater offending," blocking opportunities to participate in legitimate social activities, perceptions of injustice, and subcultures supporting deviance.[51]

In one of the few substantial studies applying social psychological theories of shame and guilt to human rights concerns, Mark Drumbl draws extensively on Braithwaite's concept of reintegrative shaming to argue in favor of the traditional Rwandan local community justice process of *gacaca* as a more effective alternative to the formal postgenocide criminal trials mounted by the International Criminal Tribunal for Rwanda, centered on guilt and punishment.[52] This conceptually sophisticated argument, however, runs counter to a substantial body of empirical research that documents the manipulation of the gacaca process by Paul Kagame's authoritarian regime to selectively control potential Hutu opposition.[53]

In devising strategies to reduce the risk that shaming and guilting will reinforce backlash and deviance, one issue is whether to put a bright spotlight on deviant behavior or to allow the violator a fig leaf to ease social reintegration. Lewis contended that openly confronting shame is needed to avoid dire social and psychological pathology. Erving Goffman's *The Presentation of Self in Everyday Life* (1959) reflects the opposite sensibility. Goffman and his followers analyze embarrassing situations in which social role expectations involving "rights and duties attached to a given status" are disrupted. This occurs when a person faces mixed audiences of different status or degrees of intimacy, placing the person under incompatible role expectations for appropriate behavior.[54] As Cooley had noted, "a man will boast to one person of an action—say some sharp transaction in trade—which he would be ashamed to own to another."[55] Goffman explores the subtle role of tact in navigating such contexts of disrupted expectations and cross-pressures, including tacit collusion by all parties to manage the resulting damage to participants' social images.[56] For Goffman the tactful agreement not to acknowledge the elephant in the room preserves the actors' "performance" of their roles and the social order.

Thinking about government performance indicators as levers of shame, a follower of Goffman might appreciate the tactful subtlety of rating a state's performance relative only to its own past without the embarrassment of an explicit ranking relative to other states, especially compared to intraregional rivals. In contrast, a follower of Lewis might see public comparative rankings of rights compliance as a much-needed reckoning with the truth.[57] Perhaps their different emphasis reflects the fact that Lewis was considering cases of clinical neurosis, whereas Goffman was concerned with normal people navigating awkward social circumstances. How to anticipate and manage the trade-off between tact and forthrightness in varied social settings is a challenge for shaming strategies.

Shame and Shaming in the Context of Group Psychology

The risk of backlash against shaming is even more apparent when group dynamics are taken into account. Scholarship on the social psychology of shame and pride generally accepts that these emotions should be studied at both the individual and the group levels, which are seen as interactive. Exactly how to merge insights at these two levels has been a long-standing subject of scholarly discussion. Tajfel's social identity theory, widely invoked in social psychology as well as in political science, has been at the center of many debates around this issue.[58] Neither social identity theory nor its theoretical variants support the idea that shaming by outsiders to the group will be effective.

Social identity theory, says Tajfel's chief collaborator, John C. Turner, "began as a way of trying to make sense of discrimination between groups and its fundamental *psychological* idea was that where people make comparisons between groups, they seek positive distinctiveness for their in-groups compared to out-groups in order to achieve a positive social identity."[59] In other words, individuals derive self-esteem from the status of their group. As Steven Ward puts it in an application to international relations, members of a respected group feel "pride," whereas members of disrespected groups feel "shame," possibly leading to anger and frustration.[60] In light of what individual-level research suggests about adverse reactions to shame, this basic hypothesis from social identity theory would not seem promising grounds for outsiders to pursue a strategy of human rights shaming.

Tajfel was reacting to Muzafer Sherif's earlier landmark study of group discrimination and conflict, which was grounded in "realistic conflict theory."[61] Sherif's Robbers Cave Experiment randomly assigned twelve-year-old, middle-class, well-behaved boys to two groups, which were pitted against each other in sports and contests, the outcome of which determined the allocation of points and prizes. Competition quickly escalated to negative stereotyping, discrimination, badmouthing, theft, and destruction of property.

Tajfel's experiments showed that discrimination and in-group bias could emerge even without stacking the deck with built-in resource competition or task-related reasons for in-group solidarity. People were randomly assigned to groups that were given no task and no reason to cooperate. These "minimal group experiments" showed that people would allocate resources preferentially to in-group members even when this discrimination would reduce the overall pool of resources for their own group.[62]

But there is an irremediable problem in this research design. Although the artificially formed groups were new and meaningless, the participants were not new to being in groups in general. Like humans everywhere, the participants had spent their whole lives being socialized to the norms and functional benefits of group loyalty. It is impossible to rule out that these habits, rather than some innate need to derive self-esteem from group status, explain in-group bias in these minimal groups.[63] This loophole opens up social identity theory to alternative interpretations.

Without renouncing social identity theory's basic self-esteem account for in-group bias, Turner complains that many applications of the theory have treated self-esteem-driven discrimination in minimal groups as "the end of the story."[64] He worries about the implication that there is nothing that can be done to counter the universal, "automatic" tendency of group members to bias against out-groups as a way of shoring up their personal pride. He argues that the minimal group condition is not representative of the situation of real groups; it is a decontextualized circumstance in which group members can achieve "positive distinctiveness" only through denigrating the out-group.[65] In real situations, according to Tajfel and Turner, the extent of bias in inter-group comparisons depends on variable factors, such as the extent to which individuals identify with an in-group and internalize group membership as part of their self-concept.[66] Also important is whether a particular out-group and a particular dimension of comparison is considered relevant to the group's status. Following this line of conjecture, other scholars have suggested that social identity and self-esteem need not rest on a zero-sum status competition if different groups value different accomplishments.[67]

Turner later supplemented social identity theory with his rather differently grounded "self-categorization" theory. Its most distinctive claim was that in-group bias stems from people's need for socially useful "reality testing," which requires convergence of opinions, attitudes, and factual assumptions of in-group members for the practical purpose of coordinating views of reality with people in their own social sphere. Turner generalized this insight further as "social influence theory," which invokes such mechanisms as socialization, the drive for conformity, the tendency toward social mimicry, and processes of cognitive framing and priming in coordinating in-group members' convergent social identity.[68] Tajfel, however, warns in passing against overstating the force of socialization to in-group favoritism, since cultures may also socialize people to a generalized norm of "fairness," even to out-groups.[69]

Apart from Tajfel's offhand remark about generalized fairness, none of these group psychology insights seem at all promising as a basis for human rights shaming, especially by outsiders. Basic social identity theory seems especially ill-suited, since it combines prejudice against out-groups with a neuralgic sensitivity to issues bearing on group status and individual self-esteem. The self-categorization and social influence approaches are little better insofar as they presume that each community tends to create its own consensus version of the truth, which is bolstered by a raft of reinforcement mechanisms. At best, this could make some in-groups indifferent rather than hostile to assertive social influence attempts by outsiders, but it hardly supports the effectiveness of shaming groups who are listening to their own drummer.

More ambiguous is the case in which a minority is socialized to its own norms and worldview and faces discrimination and stigmatization by a dominant majority identity group. This might make the oppressed minority highly receptive to a third party's universalizing rhetoric that shames the oppressive majority. If the aim is to convince the majority to stop its abusive practices, however, social identity theory would seem to recommend persuasion from inside the majority community based not on shaming but on its own vernacular concepts of decency and justice.[70]

Conditions When Shaming Might Work, and Why This Is Not the Norm

While the core arguments of these theories warrant wariness of adopting shaming strategies, some social psychologists have considered the conditions in which the beneficial effects of shaming might exceed its risks.[71] Shaming seems more likely to succeed when it is aimed at individuals, not the group in general, when shaming is respectful and is directed toward the goal of reintegration into the group, when an insider or a highly respected outsider is doing the shaming, and when the targets of influence are weak identifiers with the in-group and have an aspirational identification with a high-status out-group. Opportunities to target shaming in this way are not easily arranged, however, and when they are absent, shaming tactics often feed populist culture wars.

Shaming works best when it comes from a respected source:[72] "Only groups whose approval an actor values will have this influence."[73] A particularly effective shaming move can occur when the shamer and shamed share a social identity, the shamer points out an inconsistency between their shared identity norms and the shamed actor's deeds, and the shamer can credibly claim that the target's misbehavior is making the in-group as a whole look bad in the eyes of outsiders. Chinese nationalists were very effective in playing this card against Chinese who continued to practice foot binding, which made Chinese culture look backward and barbaric in the eyes of the world.[74] Two causal mechanisms made this work. Christian missionaries put pressure for reform on Chinese who weakly identified with traditional practices, and aspiring Chinese nationalists identified with the technological power of the modern West, if not with its other cultural attributes.[75]

Research that is mainly on guilt rather than shame finds that people who identify weakly with their in-group are more able to accept outsiders' criticism that undermines their social identity. In Germany, high and low identifiers differ in how willingly they acknowledge the Holocaust.[76] Yet, guilting or shaming weak identifiers may mean hitting exactly the wrong targets.

Notwithstanding the circumstances in which shaming from an out-group might succeed, these seem more the exception than the rule. A key goal of counter-norming is to disarm the shaming capacity of out-groups.[77] When cosmopolitan shamers from outside a culture are trying to mobilize individuals' emotions against rights abuses, it is an uphill battle. Jonathan Mercer argues that "group emotion is often stronger than individual emotion," especially among people who strongly identify with the group, as result of the group's validating "emotional consensus" and its policing of those whose emotional responses fail to conform to the expected group norm.[78]

Group leaders may exploit the contest between outside shaming and in-group loyalty to boost their legitimacy in domestic politics.[79] Although professional human rights advocacy normally tries to aim shaming at individual perpetrators or responsible state officials, broader public discourse may indulge in looser parlance that collectivizes shaming discourse, for example generalizing about "lazy Greeks" and "overbearing Germans."[80] Especially when such characterizations are seen as unjust or hypocritical, shaming provokes a collective emotion of "popular outrage."[81] Whether the target of shaming is an individual or a collectivity, "insofar as shaming promotes anger, humiliation and denial rather than empathy, guilt, and responsibility, shaming may harden rather than resolve the problem of human rights violations."[82]

In nationalist rivalries, the dynamic of shaming, humiliation, and grudge holding is common and counterproductive. For example, Peter Gries documents the Chinese obsession with past humiliations by the imperial powers dating back to the Opium Wars and the Japanese occupation. Jennifer Lind shows in turn how endless Chinese demands for ever better Japanese apologies fuel mass Japanese nationalism. Dmitri Trenin interprets contemporary Russian grudges against the West as a comparable reaction to the humiliations suffered at the hands of Western states and liberal reformers after the Cold War.[83]

In an era of populist politics, out-groups can include not only foreigners but also suspect social classes within a society, especially elite cosmopolitans who are seen as traitors to the "true people." Just as higher status groups may engage in class struggle by shaming "deplorable" lower status groups over their violations of elite social norms, conversely the impolite politics of populism can be a weapon of the weak in this struggle to delegitimize elite-dominated politics as usual.[84] The shaming tactics of such culture wars feed populist politics, which often link together the struggles against foreign, immigrant, and domestic elite enemies of the in-group.

Shaming the Masses

An especially important distinction addresses the effectiveness and risks of shaming nonelite or disadvantaged people in a society. The social psychological literature focuses heavily on feelings of shame among powerless, downtrodden, and aggrieved groups that see themselves as not being paid their due respect. For example, the literature on the American Christian Right has for the past two decades traced the mentality of those suffering deindustrialization and the contempt of cultural elites, which has fueled both social disintegration and populist backlash in the culture wars over race, immigration, gender, and sexual rights.[85] Similar points have been made about the Australian right-wing populist antimigration movement spearheaded by Pauline Hanson.[86]

Nor does shaming mass cultural practices have a good record in developing countries. Keck and Sikkink's seminal *Activists beyond Borders*, which explicates the logic of norms-based transnational information politics, includes a telling chapter on the failure of British churches' efforts in the 1920s and '30s to shame their Kenyan parishioners into abandoning the practice of female genital cutting. These shaming tactics played into the hands of independence leader Jomo Kenyatta, who exploited the issue as a prime example of British cultural imperialism, much as his son Uhuru exploits the International Criminal Court today.[87]

When NGOs initially tried to combat genital cutting in the 1990s with blunt shaming tactics based on legalism and universalistic values, they ran into stiff resistance on grounds of religion and custom.[88] Somewhat more effective were arguments offering alternative perspectives from insiders to the local's faith community, combined with health information, the provision of health services, and in a parallel to a tactic of the anti-foot-binding campaign, community pledging not to cut and not to marry girls who were cut.[89] But widespread awareness of anticutting campaigns could produce opposite effects depending on the salience of cutting in the local ethnic identity and on levels of urbanization and education.[90] Ylva Hernlund's field research in Gambia reported that the "local and national debate" was "becoming more polarized and acrimonious," with the reaction to international pressures ranging from "relief that outside help is speeding up the elimination of genital cutting to rage at what is perceived as imperialist meddling."[91]

The Double Whammy: Outsiders versus Insiders Shaming Masses

Despite the dangerous potential for popular backlash, shaming mass groups who retain illiberal attitudes and practices such as early marriage, gender and sexual inequality, child labor, and exploitation of migrant labor is part of the routine work of international human rights advocacy. Not surprisingly, shaming works better when the target already accepts the validity of the values being invoked. In statistical research using standard human rights measurements, Amanda Murdie finds, for example, that international activists' shaming of violations of physical integrity rights, such as torture, has a more positive impact in target states than does shaming over women's rights, because there is a greater divergence between shamers and targets over what women's rights should be.[92]

It is difficult for cultural outsiders to prevail in normative contests with locals when both are trying to use powerful emotions such as shame and humiliation to mobilize mass social movements (or "civil society") to support their cause. For example, Irena Sargsyan and Andrew Bennett study Muqtada al-Sadr's unexpected success in raising and sustaining an illiberal, militant Shi'a mass movement in postinvasion Iraq. They find that "leaders who maintain legitimacy among the local population, connections to indigenous social or religious networks, and a keen understanding of potential supporters' collective identity and memory are more effective in mobilizing followers than their counterparts who lack one or more of these qualities," including in this case Western states and humanitarians, foreign fighters, and returning émigré politicians.[93] They show how local militants like Sadr employ discursive "frames that evoke powerful emotions—anger, humiliation, fear, shared experiences of suffering or injustice, and a desire for honor through self-sacrifice . . . to activate collective emotions and channel them into sustained violence." "Often stressing the threat of impending violence by the outgroup against the ingroup," such militant locals "invoke shared sacred texts or metamorality endorsing violence and self-defense as legitimate in the circumstances; make a plausible claim that collective violence against the outgroup can forestall aggression; are continuously updated to maintain relevance; and are not rebutted by credible counterframes from opponents."[94] In contrast, Western efforts to shame Saddam Hussein for gassing Kurds, Sunni rebels for terror attacks, or Shi'a militias for ethnic cleansing got little traction with their core supporters. Rare US successes, such as the recruitment of Anbar province Sunni tribal fighters to give up insurgency and collaborate with the Iraqi army, came from informative dialogue and material incentives, not shaming.[95]

Shaming Elites and Their Enablers

But what about shaming elites? After all, the mainstream human rights movement and liberal rights ideology more generally prefer to think of powerful elites, especially the oppressive state, as the source of most rights abuse. Even when the abuse is a widespread cultural practice such as child labor or early marriage, rights NGOs prefer to shame state authorities for not doing enough to curtail the practice. Can hard-boiled elites be shamed without worrying about triggering a neurotic backlash?

Some social psychologists argue that elites tend to be too well insulated to be shamed effectively. Politicians are psychologically "hardened" against criticism, which is routine for them. Public relations consultants and corporate image strategists protect economic elites. They are wrapped in a cocoon of free-market ideology according to which the invisible hand determines their policies on labor and the environment. Moreover, they are good at segregating their audiences, giving different performances for supportive peers (viz., Mitt Romney's commiseration at a campaign donors' dinner over the shameful

47 percent of Americans who are freeloading on government handouts) and for the broader public, which sees them going to church on Sunday and mouthing platitudes (Google's "don't be evil").

Nonetheless, there may be chinks in elites' public relations armor of shame-lessness. These mechanisms are likely to work not by shaming the elite perpe-trators but by shaming their family members, peers, or customers, who can put them under pressure to reform.[96] Perpetrators may fear public reputational consequences (purely external shame) or disapproval from an intimate or a respected peer group (an interaction of external and internalized shame). In a final twist, the peer group (e.g., competitors of companies that exploit child labor) might exert pressure to cave in to a boycott to avoid reputational losses for the whole industry or to prevent the violator from getting a competitive advantage by hiring illegal cheap labor.[97] Apple, taking advantage of its busi-ness model, which does not rely on clickbait and fake news, has shamed big tech competitors Facebook and Google, which do.

Whether the elite targets of shaming are states or businesses, it is not simple to disentangle emotion from cunning in their reactions. For example, a 2001 assessment of the impact of shaming China for its human rights record de-scribes a mix of Chinese "indignant white papers," defensive cultural relativ-ism, and generically evasive, pro forma promises of compliance.[98] This litany fits nicely with the typical patterns found in research on the social psychology of the emotion of shame, but it could also fit the logic of a calculating public relations strategy.

Unintended Consequences of Shaming and Their Lock-in

Shamers intend to promote compliance with norms they value, but shaming often triggers unintended consequences, including shame/anger/resentment sequences and denial/hiding/deviance syndromes. In the arena of human rights, recent political science literature documents various mechanisms lead-ing to unintended consequences. Jacob Ausderan notes the tendency of sham-ing by prominent outsiders to rile up in-country constituencies who become newly aware of violations and who overestimate the likelihood of decisive help from outsiders in rectifying these wrongs.[99] He notes that this can heighten government fears of losing control and lead to a crackdown on dissent with an attendant further rise in human rights abuse. For the same reasons, rising press freedom in authoritarian states has been found to increase repressive human rights abuse.[100] In a related pattern, powerful outsiders loudly proclaiming support for abused minorities creates a moral hazard when the oppressed are misled into believing that their resistance will be backed by foreign military intervention.[101]

In accord with the denial/hiding pattern, shaming has been found to lead to "whack-a-mole" shifts from more visible means and targets of repression to less visible ones.[102] When scholars recruited the celebrity journalist/diplomat Samantha Power to a real-life experiment that shamed countries over the incarceration of human rights activists, they found that this high-profile shaming led to a much higher probability of release than for comparable prisoners whose incarcerators were not shamed. This study also found, however, that these one-off successes had no effect on the overall number of political prisoners in the country.[103]

An important question is whether adverse consequences of shaming are not only unintended and undesired, but also unanticipated, avoidable, counterproductive, and long lasting.[104] Human rights activists do not desire or intend pushback from perpetrators, but they do anticipate it under many circumstances. The influential *spiral model* foresees a temporary stage of denial and resistance in response to NGO criticism and foreign economic sanctions targeted on rights-abusing states. In the original version of the theory, this resistance was expected to collapse as the target state became caught in its own self-contradictory rhetoric in the pincer of domestic mobilization and international pressure.[105] A later restatement, however, acknowledged that resistance could be expected to persist under common adverse conditions— in wartime, in autocracies, in states that are too strong or too weak, and in cultures where rights violations are deeply entrenched in society.[106]

Most concerning is the likelihood not only that the syndrome of shame, anger, and resistance will spark short-run hostility to the rights project, but that the social context of shame will play into the hand of illiberal populist movements. Shaming and anger may have the benefit of mobilizing the shamer's own activist base, but they tend to mobilize and lock in the target's base, too.

Through the self-fulfilling prophecy of shaming and the backlash against it, both sides nurture their ideologies of hostility and contempt. Like teenagers who are labeled juvenile delinquents, pariah states and transnational antisystem groups tend to create subcultures of the ostracized, alienated, and isolationist. By "propagating the subcultural ideology," they gain "social recognition of the anti-mainstream."[107] As with the bromance among Putin, Trump, and EU right-wing populists, even nativists and nationalists find reasons to seek out membership in an international club of bad-boy sovereignty hawks. In this terrain of emotion-fueled ideology and political mobilization, humiliation hardens into grudge, and human rights can wind up worse off than they might have been with subtler tactics.[108]

Implications for a Pragmatic Theory of Shaming

The strategy of human rights promotion that gave a central role to "naming and shaming" was based on flawed social and psychological assumptions that are ripe for reassessment. These include several assumptions that bear directly on persuasion through the mobilization of shame: the innate human instinct to recoil at the exploitation of vulnerable people, the resonance of human rights ideas in the normative systems of most cultures, the persuasive potential of "information politics" to leverage the material power of liberal democracies, the sensitivity of most states to their status in an increasingly liberal international order, and the potency of shaming for isolating past perpetrators and deterring new ones. Key assumptions also include contextual factors bearing on the power of liberal social forces: the rising power of global civil society networks, their tendency to support further waves of democratization based on liberal rights principles, the feasibility of building effective domestic and international institutions that embody these mechanisms of accountability, and the inexorable tendency of all this to induce socialization to and internalization of human rights thinking.[109]

The cumulative evidence from well-established social psychology to recent international diplomacy shows that the power of these assumptions has been vastly overestimated. That is why pragmatists reach for shaming so rarely and reluctantly. Given that shaming so easily explodes in the hands of the wielder, pragmatic practitioners turn to different approaches, such as vernacularization of norms and indirect efforts to shore up the practical incentives to voluntarily join the community of rights-supportive states. Human rights are so important that they need to be promoted effectively, not jeopardized by the unintended consequences of shaming.

How should this be done? One approach might follow from the Braithwaite school of reintegrative shaming. Criticism should be respectful, focused on the deed rather than a possibly irremediable character flaw, and aimed at repairing the social rift. It should come from insiders to the social group or outsiders who are widely respected and seen as sympathetic. Forceful reminders of principled standards should be directed to everyone, not just those at risk of misbehavior. Braithwaite notes, however, that this works better in communitarian societies, in situations of cultural uniformity, and among people who are socially very interdependent, which can vary by age, gender, and other individual characteristics.[110] With respect to performance indicators, countries that are falling short of standards should be compared with their own prior performance, not shamed by comparison to neighbors and rivals.[111]

A different approach is based on the vernacularization and localization of norms.[112] Don't lecture; have a two-way conversation about normative standards. Don't insist on using the language of legalism and universalism; acknowledge the validity of local normative systems, and use generic language of respect and fairness that travels across normative systems. Reserve legal talk to subject matter where outsiders have patently legitimate standing, such as respect for legal due process as a condition of doing international business.

Another alternative to shaming is to persuade implicitly by means of narrative. Social psychologists find that people tend to react defensively to overt attempts at persuasion whenever their attitudes are being criticized as wrong or erroneous. Experimental research shows that people's "exclusionary attitudes" change much more readily when they are invited to tell a pertinent personal narrative and to listen to the personal narrative of an implicit persuader.[113] Narrative enlightens and persuades by vividly portraying a character who grapples with a personal challenge, showing—not telling—the consequences of the character's choice. For those who doubt whether this strategy will scale up, Lynn Hunt argues that human rights were "invented" when eighteenth-century novelists published vivid stories that gave insight into the rich, admirable interior life of abused but plucky heroines.[114] A later example is the overwhelming impact of Harriet Beecher Stowe's *Uncle Tom's Cabin* on Northern white attitudes on slavery.

A different tactic is to advance compliance standards not as moral or even legal imperatives but as technical advice for succeeding at a task. Ruling circles in developing countries who are skeptical about human rights are nonetheless keen to gain wealth, technological sophistication, advanced medical services, and other desirable trappings of modernity, many of which flow from advanced liberal democracies and the global capitalist system that liberal states run. States with rights-compliance shortfalls tend to be much more enthusiastic about the looser "rights-based approach" of the UN Sustainable Development Goals, which loosely link good governance targets and indicators to tangible development assistance.[115] This removes human rights advocacy from the realm of shaming and locates it nearer to management consulting. Chayes and Chayes argue that most violations of international law stem from incapacity.[116] Sometimes fixing organizational and technical problems can facilitate rights compliance. For example, Indian police with human rights training argue that rule of law might be fine in principle, but they say they have to torture detainees to protect the rights of crime victims because their local court system is so dysfunctional.[117] In hard cases that lack a favorable setting for human rights shaming, performance indicators might be more usefully designed as constructive diagnostics for institutional reform than as tools for shaming.

Finally, the credibility of human rights as a standard for social behavior depends on how attractive and dynamic the liberal international order is. It also depends in part on whether people can see themselves and their identity group fitting into that order successfully. This means that a top priority for promoting human rights is restoring the health of the liberal order and tailoring rights initiatives to the prevailing conditions in places where abuses are occurring. The social psychology of emotion suggests that transnational shaming is unlikely to make a constructive contribution to those efforts, and indeed will be counterproductive.

9

Entrenched Abuses of Women and Children

AMONG THE MOST vexing problems facing contemporary human rights activism are culturally entrenched, highly decentralized social practices that sustain endemic abuses of women and children.[1] Diffuse cultural resistance to reform makes these especially hard cases for mainstream approaches that feature legalism, moralism, and universalism. These issues might also seem challenging for a pragmatic approach that highlights bargaining over the organization of social power. But in fact, the pragmatic social power approach proves valuable in analyzing these decentralized practices and suggesting practical solutions that are tailored to complex social dilemmas.

In this chapter, I diagnose the problem of female genital mutilation (or cutting) as a much debated, intensively studied example of a socially diffuse, culturally sustained human rights abuse.[2] Just as I have used the concept of social equilibrium in previous chapters as a key analytical tool of pragmatic social power theory, so too have scholars used the concept of a perverse collective action equilibrium to study female genital cutting. Decentralized mechanisms such as market competition, anarchic security struggles, or diffuse social norms may trap individuals into conforming to patterns of socially destructive behavior. As with violence in the Hobbesian state of nature, food hoarding in a time of short supply, or a run on a bank, most or all actors might prefer to take steps to move to a cooperative equilibrium, but individuals cannot act on these preferences without guarantees that most or all other actors will simultaneously and credibly commit themselves to cooperate, too.[3] In cultures that practice female genital cutting, this kind of collective action dilemma arises from the marriage market, which requires girls to be cut.

The prominent nongovernmental organization Tostan and some scholars have proposed that the decisive solution to this dilemma is simultaneous pledging within a village not to cut daughters and not to marry women who are cut. While this approach has achieved some success, the wider angle of vision provided by the social power theory is needed to devise pragmatic strategies across varied contexts. Detailed research on strategies for combating female genital cutting echoes the findings of earlier chapters. The level of social modernization, including the development of its characteristic institutions and norms, establishes a context that conditions the effectiveness of anticutting strategies and outcomes. Strategizing for advancing rights requires tailoring tactics to fit the power, interests, and culture of actors in that context. Activist persuasion strategies that ignore local context, norms, and discourse lead to backlash, which sometimes further entrenches the practice of cutting.

Although the practice of cutting is to some extent sustained by the perverse collective action dilemma of the marriage market, this does not mean that leaping from the cutting equilibrium to a postcutting outcome can be quickly achieved by persuasion and pledging. The practice is entrenched by an interlocked set of conditions, including the lack of material and institutional preconditions of modern social organization, ethnic identity myths in which cutting serves as a salient master variable, and embedded cultural understandings that link cutting to social roles and individual interests. As with the political transitions and anticorruption measures discussed in chapter 4, the larger social system in which cutting is embedded can be unwound only through processes of change that are multidimensional and staged over time.

Focusing on the example of female genital cutting has some advantages, but also imposes some limitations. On the plus side, this topic has attracted a great deal of systematic empirical study, including statistical analysis as well as ethnographic fieldwork, much of it employing concepts of social dilemmas and low-level equilibria. This subject offers rich data to explore whether my arguments generalize to grassroots social processes in settings with weak formal institutions. On the limitations side, the particular abuses examined in this chapter are mainly problems of less modern societies, so the context of relatively weak state capacity limits these cases' relevance for studying strategies that require effective state interventions. This also means that the observed effects of variations in modernization are based mainly on comparisons within poor countries. Still, we should not think that rights abuses related to diffuse social practices appear only in traditional societies. Harassment and shaming on social media are prominent examples that appear in developed societies.

Later in the chapter, I briefly compare and contrast female genital cutting with the rather different mechanisms that lock in the equilibria of early marriage and child labor. Notwithstanding important differences that are relevant to the design of pragmatic strategies, all three of these abuses are sustained by perverse, low-level equilibrium traps. All three require pragmatic rights advocates to take processes of modernization into account and to tailor tactics to the power, interests, and culture of actors, knowing that attempted leaps from the traditional equilibrium to a reformed equilibrium risk backlash. Only through multidimensional and sequenced change are rights likely to emerge.

Female Genital Cutting as a Conventional Equilibrium Trap?

Female genital cutting is a widespread practice affecting about 90 percent or more of women and girls aged fifteen to forty-nine in Egypt, Sudan, Somalia, Eritrea, Djibouti, Mali, Guinea, and Sierra Leone, with substantial but varying incidence in a contiguous band of states across central Africa, as well as in Yemen, Iraqi Kurdistan, and Indonesia, according to 2016 data. Two-thirds of all women who have undergone cutting live in just four countries: Egypt, Ethiopia, Nigeria, and Sudan.[4] The practice varies by ethnicity. It is practiced by some Muslim and Christian groups, but not by others. Declining in recent years in some places, notably Kenya and Liberia, it has been holding steady or even increasing elsewhere, such as southern Chad.[5] In some cultures, it is part of a coming-of-age ritual for girls around puberty or before marriage, but in other cultures, cutting involves no such ritual. Increasingly cutting occurs at earlier ages. The form of cutting varies from the excision of only an exposed portion of the clitoris, to removal of the labia as well, and in the most extreme form, called *infibulation*, the sewing up of the vaginal orifice, as practiced especially in Somalia and some other East African societies. Normally justified as a measure to reduce female sexual pleasure and thus promiscuity, these usually painful cutting procedures are well documented to be associated with increased medical risks, including complications of childbirth. Not surprisingly, this has been the subject of a huge amount of activist mobilization among international rights activists; many eradication efforts, including a multiyear fifteen-country $37 million UNICEF/UNFPA campaign that began in 2008, and a considerable amount of scholarly research and empirical program evaluation.[6]

From the 1920s on, anticutting campaigns by colonial administrations, Christian churches, and later NGOs and African states have taken many forms, ranging from criminalization to excommunication to health education. Some of these went spectacularly awry. The Kenyan independence movement effectively seized on this attempt to suppress traditional culture as evidence of Britain's high-handed imperialism, and cutting continued. British authorities, seeing cutting as a barbaric custom that reinforced resistance to colonial rule, moved to criminalize female genital cutting in 1956 at the time of the Mau Mau rebellion.[7] Regional councils of indigenous elite men, not wanting to alienate the colonial administration at a politically delicate time, lacked finesse in announcing and enforcing the ban. Thousands of teenage girls, fearing they could never become married adults unless cut, fled to the forests to inflict improvised mutilations on themselves. Making matters worse, indigenous male authorities imposed and pocketed heavy fines on the girls' families.

International NGO campaigns in the 1990s likewise struggled to find a persuasive formula for success. Many were initially guided by the influential *Hoskin Report*'s exaggerated claims of medical consequences, which failed to distinguish among the various types of cutting and blamed the practice entirely on oppressive patriarchy.[8] These persuasion campaigns sometimes led with Western rights talk. They would ask what rights daughters should have, and parents would reply "the right to be circumcised."[9] Failing to get the knack of vernacularization, activists in one instance were evicted from a Somali refugee camp in Kenya at gunpoint.[10]

Faced with this kind of vivid feedback, program design quickly improved. Activists switched to science-based health information rather than international human rights law as their initial pitch, often combined with the provision of actual health services. Even this was not an easy sell. Women in societies where everyone is cut lacked a baseline for comparison. They had no idea that fistulas and other dire gynecological conditions were long-term consequences of cutting rather than just part of being female. Even when medical facts were accepted, activists usually found that this would change parents' views about the desirability of cutting their daughters but not their decision to cut.

For Muslims this decision was often due to the belief that Islam required cutting. Resourceful activists were ultimately able to convince local imams to allow them to show videotapes of prestigious Cairo religious authorities who explained that the Koran does not endorse, let alone require, cutting. Although some recalcitrants claimed that this was covered in a "secret book" of the

Koran, which was held to be all the more compelling precisely because it was secret, many accepted that they did not have to cut for religious reasons.[11] Some minority Islamic subsects, relying on their own particular interpretations of the prophet Mohammed's oral teachings, did endorse or allow cutting.[12] But even among parents who were persuaded that their version of Islam didn't require cutting, most still didn't change their behavior.

This stubborn pattern seemed to support sociologist Gerry Mackie's theory that cutting was locked in as a conventional requirement for marriage. He advanced a two-part argument to account for this convention and its staying power. He argued that female genital cutting, particularly the extreme so-called pharaonic form of infibulation, originated as a method by which the Egyptian pharaohs and other polygynous elites attempted to control the sexuality and reproduction of their harem. He analogized to the practice of foot binding, which he argued had arisen (along with eunuchs) in the Chinese imperial court for the same reason. Others have argued similarly that cutting was a strategy for ensuring virginity in the course of the transportation of enslaved females from East and West Africa to buyers in the Near East. Mackie argued that foot binding and female genital cutting spread to middling and lower orders of society as a way of increasing the chance of upward mobility for daughters through marriage to higher status husbands.

There are reasons to question some of these arguments about the origins and function of cutting. While it is true that reduced sexual desire and chastity are often given as reasons by defenders of the practice, the evidence that cutting actually has these effects is weak. In well-executed surveys in a region of Kenya where the incidence of cutting is 95 percent and in another region where it is much lower, only 1 or 2 percent of respondents gave "protects virginity" or "prevents premarital sex" as a reason for the practice.[13] In another ethnic group, girls are free to have sex, but not to get pregnant, before they are married, and then just before marriage, they must be cut.[14] Today's practices and rationales seem quite varied, and the "pharaonic" origins story and its functional rationale seem too pat.

Ultimately, though, Mackie's argument is that it doesn't matter why people started the convention linking cutting to marriageability. Regardless, this decentralized decision rule locks in a perverse equilibrium: even those parents who want to give up the practice for medical reasons fear that a failure to conform to the cultural norm of cutting will make their daughters unmarriageable.[15] Mackie proposed this theory as a result of observing the early, partial successes in the 1990s of the Tostan program, which uses health information and community dialogue to change individual preferences and then follows up with public pledging not to cut girls and not to marry girls who have been cut.[16] Campaigns against foot binding in late nineteenth-century China successfully used similar public pledges.[17]

Note the key features of the pure case of this kind of collective action dilemma. Individuals prefer to switch to the new rule, but only if others do as well. Individuals may have reason to doubt the compliance of others. A method of overcoming this doubt must make everyone's preference for the collectively superior outcome transparent, and it must provide a compelling mechanism for guaranteeing that each individual is committed to act on that preference, overcoming the fear that others might not. In a face-to-face community that operates through iterated acts of reciprocity, such as a self-contained village marriage market, a solution might rely on an informal, individualized mechanism, such as pledging one's honor.[18] In a larger, more complex community, compliance with the socially beneficial rule might require collective agreement to create some institution to incentivize compliance—for example, police and courts to punish violators, insurance to compensate steadfast cooperators who get left holding the empty bag, or monitoring systems to let people know in real time whether others are still cooperating.

Pledging not to bind feet and to marry only girls with natural feet eliminated foot binding; so too, Mackie pointed out, pledging seemed to be working with cutting. The Tostan NGO's method to end cutting was a simultaneous face-to-face ritual of the people in the village, who constituted the relevant marriage market. With Chinese foot binding, pledging was not literally simultaneous, but it spread very rapidly at the end of the nineteenth century, beginning with converts to Christianity, who formed a discrete marriage market that was influenced by foreign standards of what constituted civilized behavior. Missionaries worried, however, that the association of anti–foot binding with Christianity was ultimately limiting and stigmatizing its spread as a foreign influence. Further success came by persuading non-Christian literati that foot binding hurt China's status and exposed it to ridicule.[19] The urban upper strata led the way in adopting this change.[20]

Some evidence seems consistent with Mackie's argument. For example, the remote region in Kenya with 95 percent incidence of cutting reported only 2 percent believing that religion required cutting, 1 percent that it prevented premarital sex, and 6 percent believing that it improved hygiene, but 59 percent saying that it made marriage possible. Introducing some ambiguity into the interpretation, however, 68 percent said it was the path to adulthood, 44 percent that it gained the respect of the community, and 32 percent that it was a step to having children. Only 10 percent said that it should stop.[21]

Another source of ambiguity for Mackie's convention account is that the Tostan protocol begins with a sustained period of health education and group discussions about ethical and cultural issues, including human rights as well as local perspectives. Pledging comes only at the end of a long process. Indeed, experience has shown that longer interventions—sometimes three years—are more effective. Moreover, it's not clear that there is a credible mechanism to ensure that the pledging isn't just cheap talk for some participants. Some experts think that the real work is done by health education and community discussion rather than the binding force of the pledging.

There is also strong evidence that an attempted instant leap from one equilibrium to the opposite is not always necessary and might sometimes hinder change. In Gambia, where the nationwide incidence of cutting is about three-fourths, regions and villages often intermingle religious and ethnic groups that do and do not practice cutting. Intermarriage is becoming fairly common.[22] As a result, individuals have an option to exit the convention.[23] Among the Maasai of Kenya, there is considerable regional variation in the incidence of the practice across remote areas where it is universal, urbanized areas where it is rare, and transitional areas where individuals make different choices. In the latter situation, public pledging would be a hindrance to change. Surveys show that people often present themselves differently to different audiences, leading more worldly acquaintances to assume that they oppose cutting while leading militant traditionalists to think that they approve of cutting.[24] In Senegal, where Tostan's pledging strategy has had its greatest impact, cutting is a minority practice of only about a quarter of the population, and it has been systematically opposed by the country's moderate Sufi elites and clerics. Skeptics of pledging contend that Tostan's success there may be due to the broader social and ideological climate and to individual exit options.[25]

Based on extensive statistical and ethnographic research in several countries over two decades, the anthropologist Bettina Shell-Duncan and her co-authors have proposed an alternative social convention theory based on the centrality of women's networks.[26] Contrary to the earlier assumption that cutting is imposed by patriarchy, they point out that men are only indirectly involved in decisions about cutting. They do not make the arrangements for the cutting and are typically ill-informed about its health effects. A major 2013 UNICEF study found that the attitudes about cutting of men and women are generally similar in any given community. If anything, men are likely to be more flexible and pragmatic about its details, weighing in only insofar as it affects questions of "social acceptance."[27]

In a three-year mixed-method study to test predictions of social convention theory, beginning in 2004 in Senegal and Gambia, Shell-Duncan's team found that that female genital cutting is "most often only indirectly related to marriageability via concerns over preserving virginity." Moreover, they found, "When respondents did assert that circumcision was important or necessary for a good marriage, it was most often not because men refused to marry uncircumcised women, but because an uncircumcised woman marrying into a circumcising family would face difficult relationships with other women in her marital home."

Instead they argue for the importance of an alternative "intergenerational peer convention" among women. They "propose that being circumcised serves as a signal to other circumcised women that a girl or woman has been trained to respect the authority of her circumcised elders and is worthy of inclusion in their social network. In this manner, FGC facilitates the accumulation of social capital by younger women and of power and prestige by elder women." While this mechanism may lack the inexorability of a Mackie-style perverse equilibrium trap, they conclude that their "findings support Mackie's assertion that expectations regarding FGC are interdependent; change must therefore be coordinated among interconnected members of social networks."[28]

Modernization and the Social Equilibrium of Cutting

A more encompassing interpretation might see the whole package of fundamental norms of premodern society as sustaining the perverse equilibrium trap of female genital cutting. Following Tilly, we could see this practice as part of the overall pattern of social order based on discrimination by ascriptive categories such as family lineage, ethnic identity, and gender.[29] It is not just marriageability or virginity norms that lock in the practice but a self-reinforcing pattern of social relations that includes the hegemony of identity-group norms and gender hierarchies. In this view, the fact that women are often the immediate enforcers of FGC is not evidence against the argument that the larger social order based on patriarchy and identity hierarchies accounts for the practice. From this perspective, the likelihood that traditional abuses such as female genital cutting will fall into disuse depends on ideas about individual autonomy, equality, and personal rights being backed up by social power in a contract-based society.[30] That said, only a few traditional societies practiced female genital cutting. Elsewhere practices such as purdah or foot binding arguably substituted for cutting functionally or symbolically.

Modernization appears to have played an important role in the demise of foot binding. The rise of textile manufacturing in China created opportunities for lucrative employment of women outside the home, creating incentives for middle- and lower-class families, including non-Christians, to abandon foot binding.[31] At the same time, nationalist rhetoric around the Boxer Rebellion promoted the argument that foot binding was hobbling the power of the Chinese nation in its struggle against aggressive imperialist states. Whereas in Kenya the continuation of female genital cutting was promoted by the nationalist independence movement, in China nationalist modernizers opposed foot binding.

This modernization argument is not simple to confirm or refute because of its multifaceted nature, which encompasses material, institutional, and normative changes that unfold over time at varying tempos with intermittent reversals.[32] Moreover, its lock-in mechanism is not as straightforward to conceptualize and observe as the collective action dilemmas of game theory. Nonetheless, research on the conditions that sustain or undermine female genital cutting has often included material and cultural variables that support the modernization perspective.

From a bird's eye view, the pattern of female genital cutting seems to strongly support the modernization hypothesis insofar as countries where cutting is widespread are almost all extremely poor ones, and on average poorer communities in poor countries have a higher incidence of the practice. Nonetheless, this tendency is sometimes trumped by ethnic differences that do not correlate with modernity. Moreover, experts disagree about why modernization has this effect.

Within most African countries, indicators of modernity and development tend to correlate with lower rates of cutting, some strongly, some only mildly. In addition to greater wealth, also important are urbanization, the mother's level of education, her participation in the labor market, and access to professional health care and news media.[33] Women working outside the home for pay were found to be 43 percent less likely to have their daughters cut, according to a 2002 study that remains one of the most systematic.[34]

Comparing across African countries that practice cutting, however, economic development does not automatically bring a lesser incidence of cutting. Cutting is nearly universal in the richest per capita practicing society, Egypt.

In Nigeria, ethnicity trumps household wealth and urbanization: the wealthier, more urbanized, Christian Yoruba practice cutting, but poor, rural Muslim ethnic groups are less likely to do so.[35] As some ethnic groups in southern Chad have recently become wealthier, they have adopted the practice as a symbol of their increased status and possibly as a tactic for marrying up.[36]

Experts who accept the impact of modernization may differ in interpreting the causal mechanism. Sometimes the mother's income outside the home is seen as supporting a story of escape from patriarchy, but data showing that men are as likely or more likely to oppose cutting than women cast doubt on this interpretation. Other possibilities are that the working mother is better educated, more aware of information and attitudes in the wider society, or more able to assert herself against her community's hierarchy of older, more traditional women.

Explaining the effect of urbanization is similarly complex. Shell-Duncan notes that "rural areas are more likely to have kin-based communities with limited cultural diversity, making it difficult to deviate from longstanding social norms and conventions. Urban settings, by contrast, may be more culturally diverse, providing an opportunity to interact with a greater assortment of people, who may be both practicing and non-practicing. In urban settings, social ties may be broader and less linked to home communities, and negative social sanctions for non-adherence to FGM/C may be less common and effective."[37] Karisa Cloward, in a close study of more rural and more urban Maasai communities, emphasizes that access to news media or simply conversation in a large town's marketplace can change attitudes dramatically.[38] An Ethiopian survey study speculated that the greater incidence in rural areas "may be due to the tight tradition, religious association and loose legal concerns in the rural areas."[39]

The informational account is strongly supported by Elizabeth Boyle's 2002 research, which shows that education and especially access to international media had a more substantial impact on attitudes and, to some extent, behavior than did wealth. This, she argues, shows that the "world culture" version of modernization theory is more powerful than the strictly materialist version.[40] One major qualification is that international media exposure reduced cutting only for Christians, not Muslims.[41] Nonetheless, the latter pattern may be in flux. Janice Boddy's more recent ethnographic research shows that as rural northern Sudanese moved to Khartoum during the oil boom, young women's access to global communications media and education—including higher education—skyrocketed, outstripping young men's. These young women learned that Islam does not require female genital cutting and that it causes significant health complications. They watched Oprah Winfrey condemn "FGM" on TV. Many of them abandoned the practice.[42]

After a couple of decades of intense activism and debate over female genital cutting throughout Africa, awareness of the controversy is widespread even among those who continue the practice.[43] While economic and social modernization in most settings does undermine the practice of cutting, modernization may work through its complex effect on social power relations, social conventions, networks, and the salience of group identities.

Spoilers, Interests, and Coalitions

People's personal stake in perpetuating female genital cutting derives almost entirely from the social relations surrounding the practice. What matters to them is the role the practice plays in structuring the terms of power, status, group boundaries, and social opportunity. This is very different from the way economists talk about individuals' personal stake in early marriage. In that realm, scholars typically note the direct interest men may have in marrying younger, more malleable girls who offer more years of potential childbearing and labor. Comparable arguments about the perceived direct benefits of FGC, such as reducing promiscuity, are far less persuasive.

Activist strategies against cutting have targeted any of several categories of people who are seen as sustaining the practice. One such group are traditional circumcisers, who conventionally had been older women who used crude instruments in dubiously hygienic procedures for pay, but now may sometimes include younger, better trained women who use antibiotics. Strategies to induce them to give up the practice include paying them to turn in the knives they use for the procedure, legally banning the practice of cutting, offering them compensation to engage only in midwifery and ceremonial services, and involving the circumcisers in projects that mark and validate their changed attitude toward the practice.[44] These incentives have sometimes been combined with attempts at normative persuasion using vernacular concepts, for example, arguments that traditional coming-of-age and chastity practices are already commonly violated by early cutting and by pregnancy before marriage. None of these strategies, however, has worked well in situations where market demand for cutting continued. In these circumstances, practitioners would switch from public cutting ceremonies to back-alley operations, typically at younger ages, pocketing the incentive monies paid not to cut as well as the cutting fees. Claudie Gosselin argues that collecting fees is only a small part of the incentive for the circumcisers, whose position of status in the community and practical networking opportunities hinge on this role, which they are therefore loath to give up.[45]

Local imams are likewise seen as potential spoilers who do not want to surrender their authority to interpret Islamic doctrine to their community. Some activists have found, however, that religious leaders are eager to get NGO health clinics, and they will allow discussion of religious teachings that are carried out in religiously appropriate ways.[46] Thus, the stumbling block is not cutting per se but its implications for authority and status in the community. Men in general, including politicians and Christian church leaders, generally prefer not to get too involved in the issue, since expressing a clear view either way could stir up opposition.[47]

Older women in general constitute another group of alleged culprits. This includes the mothers who take the lead in cutting decisions as well as female elders in lineage networks who act as guardians of tradition. Controlling access to adulthood, marriage, and reproduction is a major source of women's status, legitimacy, and leverage in the community vis-à-vis younger women, who are sometimes better educated, and vis-à-vis men. Michelle Johnson reports how forcefully Muslim women defend the practice, blaming Christian opportunists who pander to get NGO money, scoffing at animist totem pole worshipers who do not cut, and alleging that non-Muslims seek to take away Muslim women's ritual purity and thus their right to pray.[48] Nonetheless, Shell-Duncan's field research team in Senegambia reports many instances of pragmatism on the part of older women who are sensitive to intergenerational differences and cultural cross-pressures in mixed communities. These older women endorse compromises that maintain their position as gatekeepers of cultural change. Although younger, better educated, urbanized, working mothers are normally expected to be in the vanguard of change, the team found that "pressure to conform was not reduced in our urban study site," and "across all study locations it was younger women who were most conservative regarding change in or abandonment of FGM/C. . . . As young women marry and move to their marital home, FGM/C signals 'insider' status among women in the extended family, and thereby helps young women access social support."[49]

Elizabeth Boyle argues that different strategies should come into play in persuading individuals as opposed to mobilizing coalitions. She suggests that concrete, narrowly targeted persuasive frames such as health effects might work on some individuals, whereas more complex, "elaborated" frames involving cultural tradition or modernity may be more effective in creating common ground across a larger coalition.[50] Issue linkage to development goals desired by everyone is also effective in forging coalitions. What works, says Boyle, is not law but "when trusted organizations work with communities to raise overall living standards as well as to combat FGCs."[51]

In short, many constituencies have an interest in the continuation of cutting, but those interests are largely a function of the role that cutting plays in the status system of these societies. Modernization is eroding that role, but in complex ways that are mediated by culture. As the social constructivists have explained, both interest and power are to some extent socially constructed, and this is especially the case in the issue of female genital cutting. Strategies of advocacy need to take into account the interaction of these structural, political, and cultural dimensions.

Cultural and Institutional Context, Normative Persuasion, and Backlash

Shell-Duncan's statistical analysis robustly supports her conclusion that "measures of ethnicity explain more variation and change in FGM/C prevalence rates than any other sociodemographic variable."[52] The respondents' ethnicity is a better predictor of their stance on female genital cutting than age, wealth, education, urbanization, gender, or religion. This is manifestly true in a descriptive sense, but how should we understand this fact?

Karisa Cloward argues that the persistence of the practice of cutting depends on its "salience" in the culture.[53] She cites Janice Boddy's research, which showed that Sudan's extreme form of infibulation takes place in a culture in which cutting not only makes a girl marriageable, but is "a necessary condition of becoming a woman, of being able to use her one great gift, fertility," in a society completely polarized between the sexes.[54] Cutting serves as a master identity symbol for the social group. In this cultural terrain, Boyle notes that "entrenched beliefs about a practice despite contrary information are often difficult to change because the cost of dissent is too high."[55] When practices are entrenched in less modernized communities, intermarriage with noncutting out-groups is likely to be rare, and if it occurs, the out-group wife will usually agree to be cut.[56] Cloward notes that conditions for cross-cultural dialogue over cutting are inauspicious when the practice is highly salient not only for the culture that practices it but also for the international activist community, as it has been lately.[57] In diaspora in the West, where maintaining cultural identity may become a heightened concern, the salience of cutting as a marker of ethnicity or religion may reinforce the practice.[58]

Cloward stresses the agency of actors in African societies that practice cutting. Not "slaves to tradition," these "cultures are always being reinterpreted and adapted" in ways that are "inherently political," often reflecting an "obsession with modernity."[59] Her Kenyan research site illustrates how politicization can be a two-edged sword. During the independence movement, Jomo Kenyatta ratcheted up the symbolic salience of cutting for the national identity, forging a coalition between opponents of colonialism and advocates of cutting.[60] Slamming the interference of missionaries and Europeans as an "attack on this country's old customs to disintegrate their social order and thereby hasten their Europeanization," Kenyatta called circumcision "the very essence of an institution which has enormous educational, social, moral, and religious implications."[61] In contrast, his successor as president, Daniel Arap Moi, sought to demote the issue and delink it from modernity by calling it a "useless" practice.[62] This gambit backfired, however, as Moi's public rebuke led more girls to be cut at an earlier age in clandestine locations.[63]

Strategies of persuasion to abandon cutting need to consider the complexities of this social and political environment. Unintended consequences have often followed from legal bans on cutting and inept persuasion strategies. In cases of perverse equilibria, criminalization attempts to suppress the human rights violation without addressing the underlying logic that motivates it and can therefore result in deeper entrenchment.[64] In the area of female genital cutting, for instance, criminalization has led to surreptitious cutting that may increase health risks. In colonial Sudan, the prospect of legislation that punished specific forms of cutting led families to have their daughters undergo the procedure before the legislation was enacted. Following widespread public protests that resulted after the first arrests, the ban was modified to allow for some cutting to be done by professional midwives.[65]

On the other hand, pragmatic colonial vernacularization strategies could also lead in unanticipated directions. Janice Boddy reports that the British women who founded Sudan's first midwifery school, knowing that native birth attendants also performed female circumcisions, "took a pragmatic stance. They did not support a peremptory ban on the procedure but, controversially, taught a less damaging operation using sterile implements, local anesthetics, and antiseptic solutions. In this way they hoped to 'reduce harm,' and gradually bring about abandonment of genital cutting as Sudanese became better educated. Because few midwifery trainees were literate, the sisters elected to work with rather than against local knowledge, . . . incorporating words from 'women's vocabulary.' They built discursive bridges between local understandings and their own by creating scientific analogies to the objects and acts of Sudanese daily life with which women's bodies are metonymously linked," referring to their bodies as a "house" or "sealed tin" that needed to be closed off against germs.[66] Their lesson book advised, "Should a midwife do circumcisions . . . she must perform the operation with all cleanliness just as she would a labour case, and attend the case daily for seven days, or more if necessary, in order to avoid infection of the wound." Boddy concludes, "such counsel insinuated biomedicine into local practice, thereby wrapping 'tradition' in biomedical mystique, lending it new authorizations . . . that seemed likely to ensure the custom's resilience."[67]

More recently in Gambia, Sierra Leone, and Guinea-Bissau, bans on cutting led to some form of public protest and backlash.[68] In Egypt, cutting declined more slowly after its legal ban in 2007.[69] Even for families that wanted to comply with the law, criminalization failed to solve the problem of the marriage market, so families turned to medicalization or went underground, avoiding public ceremonies.[70] Yet, legal bans have not always triggered backlash or evasion when the timing was right. Shell-Duncan notes, for example, that "the passage of the law in Kenya did not, however, draw the sort of mass outcries and public protests witnessed during colonial rule because it has been preceded by a fundamental shift in the perceived boundaries of parental and extended family rights toward children in relation to those of the government and church institutions."[71]

Backlash against outsider activists' shaming of those who practice cutting has also been a problem. Michelle Johnson's research among the Muslim Mandinga of Guinea-Bissau in the 1990s reports that an anticutting campaign attributed to educated non-Muslims and foreign aid organizations spurred "the largest girls' initiation ceremony in the history of the Oio region."[72] One of the reasons for trying to include traditional circumcisers in status-affirming anticutting projects is that "otherwise, they might join the active and possibly growing pro-excision movement in Mali."[73] Field interviews with men as well as women report that "in some communities deep resentments over the 'criminalization of culture' simmer just below the surface and boiled over when the subject was raised."[74] Boyle concludes, "The depiction of FGC as child abuse did little to generate local support for abandonment. . . . Rather than directly contest a practice from an outside perspective, successful approaches recruited and leveraged high status individuals who legitimized the abandonment of a long-standing practice."[75]

Persuasion efforts take place in an institutional context. In the countries that practice female genital cutting, that context is almost always institutional weakness of the state and its capacity for legal enforcement. Another limiting factor is that institutionalized civil society actors are often beholden to international donors and partners, or they are satellites of the state, which makes them suspect as credible agents of cultural change. These international obligations may also limit their use of vernacular styles of persuasion. A final feature of the institutional landscape is that political parties and officials are organized around patronage networks that are designed to discriminate on the basis of ethnicity, language, religion, or lineage. While the external trappings of multiparty democracy in these states may look superficially like modernity, underneath the veneer, the basic operating principles are those of a patronage-based society.[76] In a system that is not yet organized around rights, activism aimed at installing rights principles needs a strategy that begins by working with whatever local interests, networks, and cultural materials can be adapted to the purpose.

Local tailoring of rights solutions, however, is in tension with NGO practitioners' incentive to find solutions that can "scale up." The normal motivation for this is to gain efficiency in training and implementation through portable best practices. An example is the transitional-justice-in-a-box kit that NGOs try to bring to every postconflict and postauthoritarian environment.[77] For human rights organizations, having standardized, approved approaches helps keep the brand's reputation pure and consistent. It also facilitates the training of activists who can function as interchangeable parts across different cultural settings. Sometimes this has led to absurd NGO policies, such as the fad for promoting "alternative rites of passage" even in cultures that do not associate cutting with becoming adult and have no such traditional rite.[78]

Effective human rights campaigns may need to integrate grassroots and top-down approaches, but the emphasis they place on each strategy should differ according to the social context in which they operate. When state enforcement capacity is weak and when human rights problems are sustained by decentralized collective action, a grassroots persuasion approach is critical.[79] This means methods that focus on community empowerment, consensus building, and collective decision making.[80] In CARE's work on female genital cutting, it reports that its strategies are most effective when it employs an "inductive (bottom-up)" approach.[81] In Ethiopia, for instance, CARE workers began by asking community members to delineate their own list of rights. When they found that respondents had listed children's "right to be circumcised," they jettisoned their headquarters' template and designed a health education campaign that would resonate using different techniques.[82]

When campaigns do not use grassroots tactics, they risk having a fleeting impact. In a small minority Sabini community in Uganda, for example, one NGO tried to get local community leaders to publicly condemn the practice, and then used awards ceremonies for those leaders who did so. The NGO reported that while the majority of girls refrained from cutting in the first year, the following year the practice resumed at its initial rate.[83]

Sometimes, however, top-down strategies are needed to win over local spoilers. Some tactics may simply entail securing consent. One NGO in Egypt, the Coptic Evangelical Organization for Social Services (CEOSS), is said to be effective partly because of its policy of waiting for a written request from local community leaders before initiating its campaign.[84] Other top-down tactics might require more actively soliciting the cooperation of local elites. For instance, after facing violent backlash among Somali refugees in Kenya, CARE chose to set up camp in places where it could work with local Muslim religious authorities. CARE came to recognize the need to continuously involve religious leaders once its programs are under way, for instance by encouraging them to discuss and decide on a position on religion and FGC, or asking them to protect those in their communities who reject cutting practices.[85]

Medicalization as a Modernizing Adaptation

If community pledging is a pragmatic solution that seems to have some affinity with the communal nature of traditional society, medicalization of cutting would seem to have an affinity with the individualism and scientific rationality of a society that is in partial transition to modernity. In medicalization, parents who are trapped in the social necessity of cutting their daughters can attempt to reduce its health risks by having a medical doctor or other health professional undertake the procedure. This is a widely and increasingly used option, available especially in Egypt, Sudan, and Nigeria, affecting 16 million girls.[86] Egyptian mothers who are wealthier, better educated, and more urbanized are more likely to arrange medicalized cutting for their daughters.[87]

Proponents tend to see this as a method for moving toward safer, less extensive types of cutting, and possibly a slippery slope of norms change leading to the gradual abandonment of the practice. Skeptics argue that medicalization may be an unintended consequence of advocacy tactics that heavily stress health consequences.[88] They believe medicalization perpetuates the practice. They report cases where medicalized infibulation has occurred.[89] Empirically, medicalization has occurred alongside substantial declines in rates of cutting in Kenya, but any causal relationship is hard to judge. Based on limited data, medicalization seems associated with a trend toward less severe forms of cutting, though this may reflect some underlying factors—presumably some features of modernization—that affect both.[90]

Medical organizations worldwide oppose medicalization of female genital cutting, as do human rights activists. In contrast, some medical ethicists have argued that the slow progress toward abandonment justifies the endorsement of minimal forms of low-risk cutting. A pragmatic approach might reserve final judgment until the empirical consequences of medicalization can be established through further research.[91]

Strategizing over the Long Run

The conclusions from detailed research on strategies for combating female genital cutting echo the findings of earlier chapters on political transitions, anticorruption, media freedom, and shaming. First, the level of social modernization, including the development of its characteristic institutions and norms, establishes a context that conditions the effectiveness of anticutting strategies and outcomes. Second, strategizing for advancing rights requires tailoring tactics to fit the power, interests, and culture of actors in that context. Activist persuasion strategies that ignored local context, norms, and discourse led to backlash, which sometimes further entrenched the practice of cutting. Third, although the practice of cutting is to some extent sustained by the perverse collective action dilemma of the marriage market, this does not mean that leaping from the cutting equilibrium to a postcutting outcome can be quickly achieved by persuasion and pledging. The practice is entrenched by an interlocked set of conditions, including the lack of material and institutional preconditions of modern social organization, ethnic identity myths in which cutting serves as a salient master variable, and embedded cultural understandings that link cutting to social roles and individual interests. The larger social system in which cutting is embedded can be unwound only through processes of change that are multidimensional and staged over time.

The most rigorous and knowledgeable scholars of the subject adopt this view. Boyle's "multilevel framework" notes that "successful anti-FGC interventions worked within the layers of social, economic and political realities of communities."[92] Shell-Duncan's collaborator Amede Obiora concludes that "Tostan's program reinforces the emerging consensus among scholars and development practitioners that effective intervention strategies are not discrete and mutually exclusive, but rather multidimensional and integrated."[93]

Other Decentralized Social Dilemmas: Early Marriage

Other decentralized human rights problems, such as early marriage and child labor, have been analyzed in terms of perverse, low-level equilibrium traps associated with underdevelopment. These lack the elegant simplicity of the Mackie explanation for female genital cutting as a collective action dilemma, because self-interested exploiters or intractable resource dilemmas play a greater role in them. A look at their mechanisms helps to illustrate the diverse ways in which decentralized social equilibria contribute to entrenching human rights problems. Effective remedies need to be targeted in specific ways at these different mechanisms.

Early marriage (that is, marriage of a child before the age of eighteen according to the law in most countries) has occupied a lower profile on the agenda of international human rights activism than has female genital cutting. In recent years, however, there has been increasing attention to this entrenched, widespread practice, which some estimate to affect a third of girls in developing countries, especially in Africa and South Asia. The consequences of early marriage include increased risk of death in childbirth, dire health complications such as fistula, exposure to domestic violence, curtailment of girls' education, and violation of the right of the individual to choose a spouse and a life plan.[94]

In some cultures, early marriage is part of a syndrome of abuse that includes female genital cutting, but early marriage is also prevalent in developing countries, such as India, that do not cut girls. Where both occur, their rationales tend to intertwine. Both are commonly justified by the need to control girls' sexual behavior after puberty, with its implications for girls' marriageability and the reputation of their families.[95] Both practices are also justified as facilitating the bride's adjustment to her subordinate role in her husband's family, conforming to their cultural expectations and the authority of older women in the household. In groups that have both practices, demographic factors that affect the incidence of cutting and of early marriage are similar: rural residence, mother's lack of education, and mother's nonparticipation in the labor market are associated with cutting and early marriage of daughters.[96]

Early marriage and female genital cutting also differ in important respects. While fathers are less involved in cutting decisions unless a dispute arises, they play a large role in the details and timing of marriage. For example, among the Maasai of Kenya, the father has the right to select suitors, negotiate payments to be received by the bride's family, and make the final marriage decision.[97] Unlike a group's cutting practices, early marriage is not "salient" in the sense of distinguishing a group from others and serving a symbolic role in the group's basic identity myths.[98] Whereas activist efforts to curtail cutting in a semiurbanized, semimodernized Maasai community provoked sharp resistance from some traditionalists, efforts to eradicate early marriage did not spur much resistance.[99]

Considerable social science literature, especially by economists, has tried to analyze early marriage as a perverse equilibrium. These models are quite different, however, from Mackie's genital cutting model, in which the decision makers are trapped to continue a behavior that possibly none of them prefers. In these analyses, the early marriage equilibrium reflects the sexual, reproductive, economic, and household labor preferences of key decision makers. Men seek to marry young girls or women with many years of fertility ahead of them. Rich men, especially where polygyny or divorce is allowed, have the motive and the wherewithal, even as they age, to keep marrying young women. Girls' families typically prefer their daughters to marry economically established and thus older men, who can provide substantial payments to the bride's family and provide a secure standard of living for the bride.[100] When money in the girl's family is tight, such as when an unpayable debt is owed, cashing in sooner may be necessary, and this saves on the education and upkeep costs of the daughter. It also eliminates worry about the daughter's virginity and pregnancy, which could not only ruin the family's honor but degrade her cash value in the marriage market.[101] Girls that face few attractive opportunities for education or careers sometimes welcome early marriage as the ticket to adult status.[102]

According to such models, as well as the observations of sociologists and activists, these incentives create an equilibrium in which women in poor countries marry at younger ages than men, including ages younger than eighteen, sometimes much younger. Scope conditions for this outcome include the low expectation placed on the earning power of women, which becomes a self-fulfilling prophecy when women marry early and get little schooling. In this sense, the equilibrium of early marriage is perverse for the society as a whole, not just for the early-married women themselves, since it limits the human capital of half of its population.[103] Some argue that West European society's historical tendency toward nuclear families, which was heightened by modernization, placed a premium on the wife's maturity and immediate productive capacity in the young family, whereas extended family residence patterns place little responsibility other than procreation on young wives.[104]

Even if the mechanism supporting early marriage reflects the power of some actors' self-interest more than Mackie's theory of the cutting equilibrium does, second-order norms of upholding reciprocity in early marriage work similarly to Mackie's logic. A study in Malawi found that families that withhold their children from the early marriage market are criticized as antisocial, violating communal principles of diffuse reciprocity.[105]

Social scientists are also interested in studying perverse equilibria that may stem from the practice of bridewealth (or brideprice), in which payments go to the bride's family, and dowry, in which payments go to the groom's family. Its purported consequences include the inability of young men to afford marriage, allegedly leading to such behaviors as Islamic terrorists' requisitioning Yazidi "brides," the mistreatment of wives who fail to bring an adequate dowry or do not live up to expectations based on the price paid for them, gender imbalances due to female infanticide and starvation, and the vicious circle of families needing to sell children at a high price to buy spouses for their offspring of the other sex.[106]

Efforts to model these perverse equilibria run into logical and empirical complications. For example, early marriage has the supposed advantage of buying long years of fertility, but the disadvantage of an ignorant, unproductive wife whose remaining upbringing must be paid for. Similarly, whatever the disadvantages of brideprice may be, a systematic study of Indonesia and Zambia concludes that ethnic groups that practice brideprice invest more resources in girls' education to cash in on the higher price a more educated bride brings in the marriage market.[107] As the modelers admit, it is largely an empirical question whether these pluses or minuses weigh more heavily in a given case.[108] Moreover, modelers often find that the brideprice/dowry market puzzlingly fails to adjust when gender imbalances emerge. Likewise, age of marriage fails to adjust in response to demographic bulges and shifts that change the eligible pool of men and women. This could reflect basic flaws in these economistic models, or it could reflect cultural path dependence or other complications that create systematic biases in behavior and result in market failures.[109] For Cloward, dowry is a "salient" feature in cultural identity and thus resistant to change as a result of outside activism—and extending her argument, to temporary fluctuations in marriage market conditions.[110]

Early marriage is illegal or regulated almost everywhere, but these laws are very weakly enforced. Parental consent offers a loophole that allows the state to appear to conform to international norms while not upending traditional practices. States may have good reason to anticipate backlash against efforts to impose tighter constraints. Laws against child marriage sparked countermobilization in Sudan, where the centralization of the legal system spurred conflict with traditional authorities, but not in more decentralized Zambia. In Malawi, statements by politicians and traditional authorities against child marriage actually increased support for the practice.[111] In the absence of strong political coalitions favoring enforcement, the extreme weakness of even the most basic administration, such as a reliable system for recording birthdates, limits what can be accomplished through formal legal mechanisms in many circumstances.

Other variables affecting early marriage are the incentives in the labor market to keep girls in school and the availability of good quality, free education. By far the most successful programs at reducing child marriage have been programs that incentivize girls' education.[112] Other data suggest that choices about marriage age are responsive to economic shocks that force families to cash out their assets in children.[113] If so, a human rights pragmatist would focus on increasing investments in educational opportunities and the social safety net.

That said, considerable improvements have been made in girls' education in most developing countries in recent years, but early marriage outcomes have been slow to change, even slower than change in female genital cutting in many places.[114] Cloward's explanation for this is the low priority given to the early marriage issue by human rights activists until recently. Since she categorizes early marriage, unlike dowry, as having low cultural salience, she predicts that a bigger push of activism, comparable to that on girls' education, would produce good results.[115] This might be right, but the fact that progress on girls' education has not already brought with it noticeable progress on early marriage suggests that early marriage is entangled in family economic incentives, including brideprice and dowry, that sustain the early marriage equilibrium despite its low salience for cultural identity.[116] If so, schooling and the safety net would both be needed to accelerate change.

Assuming that intensified activism on early marriage could have a big payoff, experts have been considering what form it should take. Tostan uses its standard pledging strategy to combat early marriage, but given rich men's direct interest in perpetuating the practice, Tostan combines pledging with tangible incentives to local religious and traditional leaders to allow women to speak out in community meetings on the issue.[117] For its part, the UN Population Fund's survey of program evaluations in 2012 identified five core recommendations: empowering girls by reducing their social isolation and developing their support networks, making secondary education free and compulsory, promoting community dialogue aimed at detrimental social norms, providing economic incentives for schooling and postschool employment opportunities, and improving birth and marriage registration systems.[118] This sounds right, but the sweeping scope of these proposals suggests that only major political, economic, and social forces could drive such multidimensional changes, not just scattered NGO projects. The related topic of child labor confronts many of these same issues.

Child Labor as a Perverse Equilibrium

Economists argue that the child labor system can be self-reinforcing insofar as the widespread availability of cheap, compliant child labor drives down adult wages and job opportunities, making it impossible for families to survive without sending children to work rather than school and thus creating new generations of undereducated adults who perpetuate the perverse equilibrium.[119] Unlike the early marriage equilibrium, which seems substantially driven by the exploitive preferences of adults, especially men, almost everyone would rather educate their children and escape the child labor poverty trap if they could.

At a first cut, everyone agrees that tipping to a superior equilibrium can happen through the introduction of new production technology that increases the payoff to educated labor, government action to make school attendance compulsory, or compensation to families for the costs of school attendance. The trick in the short run is to identify catalysts that align individual short-run incentives with systemic change. Such catalysts can include economic investments in sectors that require educated labor, targeted incentives for school attendance, and factual information leading to a somewhat longer-range view of self-interest.

Economic development is the strongest predictor of child labor rates. In countries with income below $500 per capita, the percentage of children participating in the labor force ranges between 30 and 60 percent. Where per capita income falls between $500 and $1,000, child labor participation declines to 10–30 percent.[120] Reform legislation often follows shifts in market incentives that make child labor obsolescent. Improvements in industrial technology and increases in real wages shifted demand toward skilled labor and eliminated more than 90 percent of child labor in the United States before the passage of any legislation limiting it.[121]

This is not the whole story, however, since countries at similar levels of poverty show varying levels of child labor. China and Tanzania, for instance, dramatically cut their rates of child labor by making schooling compulsory, while India, with an initially similar level of economic development and labor market, has achieved only an incremental decline because school attendance is not strictly required. The veteran scholar of Indian development Myron Weiner argued that this reflected not just a difference of policy choice but of worldview: India lagged in the eradication of child labor because of the legacy of caste mentality among political and bureaucratic elites, who considered child labor among the poor to be normal and inevitable.[122] Weiner argued that indifference to child labor was rationalized by the false assumption that "the poor are always with you," and that nothing can be done to remedy the situation. Indeed, he wrote his book precisely to prove to India's elites that this was not the case.

Modernization goes hand in hand with changes in psychology, including individualism, and normative assumptions, such as meritocracy, individual opportunity, and progress, which reflect and justify the social relations of a society with a complex division of labor. While these cultural changes may sometimes be side effects of material conditions, they are also causally important facilitating conditions of modern social organization. Although China and its citizens are not liberal, they are in this respect selectively modern.

Changes must come not only in attitudes but also in the short-run vested interests and constraints that sustain the low-level equilibrium. These cannot simply be banished by a shaming campaign. In 1991, transnational activists and international labor lobbyists, largely based in the United States, launched a vocal campaign against the exploitation of child labor by exporters in Bangladesh. Local Bangladeshi rights organizations protested the campaign's one-dimensional focus, which they said disregarded the full range of local concerns.[123] They wanted not the banning of child labor, which was deemed essential to the economic viability of the children's families and the country's export economy, but the regulation of child labor to provide resources for education during nonwork hours and improvement of working conditions.[124] The Bangladeshi activists prevailed in their efforts to block the campaign, extracted concessions from employers, and helped to set in motion a successfully redirected international effort to ban the worst forms of child labor. This episode offers lessons about the advantage of true dialogue between international and local activists and the possibilities of compromise of competing rights claims based in part on differences rooted in self-interest.

When rights problems involve decentralized action in a perverse equilibrium trap, such as child labor, tactics need to target incentives of families and employers while also tapping the public resources that government officials and policy enforcers can deploy to provide a boost to a higher equilibrium.[125] Rigorous research shows that direct cash transfers to poor families with children, whether expressly linked to school attendance or not, help increase school attendance and reduce child labor. So do in-kind benefits such as free school lunch as well as basic social services such as vaccinations and health benefits.[126]

Empirical researchers generally see legal limitations on and regulation of child labor as ancillary measures to changes in other incentives, often more useful for laying down a normative principle than for wielding an enforcement cudgel. Some economists have speculated that criminalization of child labor tends to depress hourly wages of children, causing them to work longer hours to sustain overall income and to work in hidden locations or on family farms where working conditions are impossible to regulate.

In sum, a sobering thought in favor of the pragmatic social power approach to human rights is the fact that the person whose efforts have done the most to reduce child labor is almost certainly Deng Xiaoping.

Conclusions

The decentralized human rights issues treated in this chapter suggest that the basic form of social organization, defined at a general level as traditional versus modern modes, captures core aspects of these rights problems and prescribes pathways to their solution. As in Charles Tilly's formulation, the path to human rights is a journey from personalistic social relations based on in-group favoritism to rule-based equality in a state that acts in the public interest.

Discrimination-based traditional social relations are in themselves a kind of grand low-level equilibrium trap. The equilibrium traps examined in the chapter—the cutting convention, the early marriage equilibrium, and the child labor equilibrium—are nested in that larger context of social relations. Each of the specific traps helps identify the reasons that abusive practices continue and highlights possible interventions to shift to a better overall equilibrium based on human rights.

Each trap differs not only in its empirical details but also in the logical structure of the trap that locks in the undesirable behavior. Cutting is closest to a pure collective action dilemma in which everyone would be better off by shifting to behavior that creates a superior equilibrium. It is locked in mainly by identity-constituting cultural practices around which expectations converge and personal status considerations derive from the practice. Early marriage is kept in place to a substantial degree by the economic and social power of older men, which establishes an equilibrium that constrains the strategies of other actors. Child labor is mainly sustained by resource constraints that necessitate short-run choices, creating a self-perpetuating cycle.

Solutions require tactics that are specific to these mechanisms as well as a general strategy of shifting power from tradition based to liberal, modern social coalitions. To fight female genital cutting, human rights pragmatists need to invest in holistic, locally tailored campaigns of persuasion and norms change in the context of deepening economic development. To roll back child labor, they need to campaign for broad-based government investments in education and social insurance.[127]

Modernization appeared in these accounts not only as a general syndrome of social organization but also as a list of variables across which particular societies, communities, and families might vary: wealth, urbanization, education, institutional capacity, communications patterns, and cultural features. Statistical analysis that treated these attributes as causal factors shed much light on abuses and solutions. At the same time, analysis of how the social system worked as a whole, especially under conditions of partial modernity, was indispensable to understanding the incidence of rights violations and the likelihood of success or backlash from particular rights-promotion tactics.

Power, self-interest, and expedient coalitions constituted running themes in the unfolding of rights abuses and reactions to rights advocacy in these cases. It would be a mistake, however, to take too materialist or atomistic a view of these considerations. Power and interest were often a function of an individual's position in a complex social hierarchy and network. For example, the role of senior women in enforcing female genital cutting has little to do with the practice of cutting per se but mainly stems from the centrality of cutting in the legitimation of networks of social identity and power. As might be expected in an equilibrium trap, each individual's power and interest were not primitives, but rather depended on expectations about the strategies of everyone else. Power and interest were system effects.[128]

The importance of institutions was ubiquitous, if only because of their absence in societies where rights-based equilibria could not be achieved because of the lack of means to organize collective action and provide public goods. Rights enforcement capacity was often lacking. More fundamental was the dearth of institutions to coordinate activity and train citizens in basic skills needed for rights-based civic cooperation. In the long run, strengthening the capacity of a rule-enforcing, equal-access state would go a long way toward mitigating the decentralized abuses discussed in this chapter. A pragmatist needs to think about how best to accumulate the building blocks for that move and also what ameliorative measures might help in the meantime.

Ideology and culture played a role at every turn in structuring social relations around rights-harming equilibria. Ideas and culture defined social roles and group identities, shaping whether abusive practices were "salient" and problematic or easy to erode in the undertow of modernization. Culture provided both motives and tools in the mobilization of backlash against rights advocacy. Several studies suggest that access to news and communications media can play a positive and independent role in changing attitudes. Media provide information about risks and opportunities, cue audiences about appropriate social practices, and convey information about norms that others hold.[129] Media also provide role models and inspirational figures that help people to imagine different futures.[130]

Finally, these cases support the idea that the four components of the social power model—mode of organization, power and interest, institutions, and ideology—operate as integrated syndromes in more traditional and more modern settings. Yet, they also show that the real action in advancing human rights occurs in mixed settings where traditional and modern modes coexist, and where power, interest, institutions, and ideology are misaligned, in flux, and developing at an uneven pace. These are the crucial settings in which the battle between reform and backlash takes place.

10

Human Rights at a Time of Global Stalemate

THE WORLD is now precariously poised between the forces of liberalism and illiberalism. It is a moment of double equipoise: between liberal and illiberal states in the international system and between liberal and illiberal social forces within powerful transitional states. How, under these circumstances, should the promotion of human rights be carried out? Pragmatically. In this concluding chapter, I use the social power theory of human rights development, cornerstone to the pragmatic approach to human rights, to characterize and analyze the nature of the current impasse.

The human rights movement became accustomed to operating in the psychological environment of the unipolar moment, when there seemed to be no pressing reason to compromise with skeptics of the rights agenda. The movement's preferred vector of persuasion was entirely one way. Now with the rise of illiberal major powers and resistance from illiberal social forces worldwide, there is greater recognition within the movement and among liberal publics that the balance of forces is more equal. Every successful battle will be hard won, and some battles will not be won in the foreseeable future. A revised strategy will need to anticipate pushback, pick battles that can be won, flexibly recruit constituencies to support the effort, and tailor tactics to the new reality.

The first step will be righting the ship.[1] The captains of liberalism have alienated the mutinous crew by creating conditions that fostered economic inequality and mismanagement, disruptive cultural change, and a deficit of governmental accountability. The root causes of this nearly fatal alienation are the pseudo-liberal libertarians' dogmatic aversion to economic regulation and the cosmopolitan elite's lack of empathy with the demotic cultural views of their constituents. Facing what many people in the established democracies saw as an urgent social crisis, the disappointed people grew impatient with grid-locked due process, demanding direct action without the red tape of the liberal state. But this populist backlash only worsened the fate of its grassroots supporters.

The solution needs to reconcile the two indispensable elements of the liberal formula: a democratically accountable national government and a well-regulated market economy. In the postwar era, this was achieved by the national self-determination of democratic states, whose politics were made compatible with market economics by the welfare state, Keynesian methods to modulate the business cycle, and the Bretton Woods international economic institutions to smooth out trade and financial fluctuations. Another pillar of this system of *embedded liberalism* was a well-institutionalized marketplace of ideas in which civic-minded professional journalists provided the information and forums needed for coherent public deliberation. The specific format of these regulatory institutions reflected the particular circumstances of that era. They cannot be simply brought back to life unchanged from their earlier form, but an updated counterpart of that system can use the same general principles to reconstitute the cooperative league of liberal welfare states at its core.[2]

This club of liberal, rights-based societies, even when returned to a more functional state, will not be able to re-create the unipolar moment of overly ambitious human rights proselytizing, which was largely illusory in any case.[3] Instead it needs to strategize based on the realistic understanding that the international system remains at equipoise between liberal and illiberal social forces. This will remain the case even if the rising illiberal powers remain stuck in the middle-income trap and cease their rise. They will be big, illiberal, and unruly enough to continue to make trouble for the liberal design for world order.

Under these conditions, the geographical spread of human rights will mainly have to happen through the principle of the open door. Since states are the principal organizations through which rights are effectively established, this will mean creating conditions in which states will voluntarily decide to join the systems established by liberal, rights-based states, if they qualify for membership. This is the system used for EU expansion and for accession to the WTO. Its troubles arose mainly because of systemic problems and policy mistakes within the founding core states. If they are corrected, the condition-ally open door should work better, but at the pace desired by states outside the system.

Membership standards for international organizations sponsored by liberal states should be tailored to the functional requirements of the issue area. Since peace is the single strongest correlate of human rights compliance, *international security arrangements* are at the top of the human rights agenda. In a system that is at equipoise between liberal and illiberal social forces, the international security system even of the liberal powers will need to remain based on the principles of realism. The fact that democracies never fight wars against each other, given strict enough definitions of democracy and war, means that realism and rights-based liberalism are normally compatible and even mutually reinforcing. Over the past two centuries, liberal democratic states have been by far the best realists. Illiberal states can make common cause with liberal alliances on an opportunistic basis, but on operational terms that are set by the liberal realist core states. On the liberal dimension, this means observing the laws of war and supporting the right of established liberal democracies to national self-determination. On the realist dimension, it will sometimes mean deferring justice in the interests of peace (as discussed in chapter 4) and imposing strict tests of prudence in criteria for humanitarian military intervention.[4]

Among the greatest successes of the liberal rights-based social order are its *systems for governing trade, finance, technology, and investment.* This is liberalism's comparative advantage. But these systems need to be understood in Polanyi's way, as embedded in regulatory political authority that serves a broader, normative social purpose. Unregulated or badly regulated economic systems produce what Schumpeter called "creative destruction," and sometimes it is just plain destruction. In addition to the technicalities of stabilizing the fluctuations of supply and demand, two social objectives are paramount for the functioning of a liberal market system.

The first is maintaining social consensus within democratic nation-states. This has an objective dimension, managing the economy to produce reliable, widespread benefits, as well as a subjective dimension, cultivating confidence among each nation's citizens that the economic system is achieving their goals in material terms and in terms of its cultural consequences. Libertarian economics has failed on both dimensions and should not be confused with liberal rights-based economic principles.

The weakest point in the welfare state's regulatory order has been labor migration. As with trade and financial flows, democratic welfare states with aging populations and low fertility rates will need inflows of foreign labor to maintain their economic dynamism. And as with other economic flows, labor migration will need to be regulated in a way that prioritizes the maintenance of social consensus in migrant-receiving democracies. Working with refugee- and migrant-sending states to head off crisis conditions there presents a huge challenge for the embedded liberal system, but this system offers the least disruptive solution to the problem of antimigrant backlash, which will continue to threaten democracy if not managed pragmatically. Spikes in demand to cross borders are caused mainly by refugees from civil war but also from crime and exploitation. Even economic improvements in sending countries can stimulate migration because people have the resources to attempt the trip.[5] Managing these flows will require seizing the initiative and deploying sufficient investment resources just as the founders of the Bretton Woods system did. Creating incentives to improve labor opportunities and labor rights in migrant-sending countries will be a central element in this effort.

The second objective is maintaining the economic supports for liberal societies in their competition with illiberal states. In international anarchy, it is necessary to take into account not only the short-run absolute gains from the international division of labor, but also the long-run relative gains from economic and technological exchanges with illiberal states.[6] It is possible that the inefficiencies built into illiberal economies will solve the relative gains problem in the long run without the liberal democracies doing much about it. Even so, the cumulative effect of decades of mercantilism has given illiberal China a dangerous degree of market power that can be translated into a daunting level of military power. China's liberal economic partners will need to worry about the security implications of China's rise, while also realizing that any tardy, abrupt decision by liberal states to curtail economic interdependence with China could provoke a destabilizing burst of Chinese nationalism. Devising a good strategy for inducing economic and political reform in China is a human rights issue not only because we care about dissidents, minorities, and workers in China but because we care about the stability of a peaceful, liberal world order as a whole. Here as elsewhere, power politics and human rights need to be strategized together.

A target of opportunity to deepen and enhance the luster of the rules-based international economic order is *a campaign against global systemic corruption.* NGOs such as Transparency International rank the corruption of individual countries, as if all financial crime is local. In fact, the most consequential corruption is abetted by the global financial infrastructure and the laxity of legal constraints on tax avoidance and the laundering of ill-gotten gains. Much of this could be shut down if a mass social movement of voters would get behind it in the key countries that control these levers of influence.[7] Among the benefits of aiming the campaign at the global level are avoiding the appearance of imperialism and hypocrisy, which foster resentment of liberal human rights advocacy. Once the international facilitators of corruption are rooted out, global reformers should let in-country activists take the credit for finishing the job in their own backyard.

To some extent, this is happening already, but with arms-length participation by the human rights community. Amid a rising global tide of mass street protest, a third of the protests documented by the Carnegie Endowment for International Peace's "protest tracker" have anticorruption as a central theme.[8] Most of these are listed as spontaneous or organized by local single-issue movements. Large general-purpose human rights organizations such as Human Rights Watch tend to weigh in only to defend the protesters' rights to free speech and assembly in the face of government repression, not to support the anticorruption campaign per se. Stepping up their visibility in such campaigns and taking a principled stance on corruption as a human rights abuse would not be operationally difficult.

Alas, the human rights movement is not sure to what extent it wants to own the corruption issue. International lawyers agree that people have a human right to courts that are not corrupt insofar as the International Covenant on Civil and Political Rights provides for the right to equal justice and a fair trial before an impartial court. They also agree that corruption can be a cause of other kinds of rights abuses, such as discrimination and failure to provide substantively mandated protection of due process, property rights, health, education, and welfare. But progressive lawyers are not sure whether administrative corruption counts as a legal violation of international human rights standards. Moreover, they are leery of the politicization of the issue and its demagogic use in attacking political opponents.

These speedbumps require a thoughtful approach but not the avoidance of the corruption issue, which could be a wildly popular mass mobilizer for the human rights movement. One of the central theoretical points of this book has been the overcoming of favoritism in patronage relationships as a crucial impetus toward a rights-based social system. Going after corruption is not only pragmatic human rights politics; just as important, it is based on good theory.

Human rights advocacy typically talks about freedom of expression as an end in itself, which it is. But equally important, *freedom of speech, information, and the press* are instrumentally vital to the entire system of liberal rights. These rights are now exercised on a global level, thanks to new communications technology, which liberal democratic societies are mainly in charge of and responsible for. Unfortunately, the free-speech absolutism that comes most naturally to the human rights community has become part of the problem, fomenting libel and disinformation in ways that feed directly into human rights abuse, such as vigilantism in India and ethnic cleansing in Myanmar. A top priority on the global human rights agenda should be to lead the way in advocating for reform of the globalized forums of free speech to empower professional journalists and regulate monopoly tech platforms (see chapter 7). To update the Thomas Jefferson quotation, as long as we have a well-functioning media, we will be able to reinvent the rest of the human rights regime. This is yet another trump card in the long-term contest with illiberal China and Russia as well as the key to reining in our own most rights-destructive inclinations.

Finally, the human rights movement needs to be far more circumspect and consequentialist in choosing to intervene in the *entrenched cultural practices* of societies that are not yet liberal and modern. If methods of vernacularization and localization of rights advocacy can be redesigned to be highly effective, that would be splendid, but if not, it is important at this moment of backlash against the whole rights project to avoid gratuitously handing ammunition to the enemies of rights. There will be time to take on these issues later when the moment is ripe (see chapters 8 and 9).

Even more important than the substance of these issues is the need to update the human rights movement's style of work. For all the talk about global civil society as the movement's power source, unlike the populists, the religious fundamentalists, and even the liberals demonstrating for self-determination in the streets of Hong Kong, human rights professionals have no mass movement that they can mobilize toward a goal. This is a break with the successful traditions of their own heroes. To organize and mobilize a potent mass movement for the rights cause, three strategic adjustments offer promising avenues.

First, the power of religious zeal and networks should be tapped more assiduously. As Martin Luther King realized, ties of religion often provide a more inclusive bridge between otherwise divided races and ethnicities.[9] Many mass religions and godly social movements are moderate, constructive, and favorable to democracy and rights: Sufism in Islam, mainstream Catholicism and Anglicanism in Africa,[10] Catholic liberation theology in Latin America (though waning recently),[11] Mahayana Buddhism,[12] Reform and other moderate varieties of Judaism, and potentially Reformed Confucianism as imagined by the young, idealistic, perhaps naïve student generation that grew up in the Hu Jintao period of "peaceful rise." Even if human rights activists do not tap into mass religions directly, they can learn to adopt civic evangelical rhetorical styles as the secular Lincoln did.[13]

Second, human rights activism needs to focus much more on core rights values that speak to the interests of the majority groups in a society: to the majority ethnic, racial, and religious groups; to the broad middle class and dominant occupational groups; and to local civic leaders in mainstream communities. Instead of addressing mainly the powerless and downtrodden, activists need to emphasize issues in which everyone is in the same boat of exploitation by abusive elites and extractive factions. Emphasize inclusive civic rights such as equality before the law, due process, respect for the right to property *and* the fruits of one's labor, curtailment of monopoly power in markets *and* employers' coercion of labor, access to health care and pensions, and systematic checks on arbitrary abuse of official power in dealing with citizens. Activists are of course already in favor of these things. What needs to be different is that activism that highlights discrimination against weak or stigmatized groups should always be framed as a message that links abuse of the minority to similar abuse of the majority. The antislavery Quakers and Dissenters understood this connection, but most people need to have this picture painted vividly for them: "First they came for the socialists, and I did not speak out—because I was not a socialist. . . ."[14] The human rights project needs to be backed by a majority coalition that includes many powerful people.

Third, to get a big, powerful coalition, activists need to mobilize around big, hot-button grievances that unite everybody. One such issue is corruption, which is a top-priority issue for human rights activism because it links to every other kind of human rights abuse: abuse of office, due process, discrimination, torture, atrocities, and every kind of economic, social, and cultural right. In the United States the big breakthrough against organized crime came when legal strategy focused on systemic charges of racketeering and conspiracy rather than accountability for individual actions. A similar systemic approach to corruption as a human rights issue would be popular and analytically on target. It would also be in sync with the conceptual understanding of patronage-based discrimination as basic to the premodern social order that holds back human rights progress. There remains a great deal of work to be done on this project. The European Union human rights initiative of targeted sanctions on individuals guilty of human rights violations abroad, unveiled in

December 2020, declined to address violations of freedom of speech and corruption.[15]

As I argue in chapter 6, rights activism and supportive social movements need to work closely with progressive political parties. It is one thing to set forth a vision that activates the masses; it is another to drive home a bargain that can be the basis for systematic policy implementation. Both are needed. It is the progressive political party (or its functional equivalent) that can coopt fence-sitters, buy off spoilers, subsidize potential losers, and pragmatically forge a winning coalition. Social movements are generally good at building and tapping networks. Progressive parties that are in power and wield the tools of civic administration can build institutions that make rights an implemented reality. Human rights activism, at a minimum, needs to avoid undermining the practical requirements of progressive deal making, as I argue in the discussion of peace and justice in chapter 4.

Finally, the rhetoric of rights needs to avoid shaming, especially outsiders' explicit or even implicit shaming of widespread, entrenched cultural practices, which only plays into the hands of backlash against rights (chapter 8). Instead, rights persuasion will work better if the conversation is two-way, if vernacular normative ideas of the community are taken into account, and if local notables are fully engaged as intermediaries in packaging global and local concepts in a form that works in local politics. Nonetheless, activists need to find ways to vernacularize rights talk that does not proceed down the slippery slope toward "normalizing deviance": for example, torturing or lynching criminals to protect the "human rights" of the community; "persuading" refugees to agree to go back to an unsafe homeland by making their refuge even worse.[16]

Vernacularizing rights does not, however, mean wrapping the project in the aura of a backward tradition. Most people in almost every society want to be modern.[17] They want a cool smart phone and would love to have their son attend Stanford, even if it's only via a MOOC. They want to be part of a winning trend that is up to date, but they need to be shown how they can actually take part in global modernity. Persuasion works by social proof more than by logic or ethical precepts. That's why human rights needs to be pragmatic: to persuade by showing that rights work.

Liberal societies, based at their core on human rights, are so far the only form of modernity that has proved itself capable of sustaining prosperity and social peace. That's why it is so important for the human rights project to succeed, and why it has a good chance of overcoming its recent stumbles if it cleaves to the path of progressive pragmatism.

NOTES

Chapter 1. Power Leads, Rights Follow

1. Hendrik Spruyt, *The Sovereign State and Its Competitors* (Princeton, NJ: Princeton University Press, 1994); John Witte, *The Reformation of Rights: Law, Religion and Human Rights in Early Modern Calvinism* (Cambridge: Cambridge University Press, 2007), 39–80; Scott F. Abramson and Carles Boix, "Endogenous Parliaments: The Domestic and International Roots of Long-Term Economic Growth and Executive Constraints," *International Organization* 73, no. 4 (Fall 2019): 793–837.

2. Linda Colley, *Britons: Forging the Nation, 1707–1837* (New Haven, CT: Yale University Press, 2008), 25–32, 41–42, 111–13, 201, 220–22, 230–31, 363.

3. Hans Kohn, *The Idea of Nationalism: A Study in its Origins and Background* (New York: Macmillan, 1944); Anders Stephanson, *Manifest Destiny: American Exceptionalism and the Empire of Right* (New York: Hill and Wang, 1995), 7–27; Charles Tilly, *Contention and Democracy in Europe, 1650–2000* (New York: Cambridge University Press, 2004).

4. Micheline Ishay, *The History of Human Rights: From Ancient Times to the Globalization Era* (Berkeley: University of California Press, 2004), 117–72.

5. Peter Gourevitch, *Politics in Hard Times: Comparative Responses to International Economic Crises* (Ithaca, NY: Cornell University Press, 1986), 124–66; Jack Snyder, *Myths of Empire: Domestic Politics and International Ambition* (Ithaca, NY: Cornell University Press, 1991), 112–52.

6. Alexander Cooley and Daniel Nexon, *Exit from Hegemony: The Unraveling of the American Global Order* (New York: Oxford University Press, 2020). G. John Ikenberry, the leading academic theorist of the liberal international order, says "an international order is a political formation in which settled rules and arrangements exist between states to guide their interactions . . . established through an equilibrium of power." See his *Liberal Leviathan: The Origins, Crisis, and Transformation of the American International Order* (Princeton, NJ: Princeton University Press, 2011), 6.

7. Roberto Foa and Yascha Mounk, "The Democratic Disconnect," *Journal of Democracy* 28, no. 3 (July 2016): 5–17; Foa and Mounk, "The Signs of Deconsolidation," *Journal of Democracy* 28, no. 1 (January 2017): 5–15; Matthew H. Graham and Milan W. Svolik, "Democracy in America? Partisanship, Polarization, and the Robustness of Support for Democracy in the United States," *American Political Science Review* 114, no. 2 (May 2020): 392–409; G. John Ikenberry, *A World Safe for Democracy* (New Haven, CT: Yale University Press, 2020).

8. Barbara Keys, *Reclaiming American Virtue: The Human Rights Revolution in the 1970s* (Cambridge, MA: Harvard University Press, 2014).

9. Sheri Berman, *Democracy and Dictatorship in Europe: From the Ancien Régime to the Present Day* (New York: Oxford University Press, 2019).

10. Douglass C. North, John Joseph Wallis, and Barry R. Weingast, *Violence and Social Orders: A Conceptual Framework for Interpreting Recorded Human History* (New York: Cambridge University Press, 2009), discussed in chapter 3; see also Avner Greif, *Institutions and the Path to the Modern Economy: Lessons from Medieval Trade* (New York: Cambridge University Press, 2006), especially 124–52, on equilibria and endogenous institutions.

11. Anthony F. C. Wallace, "Revitalization Movements," *American Anthropologist*, n.s., 58 (1956): 264–81; Mark Juergensmeyer, *The New Cold War? Religious Nationalism Confronts the Secular State* (Berkeley: University of California Press, 1993).

12. Martha Finnemore and Kathryn Sikkink, "International Norm Dynamics and Political Change," *International Organization* 52, no. 4 (Autumn 1998): 887–918.

13. Emile Durkheim, *The Division of Labor in Society* (1893; Glencoe, IL: Free Press, 1960); Ferdinand Tönnies, *Community and Civil Society* (orig. ed. *Gemeinschaft und Gesellschaft*, 1887; Cambridge: Cambridge University Press, 2001).

14. Peter Baehr, "The 'Iron Cage' and the 'Shell as Hard as Steel': Parsons, Weber, and the Stahlhartes Gehäuse Metaphor in the Protestant Ethic and the Spirit of Capitalism," *History and Theory* 40, no. 2 (May 2001): 153–69.

15. Francis Fukuyama, "The End of History?" *National Interest*, no. 16 (September 1989): 3–18.

16. David Dollar, "Institutional Quality and Growth Traps," Pacific Trade and Development Working Paper Series, No. YF37-07, prepared for a conference at the Institute of Southeast Asian Studies, Singapore, June 3–5, 2015, http://www.eastasiaforum.org/wp-content/uploads/2015/08/PAFTAD-37-David-Dollar.pdf. More generally, see Torben Iversen and David Soskice, *Democracy and Prosperity: Reinventing Capitalism through a Turbulent Century* (Princeton, NJ: Princeton University Press, 2019), 4 and passim, on "the exceptional resilience of advanced capitalist democracies (in comparison to any other type of nation state in the last century or so)." Also, see this update from the winners of the American Political Science Association's Woodrow Wilson Prize, Dan Reiter and Allan Stam, "Democracies Have an Edge in Fighting Wars: That Will Help Them Fight Diseases Too," *Foreign Affairs*, May 7, 2020, https://www.foreignaffairs.com/articles/world/2020-05-07/democracies-have-edge-fighting-wars.

17. Alexander Gerschenkron, *Economic Backwardness in Historical Perspective* (Cambridge, MA: Belknap Press of Harvard University Press, 1962).

18. Dollar, "Institutional Quality and Growth Traps."

19. Daniel A. Bell, *The China Model: Political Meritocracy and the Limits of Democracy* (Princeton, NJ: Princeton University Press, 2015).

20. US at $65,544, PRC at $10,500, based on 2020 World Bank data, "GDP per capita (current US$)," accessed October 7, 2021, https://data.worldbank.org/indicator/ny.gdp.pcap.cd, or $17,312, using the purchasing power parity method, which favors less developed states with cheap factor inputs.

21. David Shambaugh, "Contemplating China's Future," *Washington Quarterly* 39, no. 3 (Fall 2016): 121–30.

22. Jonathan R. Stromseth, Edmund Malesky, and D. Gueorguiev, *China's Governance Puzzle: Enabling Transparency and Participation in a Single-Party State* (New York: Cambridge University Press, 2017).

23. On the growing "incongruity" between US "institutional accommodations" of political exclusions and the demand to end the exclusions that these institutions protected, see Stephen Skowronek and Karen Orren, "The Adaptability Paradox: Constitutional Resilience and Principles of Good Government in Twenty-First Century America," *Perspectives on Politics* 18, no. 2 (June 2020): 354–69, at 359.

24. John Rawls, *A Theory of Justice* (Cambridge, MA: Belknap Press of Harvard University Press, 1971), 75–82, on the "difference principle."

25. Karl Polanyi, *The Great Transformation* (New York: Farrar, 1944).

26. Mark Blyth, *Great Transformations: Economic Ideas and Institutional Change in the Twentieth Century* (New York: Cambridge University Press, 2002); Blyth, *Austerity: The History of a Dangerous Idea* (New York: Oxford University Press, 2013); Dani Rodrik, "Why Does Globalization Fuel Populism? Economics, Culture, and the Rise of Right-wing Populism," NBER Working Paper No. 27526 (July 2020), http://www.nber.org/papers/w27526.

27. Menzie Chinn and Jeffry A, Frieden, *Lost Decades: The Making of America's Debt Crisis and the Long Recovery* (New York: Norton, 2011).

28. Daniel Drezner, *The System Worked: How the World Stopped Another Great Depression* (New York: Oxford University Press, 2014); Adam Tooze, *Crashed: How a Decade of Financial Crises Changed the World* (New York: Viking, 2018).

29. John Gerard Ruggie, "International Regimes, Transactions, and Change: Embedded Liberalism in the Postwar Economic Order," *International Organization* 36, no. 2 (Spring 1982): 379–415.

30. Jessica Chen Weiss and Jeremy Wallace, "Domestic Politics, China's Rise, and the Future of the Liberal International Order," in "Challenges to the Liberal International Order," special issue, *International Organization*, 75, no. 2 (Spring 2021): 635–64, at 640–41; Carl F. Minzner, "China's Turn Against Law," *American Journal of Comparative Law* 59, no. 4 (Fall 2011): 935–84.

31. See the chapters by Stephen Hopgood, Samuel Moyn, Beth Simmons, and Anton Strezhnev, and the conclusion in Stephen Hopgood, Jack Snyder, and Leslie Vinjamuri, eds., *Human Rights Futures* (Cambridge: Cambridge University Press, 2017).

32. Alicia Mungiu-Pippidi, *The Quest for Good Governance: How Societies Develop Control of Corruption* (New York: Cambridge University Press, 2015), 11–12; United Nations Convention against Corruption, October 1, 2003, https://www.unodc.org/unodc/en/corruption/uncac.html.

33. Kenneth Roth, "The Age of Zombie Democracies: Why Autocrats Are Abandoning Even the Pretense of Democratic Rituals," *Foreign Affairs*, July 28, 2021, https://www.foreignaffairs.com/articles/americas/2021-07-28/age-zombie-democracies?.

34. Aryeh Neier, *The International Human Rights Movement: A History* (Princeton, NJ: Princeton University Press, 2012), 26–56, 93–137, 258–84.

35. Universal Declaration of Human Rights, UN Human Rights Office of the High Commissioner, accessed September 19, 2021, http://www.ohchr.org/EN/UDHR/Documents/UDHR_Translations/eng.pdf.

36. Finnemore and Sikkink, "International Norm Dynamics," 891, 894–905.

37. Margaret Keck and Kathryn Sikkink, *Activists beyond Borders: Advocacy Networks in International Politics* (Ithaca, NY: Cornell University Press, 1998), 60–86; Carlos Nino, *Radical Evil on Trial* (New Haven, CT: Yale University Press, 1996).

38. Payam Akhavan, "Beyond Impunity: Can International Criminal Justice Prevent Future Atrocities?" *American Journal of International Law* 95, no. 1 (January 2001): 31; and Akhavan, "Are International Criminal Tribunals a Disincentive to Peace? Reconciling Judicial Romanticism with Political Realism," *Human Rights Quarterly* 31, no. 3 (August 2009): 624–54. See also Patrice C. McMahon and David P. Forsythe, "The ICTY's Impact on Serbia: Judicial Romanticism Meets Network Politics," *Human Rights Quarterly* 30, no. 2 (May 2008): 414n5.

39. Thanks to Gary Bass for this point. See his *Stay the Hand of Vengeance: The Politics of War Crimes Tribunals* (Princeton, NJ: Princeton University Press, 2000), 6–7.

40. Stephen Hopgood, *The Endtimes of Human Rights* (Ithaca, NY: Cornell University Press, 2013).

41. This section is based on my original draft contribution to Stephen Hopgood, Jack Snyder, and Leslie Vinjamuri, "Introduction," in Hopgood, Snyder, and Vinjamuri, *Human Rights Futures*, where it appeared in revised form.

42. For this reason, Daniel W. Hill and K. Anne Watson argue that human rights that are distant from civil liberties should be used to test the impact of democracy on human rights. Their research note on "Democracy and Compliance with Human Rights Treaties: The Conditional Effectiveness of the Convention for the Elimination of All Forms of Discrimination against Women," *International Studies Quarterly* 63, no. 1 (March 2019), 127–38, finds that the compliance effects of CEDAW are not linear with respect to democracy or correlated with democratization, though they do not argue for any alternative interpretation.

43. Steven C. Poe, Neal Tate, and Linda Camp Keith, "Repression of the Human Right to Personal Integrity Revisited: A Global Cross-National Study Covering the Years 1976–1993," *International Studies Quarterly* 43, no. 2 (June 1999): 291–313.

44. Todd Landman and Marco Larizza, "Inequality and Human Rights: Who Controls What, When, and How," *International Studies Quarterly* 53, no. 3 (September 2009): 715–36; though for strong qualifications, see Stephan Haggard and Robert R. Kaufman, *Dictators and Democrats: Masses, Elites, and Regime Change* (Princeton, NJ: Princeton University Press, 2016).

45. In some studies, though, this apparent finding may stem from a failure to weight results by population.

46. Bruce Bueno de Mesquita, Feyral Marie Cherif, George Downs, and Alastair Smith, "Thinking Inside the Box: A Closer Look at Democracy and Human Rights," *International Studies Quarterly* 49, no. 3 (September 2005): 439–58; Helen Fein, "More Murder in the Middle: Life Integrity Violations and Democracy in the World, 1987," *Human Rights Quarterly* 17, no. 1 (February 1995): 170–91. Beth Simmons, *Mobilizing for Human Rights: International Law in Domestic Politics* (New York: Cambridge University Press, 2009), refers to this literature on p. 136, note 84. See also Christian Davenport and David Armstrong, "Democracy and the Violation of Human Rights: A Statistical Analysis from 1976 to 1996," *American Journal of Political Science* 48, no. 3 (July 2004): 538–54; and Samuel P. Huntington, *Political Order in Changing Societies* (New Haven, CT: Yale University Press, 1968), for relevant theory.

47. Simmons, *Mobilizing for Human Rights*, 153; Davenport and Armstrong, "Democracy and the Violation of Human Rights," 547; Fein, "More Murder in the Middle," 177, 179, 181, 183. Simmons's graph of the theoretically *expected* value of political mobilization begins to arc upward as soon as autocracy ends, whereas Davenport's and Fein's charts of actual outcomes shows

rights abuse remaining high and even trending slightly up at that point and declining only in complete democracy.

48. Thomas Risse, Stephen Ropp, and Kathryn Sikkink, eds., *The Persistent Power of Human Rights: From Commitment to Compliance* (New York: Cambridge University Press, 2013); see also Kenneth Roth, "Africa: The Attacks on the International Criminal Court," *New York Review of Books*, February 6, 2014, 32–35.

49. Emilie M. Hafner-Burton, *Making Human Rights a Reality* (Princeton, NJ: Princeton University Press, 2013), 3.

50. Christopher J. Fariss, "Respect for Human Rights Has Improved over Time: Modeling the Changing Standard of Accountability," *American Political Science Review* 108, no. 2 (May 2014): 297–318, proposes a very complex, indirect method for calibrating biases in measuring rights violations due to increased data availability, and historically changing standards, by making use of comparisons to continually updated historical data on the worst atrocities. Cases where data seem to be better are used as a baseline to assess overall trends. He claims this technique shows that rights outcomes are improving. Though an intriguing step forward, this methodology requires making several heroic assumptions, including confidence in updated atrocities data, which remain highly politicized. Improved data cut both ways, since civil war researchers frequently adjust casualty numbers downward as time passes and information improves. See Peter Andreas and Kelly M. Greenhill, eds., *Sex, Drugs, and Body Counts: The Politics of Numbers in Global Crime and Conflict* (Ithaca, NY: Cornell University Press, 2010), chs. 1, 6, 7, 8, and 11. For a prominent statistical critique of Fariss's method, see David Cingranelli and Mikhail Filippov, "Are Human Rights Practices Improving?" *American Political Science Review* 112, no. 4 (November 2018): 1083–89. Fariss responds in "Yes, Human Rights Practices Are Improving over Time," *American Political Science Review* 113, no. 3 (August 2019): 868–81. See also Ann Marie Clark and Kathryn Sikkink, "Information Effects and Human Rights Data: Is the Good News about Increased Human Rights Information Bad News for Human Rights Measures?" *Human Rights Quarterly* 35, no. 3 (August 2013): 539–68.

51. Thomas Risse and Kathryn Sikkink, "Conclusions," in Risse, Ropp, and Sikkink, *Persistent Power*, 281–82, 294.

52. Simmons, *Mobilizing for Human Rights*.

53. See chapters by Vinjamuri, and Cooley and Schaaf, in Hopgood, Snyder, and Vinjamuri, *Human Rights Futures*.

54. Emilie Hafner-Burton, "Sticks and Stones: Naming and Shaming the Human Rights Enforcement Problem," *International Organization* 62, no. 4 (Fall 2008): 689–716; Darius Rejali makes a similar argument, claiming that pressure from human rights advocates has driven states to adopt torture techniques that are less visible; see Darius Rejali, *Torture and Democracy* (Princeton, NJ: Princeton University Press, 2008). A factor that is not sufficiently considered by some of these studies is that disproportionate publicity may be aimed at recalcitrant actors that are hardest to change. If this were so, results would be biased against shaming tactics.

55. Ann Marie Clark, "The Normative Context of Human Rights Criticism: Treaty Ratification and UN Mechanisms," in Risse, Ropp, and Sikkink, *Persistent Power*, 143.

56. Amanda M. Murdie and David R. Davis, "Shaming and Blaming: Using Events Data to Assess the Impact of Human Rights INGOs," *International Studies Quarterly* 56, no. 1 (March 2012): 1–16.

57. Hafner-Burton, *Making Human Rights a Reality*, 21–28.

58. Anna Persson, Bo Rothstein, Jan Teorell, "Getting the Basic Nature of Systemic Corruption Right: A Reply to Marquette and Peiffer," *Governance* 32, no. 4 (October 2019): 799–810; Heather Marquette and Karen Peiffer, "Thinking Politically about Corruption as Problem-Solving: A Reply to Persson, Rothstein, and Teorell," *Governance* 32, no. 4 (October 2019): 799–810.

59. Michael Mousseau, "Market Civilization and Its Clash with Terror," *International Security* 27, no. 3 (Winter 2002–2003): 5–29.

60. Spruyt, *Sovereign State and Its Competitors*; Charles Tilly, *Coercion, Capital, and European States, AD 990–1990* (Cambridge, MA: Blackwell, 1990).

61. Imre Lakatos, "Falsification and the Methodology of Scientific Research Programmes," in *Criticism and the Growth of Knowledge*, ed. Imre Lakatos and Alan Musgrave (Cambridge: Cambridge University Press, 1970), 91–196.

62. Giovanni Sartori, "Concept Misinformation in Comparative Politics," *American Political Science Review* 64, no. 4 (December 1970): 1033–53.

63. Regina Abrami, "Worker Rights and Global Trade: The U.S.-Cambodia Bilateral Textile Trade Agreement," Harvard Business School Case 9-703-034, March 2003 (revised September 2004); Brian Greenhill, Layna Mosley, and Aseem Prakash, "Trade-Based Diffusion of Labor Rights: A Panel Study, 1986–2002," *American Political Science Review* 103, no. 4 (November 2009): 669–90; Layna Mosley and Saika Uno, "Racing to the Bottom or Climbing to the Top? Economic Globalization and Collective Labor Rights," *Comparative Political Studies* 40, no. 8 (August 2007), 923–48; Daniel Berliner and Aseem Prakash, "How Domestic Regulatory Institutions Influence the Adoption of Global Private Regimes: Firm-level Evidence from Eastern Europe and Central Asia," *International Studies Quarterly* (forthcoming); Jens Hainmueller, Michael J. Hiscox, and Sandra Sequeira, "Consumer Demand for the Fair Trade Label: Evidence from a Multi-Store Field Experiment," *Review of Economics and Statistics* 97, no. 2 (May 2015): 242–56. Thanks to Mosley and Nikhar Gaikwad for discussion on this issue.

Chapter 2. Power and Rights in the Modern State

1. Alicia Mungiu-Pippidi, *The Quest for Good Governance: How Societies Develop Control of Corruption* (New York: Cambridge University Press, 2015).

2. John Burt, *Lincoln's Tragic Pragmatism: Lincoln, Douglas, and Moral Conflict* (Cambridge, MA: Belknap Press of Harvard University Press, 2013); Ira Katznelson, *Fear Itself: The New Deal and the Origins of Our Time* (New York: Liveright, 2013).

3. Daniel Luban, "What Is Spontaneous Order?" *American Political Science Review* 114, no. 1 (February 2020): 68–80.

4. Martha Finnemore and Kathryn Sikkink, "International Norm Dynamics and Political Change," *International Organization* 52, no. 4 (Autumn 1998): 887–918; Lynn Hunt, *Inventing Human Rights* (New York: Norton, 2008).

5. Abdullahi An-Na'im, "Toward a Cross-Cultural Approach to Defining International Standards of Human Rights: The Meaning of Cruel, Inhuman, or Degrading Treatment or Punishment," in *Human Rights in Cross-Cultural Perspectives: A Quest for Consensus*, ed. Abdullahi Ahmed An-Na'im (Philadelphia: University of Pennsylvania Press, 1992), 19–44; Alison D.

Renteln, "Relativism and the Search for Human Rights," *American Anthropologist* 90, no. 1 (March 1988): 67, argues that proportional retribution is the only cross-culturally valid principle of right or justice.

6. For a modern social science argument analyzing the strategy and effectiveness of repression, see Ronald Wintrobe, *The Political Economy of Dictatorship* (New York: Cambridge University Press, 1998); and Christian Davenport and Benjamin Appel, "Stopping State Repression: An Examination of Spells, 1976–2004," American Political Science Association 2014 Annual Meeting Paper, https://ssrn.com/abstract=2452310.

7. Greenberg Research, *The People on War Report: ICRC Worldwide Consultation on the Rules of War* (Geneva: International Committee of the Red Cross, 1999), ref. 0758.

8. Andrew J. Nathan, "The Puzzle of Authoritarian Legitimacy," *Journal of Democracy* 31, no. 1 (January 2020): 158–68.

9. Leslie Vinjamuri, "Human Rights Backlash," in *Human Rights Futures*, ed. Stephen Hopgood, Jack Snyder, and Leslie Vinjamuri (New York: Cambridge University Press, 2017); Alexander Cooley and Daniel Nexon, *Exit from Hegemony: The Unraveling of the American Global Order* (New York: Oxford University Press, 2020), 141–43.

10. Brendan O'Boyle, "Did an Anti-LGBT Panic Help Defeat Colombia's Peace Deal?" *Americas Quarterly*, October 6, 2016, https://www.americasquarterly.org/article/did-an-anti-lgbt-panic-help-defeat-colombias-peace-deal/; Pawel Knut, "Poland Exit Polls Mean Victory for Homophobic Andrzej Duda," *Think*, July 13, 2020, https://www.nbcnews.com/think/opinion/poland-exit-polls-mean-victory-homophobic-andrzej-duda-misery-lgbtq-ncna1233643. More broadly, see Omar Encarnacion, "The Gay Rights Backlash: Contrasting Views from the United States and Latin America," in "Backlash Politics," special issue, *British Journal of Politics and International Relations* 22, no. 4 (November 2020): 654–65.

11. Author interview, Columbia University, 2008.

12. Tabitha Bonilla and Alvin B. Tillery, "Which Identity Frames Boost Support for and Mobilization in the #BlackLivesMatter Movement?" *American Political Science Review* 114, no. 4 (November 2020): 947–62, at 959. For evidence that gay advocacy in Bosnia boosted both gay activism and counteractivism, see Phillip A. Ayoub, Douglas Page, and Sam Whitt, "Pride amid Prejudice: The Influence of LGBT+ Rights Activism in a Socially Conservative Society," *American Political Science Review* 115, no. 2 (May 2021): 467–85.

13. Vinjamuri, "Human Rights Backlash," 115.

14. Gerardo Munck and Carol Skalnik Leff, "Modes of Transition and Democratization: South America and Eastern Europe in Comparative Perspective," in *Transitions to Democracy*, ed. Lisa Anderson (New York: Columbia University Press, 1999), 193–216, at 195.

15. V. I. Lenin, *Left-Wing Communism: An Infantile Disorder* (Detroit, MI: Marxian Educational Society, 1921).

16. Michael Mousseau, "Market Civilization and Its Clash with Terror," *International Security* 27, no. 3 (Winter 2002–2003), 5–29; "Backlash Politics," special issue, *British Journal of Politics and International Relations* 22, no. 4 (November 2020); Barnett R. Rubin, *The Fragmentation of Afghanistan: State Formation and Collapse in the International System* (New Haven, CT: Yale University Press, 1995); Sameer Yasir, "Gandhi's Killer Evokes Admiration as Never Before," *New York Times*, February 4, 2020; Vinjamuri, "Human Rights Backlash," 124–31; Alexander Cooley and Matthew Schaaf, "Grounding the Backlash: Regional Security Treaties, Counternorms, and

Human Rights in Eurasia," in Hopgood, Snyder, and Vinjamuri, *Human Rights Futures*, 159–88; Kevin L. Cope and Charles Crabtree, "A Nationalist Backlash to International Refugee Law: Evidence from a Survey Experiment in Turkey," *Journal of Empirical Legal Studies* 17, no. 4 (December 2020): 752–88.

17. Editorial, "Justice Ginsburg's Misdirection: The Lesson of Roe v. Wade Is that the Supreme Court Must Not Wait on Fundamental Rights," *New York Times*, April 3, 2013, A26.

18. Margaret E. Tankard and Elizabeth Levy Paluck, "The Effect of a Supreme Court Decision Regarding Gay Marriage on Social Norms and Personal Attitudes," *Psychological Science* 28, no. 9 (2017): 1334–44. Thanks to Dylan Groves for this reference. Myra Marx Ferree, "Resonance and Radicalism: Feminist Framing in the Abortion Debates of the United States and Germany," *American Journal of Sociology* 109, no. 2 (September 2003): 304–44.

19. Sarah Zukerman Daly, "Voting for Victors: Why Violent Actors Win Postwar Elections," *World Politics* 71, no. 4 (October 2019): 747–805.

20. Rodney Stark, *The Rise of Christianity* (Princeton, NJ: Princeton University Press, 1996).

21. Richard Primus, *The American Language of Rights: Ideas in Context* (New York: Cambridge University Press, 1999).

22. "The End of Child Labour: Within Reach," Report of the Director-General, International Labour Conference, 95th Session, Report I(B), (2006), 11, says "In the past 25 years, China has taken more people out of poverty and enrolled more children in school than any other country," having "a dramatic impact on child labour in China."

23. Rosemary Foot, *China, the UN, and Human Protection: Beliefs, Power, Image* (New York: Oxford University Press, 2020), 207.

24. Jonathan R. Stromseth, Edmund Malesky, and D. Gueorguiev, *China's Governance Puzzle: Enabling Transparency and Participation in a Single-Party State* (New York: Cambridge University Press, 2017).

25. Alasdair MacIntyre, *After Virtue*, 2d ed. (London: Duckworth, 1985).

26. Reinhold Niebuhr, *Moral Man and Immoral Society: A Study in Ethics and Politics* (New York; Scribner's, 1932); Ben Rhodes, *The World as It Is: A Memoir of the Obama White House* (New York: Random House, 2018).

27. See Aryeh Neier's account of the antislavery movement in *The International Human Rights Movement: A History* (Princeton, NJ: Princeton University Press, 2012), 33–36.

28. Neier, *International Human Rights Movement*, 205–7; Margaret Keck and Kathryn Sikkink, *Activists beyond Borders: Advocacy Networks in International Politics* (Ithaca: Cornell University Press, 1998), 24; Finnemore and Sikkink, "International Norm Dynamics," 899–900; Kathryn Sikkink, *The Justice Cascade: How Human Rights Prosecutions Are Changing World Politics* (New York: Norton, 2011), 115–21; and more generally John G. Ruggie, "What Makes the World Hang Together? Neo-Utilitarianism and the Social Constructivist Challenge," *International Organization* 52, no. 4 (Autumn 1998): 855–85; and Alexander Wendt, *Social Theory of International Politics* (New York: Cambridge University Press, 1999).

29. Ann Marie Clark, "The Normative Context of Human Rights Criticism: Treaty Ratifications and UN Mechanisms," in *The Persistent Power of Human Rights: From Commitment to Compliance*, ed. Thomas Risse, Stephen Ropp, and Kathryn Sikkink (New York: Cambridge University Press, 2013), 125–44.

30. Jürgen Habermas, "Discourse Ethics: Notes on a Program of Philosophical Justification," in *Moral Consciousness and Communicative Action* (Cambridge, MA: MIT, 1990), 43–116; Thomas Risse, "Let's Argue! Communicative Action in World Politics," *International Organization* 54 (Winter 2000): 1–39.

31. See the list of mechanisms in Keck and Sikkink, *Activists beyond Borders*, 16–25.

32. Patrick T. Jackson and Ronald R. Krebs, "Twisting Tongues and Twisting Arms: The Power of Political Rhetoric," *European Journal of International Relations* 13, no. 1 (March 2007): 35–66.

33. Jack Snyder and Leslie Vinjamuri, "Trials and Errors: Principle and Pragmatism in International Justice," *International Security* 28, no. 3 (Winter 2003–2004): 5–44.

34. Neier, *International Human Rights Movement*, 30–32, 47, 55.

35. Richard Rorty, "Human Rights, Rationality, and Sentimentality," in *On Human Rights: The Oxford Amnesty Lectures, 1993*, ed. Stephen Shute and Susan Hurley (New York: Basic, 1993), 111–34, at 118.

36. In the academic field of international relations, any pragmatic approach that features power and interest is likely to be seen as some version of realism. This label is often applied to any of the following arguments: (1) effective political action requires prudent consequentialism and an ethic of responsibility; (2) clubs are trump in international politics, and war is necessarily an omnipresent concern of states; (3) states in the anarchical international system necessarily define interest as power; and (4) states should and do base their policy on selfish national interests because of the reciprocal commitment of their citizens to die if necessary in defense of each other. Among these four points, my arguments about human rights pragmatism are realist only in the first sense—that is, they are consequentialist. Taking a very broad view of power, my argument is also compatible with point 3 in the sense that any consequentialist ethic must consider how to mobilize the power needed to achieve ethical goals. In that view, power is an interest, but not the only interest. The other points are not logically entailed in any of the arguments I am making here, so if points 2 and 4 were the criteria, my arguments would not be realist. See Hans Morgenthau, *In Defense of the National Interest* (New York: Knopf, 1951).

37. Wex Legal Dictionary, Legal Information Institute, Cornell University.

38. Thomas Nagel, *The View from Nowhere* (New York: Oxford University Press, 1986); and Nagel, *The Last Word* (New York: Oxford University Press, 1997), 101–26.

39. Edna Ulmann-Margalit, *The Emergence of Norms* (Oxford: Clarendon Press, 1977). Assessing both sides of this issue is Jon Elster, *The Cement of Society: A Study of Social Order* (New York: Oxford University Press, 1989).

40. Nagel, *Last Word*, 102, remarks: "Empirical confirmation plays a vital role in this process, but it cannot do so without theory."

41. Ronald Dworkin, "Objectivity and Truth: You'd Better Believe It," *Philosophy and Public Affairs* 25, no. 2 (Spring 1996): 87–139.

42. Herbert Croly, *The Promise of American Life* (New York: Macmillan, 1909); Daniel DiSalvo, *Engines of Change: Party Factions in American Politics, 1868–2010* (New York: Oxford University Press, 2012). Nagel, *Last Word*, 103, says, "Moral reasoning is a species of practical reasoning."

43. Upton Sinclair, *The Jungle* (New York: Doubleday, 1906); John Dewey, *Democracy and Education* (New York: Institute for Learning Technologies, 1995).

44. Richard A. Wilson, "Human Rights, Culture, and Context: An Introduction," in *Human Rights, Culture, and Context: Anthropological Perspectives*, ed. Richard A. Wilson (London: Pluto, 1997), 16.

45. Jack Knight, *Institutions and Social Conflict* (New York: Cambridge University Press, 1992).

46. Robert Gilpin, *War and Change in World Politics* (New York: Cambridge University Press, 1981).

47. G. John Ikenberry, *After Victory: Institutions, Strategic Restraint, and the Rebuilding of Order after Major Wars*, 2d ed. (Princeton, NJ: Princeton University Press, 2019); for the human rights aspect, see Ikenberry, *Liberal Leviathan: The Origins, Crisis, and Transformation of the American World Order* (Princeton, NJ: Princeton University Press, 2011), 246–47.

48. Seymour Martin Lipset and Stein Rokkan, "Cleavage Structures, Party Systems, and Voter Alignments: An Introduction," in *Party Systems and Voter Alignments: Cross-National Perspectives*, ed. Seymour Martin Lipset and Stein Rokkan (New York: Free Press, 1967), 1–64.

49. David Scheffer, *All the Missing Souls: A Personal History of the War Crimes Tribunals* (Princeton, NJ: Princeton University Press, 2012), 199–226.

50. Priscilla Hayner, *The Peacemaker's Paradox: Pursuing Justice in the Shadow of Conflict* (New York: Routledge, 2018), 145–59, covers the evidence about bargaining leverage in this case in full complexity from both viewpoints. Gary Bass, *Stay the Hand of Vengeance: The Politics of War Crimes Tribunals* (Princeton, NJ: Princeton University Press, 2000), 290–95, was an early challenger of the claim that holding trials deters future atrocities.

51. Michael Latham, *Modernization as Ideology: American Social Science and "Nation Building" in the Kennedy Era* (Chapel Hill: University of North Carolina, 2000).

52. Barrington Moore, *Social Origins of Dictatorship and Democracy: Lord and Peasant in the Making of the Modern World* (Boston: Beacon, 1966); Alexander Gerschenkron, *Economic Backwardness in Historical Perspective: A Book of Essays* (Cambridge, MA: Harvard University Press, 1962); Samuel P. Huntington, *Political Order in Changing Societies* (New Haven, CT: Yale University Press, 1968).

53. Speech in the House of Commons, November 11, 1947.

54. See Jon Elster, *Ulysses and the Sirens* (Cambridge: Cambridge University Press, 1979), for a critique of functional theory in the social sciences.

55. Hendrik Spruyt, *The Sovereign State and Its Competitors* (Princeton, NJ: Princeton University Press, 1994), 106, on the shift from feudalism to a rule-based state.

56. Shmuel N. Eisenstadt, "Multiple Modernities," *Daedalus* 129, no. 1 (Winter 2000): 1–29; Peter Katzenstein, ed., *Civilizations in World Politics* (New York: Routledge, 2010), ch. 1.

57. Jack Donnelly, *Universal Human Rights in Theory and Practice*, 2d ed. (Ithaca, NY: Cornell University Press, 2003), 107–26; Stephen Krasner, *Structural Conflict: The Third World Against Global Liberalism* (Berkeley: University of California Press, 1985).

58. Francis Fukuyama, *The Origins of Political Order from Prehuman Times to the French Revolution* (New York: Farrar, Straus and Giroux, 2011); Fukuyama, *Political Order and Political Decay* (New York: Farrar, Straus, 2014); Fukuyama, "Why Is Democracy Performing So Poorly?" *Journal of Democracy* 26, no. 1 (January 2015): 11–20; see also Daron Acemoglu and James A. Robinson, *Why Nations Fail: The Origins of Power, Prosperity, and Poverty* (New York: Crown, 2012).

59. Douglass C. North, John Joseph Wallis, and Barry R. Weingast, *Violence and Social Orders: A Conceptual Framework for Interpreting Recorded Human History* (New York: Cambridge University Press, 2009).

60. Kevin Narizny, "The Political-Economic Foundations of Representative Government," *Perspectives on Politics* 18, no. 2 (June 2020): 454–69.

61. Barbara Geddes, *How Dictatorships Work* (New York: Cambridge University Press, 2018); Milan Svolik, *The Politics of Authoritarian Rule* (New York: Cambridge University Press, 2012); Beatriz Magaloni, *Voting for Autocracy: Hegemonic Party Survival and Its Demise in Mexico* (New York: Cambridge University Press, 2006); Jessica L. P. Weeks, *Dictators at War and Peace* (Ithaca, NY: Cornell University Press, 2014); Jennifer Gandhi, *Political Institutions under Dictatorship* (New York: Cambridge University Press, 2008).

62. Svolik, *Politics of Authoritarian Rule*, 116–17.

63. Svolik, *Politics of Authoritarian Rule*, 192–95.

64. Weeks, *Dictators at War*, 54–66.

65. Stephan Haggard and Robert R. Kaufman, *Dictators and Democrats: Masses, Elites, and Regime Change* (Princeton, NJ: Princeton University Press, 2016), 348; Dan Slater and Joseph Wong, "The Strength to Concede: Ruling Parties and Democratization in Developmental Asia," *Perspectives on Politics* 11, no. 3 (September 2013): 717–33; Anna Grzymala-Busse, *Rebuilding Leviathan: Party Competition and State Exploitation in Post-Communist Democracies* (New York: Cambridge University Press, 2007).

66. Alena Ledeneva, *Can Russia Modernise? Sistema, Power Networks and Informal Governance* (Cambridge: Cambridge University Press, 2013).

67. Charles Tilly, *Contention and Democracy in Europe, 1650–2000* (New York: Cambridge University Press, 2004), 17–20.

68. Fredrik Barth, *Ethnic Groups and Boundaries* (Boston: Little, Brown, 1969).

69. For a somewhat parallel analysis of traditional versus postmodern values based on attitude surveys, see Ronald Inglehart, "Findings and Insights," WVS Database, World Values Survey Association, 2015, http://www.worldvaluessurvey.org/WVSContents.jsp, p. 4. Inglehart says that "traditional values emphasize the importance of religion, parent-child ties, deference to authority and traditional family values. People who embrace these values also reject divorce, abortion, euthanasia and suicide. These societies have high levels of national pride and a nationalistic outlook." Thanks to Elektra Williams for this reference.

70. Tilly, *Contention and Democracy*, 20.

71. Adam Przeworski, Michael Alvarez, Jose Cheibub, and Fernando Limongi, *Democracy and Development* (New York: Cambridge University Press, 2000); Stephan Haggard and Robert R. Kaufman, "Democratization During the Third Wave," *Annual Review of Political Science* 19 (2016): 125–44, at 129–30.

72. For the argument that technocracy will suffice for success, see Daniel A. Bell, *The China Model: Political Meritocracy and the Limits of Democracy* (Princeton, NJ: Princeton University Press, 2015).

73. Jeffrey C. Alexander, *The Dark Side of Modernity* (Cambridge: Polity, 2013).

74. Karl Polanyi, *The Great Transformation* (New York: Farrar, 1944).

75. Ernest Gellner, *Nations and Nationalism* (Ithaca, NY: Cornell University Press, 1983); Gerschenkron, *Economic Backwardness in Historical Perspective*; B. Moore, *Social Origins of Dictatorship and Democracy*; Huntington, *Political Order in Changing Societies*.

76. James D. Fearon, "Self-Enforcing Democracy," *Quarterly Journal of Economics* 126, no. 4 (November 2011): 1661–1708; Barry Weingast, "The Political Foundations of Democracy and Rule of Law," *American Political Science Review* 91, no. 2 (June 1997): 245–63.

77. For a good application to Putin's Russia, see Timothy Frye, *Weak Strongman: The Limits of Power in Putin's Russia* (Princeton, NJ: Princeton University Press, 2021), ch. 2.

78. Scott Gates, Håvard Hegre, Mark P. Jones, and Håvard Strand, "Institutional Inconsistency and Political Stability: Polity Duration, 1800–2000," *American Journal of Political Science* 50, no. 4 (October 2006): 893–908; Carl Henrik Knutsen and Håvard Mokleiv Nygård, "Institutional Characteristics and Regime Survival: Why Are Semi-Democracies Less Durable than Autocracies and Democracies?" *American Journal of Political Science* 59, no. 3 (July 2015): 656–70; Harry Eckstein, "Authority Patterns: A Structural Pattern for Inquiry," *American Political Science Review* 67, no. 4 (December 1973): 1143–61; Steven Levitsky and Lucan A. Way, *Competitive Authoritarianism: Hybrid Regimes after the Cold War* (New York: Cambridge University Press, 2010); Jennifer Gandhi and Ellen Lust-Okar, "Elections under Authoritarianism," *Annual Review of Political Science* 12 (June 2009): 403–22.

79. Emilie Hafner-Burton, Susan Hyde, and Ryan Jablonski, "When Do Governments Resort to Election Violence?" *British Journal of Political Science* 44, no. 1 (January 2014): 149–79; Steven I. Wilkinson, *Votes and Violence: Electoral Competition and Ethnic Riots in India* (New York: Cambridge University Press, 2004); Dawn Brancati and Jack Snyder, "Time to Kill: The Impact of Election Timing on Post-Conflict Stability," *Journal of Conflict Resolution* 57, no. 5 (October 2013): 822–53.

80. Mark R. Beissinger, "Structure and Example in Modular Political Phenomena: The Diffusion of the Bulldozer/Rose/Orange/Tulip Revolutions," *Perspectives on Politics* 5, no. 2 (June 2007): 259–76; Henry Hale, "Regime Cycles: Democracy, Autocracy, and Revolution in Post-Soviet Eurasia," *World Politics* 58, no. 1 (October 2005): 133–65; Ora John Reuter and David Szakonyi, "Electoral Manipulation and Regime Support: Survey Evidence from Russia," *World Politics* 73, no. 2 (April 2021): 275–314.

81. Giacomo Chiozza and Hein Goemans, *Leaders and International Conflict* (New York: Cambridge University Press, 2011).

82. Håvard Hegre, Tanja Ellingsen, Scott Gates, and Nils Petter Gleditsch, "Toward a Democratic Civil Peace? Democracy, Political Change, and Civil War, 1816–1992," *American Political Science Review* 95, no. 1 (March 2001): 33–48; Helen Fein, "More Murder in the Middle: Life Integrity Violations and Democracy in the World, 1987," *Human Rights Quarterly* 17, no. 1 (February 1995): 170–91.

83. Seva Gunitsky, "Lost in the Gray Zone: Competing Measures of Democracy in the Former Soviet Republics," in *Ranking the World*, ed. Alexander Cooley and Jack Snyder (New York: Cambridge University Press, 2015), 113, finds that different democracy indexes' "measures of hybrid regimes are particularly unreliable."

84. Beatriz Magaloni and Ruth Kricheli, "Political Order and One-Party Rule," *Annual Review of Political Science* 13 (2010): 123–43; Huntington, *Political Order in Changing Societies*. Knutsen and Nygård, "Institutional Characteristics and Regime Survival," 664, find that the superior durability of single-party regimes disappears when level of democracy is taken into account. Weeks, *Dictators at War*, 49, finds that the less belligerent foreign policy behavior of single-party regimes is not due to any difference in their degree of democracy.

85. Jean Lachapelle, Steven Levitsky, Lucan Way, and Adam Casey, "Social Revolution and Authoritarian Durability," *World Politics* 72, no. 4 (October 2020): 557–600.

86. Magaloni and Kricheli, "Political Order and One-Party Rule," 131. Huntington claimed that "liberalized authoritarianism is not a stable equilibrium; the half way house does not stand." Samuel P. Huntington, *The Third Wave: Democratization in the Late Twentieth Century* (Norman: University of Oklahoma, 1993), 174–75.

87. Samuel Moyn, *The Last Utopia: Human Rights in History* (Cambridge, MA: Belknap Press of Harvard University Press, 2010).

88. Hunt, *Inventing Human Rights*.

89. Samuel Moyn, "Human Rights and the Crisis of Liberalism," in Hopgood, Snyder, and Vinjamuri, *Human Rights Futures*, 261–83; Moyn, *Not Enough: Human Rights in an Unequal World* (Cambridge, MA: Belknap Press of Harvard University Press, 2018); Moyn, *Humane* (Farrar, Straus and Giroux, 2021).

90. Luis Moreno Ocampo, "Keynote Address: Integrating the Work of the ICC into Local Justice Initiatives," Symposium: International Criminal Tribunals in the 21st Century, *American University International Law Review* 21, no. 4 (2006): 497–504, at 502.

91. Mancur Olson, "Dictatorship, Democracy, and Development," *American Political Science Review* 87, no. 3 (September 1993): 567–76; but see also Kimberly Marten, "Debunking the Stationary Bandit Myth: Violence and Governance in Statebuilding History," in *Non-State Challenges in a Re-ordered World: The Jackals of Westphalia*, ed. Stefano Ruzza, Anja P. Jakobi, and Charles Geisler (New York: Routledge, 2016), 175–90.

92. Alberto Alesina and Enrico Spolaore, *The Size of Nations* (Cambridge, MA: MIT, 2003).

93. Karl Deutsch, *Nationalism and Social Communication* (Cambridge, MA: MIT, 1966).

94. Allison Carnegie, *Power Plays: How International Institutions Reshape Coercive Diplomacy* (New York: Cambridge University Press, 2015).

95. As an empirical matter, however, reciprocity does affect states' compliance with the laws of war. See James D. Morrow, "When Do States Follow the Laws of War?" *American Political Science Review* 101, no. 3 (August 2007): 559–72.

96. Carles Boix, "Democracy, Development, and the International System," *American Political Science Review* 105, no. 4 (November 2011): 809–28.

97. Seva Gunitsky, *Aftershocks: Great Powers and Domestic Reforms in the Twentieth Century* (Princeton, NJ: Princeton University Press, 2017).

98. Rajan Menon, *The Conceit of Humanitarian Intervention* (New York: Oxford University Press, 2016).

99. Michael McFaul, *From Cold War to Hot Peace: An American Ambassador in Putin's Russia* (Boston: Houghton Mifflin Harcourt, 2018), 217–27.

100. Andreas Mehler, "From 'Protecting Civilians' to 'For the Sake of Democracy' (and Back Again): Justifying Intervention in Côte D'Ivoire," *African Security* 5, nos. 3–4 (July–December 2012): 199–216.

101. Global Centre for the Responsibility to Protect, "Atrocity Alert No. 227: Côte d'Ivoire, Myanmar (Burma) and Democratic Republic of the Congo," November 4, 2020.

102. Transcript: Aung San Suu Kyi's speech at the ICJ in full, Online Burma/Myanmar Library, December 5, 2019, https://www.burmalibrary.org/en/transcript-aung-san-suu-kyis-speech-at-the-icj-in-full.

103. Daniel R. Lake, "The Limits of Coercive Airpower: NATO's 'Victory' in Kosovo Revisited," *International Security* 34, no. 1 (Summer 2009): 83–112; Barry Posen, "The War for Kosovo: Serbia's Political-Military Strategy," *International Security* 24, no. 4 (Spring 2000): 39–84; Timothy W. Crawford, "Pivotal Deterrence and the Kosovo War: Why the Holbrooke Agreement Failed," *Political Science Quarterly* 116, no. 4 (Winter 2001–2002): 499–523.

104. Shareen Hertel, *Unexpected Power: Conflict and Change among Transnational Activists* (Ithaca, NY: Cornell University Press, 2006).

105. Alexandra Gillies, *Crude Intentions: How Oil Corruption Contaminates the World* (New York: Oxford University Press, 2020).

106. Levitsky and Way, *Competitive Authoritarianism*, stress the democratizing impact of extensive material linkages between established democracies and authoritarian states, and the effectiveness (or not) of authoritarian institutions, especially the scope and cohesion of their repressive capacity, in cases of weak linkage with established democracies.

Chapter 3. Building Blocks and Sequences

1. Daniel Lerner, *The Passing of Traditional Society* (New York: Free Press, 1958); Seymour Martin Lipset, "Some Social Requisites of Democracy: Economic Development and Political Legitimacy," *American Political Science Review* 53, no. 1 (March 1959): 69–105.

2. Barrington Moore, *Social Origins of Dictatorship and Democracy: Lord and Peasant in the Making of the Modern World* (Boston: Beacon, 1966); Daron Acemoglu and James Robinson, *Economic Origins of Dictatorship and Democracy* (New York: Cambridge University Press, 2006).

3. Sheri Berman, *Democracy and Dictatorship in Europe: From the Ancien Régime to the Present Day* (New York: Oxford University Press, 2019).

4. The term is from Douglass C. North, John Joseph Wallis, and Barry R. Weingast, *Violence and Social Orders: A Conceptual Framework for Interpreting Recorded Human History* (New York: Cambridge University Press, 2009).

5. Robert A. Dahl, *Polyarchy: Participation and Opposition* (New Haven, CT: Yale University Press, 1972), 33–47; Samuel P. Huntington, *Political Order in Changing Societies* (New Haven, CT: Yale University Press, 1968).

6. David Lake and Robert Powell, eds., *Strategic Choice and International Relations* (Princeton, NJ: Princeton University Press, 1999), especially chapters by Lake and Powell, 3–38, and Jeffry Frieden, 39–76.

7. Jack Knight, *Institutions and Social Conflict* (New York: Cambridge University Press, 1992).

8. Peter L. Berger and Thomas Luckmann, *The Social Construction of Reality: A Treatise in the Sociology of Knowledge* (Garden City, NY: Doubleday, 1966); Clifford Geertz, *The Interpretation of Cultures* (New York: Basic, 1973); John G. Ruggie, "What Makes the World Hang Together? Neo-Utilitarianism and the Social Constructivist Challenge," *International Organization* 52, no. 4 (Autumn 1998): 855–85; Alexander Wendt, *Social Theory of International Politics* (New York: Cambridge University Press, 1999); Dietrich Rueschemeyer, Evelyne Huber Stephens, and John D. Stephens, *Capitalist Development and Democracy* (Chicago: University of Chicago Press, 1992), 53–57.

9. James Fearon and Alexander Wendt, "Rationalism v. Constructivism: A Skeptical View," in *Handbook of International Relations*, ed. Walter Carlsnaes, Thomas Risse, and Beth Simmons (London: SAGE, 2002), 52–72.

10. Lipset, "Some Social Requisites of Democracy"; Rueschemeyer, Stephens, and Stephens, *Capitalist Development and Democracy*; Peggy Levitt and Sally Engle Merry, "Vernacularization on the Ground: Local Uses of Global Women's Rights in Peru, China, India, and the United States," *Global Networks* 9, no. 4 (2009): 441–61; Sirianne Dahlum, Carl Henrik Knutsen, and Tore Wig, "Who Revolts? Empirically Revisiting the Social Origins of Democracy," *Journal of Politics* 81, no. 4 (October 2019): 1494–99.

11. Eva R. Bellin, *Stalled Democracy: Capital, Labor, and the Paradox of State-Sponsored Development* (New York: Cornell University Press, 2002).

12. Seymour Martin Lipset, "Democracy and Working-Class Authoritarianism," *American Sociological Review* 24, no. 4 (August 1959): 482–50.

13. Ronald Inglehart and Pippa Norris, "The Developmental Theory of the Gender Gap: Women's and Men's Voting Behavior in Global Perspective," *International Political Science Review* 21, no. 4 (2000): 441–63; Richard C. Feinberg, *Gender, War, and World Order: A Study of Public Opinion* (Ithaca, NY: Cornell University Press, 2019); Joslyn Barnhart, Robert Trager, Elizabeth Saunders, and Allan Dafoe, "The Suffragist Peace," *International Organization* 74, no. 4 (Fall 2020), 633–70.

14. Mala Htun, *Sex and the State: Abortion, Divorce, and the Family under Latin American Dictatorships and Democracies* (New York: Cambridge University Press, 2003); see also Saba Mahmood, *The Politics of Piety: The Islamic Revival and the Feminist Subject* (Princeton, NJ: Princeton University Press, 2012), about women's complicated relationship to the veil and other patriarchal norms in Egypt.

15. Cas Mudde and Cristóbal Rovira Kaltwasser, eds., *Populism in Europe and the Americas: Threat or Corrective for Democracy?* (New York: Cambridge University Press, 2012).

16. John Witte, *The Reformation of Rights: Law, Religion and Human Rights in Early Modern Calvinism* (Cambridge: Cambridge University Press, 2007), 39–80, 265–66, 336–39.

17. Robert A. Dahl, "The Concept of Power," *Behavioral Science* 2, no. 3 (January 1957): 201–15.

18. Michael Barnett and Raymond Duvall, "Power in International Politics," *International Organization* 59, no. 1 (January 2005): 39–75, discusses four types of power based on whether they are compulsory, institutional, structural, or productive.

19. Michael Mann, *The Sources of Social Power*, vol. 1 (New York: Cambridge University Press, 1986), calls this infrastructural power.

20. Michael Hechter, *Principles of Group Solidarity* (Berkeley: University of California Press, 1987); Russell Hardin, *One for All: The Logic of Group Conflict* (Princeton, NJ: Princeton University Press, 1995); Anthony Smith, *The Ethnic Origins of Nations* (Oxford: Basil Blackwell, 1986); Dan Reiter, "Avoiding the Coup-Proofing Dilemma: Consolidating Political Control while Maximizing Military Power," *Foreign Policy Analysis* 16, no. 3 (July 2020): 312–31.

21. Christopher H. Achen and Larry M. Bartels, *Democracy for Realists: Why Elections Do Not Produce Responsive Government* (Princeton, NJ: Princeton University Press, 2016), chs. 8–9.

22. Daniel Schlozman, *When Movements Anchor Parties: Electoral Alignments in American History* (Princeton, NJ: Princeton University Press, 2015), and chapter 6 in this volume.

23. Megumi Naoi, *Building Legislative Coalitions for Free Trade in Asia: Globalization as Legislation* (New York: Cambridge University Press, 2015).

24. William Riker, "The Number of Political Parties: A Reexamination of Duverger's Law," *Comparative Politics* 9, no. 1 (October 1976): 93–106; Beatriz Magaloni, *Voting for Autocracy: Hegemonic Party Survival and Its Demise in Mexico* (New York: Cambridge University Press, 2006), 176.

25. Chaim Kaufmann and Robert Pape, "Explaining Costly International Moral Action: Britain's Sixty-Year Campaign against the Atlantic Slave Trade," *International Organization* 53, no. 4 (Autumn 1999): 654–57.

26. Eric Foner, *Free Soil, Free Labor, Free Men* (New York: Oxford University Press, 1970), 266.

27. Marc van de Wardt, Catherine E. De Vries, and Sara B. Hobolt, "Exploiting the Cracks: Wedge Issues in Multiparty Competition," *Journal of Politics* 76, no. 4 (July 2014): 986–99.

28. Brett Fairbairn, "Interpreting Wilhelmine Elections: National Issues, Fairness Issues, and Electoral Mobilization," in *Elections, Mass Politics, and Social Change in Modern Germany: New Perspectives*, ed. Larry Eugene Jones and James N. Retallack (Cambridge: Cambridge University Press, 1992), 22–30; Berman, *Democracy and Dictatorship*, 387–88.

29. Dafna Hochman Rand, *Roots of the Arab Spring: Contested Authority and Political Change in the Middle East* (Philadelphia: University of Pennsylvania Press, 2013).

30. Magaloni, *Voting for Autocracy*, 10.

31. Seymour Martin Lipset and Stein Rokkan, "Cleavage Structures, Party Systems, and Voter Alignments: An Introduction," in *Party Systems and Voter Alignments: Cross-National Perspectives*, ed. Seymour Martin Lipset and Stein Rokkan (New York: Free Press, 1967), 1–64.

32. Lipset and Rokkan, "Cleavage Structures," four-variable chart on pp. 27–29. For an update on the Lipset and Rokkan framework that applies it to the post–industrial revolution, postmaterialism in Europe and contemporary globalization, see Daniele Caramani, *The Europeanization of Politics: The Formation of a European Electorate and Party System in Historical Perspective* (Cambridge: Cambridge University Press, 2015), 48–50.

33. Gregory Luebbert, *Liberalism, Fascism, or Social Democracy: Social Classes and the Political Origins of Regimes in Interwar Europe* (New York: Oxford University Press, 1991), 306–15.

34. Charles Tilly and Lesley J. Wood, *Social Movements, 1768–2012*, 2d ed. (Boulder, CO: Paradigm, 2009), 3–5, 25–29, 33–37.

35. Lars-Erik Cederman, *Emergent Actors in World Politics: How States and Nations Develop and Dissolve* (Princeton, NJ: Princeton University Press, 1997), chs. 6–7.

36. Fotini Christia, *Alliance Formation in Civil Wars* (New York: Cambridge University Press, 2012).

37. Liah Greenfeld, *Nationalism: Five Roads to Modernity* (Cambridge, MA: Harvard University Press, 1992).

38. Martha Finnemore, *The Purpose of Intervention: Changing Beliefs about the Use of Force* (Ithaca, NY: Cornell University Press, 2003).

39. Thomas Pepinsky, "The Institutional Turn in Comparative Authoritarianism," *British Journal of Political Science* 44, no. 3 (July 2014): 631–53, on the need for analysts to distinguish between institutions as causes and institutions as epiphenomena.

40. John D. Huber, *Exclusion by Elections: Inequality, Ethnic Identity, and Democracy* (New York: Cambridge University Press, 2017), 3–9, 55–58.

41. For a well-supported example of this logic, see Daniel N. Posner, *Institutions and Ethnic Politics in Africa* (New York: Cambridge University Press, 2005).

42. Huber, *Exclusion by Elections*, 158. For an example based on evidence from Indian trade protectionism, see Nikhar Gaikwad, "Identity Politics and Economic Policy," paper presented at the American Political Science Association Annual Conference, 2018, and his forthcoming book of the same title.

43. Huber, *Exclusion by Elections*, 58, 189–91. For a similar logic on the tendency toward economic nationalism in plurality systems, see Ronald Rogowski, "Trade and the Variety of Democratic Institutions," *International Organization* 41, no. 2 (1987): 203–23, and references to more conditional findings of the subsequent debate in Patrick Wagner and Michael Plouffe, "Electoral Systems and Trade-Policy Outcomes: The Effects of Personal-Vote Incentives on Barriers to International Trade," *Public Choice* 180, nos. 3–4 (September 2019): 333–52.

44. Huber, *Exclusion by Elections*, 13–15, 51–55.

45. Donald Horowitz, "Making Moderation Pay," in *Conflict and Peacemaking in Multiethnic Societies*, ed. Joseph V. Montville (Lexington, MA: Lexington, 1990), ch. 25; Jack Snyder, *From Voting to Violence: Democratization and Nationalist Conflict* (New York: Norton, 2000), 273–87.

46. Richard C. Paddock, "Fierce but Frail, Malaysia's Mahathir, 92, Aims to Topple Protégé," *New York Times,* February 17, 2018, https://www.nytimes.com/2018/02/17/world/asia /malaysia-mahathir-mohamad-najib-razak.html.

47. For the contrary view, see John Mearsheimer, *The Great Delusion: Liberal Dreams and International Realities* (New Haven, CT: Yale University Press, 2018), 82–119.

48. Kenneth Roth, "Defending Economic, Social and Cultural Rights: Practical Issues Faced by an International Human Rights Organization," *Human Rights Quarterly* 26, no. 1 (February 2004): 63–74; Aryeh Neier, *International Human Rights Movement: A History* (Princeton, NJ: Princeton University Press, 2012), ch. 3.

49. Neier, *International Human Rights Movement*, 33–37.

50. Michael Young, "A Revolution of the Soul: Transformative Experiences and Immediate Abolition," in *Passionate Politics: Emotions and Social Movements*, ed. Jeff Goodwin, James Jasper, and Francesca Polletta (Chicago: University of Chicago Press, 2001), 102–3, argues that "white abolitionists were self-absorbed eccentrics more concerned with personal perfection than practical solutions for a complex social problem."

51. Judith M. Brown, *Gandhi's Rise to Power: Indian Politics, 1915–1922* (Cambridge: Cambridge University Press, 1972); Ramachandra Guha, *Gandhi: The Years that Changed the World, 1914–1948* (New York: Knopf, 2018).

52. For a theoretical discussion of contemporary approaches that avoid the reification of rights and of culture, and thus pose a flexible interaction between them, see Sally Engle Merry, "Changing Rights, Changing Culture," in *Culture and Rights: Anthropological Perspectives*, ed. J. Cowan, M. Dembour, and R. Wilson (Cambridge: Cambridge University Press, 2001), 31–55.

53. Levitt and Merry, "Vernacularization on the Ground," 441–61, explores both sides of this tradeoff. See also Amitav Acharya, "How Ideas Spread: Whose Norms Matter? Norm Localization and Institutional Change in Asian Regionalism," *International Organization* 58, no. 2 (Spring 2004): 239–75.

54. Levitt and Merry, "Vernacularization on the Ground," 452–53.

55. Charles Tilly, *Contention and Democracy in Europe, 1650–2000* (New York: Cambridge University Press, 2004), 17–20.

56. Levitt and Merry, "Vernacularization on the Ground," 448.

57. Levitt and Merry, "Vernacularization on the Ground," 447–48.

58. Rachel Wahl, *Just Violence: Torture and Human Rights in the Eyes of the Police* (Stanford, CA: Stanford University Press, 2017).

59. Acharya, "How Ideas Spread."

60. Moses Shayo, "A Model of Social Identity with an Application to Political Economy: Nation, Class, and Redistribution," *American Political Science Review* 103, no. 2 (May 2009): 147–74.

61. Micah English and Joshua Kalla, "Racial Equality Frames and Public Policy Support: Survey Experimental Evidence," OSF Preprints, April 23, 2021, doi:10.31219/osf.io/tdkf3.

62. Fairbairn, "Interpreting Wilhelmine Elections," 22–30.

63. Steven I. Wilkinson, *Votes and Violence: Electoral Competition and Ethnic Riots in India* (New York: Cambridge University Press, 2004).

64. Dahl, *Polyarchy*, 33–47.

65. Fareed Zakaria, "The Rise of Illiberal Democracy," *Foreign Affairs* 76, no. 6 (November-December 1997): 22–43.

66. Edward D. Mansfield and Jack Snyder, "Democratization and the Arab Spring," *International Interactions* 38, no. 5 (2012): 722–33.

67. Daniel Byman, "Constructing a Democratic Iraq: Challenges and Opportunities," *International Security* 28, no. 1 (Summer 2003): 47–78.

68. Kathryn Sikkink, *Evidence for Hope: Making Human Rights Work in the 21st Century* (Princeton, NJ: Princeton University Press, 2017), 194–95, says that "democracy is essential for human rights to succeed, but not sufficient."

69. Dankwart Rustow, "Transitions to Democracy: Toward a Dynamic Model," *Comparative Politics* 2, no. 2 (April 1970): 337–63.

70. This is the commonly used definition of Ernest Gellner.

71. Rogers Brubaker, "Aftermaths of Empire and the Unmixing of Peoples: Historical and Comparative Perspectives," *Ethnic and Racial Studies* 18, no. 2 (April 1995): 189–218.

72. Eugen Weber, *Peasants into Frenchmen: The Modernization of Rural France, 1870–1914* (Stanford, CA: Stanford University Press, 1976).

73. Dawn Brancati, *Peace by Design: Managing Intrastate Conflict through Decentralization* (New York: Oxford University Press, 2009).

74. Posner, *Institutions and Ethnic Politics in Africa*.

75. Lisa Blaydes, *State of Repression: Iraq under Saddam Hussein* (Princeton, NJ: Princeton University Press, 2018).

76. Daniel Byman, "Forever Enemies? The Manipulation of Ethnic Identities to End Ethnic Wars," *Security Studies* 9, no. 3 (Spring 2000): 149–90.

77. Arend Lijphart, *Democracy in Plural Societies* (New Haven, CT: Yale University Press, 1977).

78. Alvin Rabushka and Kenneth A. Shepsle, *Politics in Plural Societies: A Theory of Democratic Instability* (Columbus, OH: Merrill 1972); Andrew Kydd and Barbara Walter, "The Strategies of Terrorism," *International Security* 31, no. 1 (Summer 2006): 49–79.

79. Horowitz, "Making Moderation Pay."

80. Guillermo O'Donnell, *Modernization and Bureaucratic-Authoritarianism: Studies in South American Politics* (Berkeley: Institute of International Studies, University of California, 1973);

Beatriz Magaloni and Ruth Kricheli, "Political Order and One-Party Rule," *Annual Review of Political Science* 13 (2010): 123–43.

81. V. I. Lenin, *Left-Wing Communism: An Infantile Disorder* (Detroit, MI: Marxian Educational Society, 1921).

82. Micheline Ishay, *The History of Human Rights: From Ancient Times to the Globalization Era* (Berkeley: University of California Press, 2004), 117–72.

Chapter 4. Crossing the Political Threshold

1. Azar Gat, *Nations: The Long History and Deep Roots of Political Ethnicity and Nationalism* (Cambridge: Cambridge University Press, 2013), ch. 2.

2. Francis Fukuyama, *The Origins of Political Order from Prehuman Times to the French Revolution* (New York: Farrar, Straus and Giroux, 2011); Douglass C. North, John Joseph Wallis, and Barry R. Weingast, *Violence and Social Orders: A Conceptual Framework for Interpreting Recorded Human History* (New York: Cambridge University Press, 2009); Gat, *Nations*.

3. Karen Barkey, *Bandits and Bureaucrats: The Ottoman Route to State Centralization* (Ithaca, NY: Cornell University Press, 1994).

4. Margaret Levi, *Of Rule and Revenue* (Berkeley: University of California, 1988), 122–44.

5. North, Wallis, and Weingast, *Violence and Social Orders*, 25–27, 148–250.

6. Interviews with NGO activists, local officials, journalists, political party activists, militia members, and scholars in Dnipropetrovsk, Kyiv, and Lviv, 2015.

7. Nicolas van de Walle, *African Economies and The Politics of Permanent Crisis, 1979–1999* (New York: Cambridge University Press, 2001), 127, notes that the patrimonialism of postcolonial African states such as Senegal, which confounds international financial organizations' attempts to impose conditions conducive to the consolidation of an open order, is not only a hangover from traditional practice of clientelism but also a reflection of modernization under conditions of state incapacity and the heightening of ethnic identity under divide and rule. Also see Stephen P. Riley, "The Political Economy of Anti-Corruption Strategies in Africa," *European Journal of Development Research* 10, no. 1 (June 1998): 129–59, at 142, on rising corruption in relatively democratic periods in Gambia and Nigeria.

8. Kurt Weyland, *Making Waves: Democratic Contention in Europe and Latin America since the Revolutions of 1848* (New York: Cambridge University Press, 2014); Alicia Mungiu-Pippidi, *The Quest for Good Governance: How Societies Develop Control of Corruption* (New York: Cambridge University Press, 2015). For an overview of the literature of democratization and consolidation, see Gerardo L. Munck, "The Regime Question: Theory Building in Democracy Studies," *World Politics* 54, no. 1 (October 2001): 119–44.

9. Sheri Berman, *Democracy and Dictatorship in Europe: From the Ancien Régime to the Present Day* (New York: Oxford University Press, 2019), 77–105.

10. Weyland, *Making Waves*, 121.

11. Beverly Heckart, *From Bassermann to Bebel: The Grand Bloc's Quest for Reform in the Kaiserreich, 1900–1914* (New Haven, CT: Yale University Press, 1975), on the failure of a progressive alliance to emerge between middle-class and working-class parties.

12. Daniel Ziblatt, *Conservative Parties and the Birth of Democracy* (New York: Cambridge University Press, 2017).

13. Weyland, *Making Waves*, 69–72; Jeffry Frieden, *Debt, Development, and Democracy: Modern Political Economy and Latin America, 1965–1985* (Princeton, NJ: Princeton University Press, 1992).

14. Weyland, *Making Waves*, 201–2.

15. Weyland, *Making Waves*, 209–10.

16. Weyland, *Making Waves*, 231–54.

17. Erica Chenoweth, "The Future of Nonviolent Resistance," *Journal of Democracy* 31, no. 3 (July 2020): 69–84.

18. Mungiu-Pippidi, *Quest for Good Governance*, 10, 75–76. See also Bo Rothstein, "Fighting Systemic Corruption: The Indirect Strategy," *Daedalus* 147, no. 3 (Summer 2018): 35–49; Mlada Bukovansky, "The Hollowness of Anti-Corruption Discourse," *Review of International Political Economy* 13, no. 2 (2006): 181–209.

19. Mungiu-Pippidi, *Quest for Good Governance*, 4–9, 65. See also Susan Rose-Ackerman and Paul Lagunes, eds., *Greed, Corruption, and the Modern State: Essays in Political Economy* (Northampton, MA: Edward Elgar, 2015).

20. Mungiu-Pippidi, *Quest for Good Governance*, 10–11, 75; Stanislas Andreski, "Kleptocracy or Corruption as a System of Government," in *The African Predicament: A Study in the Pathology of Modernization* (London: Joseph, 1968), 92–109, at 109, points out that pure kleptocracy as regulated by "supply and demand" is mitigated in ethnic settings by customary rules of favoritism to kin.

21. Mungiu-Pippidi, *Quest for Good Governance*, 88; Samuel P. Huntington, *Political Order in Changing Societies* (New Haven, CT: Yale University Press, 1968), 59–71, section on "Modernization and Corruption"; Daniel Treisman, "The Causes of Corruption: A Cross-National Study," *Journal of Public Economics* 76, no. 3 (2000): 399–457.

22. Mungiu-Pippidi, *Quest for Good Governance*, 76.

23. Huntington cited in Mungiu-Pippidi, *Quest for Good Governance*, 75, 114–15.

24. Mungiu-Pippidi, *Quest for Good Governance*, 80.

25. Mungiu-Pippidi, *Quest for Good Governance*, 129.

26. Mungiu-Pippidi, *Quest for Good Governance*, 72.

27. Mungiu-Pippidi, *Quest for Good Governance*, 10–11, 123.

28. Mungiu-Pippidi, *Quest for Good Governance*, 138–39. For examples in other settings, see the Tanzanian government's self-initiated anticorruption investigation, the Warioba Commission, discussed in Riley, "Political Economy of Anti-Corruption Strategies in Africa," 143–44; and Rahul Mukherji and Seyed Hossein Zarhani, "Governing India: Evolution of Programmatic Welfare in Andhra Pradesh," *Studies in Indian Politics* 8, no. 1 (2020): 7–21.

29. Ramachandra Guha, "India Was a Miracle Democracy, but It's Time to Downgrade Its Credentials," *Washington Post*, August 14, 2019, https://www.washingtonpost.com/opinions/2019/08/14/india-was-miracle-democracy-its-time-downgrade-its-credentials/.

30. Hans-Ulrich Wehler, *The German Empire, 1871–1918* (Dover, NH: Berg, 1985); David Blackbourn and Geoff Eley, *The Peculiarities of German History: Bourgeois Society and Politics in Nineteenth-Century Germany* (New York: Oxford University Press, 1984).

31. Joel Hellman, "Winners Take All: The Politics of Partial Reform in Postcommunist Transitions," *World Politics* 50, no. 2 (January 1998): 203–34.

32. Peter Gourevitch, *Politics in Hard Times: Comparative Responses to International Economic Crises* (Ithaca, NY: Cornell University Press, 1986), ch. 4.

33. Heckart, *From Bassermann to Bebel.*

34. Geoff Eley, *Reshaping the German Right: Radical Nationalism and Political Change after Bismarck* (New Haven, CT: Yale University Press, 1980).

35. Weyland, *Making Waves,* 166–86.

36. Frieden, *Debt, Development, and Democracy;* Barbara Geddes, *Politician's Dilemma: Building State Capacity in Latin America* (Berkeley: University of California Press, 1994).

37. Weyland, *Making Waves,* 10.

38. John K. Glenn, *Framing Democracy: Civil Society and Civic Movements in Eastern Europe* (Stanford, CA: Stanford University Press, 2001).

39. Beth Simmons, *Mobilizing for Human Rights: International Law in Domestic Politics* (New York: Cambridge University Press, 2009); Amanda M. Murdie and David R. Davis, "Shaming and Blaming: Using Events Data to Assess the Impact of Human Rights INGOs," *International Studies Quarterly* 56, no. 1 (March 2012): 1–16.

40. Weyland, *Making Waves,* 69–72. Whitney K. Taylor, "On the Social Construction of Legal Grievances: Evidence from Colombia and South Africa," *Comparative Political Studies* 53, no. 8 (July 2020): 1326–56, has described how activists in South Africa and Colombia have engaged in "legal mobilization" to demand rights in courts, sometimes with international support, but with locally defined needs in the forefront.

41. Jack Snyder and Leslie Vinjamuri, "Trials and Errors: Principle and Pragmatism in International Justice," *International Security* 28, no. 3 (Winter 2003–2004): 5–44; Martha Finnemore and Kathryn Sikkink, "International Norm Dynamics and Political Change," *International Organization* 52, no. 4 (Autumn 1998): 887–918; E. Tory Higgins, "Making a Good Decision: Value from Fit," *American Psychologist* 55 (2000): 1217–30; Christopher Camacho, E. Tory Higgins, and Lindsay Luger, "Moral Value Transfer from Regulatory Fit: 'What Feels Right *Is* Right' and 'What Feels Wrong *Is* Wrong,'" *Journal of Personality and Social Psychology* 84 (2003): 498–510. Transitional justice is the set of institutions, policies, and practices designed to deal with atrocities and major politically motivated human rights violations in the process, anticipation, or aftermath of regime change or violent conflict. See Ruti G. Teitel, *Transitional Justice* (New York: Oxford University Press, 2000); Lara Nettelfield, *Courting Democracy in Bosnia and Herzegovina: The Hague Tribunal's Impact in a Postwar State* (New York: Cambridge University Press, 2010).

42. Christopher Rudolph, *Power and Principle: The Politics of International Criminal Courts* (Ithaca, NY: Cornell University Press, 2017).

43. "International Justice," Human Rights Watch website, current as of March 2020, as of August 28, 2020 moved to https://www.hrw.org/legacy/justice/about.htm; revised as of August 28, 2020, to say "Human Rights Watch considers international justice—accountability for genocide, war crimes, and crimes against humanity—to be an essential element of building respect for human rights," at "International Justice," Human Rights Watch, http://www.hrw.org/justice.

44. Teitel, *Transitional Justice,* 28–30.

45. José Alvarez, "Crimes of States/Crimes of Hate: Lessons from Rwanda," *Yale Journal of International Law* 24, no. 2 (Summer 1999): 365–483.

46. For a normative discussion of amnesties and some historical examples, see W. James Booth, "The Unforgotten: Memories of Justice," *American Political Science Review* 95, no. 4 (December 2001): 783–85.

47. Neil J. Kritz, "Coming to Terms with Atrocities: A Review of Accountability Mechanisms for Mass Violations of Human Rights," *Law and Contemporary Problems* (Duke University School of Law) 59, no. 4 (Autumn 1996): 127–52; Martha Minow, *Between Vengeance and Forgiveness: Facing History after Genocide and Mass Violence* (Boston: Beacon, 1998).

48. Kate Cronin-Furman, "Human Rights Half Measures: Avoiding Accountability in Postwar Sri Lanka," *World Politics* 72, no. 1 (January 2020): 121–63; Cronin-Furman's book on transitional justice, forthcoming from Cornell University Press.

49. Marlise Simons, "Briton Gives Testimony on Warning to Milosevic," *New York Times*, March 17, 2002, p. 7, on the testimony of former British Member of Parliament Paddy Ashdown.

50. "Macedonia Bolsters Albanian Rights: After Constitutional Change, Amnesty Is Declared for Former Rebels," *International Herald Tribune*, November 17–18, 2001; Timothy Garton Ash, "Is There a Good Terrorist?" *New York Review of Books*, November 29, 2001, 30–33; "Macedonia Is Seeking Control of Land Harboring Ex-Rebels," *New York Times*, November 26, 2001, A11.

51. Extensive interview-based research on the Macedonian clash finds that the tribunal did deter groups who were dependent on Western democracies' support from perpetrating atrocities. Jacqueline R. McAllister, "Deterring Wartime Atrocities: Hard Lessons from the Yugoslav Tribunal," *International Security* 44, no. 3 (Winter 2019/20): 84–128.

52. Payam Akhavan, "Beyond Impunity: Can International Criminal Justice Prevent Future Atrocities?" *American Journal of International Law* 95, no. 1 (January 2001): 16; José Alvarez, "Rush to Closure: Lessons of the Tadic Judgment," *Michigan Law Review* 96, no. 7 (June 1998): 2031–2113.

53. Chaim Kaufmann, "Possible and Impossible Solutions to Ethnic Civil Wars," *International Security* 20, no. 4 (Spring 1996): 136–75.

54. "A Survey of Voter Attitudes in B&H, Summary Report," National Democratic Institute for International Affairs, Bosnia and Herzegovina, May 31, 2002, p. 21.

55. "Serbia: Reform Constituency Shrinks," Results of the Nationwide Survey Conducted by Greenberg Quinlan Rosner Research, National Democratic Institute, June 2002, p. 2.

56. Jelena Subotic, *Hijacked Justice: Dealing with the Past in the Balkans* (Ithaca, NY: Cornell University Press, 2009).

57. Nettelfield, *Courting Democracy in Bosnia and Herzegovina*.

58. Paola Cesarini, "Legacies of Injustice in Italy and Argentina," in *Authoritarian Legacies and Democracy in Latin America and Southern Europe*, ed. Paola Cesarini and Katherine Hite (Notre Dame: Notre Dame Press, 2004), 159–90; Paola Cesarini, "The Politics of Transitional Justice in Italy and Portugal" (PhD diss., Columbia University, 2010).

59. Carlos Nino, *Radical Evil on Trial* (New Haven, CT: Yale University Press, 1996), 116.

60. Priscilla B. Hayner, *Unspeakable Truths: Confronting State Terror and Atrocity* (New York: Routledge, 2001), 187.

61. Margaret Popkin, "El Salvador: A Negotiated End to Impunity?" in *Impunity and Human Rights in International Law and Practice*, ed. Naomi Roht-Arriaza (New York: Oxford University Press, 1995), 198–217.

62. William Stanley, *The Protection Racket State: Elite Politics, Military Extortion, and Civil War in El Salvador* (Philadelphia: Temple University Press, 1996), 218–55; Elisabeth Wood, *Forging Democracy from Below: Insurgent Transitions in South Africa and El Salvador* (Cambridge: Cambridge University Press, 2000). For a similar point regarding the Guatemala settlement,

see Mark Peceny and William Stanley, "Liberal Social Reconstruction and the Resolution of Civil Wars in Central America," *International Organization* 55, no. 1 (Winter 2001): 171–75.

63. Human Rights Watch Briefing Paper, *Serious Flaws: Why the U.N. General Assembly Should Require Changes to the Draft Khmer Rouge Tribunal Agreement*, April 2003.

64. George W. Bush speech, March 18, 2003.

65. Erik Voeten, "Populism and Backlashes against International Courts," *Perspectives on Politics* 18, no. 2 (June 2020): 407–22, at 417–18.

66. Doug Saunders, "Why Louise Arbour Is Thinking Twice," *Toronto Globe and Mail*, March 28, 2015, updated May 12, 2018, https://www.theglobeandmail.com/opinion/why-louise-arbour-is-thinking-twice/article23667013/.

67. Hyeran Jo and Beth Simmons, "Can the International Criminal Court Deter Atrocity?" *International Organization* 70, no. 3 (Summer 2016): 443–75; Simmons, *Mobilizing for Human Rights*.

68. Barry Hashimoto, "Autocratic Consent to International Law: The Case of the International Criminal Court's Jurisdiction, 1998–2017," *International Organization* 74, no. 2 (Spring 2020): 331–62.

69. Geoff Dancy, "Deals with the Devil? Conflict, Amnesties, and Civil War," *International Organization* 72, no. 2 (Spring 2018): 387–421, at 387.

70. Lesley-Ann Daniels, "How and When Amnesty during Conflict Affects Conflict Termination," *Journal of Conflict Resolution* 64, no. 9 (October 2020): 1612–37.

71. Dancy, "Deals with the Devil?," 407–8.

72. Priscilla Hayner, *The Peacemaker's Paradox: Pursuing Justice in the Shadow of Conflict* (New York: Routledge, 2018).

73. Hayner, *Peacemaker's Paradox*, 56–57.

74. Hayner, *Peacemaker's Paradox*, 78.

75. Hayner, *Peacemaker's Paradox*, 82, also 75.

76. Hayner, *Peacemaker's Paradox*, 82.

77. Hayner, *Peacemaker's Paradox*, 48, 50.

78. Hayner, *Peacemaker's Paradox*, 60; also Daniel Krcmaric, *The Justice Dilemma* (Ithaca, NY: Cornell University Press, 2020), 97–104, 137–38, 182–84.

79. Hayner, *Peacemaker's Paradox*, 194–216.

80. Allan S. Weiner, "Ending Wars, Doing Justice: Colombia, Transitional Justice, and the International Criminal Court," *Stanford Journal of International Law* 52, no. 2 (Summer 2016): 211–42.

81. Hayner, *Peacemaker's Paradox*, 210.

82. Hayner, *Peacemaker's Paradox*, 211–12; and see chapter 3 in this volume.

83. Robert A. Karl, *Forgotten Peace: Reform, Violence, and the Making of Contemporary Colombia* (Berkeley: University of California Press, 2017), 35–44, 53–54.

84. Hayner, *Peacemaker's Paradox*, 12–13, 99–110, 118, 201.

85. Hayner, *Peacemaker's Paradox*, 73, 84, note 12, citing Dancy, "Deals with the Devil?"

86. David Bosco, *Rough Justice: The International Criminal Court in a World of Power Politics* (New York: Oxford University Press, 2014); Sarah Nouwen, *Complementarity in the Line of Fire: The Catalysing Effect of the International Criminal Court in Uganda and Sudan* (New York: Cambridge University Press, 2013).

87. George W. Bush, Remarks by the President at the 20th Anniversary of the National Endowment for Democracy, Washington, DC, November 6, 2003.

88. Dawn Brancati and Jack Snyder, "Time to Kill: The Impact of Election Timing on Post-Conflict Stability," *Journal of Conflict Resolution* 57, no. 5 (October 2013): 822–53.

89. Page Fortna, "Has Violence Declined in World Politics?" *Perspectives on Politics* 11, no. 2 (June 2013), 566–70.

90. Séverine Autesserre, *The Trouble with the Congo: Local Violence and the Failure of International Peacebuilding* (New York: Cambridge University Press, 2010).

91. Dawn Brancati and Jack Snyder, "Rushing to the Polls: The Causes of Premature Post-Conflict Elections," *Journal of Conflict Resolution* 55, no. 3 (June 2011): 469–92; Brancati and Snyder, "Time to Kill." For similar findings, see Thomas Edward Flores and Irfan Nooruddin, "The Effect of Elections on Postconflict Peace and Reconstruction," *Journal of Politics* 74, no. 2 (April 2012): 558–70.

92. Roland Paris, *At War's End: Building Peace after Civil Conflict* (New York: Cambridge University Press; CO: Lynne Rienner, 2002).

93. Caroline A. Hartzell and Matthew Hoddie, *Power Sharing and Democracy in Post-Civil War States* (New York: Cambridge University Press, 2020).

94. Philip G. Roeder and Donald Rothchild, *Sustainable Peace: Power and Democracy after Civil Wars* (Ithaca, NY: Cornell University Press, 2005), recommends "power dividing" arrangements that separate powers in different branches of government in a way that encourages alliances that cut across rival factions. Although Brancati and Snyder did not test this hypothesis, this arrangement may have long-term advantages that could serve as a corrective to power sharing's tendency to reify groups.

95. Suzanne Werner and Amy Yuen, "Making and Keeping Peace," *International Organization* 59, no. 2 (Spring 2005): 261–92.

Chapter 5. Crossing the Economic Threshold in China

1. Avinash K. Dixit, *Lawlessness and Economics: Alternative Modes of Governance* (Princeton, NJ: Princeton University Press, 2004); Graeme Thompson, Jennifer Frances, Rosalind Levacic, and Jeremy Mitchell, eds., *Markets, Hierarchies and Networks* (London: Sage, 1991); Christopher Clapham, ed., *Private Patronage and Public Power: Political Clientelism in the Modern State* (London: Frances Pinter, 1982); Andrei Shleifer and Robert W. Vishny, *The Grabbing Hand* (Cambridge, MA: Harvard University Press, 1998); Suzanne Berger and Ronald Dore, *National Diversity and Global Capitalism* (Ithaca, NY: Cornell University Press, 1996).

2. Guillermo O'Donnell, *Bureaucratic Authoritarianism: Argentina, 1966–1973, in Comparative Perspective* (Berkeley: University of California, 1988).

3. Alexander Gerschenkron, *Economic Backwardness in Historical Perspective* (Cambridge, MA: Harvard University Press, 1962). On the mobilization of underutilized rural labor, see Kristen E. Looney, "Mobilization Campaigns and Rural Development: The East Asian Model Reconsidered," *World Politics* 73, no. 2 (April 2021): 205–42.

4. David Dollar, "Institutional Quality and Growth Traps," Pacific Trade and Development Working Paper Series, No. YF37-07, prepared for a conference at the Institute of Southeast Asian Studies, Singapore, June 3–5, 2015; and Dollar, "Institutional Quality and Growth Traps," in *Asia*

and the Middle-Income Trap, Pacific Trade and Development Conference Series, ed. Francis Hutchinson and Sanchita Basu Das (New York: Routledge, 2016), 159–78. For an update on the issue, see Antonio Alonso and Antonio Ocampo, eds., *Trapped in the Middle? Developmental Challenges for Middle-Income Countries* (New York: Oxford University Press, 2020).

5. On the impact of size and lawlessness of the informal sector on economic growth, see Richard F. Doner and Ben Ross Schneider, "The Middle-Income Trap: More Politics than Economics," *World Politics* 68, no. 4 (October 2016): 1–37. The informal sector in this sense means very small-scale commerce conducted by poor people that avoids licenses, regulation, and taxes.

6. Edmund Malesky, "Gerrymandering—Vietnamese Style: Escaping the Partial Reform Equilibrium in a Nondemocratic Regime," *Journal of Politics* 71, no. 1 (January 2009): 132–59.

7. On illiberal logrolling among interest groups in China, see Mario Gilli, Yuan Li, and Jiwei Qian, "Logrolling under Fragmented Authoritarianism: Theory and Evidence from China," *Public Choice* 175, no. 1–2 (April 2018): 197–214.

8. Yuen Yuen Ang, *How China Escaped the Poverty Trap* (Ithaca, NY: Cornell University Press, 2016), figures C.1 and C.2; 243–47.

9. Dani Rodrik, "Second-Best Institutions," *American Economic Review* 98, no. 2 (May 2008): 100–104.

10. Ang, *How China Escaped the Poverty Trap*, 248.

11. Ang, *How China Escaped the Poverty Trap*, 249; see also Yuen Yuen Ang, *China's Gilded Age: The Paradox of Economic Boom and Vast Corruption* (New York: Cambridge University Press, 2020); and Ang, "The Robber Barons of Beijing: Can China Survive Its Gilded Age?" *Foreign Affairs* 100 (July-August 2021): 30–39.

12. Alexander Gerschenkron, *Bread and Democracy in Germany* (Berkeley: University of California Press, 1943); Eckart Kehr, *Battleship Building and Party Politics in Germany, 1894–1901* (Chicago: University of Chicago Press, 1975).

13. Menzie Chinn and Jeffry A. Frieden, *Lost Decades: The Making of America's Debt Crisis and the Long Recovery* (New York: Norton, 2011).

14. Daniel H. Rosen, "China's Economic Reckoning: The Price of Failed Reforms," *Foreign Affairs* 100, no. 4 (July/August 2021): 20–29.

15. Barry Naughton, "China's Economy: Complacency, Crisis and the Challenge of Reform," *Daedalus* 143, no. 2 (Spring 2014): 14–25.

16. Ligang Song, Yixiao Zhou, Luke Hurst, eds., *The Chinese Economic Transformation: Views from Young Economists* (Canberra: ANU Press, 2019).

17. Min Ye, "Fragmentation and Mobilization: Domestic Politics of the Belt and Road in China," *Journal of Contemporary China* 28, no. 119 (February 2019): 696–711; Deborah Brautigam, *The Dragon's Gift: The Real Story of China in Africa* (New York: Oxford University Press, 2009); Thomas J. Christensen, "No New Cold War: Why US-China Strategic Competition Will Not Be Like the US-Soviet Cold War," Asian Institute for Policy Studies, September 10, 2020, https://en.asaninst.org/contents/no-new-cold-war-why-us-china-strategic-competition-will-not-be-like-the-us-soviet-cold-war/, citing Agatha Kratz, Allen Feng, and Logan Wright, "New Data on the 'Debt Trap' Question," Rhodium Group Report, April 29, 2019, https://rhg.com/research/new-data-on-the-debt-trap-question/, and Deborah Brautigam, "A Critical Look at Chinese 'Debt-Trap Diplomacy': The Rise of a Meme," *Area Development and Policy* 5, no. 1 (December 6, 2019): 1–14; Alexander Cooley and Daniel Nexon, *Exit*

from Hegemony: The Unraveling of the American Global Order (New York: Oxford University Press, 2020), 123–24.

18. On logrolling among interests in imperial expansion, in general see Jack Snyder, *Myths of Empire: Domestic Politics and International Ambition* (Ithaca, NY: Cornell University Press, 1991), and in China see Gilli, Li, and Qian, "Logrolling under Fragmented Authoritarianism." Thanks to Susan Shirk for discussion on this point.

19. Susan Shirk, "China in Xi's 'New Era': The Return to Personalistic Rule," *Journal of Democracy* 29, no. 2 (April 2018): 22–36.

20. Ang, *China's Gilded Age*.

21. Thomas Fingar and Jean C. Oi, "China's Challenges: Now It Gets Much Harder," *Washington Quarterly* 43, no. 1 (2020): 65–82, at 72–73; Andrew Wedeman, "Anti-Corruption Forever?" and Oi, "Future of Center-Local Relations," in *Fateful Decisions: Choices that Will Shape China's Future*, ed. Thomas Fingar and Jean C. Oi (Stanford, CA: Stanford University Press, 2020), 84–108.

22. Christopher Cairns and Allen Carlson, "Real World Islands in a Social Media Sea: Nationalism and Censorship on Weibo during the 2012 Diaoyu/Senkaku Crisis," *China Quarterly* 225 (March 2016): 23–49; Andrew Chubb, "Assessing Public Opinion's Influence on Foreign Policy: The Case of China's Assertive Maritime Behavior," *Asian Security* 15, no. 2 (March 2018): 159–79.

23. On Germany's provocations leading to its encirclement by hostile powers before World War I, see Snyder, *Myths of Empire*, ch. 3.

24. Matthew McCubbins and Thomas Schwartz, "Congressional Oversight Overlooked: Police Patrols versus Fire Alarms," *American Journal of Political Science* 28, no. 1 (February 1984): 165–79; Jonathan R. Stromseth, Edmund Malesky, and D. Gueorguiev, *China's Governance Puzzle: Enabling Transparency and Participation in a Single-Party State* (New York: Cambridge University Press, 2017).

25. Stromseth, Malesky, and Gueorguiev, *China's Governance Puzzle*, 17, 21, 22.

26. Stromseth, Malesky, and Gueorguiev, *China's Governance Puzzle*, ch. 8; Joseph Fewsmith, *The Logic and Limits of Political Reform in China* (New York: Cambridge University Press, 2013).

27. Stromseth, Malesky, and Gueorguiev, *China's Governance Puzzle*, 19, 21; Ang, *China's Gilded Age*.

28. Dan Slater and Joseph Wong, "The Strength to Concede: Ruling Parties and Democratization in Developmental Asia," *Perspectives on Politics* 11, no. 3 (September 2013): 717–33.

29. Stromseth, Malesky, and Gueorguiev, *China's Governance Puzzle,* 20, 24; John Garrick and Yan Chang Bennett, eds., *China's Socialist Rule of Law Reforms under Xi Jinping* (New York: Routledge, 2016).

30. Stromseth, Malesky, and Gueorguiev, *China's Governance Puzzle,* 24.

31. Fingar and Oi, "China's Challenges," 70; Qiran Zhao, Xiaobing Wang, and Scott Rozelle, "Better Cognition, Better School Performance? Evidence from Primary Schools in China," *China Economic Review* 55 (June 2019): 199–217, https://doi.org/10.1016/j.chieco.2019.04.005.

32. Yang Song and Guangsu Zhou, "Inequality of Opportunity and Household Education Expenditures: Evidence from Panel Data in China," *China Economic Review* 55 (June 2019): 85–98, at 96.

33. Susan L. Shirk, *China: Fragile Superpower* (New York: Oxford University Press, 2007).

34. Peter Hays Gries, *China's New Nationalism: Pride, Politics, and Diplomacy* (Berkeley: University of California, 2004), especially chs. 1–3.

35. Rohan Mukherjee, *Ascending Order: Rising Powers and the Institutional Politics of Status* (New York: Cambridge University Press, forthcoming).

36. Henri Tajfel and J. C. Turner, "An Integrative Theory of Intergroup Conflict," in *The Social Psychology of Intergroup Relations*, ed. W. G. Austin and S. Worchel (Monterey, CA: Brooks/ Cole, 1979), 33–47.

37. Jon Elster, *Closing the Books: Transitional Justice in Historical Perspective* (New York: Cambridge University Press, 2004); Paul Midford, *Rethinking Japanese Public Opinion and Security: From Pacifism to Realism?* (Stanford: Stanford University Press, 2011); Shirk, *China*; Suisheng Zhao, *A Nation-State by Construction: Dynamics of Modern Chinese Nationalism* (Stanford, CA: Stanford University Press, 2004); Suisheng Zhao, "A State-Led Nationalism: The Patriotic Education Campaign in Post-Tiananmen China," *Communist and Post-Communist Studies* 31, no. 3 (September 1998): 287–302.

38. Song Qiang, Zhang Zangzang, Qiao Bian, Tang Zhengyu, and Gu Qingsheng, eds., *China Can Say No* (Beijing: China Federation of Literary and Arts Circles, 1996).

39. Zhao Dingxin, "An Angle on Nationalism in China Today: Attitudes among Beijing Students after Belgrade 1999," *China Quarterly* 172 (December 2002): 49–69.

40. Jessica Chen Weiss, "How Hawkish Is the Chinese Public? Another Look at 'Rising Nationalism' and Chinese Foreign Policy," *Journal of Contemporary China* 28, no. 119 (March 2019): 679–95; Margaret E. Roberts, *Censored: Distraction and Diversion inside China's Great Firewall* (Princeton, NJ: Princeton University Press, 2018); Chubb, "Assessing Public Opinion's Influence on Foreign Policy," 159–79.

41. Cairns and Carlson, "Real World Islands"; Yinxian Zhang, Jiajun Liu, and Ji-Rong Wen, "Nationalism on Weibo: Towards a Multifaceted Understanding of Chinese Nationalism," *China Quarterly* 235 (September 2018): 758–83.

42. Taylor Washburn, "How an Ancient Kingdom Explains Today's China-Korea Relations," *Atlantic*, April 15, 2013, https://www.theatlantic.com/china/archive/2013/04/how-an-ancient-kingdom-explains-todays-china-korea-relations/274986/; Christina Lai, "Realism Revisited: China's Status-Driven Wars against Koguryo in the Sui and Tang Dynasties," *Asian Security* (June 2020): 1–16, https://doi.org/10.1080/14799855.2020.1782887.

43. Edward Friedman and Barrett L. McCormick, eds., *What If China Doesn't Democratize?* (Armonk, NY: M. E. Sharpe, 2000); Andrew Nathan, *Chinese Democracy* (Berkeley: University of California Press, 1986).

44. Alastair Iain Johnston, "Is Chinese Nationalism Rising?" *International Security* 41, no. 3 (Winter 2016–17): 7–43.

45. Andrew J. Nathan, "The Puzzle of the Chinese Middle Class," *Journal of Democracy* 27, no. 2 (2016): 5–19.

46. Edmund J. Malesky and Layna Mosley, "Chains of Love? Global Production and the Firm-Level Diffusion of Labor Standards," *American Journal of Political Science* 62, no. 3 (July 2018): 712–28.

47. Yuhua Wang, *Tying the Autocrat's Hands: The Rise of the Rule of Law in China* (Cambridge: Cambridge University Press, 2014); Benjamin L. Liebman, "Legal Reform: China's Law-Stability Paradox," *Daedalus* 143, no. 2 (Spring 2014): 96–109.

48. Linda Yueh, "The Law and Growth Nexus in China," in *China's Socialist Rule of Law Reforms under Xi Jinping*, ed. John Garrick and Yan Chang Bennett (London: Routledge, 2016), 77–93.

49. For historical and strategic context on trade bargaining over this period, see Thomas Christensen, *The China Challenge: Shaping the Choices of a Rising Power* (New York: Norton, 2015); and Robert Zoellick, "The China Challenge," *National Interest*, February 14, 2020, https://nationalinterest.org/feature/china-challenge-123271.

50. Even Taiwan has been able to diversify its trading partners to decrease its dependence on Beijing. Christina Lai, "More than Carrots and Sticks: Economic Statecraft and Coercion in China–Taiwan relations from 2000 to 2019," *Politics* (February 2021): 1–16, https://doi.org/10.1177/0263395720962654.

51. John Gerard Ruggie, "International Regimes, Transactions, and Change: Embedded Liberalism in the Postwar Economic Order," *International Organization* 36, no. 2 (Spring 1982): 379–415.

52. World Bank data at "Trade (% of GDP)—China," accessed September 19, 2021, https://data.worldbank.org/indicator/NE.TRD.GNFS.ZS?locations=CN.

53. Christopher A. Ford, "Realpolitik with Chinese Characteristics: Chinese Strategic Culture and the Modern Communist Party-State," in *Understanding Strategic Cultures in the Asia-Pacific*, ed. Ashley J. Tellis, Alison Szalwinski, and Michael Wills (Washington DC: National Bureau of Asian Research, 2016), 60.

54. S.1309—Combating Global Corruption Act of 2019, 116 Cong., 1st sess. (2019), https://www.congress.gov/bill/116th-congress/senate-bill/1309/text.

55. Sarah Chayes, *Thieves of the State: Why Corruption Threatens Global Security* (New York: Norton, 2015).

56. Andrew Nathan and Perry Link, eds., *The Tiananmen Papers* (New York: Public Affairs, 2001); Jessica Chen Weiss, "The Stories China Tells: The New Historical Memory Reshaping Chinese Nationalism," *Foreign Affairs* 100, no. 2 (March/April 2021): 90, https://www.foreignaffairs.com/reviews/review-essay/2021-02-16/stories-china-tells; Rana Mitter, *China's Good War: How World War II Is Shaping a New Chinese Nationalism* (Cambridge: Harvard University Press, 2020).

57. "Khrushchev's Secret Speech, 'On the Cult of Personality and Its Consequences,' Delivered at the Twentieth Party Congress of the Communist Party of the Soviet Union," February 25, 1956, History and Public Policy Program Digital Archive, From the Congressional Record: Proceedings and Debates of the 84th Congress, 2nd Session (May 22, 1956–June 11, 1956), C11, Part 7 (June 4, 1956), pp. 9389–9403, Wilson Center, http://digitalarchive.wilsoncenter.org/document/115995.

Chapter 6. Aligning with Mass Movements, Reform Parties, and Religion

1. Margaret Keck and Kathryn Sikkink, *Activists beyond Borders: Advocacy Networks in International Politics* (Ithaca, NY: Cornell University Press, 1998), 32–34, prefers the formulation "transnational civil society."

2. Human Rights Watch, "about us," n.d., quoted by the SUNY Levin Institute, "Social Movements and NGOs," accessed September 20, 2021, http://www.globalization101.org/the-rise-of-non-governmental-organizations-ngos-and-global-civil-society/. As of August 29, 2014,

Human Rights Watch says simply, "We work closely with a broad range of local and international civil society actors to maximize our impact." "About Us," Human Rights Watch, http://www.hrw.org/about.

3. Aryeh Neier, *The International Human Rights Movement: A History* (Princeton, NJ: Princeton University Press, 2012), 33–37.

4. Keck and Sikkink, *Activists beyond Borders*, 41–51.

5. Kenneth Roth, "Defending Economic, Social and Cultural Rights: Practical Issues Faced by an International Human Rights Organization," *Human Rights Quarterly* 26, no. 1 (February 2004): 63–74, at 72.

6. Stephen Hopgood, *The Endtimes of Human Rights* (Ithaca, NY: Cornell University Press, 2013), ch. 2.

7. On the crucial role of "protest brokers," see Sarah J. Lockwood, "Making Protest Work: Protest Brokers and the Technology of Mobilization," *Comparative Political Studies*, forthcoming; and Robert Mattes, Sarah J. Lockwood, and Matthias Krönke, "Party Footprints in Africa: Measuring Party Organizational Capacity Across the Continent" (2019) at https://www.sarahjlockwood.com/research/. On the connection between the emotional register of religious experience and mass social movements, drawing on Emile Durkheim, see Randall Collins, "Social Movements and the Focus of Emotional Attention," in *Passionate Politics: Emotions and Social Movements*, ed. Jeff Goodwin, James Jasper, and Francesca Polletta (Chicago: University of Chicago, 2001), 27–44.

8. Charles Tilly and Lesley J. Wood, *Social Movements, 1768–2012*, 2d ed. (Boulder, CO: Paradigm, 2009), 3–5, 25–29, 33–37.

9. Chaim Kaufmann and Robert Pape, "Explaining Costly International Moral Action: Britain's Sixty-year Campaign against the Atlantic Slave Trade," *International Organization* 53, no. 4 (Autumn 1999): 654–57.

10. Jack Snyder, *Myths of Empire: Domestic Politics and International Ambition* (Ithaca, NY: Cornell University Press, 1991), 192–97; Lucy Brown, *The Board of Trade and the Free Trade Movement* (Oxford: Oxford University Press, 1958), 57–60.

11. Charles Tilly, *Contentious Performances* (New York: Cambridge University Press, 2008), 72, 87.

12. Daniel Schlozman, *When Movements Anchor Parties: Electoral Alignments in American History* (Princeton, NJ: Princeton University Press, 2015), 243.

13. Schlozman, *When Movements Anchor Parties*, 5–9, quotation at 9.

14. Jack M. Balkin, "How Social Movements Change (or Fail to Change) the Constitution: The Case of the New Departure," *Suffolk University Law Review* 39, no. 1 (2005): 57–58, quoted and discussed by Schlozman, *When Movements Anchor Parties*, 248.

15. Tilly and Wood, *Social Movements*, 56–58.

16. Jack Snyder, *From Voting to Violence: Democratization and Nationalist Conflict* (New York: Norton, 2000), 273–87.

17. Tilly and Wood, *Social Movements*, 153–57.

18. Neier, *International Human Rights Movement*, ch. 2.

19. J. R. Goody, "Civil Society in an Extra-European Perspective," in *Civil Society: History and Possibilities*, ed. Sudipta Kaviraj and Sunil Khilnani (Cambridge: Cambridge University Press, 2001), 149.

20. Micheline Ishay, *The History of Human Rights: From Ancient Times to the Globalization Era* (Berkeley: University of California Press, 2004).

21. Miguel Carter, "Ideal Interest Mobilization: Explaining the Formation of Brazil's Landless Social Movement" (PhD diss., Columbia University, 2002), ch. 1, p. 43.

22. Sidney Tarrow, *Power in Movement: Social Movements and Contentious Politics*, 3d ed. (New York: Cambridge University Press, 2011), ch. 8.

23. Frances Fox Piven and Richard A. Cloward, *Poor People's Movements: Why They Succeed, How They Fail* (New York: Vintage, 1979); on the decline of the civil rights movement, see Douglas McAdam, *Political Process and the Development of Black Insurgency, 1930–1970* (Chicago: University of Chicago Press, 1982), ch. 8.

24. Stewart Winger, *Lincoln, Religion, and Romantic Cultural Politics* (DeKalb: Northern Illinois University, 2003), 185, quotation from 1837.

25. John Burt, *Lincoln's Tragic Pragmatism: Lincoln, Douglas, and Moral Conflict* (Cambridge, MA: Belknap Press of Harvard University Press, 2013), 225, 401, 403, 405–7.

26. Richard J. Carwardine, *Lincoln: Profiles in Power* (Harlow, UK: Pearson Longman, 2003), 104.

27. Stewart Winger, *Lincoln, Religion, and Romantic Cultural Politics* (DeKalb: Northern Illinois University, 2003), 192.

28. McAdam, *Political Process*, 45.

29. Donatella Della Porta and Mario Diani, *Social Movements: An Introduction*, 2d ed. (Oxford: Blackwell, 2006), 145.

30. Risa L. Goluboff, *The Lost Promise of Civil Rights* (Cambridge, MA: Harvard University Press, 2007), 37.

31. Goluboff, *Lost Promise*, 223–30, 251.

32. McAdam, *Political Process*, 129–33, 152.

33. Piven and Cloward, *Poor People's Movements*, 240.

34. Piven and Cloward, *Poor People's Movements*, 252; McAdam, *Political Process*.

35. Della Porta and Diani, *Social Movements*, 28, 107; John D'Emilio, "The Gay Liberation Movement," in *The Social Movements Reader*, ed. Jeff Goodwin and J. Jasper, 2d ed. (Oxford: Blackwell, 2009), 38, reprinted from D'Emilio, *Sexual Politics, Sexual Communities* (Chicago: University of Chicago Press, 1998).

36. Della Porta and Diani, *Social Movements*, 24.

37. Clifford Bob, *The Marketing of Rebellion* (New York: Cambridge University Press, 2005), 27–28.

38. Tarrow, *Power in Movement*, 248.

39. Conny Roggeband, "Transnational Networks and Institutions: How Diffusion Shaped the Politicization of Sexual Harassment in Europe," in *The Diffusion of Social Movements*, ed. Rebecca Kolins Givan, Kenneth M. Roberts, and Sarah Soule (New York: Cambridge University Press, 2010), 23–30.

40. Labor lawyer Jay Youngdahl, "Solidarity First: Labor Rights Are Not the Same as Human Rights," *New Labor Forum* 18, no. 1 (Winter 2009): 31–37, at 31. See also Lance Compa, "Framing Labor's New Human Rights Movement," in Givan, Roberts, and Soule, *Diffusion of Social Movements*, 71.

41. Cathy Albisa, "Drawing Lines in the Sand: Building Economic and Social Rights Norms in the United States," in *Human Rights in the United States: Beyond Exceptionalism*, ed. Shareen Hertel and Kathryn Libal (New York: Cambridge University Press, 2011), 68–88, at 85.

42. Makau Mutua, "Savages, Victims, and Saviors: The Metaphor of Human Rights," *Harvard International Law Journal* 42, no. 1 (Winter 2001): 201–45.

43. Lynn Hunt, *Inventing Human Rights* (New York: Norton, 2008). To be fair, one of the victims in *The Help* shows a great deal of pluck, even if the white aspiring journalist is still her voice to the outside world.

44. Conor O'Dwyer, "From NGOs to Naught: The Rise and Fall of the Czech Gay Rights Movement," in *Beyond NGO-ization: The Development of Social Movements in Central and Eastern Europe*, ed. Kerstin Jacobsson and Steven Saxonberg (Burlington, VT: Ashgate, 2013), 117–38.

45. Erica Chenoweth and Maria J. Stephan, *Why Civil Resistance Works: The Strategic Logic of Nonviolent Conflict* (New York: Columbia University Press, 2011), 55; Chenoweth, *Civil Resistance: What Everyone Needs to Know* (New York: Oxford University Press, 2021).

46. Herbert Kitschelt, "Landscapes of Political Interest Intermediation: Social Movements, Interest Groups, and Parties in the Early Twenty-First Century," in *Social Movements and Democracy*, ed. Pedro Ibarra (New York: Palgrave, 2003), 84.

47. Brayden G. King, Keith G. Bentele, and Sarah Anne Soule, "Protest and Policymaking: Explaining Fluctuation in Congressional Attention to Rights Issues, 1960–1986," *Social Forces* 86, no. 1 (September 2007): 137–63.

48. Kitschelt, "Landscapes of Political Interest Intermediation," 84.

49. Neier, *International Human Rights Movement*, 42.

50. Jo Freeman, "The Women's Movement," in Goodwin and Jasper, *Social Movements Reader*, 29, reprinted from Freeman, "The Origins of the Women's Liberation Movement," *American Journal of Sociology* 78, no. 4 (January 1973): 792–811.

51. Mary Kaldor, *Global Civil Society: An Answer to War* (Cambridge: Polity, 2003), 92.

52. Sarah E. Mendelson and John K. Glenn, eds., *The Power and Limits of NGOs* (New York: Columbia University Press, 2003).

53. Kenneth Roth, "The Age of Zombie Democracies: Why Autocrats Are Abandoning Even the Pretense of Democratic Rituals," *Foreign Affairs*, July 28, 2021, https://www.foreignaffairs.com/articles/americas/2021-07-28/age-zombie-democracies?.

54. Even Stalin's Soviet Union was able to sign on to this general statement.

55. Aryeh Neier, "Misunderstanding Our Mission," *OpenGlobalRights*, July 23, 2013, https://www.opendemocracy.net/openglobalrights/aryeh-neier/misunderstanding-our-mission.

56. Neier, *International Human Rights Movement*, 42, 53, 56, 312; Davide Rodogno, *Against Massacre: Humanitarian Interventions in the Ottoman Empire, 1815–1914* (Princeton, NJ: Princeton University Press, 2012); but see Gary Bass, *Freedom's Battle: The Origins of Humanitarian Intervention* (New York: Knopf, 2008), 305–10, on early glimmerings of a more universalist outlook.

57. Finnemore, *Intervention*; Jack Snyder, "Realism, Refugees, and Strategies of Humanitarianism," in *Refugees in International Relations*, ed. Alexander Betts and Gil Loescher (New York: Oxford, 2010), 29–52; Jon Western, "Sources of Humanitarian Intervention: Beliefs, Information, and Advocacy in the U.S. Decisions on Somalia and Bosnia," *International Security* 26, no. 4 (Spring 2002): 112–42.

58. John Witte, *The Reformation of Rights: Law, Religion and Human Rights in Early Modern Calvinism* (Cambridge: Cambridge University Press, 2007); Winger, *Lincoln, Religion, and Romantic Cultural Politics*; Michael Barnett, "Another Great Awakening? International Relations

Theory and Religion," in *Religion and International Relations Theory*, ed. Jack Snyder (New York: Columbia University Press, 2011), 91–114, at 101–2; McAdam, *Political Process*.

59. Robin Blackburn, *The Overthrow of Colonial Slavery, 1776–1848* (London: Verso. 1988), 95–102; Thomas Clarkson, *The History of the Rise, Progress and Accomplishment of the Abolition of the Slave-Trade by the British Parliament* (Philadelphia: James P. Parke, 1808).

60. Robert W. Hefner, *Civil Islam: Muslims and Democratization in Indonesia* (Princeton, NJ: Princeton University Press, 2000).

61. Dan Slater, "Party Cartelization, Indonesian-Style: Presidential Powersharing and the Contingency of Democratic Opposition," *Journal of East Asian Studies* 18, no. 1 (March 2018): 23–46; Slater, "Indonesia's Tenuous Democratic Success and Survival," in *Democracy in Indonesia: From Stagnation to Regression*, ed. Thomas Power and Eve Warburton (Singapore: ISEAS, 2020), 45–62; Mirjam Künkler and Alfred Stepan, eds., *Democracy and Islam in Indonesia* (New York: Columbia University Press, 2013).

62. Jack Snyder and Leslie Vinjamuri, "Trials and Errors: Principle and Pragmatism in International Justice," *International Security* 28, no. 3 (Winter 2003–2004): 5–44.

63. Douglas McAdam and Sidney Tarrow, "Social Movements and Elections: Toward a Broader Understanding of the Political Context of Contention," in *The Future of Social Movement Research: Dynamics, Mechanisms, and Processes*, ed. Jacqueline van Stekelberg, Conny Roggeband, and Bert Klandermans (Minneapolis: University of Minnesota, 2013), 329.

64. Leslie Vinjamuri, "Human Rights Backlash," in *Human Rights Futures*, ed. Stephen Hopgood, Jack Snyder, and Leslie Vinjamuri (New York: Cambridge University Press, 2017), 114–34.

65. Neier, *International Human Rights Movement*, 33–37; Keck and Sikkink, *Activists beyond Borders*, 41–51.

66. For commentary, see Howard Temperley, "Anti-slavery as a Form of Cultural Imperialism," in *Anti-slavery, Religion, and Reform*, ed. Christine Bolt and Seymour Drescher (Hamden, CT: Dawson, 1980), 338.

67. Seymour Drescher, *Capitalism and Antislavery* (Oxford: Oxford University Press, 1987), chs. 4, 6; David Turley, *The Culture of English Antislavery, 1780–1860* (London: Routledge, 1991), chs. 3, 5; Edith Hurwitz, *The Politics of Public Conscience: Slave Emancipation and the Abolitionist Movement in Britain* (London: Allen and Unwin, 1973), 23; Robin Blackburn, *The Overthrow of Colonial Slavery, 1776–1848* (London: Verso, 1988), 96, 102.

68. Blackburn, *Overthrow*, ch. 2.

69. Kaufmann and Pape, "Explaining Costly International Moral Action," 651–57; Blackburn, *Overthrow*, 76–77, 307–15; Hurwitz, *Politics of Public Conscience*, 49–54; Brian Harrison, "A Genealogy of Reform," in Bolt and Drescher, *Anti-slavery, Religion, and Reform*, 119–48; G. M. Ditchfield, "Repeal, Abolition, and Reform: A Study in the Interaction of Reforming Movements in the Parliament of 1790–96," in Bolt and Drescher, *Anti-slavery, Religion, and Reform*, 101–18.

70. John K. Glenn, *Framing Democracy: Civil Society and Civic Movements in Eastern Europe* (Stanford, CA: Stanford University Press, 2001), chs. 3–4.

71. Glenn, *Framing Democracy*, chs 5–6.

72. Víctor Pérez-Díaz, *The Return of Civil Society: The Emergence of Democratic Spain* (Cambridge, MA: Harvard University Press, 1993); Juan J. Linz and Alfred Stepan, *Problems of*

Democratic Transition and Consolidation (Baltimore, MD: Johns Hopkins University Press, 1996), ch. 6.

73. Ruth Berins Collier, *Paths toward Democracy: The Working Class and Elites in Western Europe and South America* (New York: Cambridge University Press, 1999), 132–38; Linz and Stepan, *Problems of Democratic Transition*, ch. 11; Weyland, *Making Waves*, ch. 6.

74. Elke Zuern, *The Politics of Necessity: Community Organizing and Democracy in South Africa* (Madison: University of Wisconsin Press, 2011), 30–31.

75. Künkler and Stepan, *Democracy and Islam in Indonesia*.

76. Santiago Anria, *When Movements Become Parties: The Bolivian MAS in Comparative Perspective* (New York: Cambridge University Press, 2018).

77. Carlos Nino, *Radical Evil on Trial* (New Haven, CT: Yale University Press, 1996), 116.

Chapter 7. Regulating the Marketplace of Ideas

1. See Article 19 of the Universal Declaration of Human Rights and Article 19 of the International Covenant on Civil and Political Rights.

2. Aernout Nieuwenhuis, "Freedom of Speech: USA vs Germany and Europe," *Netherlands Quarterly of Human Rights* 18, no. 2 (June 2000): 195–214.

3. Thomas Jefferson, *The Works of Thomas Jefferson*, vol. 5, *Correspondence 1786–1789*, ed. Paul Leicester Ford (London: Putnam, 1905), 253.

4. Joshua A. Tucker, Yannis Theocharis, Margaret Roberts, and Pablo Barbera, "From Liberation to Turmoil: Social Media and Democracy," *Journal of Democracy* 28, no. 4 (2017): 46–59; Yochai Benkler, Robert Faris, and Hal Roberts, *Network Propaganda: Manipulation, Disinformation, and Radicalization in American Politics* (New York: Oxford University Press, 2018); David Kaye, *Speech Police: The Global Struggle to Govern the Internet* (New York: Columbia Global Reports, 2019).

5. Whitney v. California, Louis Brandeis opinion, 1927. See also Nadine Strossen, *Hate: Why We Should Resist It with Counterspeech, Not Censorship* (New York: Oxford University Press, 2018). The media NGO Article 19 worries in its 2019 annual report (*International Annual Report 2019: Defending Freedom of Expression and Information around the World*, https://www.article19 .org/wp-content/uploads/2020/06/A19_AnnualReport_2019_Final_22June2020-min.pdf) that "under their community guidelines, social media companies can restrict a lot of content— not just content that is illegal but also content they deem distasteful or unpopular." "Proposals to force companies to remove 'legal but harmful' speech are misguided and dangerous for freedom of speech."

6. Youjung Jun, Rachel Meng, and Gita Venkataramani Johar, "Perceived Social Presence Reduces Fact-Checking," *Proceedings of the National Academy of Sciences of the United States of America* 114, no. 23 (June 6, 2017): 5976–81; Brendan Nyhan and Jason Reifler, "The Effect of Fact-Checking on Elites: A Field Experiment on U.S. State Legislators," *American Journal of Political Science* 59, no. 3 (July 2015): 628–40.

7. Aja Romano, "Kicking People off Social Media Isn't about Free Speech," *Vox*, January 21, 2021, https://www.vox.com/culture/22230847/deplatforming-free-speech-controversy-trump.

8. Nicholas Lemann, "Can Journalism Be Saved?" *New York Review of Books* (February 27, 2020): 39–42; Anne Nelson, *Shadow Network: Media, Money, and the Secret Hub of the Radical Right* (New York: Bloomsbury, 2019).

9. Christopher Achen and Larry Bartels, *Democracy for Realists: Why Elections Do Not Produce Responsive Government* (Princeton, NJ: Princeton University Press, 2016) on the folk theory of democracy.

10. R. H. Coase, "The Economics of the First Amendment: The Market for Goods and the Market for Ideas," *American Economic Review* 64, no. 2 (1974): 384–91.

11. Amy Guttmann, *Why Deliberative Democracy?* (Princeton, NJ: Princeton University Press, 2004).

12. Fred S. Siebert, Theodore Peterson, and Wilbur Schramm, *Four Theories of the Press: The Authoritarian, Libertarian, Social Responsibility, and Soviet Communist Concepts of What the Press Should Be and Do* (Urbana: University of Illinois Press, 1956).

13. Jenifer Whitten-Woodring, "Watchdog or Lapdog? Media Freedom, Regime Type, and Government Respect for Human Rights," *International Studies Quarterly* 53, no. 3 (September 2009): 595–625; Jack Snyder and Karen Ballentine, "Nationalism and the Marketplace of Ideas," *International Security* 21, no. 2 (Fall 1996): 5–40; Jack Snyder, *From Voting to Violence: Democratization and Nationalist Conflict* (New York: Norton, 2000), ch. 2 and sections on media: 121–28, 146–49, 154–57, 213–20, 235–37, 242–50, 334–38.

14. Mary Myers, *Is There a Link between the Media and Good Governance? What the Academics Say* (Report to the Center for International Media Assistance, June 28, 2012), https://www .cima.ned.org/wp-content/uploads/2015/02/Myers-Mary-Good-Governance-Academics -Survey-07-06-12-FINAL.pdf; and see Article 19, *International Annual Report 2019*, for claims about the beneficial effects of free expression and media on citizen knowledge, civil society vibrancy, good governance, corruption, accountability, and our other mechanisms and outcome variables.

15. Coase, "Economics of the First Amendment," 384–91. Oliver Wendell Holmes's dissent in Abrams v. United States, 250 U.S. 616 (1919), asserts that "the best test of truth" is "to get itself accepted in the competition of the market." The invisible hand analogy originates in Adam Smith, *An Inquiry into the Nature and Causes of the Wealth of Nations* (1776): "By directing that industry in such a manner as its produce may be of the greatest value, he intends only his own gain, and he is in this, as in many other cases, led by an invisible hand to promote an end which was no part of his intention." See also Daniel E. Ho and Frederick Schauer, "Testing the Marketplace of Ideas," *New York University Law Review* 90 (2015): 1160–1228.

16. John Milton, *Areopagitica: A Speech for the Liberty of Unlicensed Printing*, ed. H. B. Cotterill (1920; New York: Macmillan, 1959), 44–45.

17. Milton, *Areopagitica*, 27.

18. Milton, *Areopagitica*, 25, 47. A later landmark in the liberal canon is John Stuart Mill's *On Liberty* (1859). See also Kaye, *Speech Police*, 47, and American Civil Liberties Union, "Freedom of Expression, ACLU Position Paper," accessed August 23, 2020, https://www.aclu.org/other /freedom-expression-aclu-position-paper.

19. On Thomas Jefferson's view of the shortcomings of the free press, see Merrill D. Peterson, ed., *The Portable Thomas Jefferson* (New York: Viking, 1975), 505.

20. Jefferson, *Correspondence 1786–1789*, 253.

21. Walter Lippmann, *Public Opinion* (London: Allen and Unwin, 1922), 31–32, 358–65; Eric Van Rythoven, "Walter Lippmann, Emotion, and the History of International Theory," *International Theory, First View* (October 2021): 1–25, https://doi.org/10.1017/S1752971921000178.

22. Commission of the Freedom of Press, *A Free and Responsible Press* (Chicago: University of Chicago Press, 1947), 10.

23. Siebert, Peterson, and Schramm, *Four Theories of the Press*, 100–102; Vincent Blasi, "Holmes and the Marketplace of Ideas," *Supreme Court Review* 2004 (2004): 46.

24. Paul Starr, *The Creation of the Media: Political Origins of Modern Communications* (New York: Basic Books, 2004), ch. 11.

25. Richard H. Thaler and Cass R. Sunstein, *Nudge: Improving Decisions about Health, Wealth, and Happiness* (New Haven, CT: Yale University Press, 2008).

26. Markus Prior, *Post-Broadcast Democracy: How Media Choice Increases Inequality in Political Involvement and Polarizes Elections* (New York: Cambridge University Press, 2007), 257–58.

27. Kathleen Ann Ruane, "Fairness Doctrine: History and Constitutional Issues," Congressional Research Service, July 13, 2011.

28. Aleksi Aaltonen and Giovan Lanzara, "Building Governance Capability in Online Social Production: Insights from Wikipedia," *Organization Studies* 36, no. 12 (2015): 1649–73, https://journals.sagepub.com/doi/10.1177/0170840615584459; Csilla Rudas and János Török, "Modeling the Wikipedia to Understand the Dynamics of Long Disputes and Biased Articles," *Historical Social Research / Historische Sozialforschung* 43, no. 1 (2018): 72–88, https://www.researchgate.net/publication/325100810_Modeling_the_wikipedia_to_understand_the_dynamics_of_long_disputes_and_biased_articles.

29. Tim Wu, *The Curse of Bigness: Antitrust in the New Gilded Age* (New York: Columbia Global Reports, 2018); Lemann, "Can Journalism Be Saved?"; Ronald R. Krebs, *Narrative and the Making of US National Security* (New York: Cambridge University Press, 2015).

30. Kaye, *Speech Police*, 112–26, Benkler, Faris, and Roberts, *Network Propaganda*, conclusion.

31. Freedom House, "Freedom of the Press 2017 Methodology" (2017), https://freedomhouse.org/report/freedom-press-2017-methodology.

32. Whitten-Woodring, "Watchdog or Lapdog?"; Marc L. Hutchison and Salvatore Schiano, "When the Fourth Estate Becomes a Fifth Column: The Effect of Media Freedom and Social Intolerance on Civil Conflict," *International Journal of Press/Politics* 21, no. 2 (April 2016): 165–87.

33. Thomas Hanitzsch, Folker Hanusch, Jyotika Ramaprasad, and Arnold S. De Beer, eds., *Worlds of Journalism: Journalistic Cultures around the Globe* (New York: Columbia University Press, 2019).

34. Margaret E. Roberts, *Censored: Distraction and Diversion inside China's Great Firewall* (Princeton, NJ: Princeton University Press, 2018).

35. The appendix provides details on the measurement of the variables.

36. See Stephen Van Evera, *Guide to Methods for Students of Political Science* (Ithaca, NY: Cornell University Press, 1997), 31–32, on the "hoop test."

37. Freedom House, "Freedom of the Press 2017 Methodology."

38. Michael Coppedge et al., *V-Dem Codebook v9*, April 2019, https://www.v-dem.net/media/filer_public/e6/d2/e6d27595-9d69-4312-b09f-63d2a0a65df2/v-dem_codebook_v9.pdf.

39. David Cingranelli, David Richards, and K. Chad Clay, "The CIRI Human Rights Dataset," Version 2014.04.14. (2014), http://www.humanrightsdata.com.

40. Monty G. Marshall, "Major Episodes of Political Violence (MEPV) and Conflict Regions, 1946–2015," Center for Systemic Peace 25 (2016).

41. Jan Teorell, Stefan Dahlberg, Sören Holmberg, Bo Rothstein, Anna Khomenko, and Richard Svensson, "The Quality of Government Standard Dataset, Version Jan17," University of Gothenburg: The Quality of Government Institute, April 30, 2020, http://www.qog.pol.gu .se, doi:10.18157/QoGStdJan17.

42. Monty G. Marshall, Ted Robert Gurr, and Keith Jaggers, "Polity IV Project: Political Regime Characteristics and Transitions, 1800–2013," Center for Systemic Peace (2016), http:// www.systemicpeace.org/polity/polity4.htm.

43. Cingranelli, Richards, and Clay, "CIRI Human Rights Dataset."

44. Marshall, "Major Episodes."

45. We use the Political Corruption Index from the Varieties of Democracy project (Coppedge et al., *V-Dem Codebook v9*, 266).

46. Teorell et al., "Quality of Government," 77.

47. Coppedge et al., *V-Dem Codebook v9*, 187.

48. Coppedge et al., *V-Dem Codebook v9*, 179, 149.

49. V. Mechkova, D. Pemstein, B. Seim, and S. Wilson, "Measuring Internet Politics: Introducing the Digital Society Project," Digital Society Project Working Paper no. 1, May 2019, http://digitalsocietyproject.org/wp-content/uploads/2019/05/DSP_WP_01-Introducing-the -Digital-Society-Project.pdf.

50. Mechkova et al., "Measuring Internet Politics," 22.

51. Mechkova et al., "Measuring Internet Politics," 26.

52. Coppedge et al., *V-Dem Codebook v9*, 187.

53. Thomas Carothers, *Assessing Democracy Assistance: The Case of Romania* (Washington, DC: Carnegie Endowment for International Peace, 1996), 80–89.

54. Peter T. Leeson, "Media Freedom, Political Knowledge, and Participation," *Journal of Economic Perspectives* 22, no. 2 (Spring 2008): 155–69.

55. We use survey data from the Afrobarometer (waves 1–5, collected between 1999 and 2013), the Arab Barometer (first three waves, collected between 2006 and 2014), the Asian Barometer (first three waves, collected between 2001 and 2012), the Comparative Study of Electoral Systems (survey models 1 through 4, collected between 1996 and 2016), and the Latin American Public Opinion Project (collected between 2004 and 2014).

56. We find a high degree of variation in political knowledge across countries, with some having less than 20 percent of respondents answering political knowledge questions correctly, and others with over 90 percent correct responses.

57. Guttmann, *Why Deliberative Democracy?*; Jane Mansbridge, "The Place of Self-Interest and the Role of Power in Deliberative Democracy," *Journal of Political Philosophy* 18, no. 1 (March 2010): 64–100.

58. Beth A. Simmons, *Mobilizing for Human Rights: International Law in Domestic Politics* (New York: Cambridge University Press, 2009).

59. Sheri Berman, "Civil Society and the Collapse of the Weimar Republic," *World Politics* 49, no. 3 (April 1997): 401–29.

60. Achen and Bartels, *Democracy for Realists*.

61. Carew Boulding, *NGOs, Political Protest, and Civil Society* (New York: Cambridge University Press, 2014), 98.

62. Coppedge et al., *V-Dem Codebook v9*, 149, 179.

63. Jürgen Habermas, *The Structural Transformation of the Public Sphere: An Inquiry into a Category of Bourgeois Society* (Cambridge: Polity, 1989); Benedict Anderson, *Imagined Communities* (New York: Verso, 1983).

64. Shibley Telhami, *The World through Arab Eyes* (New York: Basic, 2003), 42–44, 47–50; Cass Sunstein, *Republic.com* (Princeton, NJ: Princeton University Press, 2001); Benkler, Faris, and Roberts, *Network Propaganda*, 79; Jennifer Forestal, "Beyond Gatekeeping: Propaganda, Democracy, and the Organization of Digital Publics," *Journal of Politics* 83, no. 1 (January 2021): 306–20; R. Kelly Garrett, "Echo Chambers Online? Politically Motivated Selective Exposure among Internet News Users," *Journal of Computer Mediated-Communication* 14, no. 2 (2009): 265–85, http://onlinelibrary.wiley.com/doi/10.1111/j.1083-6101.2009.01440.x/full.

65. Andrew Kydd and Barbara Walter, "The Strategies of Terrorism," *International Security* 31, no. 1 (2006): 49–80.

66. Prior, *Post-Broadcast Democracy*.

67. Benkler, Faris, and Roberts, *Network Propaganda*, 13–14.

68. Benjamin I. Page and Robert Y. Shapiro, *The Rational Public* (Chicago: University of Chicago Press 1992), 15–27.

69. Miroslav Nincic, "The United States, the Soviet Union, and the Politics of Opposites," *World Politics* 40, no. 4 (July 1988): 452–75.

70. Anthony Downs, "An Economic Theory of Political Action in a Democracy," *Journal of Political Economy* 65, no. 2 (April 1957): 135–50, at 149; Downs, *An Economic Theory of Democracy* (New York: Harper and Brothers, 1957); Phillip Converse, "The Nature of Belief Systems in Mass Publics," in *Ideology and Discontent*, ed. David E. Apter (New York: Free Press, 1964), 206–61.

71. John R. Zaller, *The Nature and Origins of Mass Opinion* (New York: Cambridge University Press, 1992), 16–28.

72. Michaela Mattes and Jessica Weeks, "Hawks, Doves, and Peace: An Experimental Approach," *American Journal of Political Science* 63, no. 1 (January 2019): 53–66; Keith Krehbiel, *Information and Legislative Organization* (Ann Arbor: University of Michigan Press, 1991), ch. 3, for hypotheses about expertise and preference outliers.

73. Arthur Lupia and Matthew D. McCubbins, *The Democratic Dilemma: Can Citizens Learn What They Need to Know?* (New York: Cambridge University Press, 1998), 13, 205–25.

74. Benkler, Faris, and Roberts, *Network Propaganda*.

75. Andreas Wimmer, *Nation Building: Why Some Countries Come Together While Others Fall Apart* (Princeton, NJ: Princeton University Press, 2018), 30–31.

76. In the technical appendix, we analyze the same data using multivariate regressions that account for country fixed effects and the level of democracy, GDP per capita, and population size. We find similar results.

77. Coppedge et al., *V-Dem Codebook v9*, 187.

78. Mechkova et al., "Measuring Internet Politics," 20.

79. Mechkova et al., "Measuring Internet Politics," 21.

80. Mechkova et al., "Measuring Internet Politics," 12–13, 26.

81. Tucker et al., "From Liberation to Turmoil."

82. Robert A. Dahl, *Polyarchy: Participation and Opposition* (New Haven, CT: Yale University Press, 1972); Samuel P. Huntington, *Political Order in Changing Societies* (New Haven, CT: Yale University, 1968).

83. Jeremy Popkin, *Revolutionary News: The Press in France, 1789–1799* (Durham, NC: Duke University Press, 1990), 41; Simon Schama, *Citizens* (New York: Knopf, 1992), 582.

84. Håvard Hegre, Tanja Ellingsen, Scott Gates, and Nils Peter Gleditsch, "Toward a Civil Democratic Peace? Democracy, Political Change, and Civil War, 1816–1992," *American Political Science Review* 95, no. 1 (March 2001): 33–48; Christian Davenport and David Armstrong, "Democracy and the Violation of Human Rights: A Statistical Analysis from 1976 to 1996," *American Journal of Political Science* 48, no. 3 (July 2004): 538–54; David E. Cunningham, Kristian Skrede Gleditsch, Belen Gonzalez, Dragana Vidovic, and Peter White, "Words and Deeds: From Incompatibilities to Outcomes in Anti-Government Disputes," *Journal of Peace Research* 54, no. 4 (July 2017): 468–83; Helen Fein, "More Murder in the Middle: Life Integrity Violations and Democracy in the World, 1987," *Human Rights Quarterly* 17, no. 1 (February 1995): 170–91; Zachary M. Jones and Yonatan Lupu, "Is There More Violence in the Middle?" *American Journal of Political Science* 62, no. 3 (July 2018): 652–67; Snyder, *From Voting to Violence*; Edward D. Mansfield and Jack Snyder, "Democratization and Civil War," in *Power and Progress*, ed. Jack Snyder (London: Routledge, 2012), 175–200.

85. Modris Eksteins, *The Limits of Reason: The German Democratic Press and the Collapse of Weimar Democracy* (London: Oxford, 1975).

86. Richard L. Merritt, *Democracy Imposed: U.S. Occupation Policy and the German Public, 1945–1949* (New Haven, CT: Yale University Press, 1996), 291–315, esp. 296.

87. Mark Thompson, *Forging War: The Media in Serbia, Croatia, and Bosnia-Herzegovina* (London: Article 19, International Center Against Censorship, May 1994); Snyder, *From Voting to Violence*, 213–20.

88. V. P. Gagnon, "Ethnic Nationalism and International Conflict: The Case of Serbia," *International Security* 19, no. 3 (Winter 1994–95): 130–66; Gagnon, *The Myth of Ethnic War: Serbia and Croatia in the 1990s* (Ithaca, NY: Cornell University Press, 2004).

89. Snyder and Ballentine, "Nationalism and the Marketplace of Ideas"; for comparable cases, see Katrin Voltmer, *The Media in Transitional Democracies* (New York: Polity, 2013), 187–88.

90. Newley Purnell and Jeff Horwitz, "Facebook's Hate-Speech Rules Collide with Indian Politics," *Wall Street Journal* (online), August 14, 2020; Kaye, *Speech Police*, 28–34.

91. Simmons, *Mobilizing for Human Rights*, 276; Patrick M. Regan and Errol A. Henderson, "Threats and Political Repression in Developing Countries: Are Democracies Internally Less Violent?" *Third World Quarterly* 23, no. 1 (February 2002): 119–36.

92. Marc Lynch, *Voices of the New Arab Public: Iraq, Al-Jazeera, and Middle East Politics Today* (New York: Columbia University Press, 2006), 24, 37.

93. Michael Barnett, *Dialogues in Arab Politics* (New York: Columbia University Press, 1998).

94. Telhami, *World through Arab Eyes*, 28–33.

95. Erik C. Nisbet, Magdalena Saldaña Thomas, J. Johnson, Guy Golan, and Anita Day, "Credibility Gaps and Public Opinion in a Competitive Media Environment: The Case of Arab Satellite TV News in Lebanon," *International Journal of Communication* 11 (August 2017): 3072–95.

96. Lynch, *Voices*, 26.

97. Lynch, *Voices*, 35.

98. Marc Lynch, "After the Arab Spring: How the Media Trashed the Transitions," *Journal of Democracy* 26, no. 4 (October 2015): 90–99; Marc Lynch, Deen Freelon, and Sean Aday, *Blogs*

and Bullets III: Syria's Socially Mediated Civil War (Washington, DC: United States Institute of Peace, 2014); Marc Lynch, Deen Freelon, and Sean Aday, *Blogs and Bullets IV: How Social Media Undermines Transitions to Democracy* (Washington, DC: United States Institute of Peace, 2016).

99. Kaye, *Speech Police*; Philip Napoli, *Social Media and the Public Interest: Media Regulation in the Disinformation Age* (New York: Columbia University Press, 2019).

100. Richard Ashby Wilson and Molly K. Land, "Hate Speech on Social Media: Content Moderation in Context," *Connecticut Law Review* 52, no. 1029 (2021): 449.

101. Evelyn Douek, "It's Not Over: The Oversight Board's Trump Decision Is Just the Start," *Lawfare*, May 5, 2021, https://www.lawfareblog.com/its-not-over-oversight-boards-trump-decision-just-the-start.

102. Amy Mitchell, https://www.pewresearch.org/staff/jeffrey-gottfried, Jeffrey Gottfried, https://www.pewresearch.org/staff/michael-barthel, Michael Barthel, and https://www.pewresearch.org/staff/nami-sumida, Nami Sumida, *Distinguishing between Factual and Opinion Statements in the News*, Pew Research Center, Journalism and Media (Washington, DC: June 18, 2018), https://www.journalism.org/2018/06/18/distinguishing-between-factual-and-opinion-statements-in-the-news/.

103. Benkler, Faris, and Roberts, *Network Propaganda*, 91–92.

104. Maira T. Vaca-Baquiero, *Four Theories of the Press: 60 Years and Counting* (New York: Routledge, 2018), 81–83.

105. Mark Jurkowitz, Amy Mitchell, Elisa Shearer, and Mason Walker, *U.S. Media Polarization and the 2020 Election: A Nation Divided*, Pew Research Center, January 24, 2020, at https://www.journalism.org/2020/01/24/u-s-media-polarization-and-the-2020-election-a-nation-divided/.

106. Percentages do not add to 100 because each respondent was randomly shown one of the options and asked to agree or disagree. See the technical appendix.

Chapter 8. Backlash against Human Rights Shaming

1. Aryeh Neier, "'Naming and Shaming': Still the Human Rights Movement's Best Weapon," *OpenGlobalRights*, July 11, 2018, https://www.openglobalrights.org/Naming-and-shaming-still-the-human-rights-movements-best-weapon/?lang=English.

2. César Rodríguez-Garavito and Krizna Gomez, "Illiberal Democracies and Human Rights: A New Playbook," *OpenGlobalRights*, June 28, 2018, https://www.openglobalrights.org/illiberal-democracies-and-human-rights-a-new-playbook/?lang=English; Yasmine Ergas, "Take Back the Future: Feminisms and the Coming Crisis of the Beijing Settlement," in "Dynamics of Global Feminism," special issue, *Journal of International Affairs* 72, no. 2 (Spring/Summer 2019): 19–36.

3. Alison Brysk, *The Future of Human Rights* (Cambridge: Polity, 2018), 21, also 13, 55, 99–103.

4. Vanessa Friedman and Elizabeth Paton, "What Is Going on with China, Cotton, and All of These Clothing Brands?," *New York Times*, April 2, 2021, https://www.nytimes.com/2021/03/29/style/china-cotton-uyghur-hm-nike.html.

5. Judith G. Kelley and Beth A. Simmons, "Indicators as Social Pressure in International Relations," *American Journal of Political Science* 59, no. 1 (January 2015): 55–70; Kelley and

Simmons, "Introduction: The Power of Global Performance Indicators," in *The Power of Global Performance Indicators*, ed. Judith G. Kelley and Beth A. Simmons (New York: Cambridge University Press, 2020), 5–6, 11.

6. Emilie Hafner-Burton, "Sticks and Stones: Naming and Shaming the Human Rights Enforcement Problem," *International Organization* 62, no. 4 (Fall 2008): 689–716; Amanda Murdie and David R. Davis, "Shaming and Blaming: Using Events Data to Assess the Impact of Human Rights INGOs," *International Studies Quarterly* 56, no. 1 (March 2012): 1–16.

7. Thomas Risse, Stephen Ropp, and Kathryn Sikkink, eds., *The Power of Human Rights* (New York: Cambridge University Press, 1999).

8. Giovanni Mantilla, "Forum Isolation: Social Opprobrium and the International Law of Internal Conflict," *International Organization* 72, no. 2 (Spring 2018): 317–50.

9. Among the numerous recent efforts to theorize the role of emotion in international relations more generally, see Neta Crawford, "The Passion of World Politics: Propositions on Emotion and Emotional Relationships," *International Security* 24, no. 4 (Spring 2000): 116–56; Jonathan Mercer, "Emotional Beliefs," *International Organization* 64, no. 1 (January 2010): 1–31; Mercer, "Feeling Like a State: Social Emotion and Identity," *International Theory* 6, no. 3 (November 2014): 515–35.

10. Donald L. Horowitz, *Ethnic Groups in Conflict* (Berkeley: University of California Press,1985), 143–49, 167–68; Horowitz, *The Deadly Ethnic Riot* (Berkeley: University of California Press, 2001), 540–53; Henri Tajfel, *Human Groups and Social Categories* (Cambridge: Cambridge University Press, 1981).

11. Marilyn Brewer, "Ingroup Identification and Intergroup Conflict," in *Social Identity, Intergroup Conflict, and Conflict Resolution*, ed. Richard Ashmore, David Wilder, and Lee Jussim (New York: Oxford University Press, 2001), 17–41; John C. Turner, *Rediscovering the Social Group: A Self-Categorization Theory* (Oxford: Basil Blackwell, 1987); Turner, "Social Identity Theory: Where Are We Now?" in *Social Identity: Context, Commitment, Content*, ed. Naomi Ellemers, R. Spears, and B. Doosje (New York: Wiley-Blackwell, 1999).

12. Thomas J. Scheff, "Shame and the Social Bond," *Sociological Theory* 18, no. 1 (March 2000): 84–99; Thomas J. Scheff and Suzanne M. Retzinger, *Emotions and Violence: Shame and Rage in Destructive Conflict* (Lexington, MA: Lexington Books, 1991).

13. An excellent survey of this literature written for an international relations audience is Robin Markwica, *Emotional Choices* (New York: Oxford University Press, 2018).

14. Scheff, "Shame and the Social Bond," 84–99.

15. Alfred Adler, *The Individual Psychology of Alfred Adler* (New York: Basic, 1956); Scheff, "Shame and the Social Bond," 86.

16. Karen Horney, *Neurosis and Human Growth* (New York: Norton, 1950).

17. Charles H. Cooley, *Human Nature and the Social Order* (New York: Scribner's, 1902), 183–84; Scheff, "Shame and the Social Bond," 88.

18. Keren Yarhi-Milo, *Who Fights for Reputation?* (Princeton, NJ: Princeton University Press, 2018).

19. Helen B. Lewis, *Shame and Guilt in Neurosis* (New York: International Universities Press, 1971).

20. Scheff, "Shame and the Social Bond," 95.

21. Scheff, "Shame and the Social Bond," 94–95; Lewis, *Shame and Guilt*, 37, 44–45, 248–49, 323.

22. D. F. Greenwald and D. W. Harder, "Domains of Shame," in *Shame: Interpersonal Behavior, Psychopathology, and Culture*, ed. Paul Gilbert (New York: Oxford University Press, 1998).

23. Daniel Sznycer, John Tooby, Leda Cosmides, Roni Porat, Shaul Shalvi, and Eran Halperin, "Shame Closely Tracks the Threat of Devaluation by Others, Even across Cultures," *PNAS* 113, no. 10 (March 2016): 2625–30, https://doi.org/10.1073/pnas.1514699113.

24. Paul Gilbert, "Evolution, Social Roles, and the Differences in Shame and Guilt," *Social Research* 70, no. 4 (Winter 2003): 1205–30, at 1213, 1225.

25. Markwica, *Emotional Choices*, 82.

26. Karisa Cloward, *When Norms Collide: Local Responses to Activism against Female Genital Mutilation and Early Marriage* (New York: Oxford University Press, 2016), 19–20, 228–51; Janice Boddy, "Womb as Oasis: The Symbolic Context of Pharaonic Circumcision in Rural Northern Sudan," *American Ethnologist* 9, no. 4 (November 1982): 682–98.

27. Michael Barnett, "Humanitarianism Transformed," *Perspectives on Politics* 3, no. 4 (December 2005): 723–40.

28. Human Rights Watch, "Reports," accessed March 20, 2019, http://www.hrw.org/publications.

29. See, for example, coverage in *Times of India*, https://timesofindia.indiatimes.com/topic/Cow-Vigilantes.

30. Simon Lewis and Shoon Naing, "Two Reuters Reporters Freed in Myanmar after More than 500 Days in Jail," *Reuters*, May 6, 2019, https://www.reuters.com/article/us-myanmar-journalists/two-reuters-reporters-freed-in-myanmar-after-more-than-500-days-in-jail-idUSKCN1SD056; Linda Lakhdhir, "Two Myanmar Journalists Freed, but Many Face Charges: Government Uses Draconian Laws to Keep a Grip on Media," Human Rights Watch, May 7, 2019, https://www.hrw.org/news/2019/05/07/two-myanmar-journalists-freed-many-face-charges#.

31. Sally Engle Merry, Kevin E. Davis, and Benedict Kingsbury, eds., *The Quiet Power of Indicators: Measuring Governance, Corruption, and the Rule of Law* (New York: Cambridge University Press, 2015).

32. Kelley and Simmons, *Power of Global Performance Indicators*, 5–6.

33. Judith G. Kelley, *Scorecard Diplomacy: Grading States to Influence Their Reputation and Behavior* (New York: Cambridge University Press, 2017), 12, 246–47, notes that indicators have the advantages over simple shaming of being comparative, potentially praising, and recurrent.

34. Kelley and Simmons, *Power of Global Performance Indicators*.

35. Thomas Risse, Stephen Ropp, and Kathryn Sikkink, eds., *The Persistent Power of Human Rights: From Commitment to Compliance* (New York: Cambridge University Press, 2013); Beth A. Simmons, *Mobilizing for Human Rights: International Law in Domestic Politics* (New York: Cambridge University Press, 2009). Kathryn Sikkink, in *Evidence for Hope: Making Human Rights Work in the 21st Century* (Princeton, NJ: Princeton University Press, 2017), 179, 212, expresses misgivings about the term *shaming* and says she prefers "shining a light." More generally on the debate over the effectiveness of human rights advocacy, see Christopher J. Fariss, "Respect for Human Rights Has Improved over Time: Modeling the Changing Standard of Accountability," *American Political Science Review* 108, no. 2 (May 2014): 297–318, with rebuttal in David Cingranelli and Mikhail Filippov, "Are Human Rights Practices Improving?" *American Political Science Review* 112, no. 4 (November 2018): 1083–89, and surrebuttal in

Christopher J. Fariss, "Yes, Human Rights Practices Are Improving over Time," *American Political Science Review* 113, no. 3 (August 2019): 868–81.

36. Murdie and Davis, "Shaming and Blaming."

37. Hafner-Burton, "Sticks and Stones."

38. Ann Marie Clark, "The Normative Context of Human Rights Criticism: Treaty Ratification and UN Mechanisms," in *The Persistent Power of Human Rights: From Commitment to Compliance*, ed. Thomas Risse, Stephen Ropp, and Kathryn Sikkink (New York: Cambridge University Press, 2013), 125–44.

39. Alexander Cooley and Matthew Schaaf, "Grounding the Backlash: Regional Security Treaties, Counternorms, and Human Rights in Eurasia," in *Human Rights Futures*, ed. Stephen Hopgood, Jack Snyder, and Leslie Vinjamuri (New York: Cambridge University Press, 2017), 159–88. For related works, see James C. Franklin, "Shame on You: The Impact of Human Rights Criticism on Political Repression in Latin America," *International Studies Quarterly* 52, no. 1 (March 2008): 187–211; Faradj Koliev, "Selecting for Shame: The Monitoring of Workers' Rights by the International Labour Organization, 1989 to 2011," *International Studies Quarterly* 62, no. 2 (June 2018): 437–52; Matthew Krain, "J'accuse! Does Naming and Shaming Perpetrators Reduce the Severity of Genocides or Politicides?" *International Studies Quarterly* 56, no. 3 (September 2012): 574–89; Darius Rejali, *Torture and Democracy* (Princeton, NJ: Princeton University Press, 2008).

40. Scheff and Retzinger, *Emotions and Violence*, 65.

41. Lewis, *Shame and Guilt*, 30, 37, 40.

42. June P. Tangney and Ronda L. Dearing, *Shame and Guilt* (New York: Guilford, 2002); Markwica, *Emotional Choices*, 19.

43. John Braithwaite, *Crime, Shame, and Reintegration* (New York: Cambridge University Press, 1989), 69–77.

44. Danielle Every, "'Shame on You': The Language, Practice, and Consequences of Shame and Shaming in Asylum Seeker Advocacy," *Discourse and Society* 24, no. 6 (November 2013): 667–86, at 670.

45. Nathan Harris, "Shame in Regulatory Settings," in *Regulatory Theory*, ed. Peter Drahos (Acton, Australia: ANU Press, 2017), 69–70.

46. Katherine J. Kramer, *The Politics of Resentment: Rural Consciousness in Wisconsin and the Rise of Scott Walker* (Chicago: University of Chicago Press, 2016); Claudia Wallis, "Trump's Victory and the Politics of Resentment," *Scientific American*, November 12, 2016, interview with Katherine Kramer.

47. Tangney and Dearing, *Shame and Guilt*.

48. Brené Brown, *I Thought It Was Just Me* (New York: Gotham, 2008).

49. Eliza Ahmed, John Braithwaite, Nathan Harris, and Valerie Braithwaite, *Shame Management through Reintegration* (New York: Cambridge University Press, 2001); Braithwaite, *Crime, Shame, and Reintegration*.

50. Braithwaite, *Crime, Shame, and Reintegration*, 83.

51. Harris, "Shame in Regulatory Settings," 59–61; Braithwaite, *Crime, Shame, and Reintegration*, 65–68.

52. Mark A. Drumbl, "Punishment, Postgenocide: From Guilt to Shame to Civis in Rwanda," *New York University Law Review* 75, no. 5 (November 2000): 1221–1323, at 1256.

53. Bert Ingelaire, "The Gacaca Courts in Rwanda," in *Traditional Justice and Reconciliation after Violent Conflict*, ed. Luc Huyse and Mark Salter (Stockholm: International Idea, 2008); Phil Clark, *The Gacaca Courts, Post-Genocide Justice and Reconciliation in Rwanda: Justice without Lawyers* (Cambridge: Cambridge University Press, 2010).

54. Erving Goffman, *The Presentation of Self in Everyday Life* (Garden City, NY: Doubleday, 1959), 13, 16, 49; Omar Lizardo and Jessica L. Collett, "Embarrassment and Social Organization: A Multiple Identities Model," *Social Forces* 92, no. 1 (September 2013): 353–75.

55. C. Cooley, *Human Nature and the Social Order*, 184–85.

56. Goffman, *Presentation of Self*, 14, 234; Erving Goffman, "On Cooling the Mark Out," *Psychiatry* 15, no. 4 (November 1952): 451–63.

57. Alexander Cooley, "The Emerging Politics of International Rankings and Ratings: A Framework for Analysis," in *Ranking the World: Grading States as a Tool of Global Governance*, ed. Alexander Cooley and Jack Snyder (New York: Cambridge University Press. 2015), 13–14.

58. Tajfel, *Human Groups and Social Categories*, 41–53.

59. John C. Turner, "Foreword to the First Edition: What the Social Identity Approach Is and Why It Matters," in *Psychology in Organizations: The Social Identity Approach*, ed. S. Alexander Haslam, 2d ed. (London: Sage, 2004), xvii–xx at xix; Henri Tajfel and John C. Turner, "An Integrative Theory of Intergroup Conflict," in *The Social Psychology of Intergroup Relations*, ed. W. G. Austin and S. Worchel (Monterey, CA: Brooks/Cole, 1979), 33–47, at 40–41.

60. Steven Ward, *Status and the Challenge of Rising Powers* (Cambridge: Cambridge University Press, 2017), 37–38. As Jonathan Mercer notes regarding British feelings of guilt and shame during the Boer War, these notions may be self-generated. The British experienced either pride or shame based on their own assessment of their behavior, which they then used as evidence of what others thought. See Jonathan Mercer, "The Illusion of International Prestige," *International Security* 41, no. 4 (Spring 2017): 133–68.

61. Muzafer Sherif, O. Harvey, B. White, W. Hood, and C. Sherif, *Experimental Study of Positive and Negative Intergroup Attitudes between Experimentally Produced Groups: Robbers Cave Study* (Norman: University of Oklahoma Press, 1954); Muzafer Sherif, O. Harvey, B. White, W. Hood, and C. Sherif, *Intergroup Conflict and Cooperation: The Robbers Cave Experiment* (Norman, OK: University Book Exchange, 1961).

62. Henri Tajfel, M. G. Billig, R. P. Bundy, and Claude Flament, "Social Categorization and Intergroup Behaviour," *European Journal of Social Psychology* 1, no. 2 (April/June 1971): 149–78.

63. Tajfel, *Human Groups and Social Categories*, 236.

64. John C. Turner, "Social Identity Theory: Where Are We Now?" in *Social Identity: Context, Commitment, Content*, ed. Naomi Ellemers, R. Spears, and B. Doosje (New York: Wiley-Blackwell, 1999), 7–8.

65. Frank Mols and Martin Weber, "Laying Sound Foundations for Social Identity Theory-Inspired European Union Attitude Research: Beyond Attachment and Deeply Rooted Identities," *Journal of Common Market Studies* 51, no. 3 (May 2013): 505–21, at 507.

66. Tajfel and Turner, "Integrative Theory of Intergroup Conflict," 41.

67. Brewer, "Ingroup Identification and Intergroup Conflict"; Deborah Welch Larson and Alexei Shevchenko, *Quest for Status: Chinese and Russian Foreign Policy* (New Haven, CT: Yale University Press, 2019).

68. Alastair Iain Johnston, "Treating International Institutions as Social Environments," *International Studies Quarterly* 45, no. 4 (December 2001): 487–515, at 494; John C. Turner, *Social Influence* (Bristol, PA: Open University Press, 1991).

69. Tajfel, *Human Groups and Social Categories*, 270–71.

70. Peggy Levitt and Sally Engle Merry, "Vernacularization on the Ground: Local Uses of Global Women's Rights in Peru, China, India, and the United States," *Global Networks* 9, no. 4 (October 2009): 441–61.

71. John Braithwaite and Peter Drahos, "Zero Tolerance, Naming and Shaming: Is There a Case for It with Crimes of the Powerful?" *Australian and New Zealand Journal of Criminology* 35, no. 3 (December 2002): 269–88.

72. Braithwaite and Drahos, "Zero Tolerance," 273.

73. Alastair Iain Johnston, *Social States: China in International Institutions, 1980–2000* (Princeton, NJ: Princeton University Press, 2008), 80; also Mantilla, "Forum Isolation," 324.

74. Margaret E. Keck and Kathryn Sikkink, *Activists beyond Borders: Advocacy Networks in International Politics* (Ithaca, NY: Cornell University Press 1998), 39–40, 59–66, 73–74.

75. Kwame Anthony Appiah, *The Honor Code: How Moral Revolutions Happen* (New York: Norton 2010), 53–100.

76. Lars Rensman, "Collective Guilt, National Identity, and Political Processes in Contemporary Germany," in *Collective Guilt*, ed. Nyla R. Branscombe and Bertjan Doosje (New York: Cambridge University Press, 2004), 169–92. When the in-group is the source of the negative information, this increases high-identifiers' feelings of guilt, while diminishing low-identifiers' feelings of guilt (because they think the group acknowledges the criticism). On "backdoor shaming" that evades social norms against shaming by using rhetorical moves such as decontextualization to conflate the difference between guilt and shame, see Roger Petersen, "Guilt, Shame, Balts, Jews," in *Confronting Memories of World War II*, ed. Daniel Chirot (Seattle: University of Washington, 2014), 258–82.

77. A. Cooley and Scharf, "Grounding the Backlash"; Randall Schweller and Xiaoyu Pu, "After Unipolarity: China's Visons of International Order in an Era of U.S. Decline," *International Security* 36, no. 1 (Summer 2011): 41–72.

78. Mercer, "Feeling Like a State," 515–35, at 515–26.

79. Ward, *Status and the Challenge of Rising Powers*, 38, 55–56.

80. Rebecca Adler-Nissen, "Stigma Management in IR: Transgressive Identities, Norms and Order in International Society," *International Organization* 68, no. 1 (January 2014): 143–76; Adler-Nissen, "Are We 'Lazy Greeks' or 'Nazi Germans'?" in *Hierarchies in World Politics*, ed. Ayse Zarakol (New York: Cambridge University Press, 2017), 198–218.

81. Todd H. Hall, "On Provocation: Outrage, International Relations, and the Franco–Prussian War," *Security Studies* 26, no. 1 (January 2017): 1–29; Ward, *Status and the Challenge of Rising Powers*, 50–51.

82. Brian Lickel, Toni Schmader, and Marchelle Barquissau, "The Evolution of Moral Emotions in Intergroup Contexts: The Distinction between Collective Guilt and Collective Shame," in Branscombe and Doosje, *Collective Guilt*, 52.

83. Peter Hays Gries, *China's New Nationalism: Pride, Politics, Diplomacy* (Berkeley: University of California Press, 2004); Jamie Gruffydd-Jones, "Citizens and Condemnation: Strategic Uses of International Human Rights Pressure in Authoritarian States," *Comparative Political*

Studies 52, no. 4 (March 2019): 579–612; Dmitri Trenin, *Should We Fear Russia?* (New York: Polity, 2016); Jennifer Lind, *Sorry States: Apologies in International Politics* (Ithaca, NY: Cornell University Press, 2008).

84. Mantilla, "Forum Isolation," 326; James C. Scott, *Weapons of the Weak: Everyday Forms of Peasant Resistance* (New Haven, CT: Yale University Press, 1985); Benjamin Moffitt, *The Global Rise of Populism: Performance, Style, and Representation* (Stanford, CA: Stanford University Press, 2016).

85. Arlene Stein, "Revenge of the Shamed: The Christian Right's Emotional Culture War," in *Passionate Politics: Emotions and Social Movements*, ed. Jeff Goodwin, James Jasper, and Francesca Polletta (Chicago: University of Chicago, 2001), 115–31.

86. Every, "Shame on You," 2013.

87. Keck and Sikkink, *Activists beyond Borders*, 66–72.

88. Henrietta Rajadurai and Susan Igras, *At the Intersection of Health, Social Well-Being and Human Rights: CARE's Experience Working with Communities towards the Abandonment of Female Genital Cutting* (Atlanta: CARE, 2004).

89. Gerry Mackie, "Ending Footbinding and Infibulation: A Convention Account," *American Sociological Review* 61, no. 6 (December 1996): 999–1017.

90. Cloward, *When Norms Collide*; Bettina Shell-Duncan, R. Naik, and C. Feldman-Jacobs, *A State-of-the-Art Synthesis on Female Genital Mutilation/Cutting: What Do We Know Now?* (New York: Population Council, 2016).

91. Ylva Hernlund, "Cutting without Ritual and Ritual without Cutting: Female 'Circumcision' and the Re-ritualization of Initiation in the Gambia," in *Female "Circumcision" in Africa: Culture, Controversy, and Change*, ed. Bettina Shell-Duncan and Ylva Hernlund (Boulder, CO: Lynn Rienner, 2000), 242.

92. Amanda Murdie, *Help or Harm? The Human Security Effects of NGOs* (Stanford, CA: Stanford University Press, 2014), 193.

93. Irena L. Sargsyan and Andrew Bennett, "Discursive Emotional Appeals in Sustaining Violent Social Movements in Iraq, 2003–11," *Security Studies* 25, no. 4 (October 2016): 608–45, at 609.

94. Sargsyan and Bennett, "Discursive Emotional Appeals," 618.

95. Marc Lynch, "Explaining the Awakening: Engagement, Publicity, and the Transformation of Iraqi Sunni Political Attitudes," *Security Studies* 20, no. 1 (January 2011): 36–72; Stephen Biddle, Jeffrey Friedman, and Jacob Shapiro, "Testing the Surge: Why Did Violence Decline in Iraq in 2007?" *International Security* 37, no. 1 (Summer 2012): 7–40.

96. Braithwaite and Drahos, "Zero Tolerance," 273–74.

97. John Gerard Ruggie, *Just Business: Multinational Corporations and Human Rights* (New York: Norton, 2013).

98. Alan M. Wachman, "Does the Diplomacy of Shame Promote Human Rights in China?" *Third World Quarterly* 22, no. 2 (April 2001): 257–81.

99. Jacob Ausderan, "How Naming and Shaming Affects Human Rights Perceptions in the Shamed Country," *Journal of Peace Research* 51, no. 1 (January 2014): 81–95.

100. Jenifer Whitten-Woodring, "Watchdog or Lapdog? Media Freedom, Regime Type, and Government Respect for Human Rights," *International Studies Quarterly* 53, no. 3 (September 2009): 595–625.

101. Timothy W. Crawford and Alan J. Kuperman, eds., *Gambling on Humanitarian Intervention: Moral Hazard, Rebellion and Civil War* (New York: Routledge, 2006).

102. Hafner-Burton, "Sticks and Stones."

103. Rachel Myrick and Jeremy Weinstein, "Making Sense of Human Rights Diplomacy: Symbolism or Concrete Impact?" Stanford University, manuscript, May 1, 2019.

104. Vinjamuri, "Human Rights Backlash," in Hopgood, Snyder, and Vinjamuri, *Human Rights Futures*, 114–34; Stein, "Revenge of the Shamed," 382.

105. Risse, Ropp, and Sikkink, *Power of Human Rights*.

106. Risse, Ropp, and Sikkink, *Persistent Power*.

107. Shogo Suzuki, "'Delinquent Gangs' in International System Hierarchy," in *Hierarchies in World Politics*, ed. Ayse Zarakol (New York: Cambridge University Press, 2017), 219–40, at 227–28, 231.

108. Markwica, *Emotional Choices*, 83.

109. Keck and Sikkink, *Activists beyond Borders*; Finnemore and Sikkink, "International Norm Dynamics"; Risse, Ropp, Sikkink, *Power of Human Rights*; Kathryn Sikkink, *The Justice Cascade: How Human Rights Prosecutions Are Changing World Politics* (New York: Norton, 2011); Sidney Tarrow, *Power in Movement* (New York: Cambridge University Press, 1998).

110. Braithwaite, *Crime, Shame, and Reintegration*, 84–97.

111. Jack Snyder and Alexander Cooley, "Conclusion: Rating the Rankings Craze," in Cooley and Snyder, *Ranking the World*, 178–93.

112. Levitt and Merry, "Vernacularization on the Ground"; Amitav Acharya, "How Ideas Spread: Whose Norms Matter? Norm Localization and Institutional Change in Asian Regionalism," *International Organization* 58, no. 2 (Spring 2004): 239–75.

113. Joshua L. Kalla and David E. Broockman, "Reducing Exclusionary Attitudes through Interpersonal Conversation: Evidence from Three Field Experiments," *American Political Science Review* 114, no. 2 (May 2020), 410–25.

114. Lynn Hunt, *Inventing Human Rights* (New York: Norton, 2008).

115. United Nations, "Transforming Our World: The 2030 Agenda for Sustainable Development," 2015, https://sustainabledevelopment.un.org/post2015/transformingourworld.

116. Abram Chayes and Antonia Handler Chayes, "On Compliance," *International Organization* 47, no. 2 (Spring 1993): 175–206.

117. Rachel Wahl, *Just Violence: Torture and Human Rights in the Eyes of the Police* (Stanford, CA: Stanford University Press, 2017).

Chapter 9. Entrenched Abuses of Women and Children

1. Thomas Risse, Stephen Ropp, and Kathryn Sikkink, eds., *The Persistent Power of Human Rights: From Commitment to Compliance* (New York: Cambridge University Press, 2013), 18–23.

2. The ideas in this chapter build on Suzanne Katzenstein and Jack Snyder, "Human Rights Pragmatism: Strategy, Context, and Effectiveness," presented at the International Relations Faculty Colloquium, Department of Politics, Princeton University, September 22, 2008; and Suzanne Katzenstein and Jack Snyder, "Expediency of the Angels," *National Interest*, no. 100 (March/April 2009), 58–65.

3. Gerry Mackie, "Ending Footbinding and Infibulation: A Convention Account," *American Sociological Review* 61, no. 6 (December 1996): 999–1017.

4. Bettina Shell-Duncan, R. Naik, and C. Feldman-Jacobs, *A State-of-the-Art Synthesis on Female Genital Mutilation/Cutting: What Do We Know Now?* (New York: Population Council, 2016).

5. Shell-Duncan, Naik, and Feldman-Jacobs, *State-of-the-Art Synthesis.*

6. Elizabeth Heger Boyle and Joseph Svec, "Success in Reducing Female Genital Cutting: A Multilevel Framework for Social Change," in *Alleviating World Suffering: The Challenge of Negative Quality of Life,* ed. Ronald E. Anderson (Cham, Switzerland: Springer, Social Indicators Research Series, 2017), 353–54; Bettina Shell-Duncan, David Gathara, and Zhuzhi Moore, *Female Genital Mutilation/Cutting in Kenya: Is Change Taking Place? Descriptive Statistics from Four Waves of Demographic and Health Surveys* (New York: Population Council, February 2017).

7. Lynn Thomas, "'Ngaitana (I Will Circumcise Myself)': Lessons from Colonial Campaigns to Ban Excision in Meru, Kenya," in *Female "Circumcision" in Africa: Culture, Controversy, and Change,* ed. Bettina Shell-Duncan and Ylva Hernlund (Boulder, CO: Lynne Rienner, 2000), 141.

8. Fran Hosken, *The Hosken Report: Genital and Sexual Mutilation of Females* (Lexington, MA: Women's International Network News, 1982 and 1993); Bettina Shell-Duncan and Ylva Hernlund, "Female 'Circumcision' in Africa: Dimensions of the Practice and Debates," in Shell-Duncan and Hernlund, *Female "Circumcision" in Africa,* 7.

9. CARE, "Integrating Rights-Based Approaches into Community-Based Health Projects: Experiences from the Prevention of Female Genital Cutting Project in East Africa," 20, published under the same title by Susan Igras, Jacinta Muteshi, Asmelash WoldeMariam, and Saida Ali, in *Health and Human Rights* 7, no. 2 (2004): 251–71.

10. Henrietta Rajadurai and Susan Igras, *At the Intersection of Health, Social Well-Being and Human Rights: CARE's Experience Working with Communities towards the Abandonment of Female Genital Cutting* (Atlanta: CARE, 2005).

11. Michelle C. Johnson, "Becoming a Muslim, Becoming a Person: Female 'Circumcision,' Religious Identity, and Personhood in Guinea-Bissau," in Shell-Duncan and Hernlund, *Female "Circumcision" in Africa,* 221–22.

12. Yasmin Bootwala, "A Review of Female Genital Cutting in the Dawoodi Bohra Community: Part 3—the Underpinnings of FGC in the Dawoodi Bohras," *Current Sexual Health Reports* 11, no. 3 (2019): 228–35, https://doi.org/10.1007/s11930-019-00214-x.

13. Karisa Cloward, *When Norms Collide: Local Responses to Activism against Female Genital Mutilation and Early Marriage* (New York: Oxford University Press, 2016), 120, 132.

14. Bettina Shell-Duncan, W. Obiero, and L. Muruli, "Women without Choices: The Debate over Medicalization of Female Genital Cutting and Its Impact on a Northern Kenyan Community," in Shell-Duncan and Hernlund, *Female "Circumcision" in Africa,* 109–28.

15. Mackie, "Ending Footbinding and Infibulation," 999–1017.

16. The Population Council, GTZ, and TOSTAN, "The Tostan Program: Evaluation of a Community Based Program in Senegal," August 2004.

17. Margaret E. Keck and Kathryn Sikkink, *Activists beyond Borders: Advocacy Networks in International Politics* (Ithaca, NY: Cornell University Press, 1998), 63.

18. Elinor Ostrom, *Governing the Commons: The Evolution of Institutions for Collective Action* (New York: Cambridge University Press, 1990), on Turkish fishermen.

19. Kwame Anthony Appiah, *The Honor Code: How Moral Revolutions Happen* (New York: Norton, 2010), 86–87.

20. Appiah, *Honor Code*, 98.

21. Cloward, *When Norms Collide*, 131–32.

22. Ylva Hernlund, "Cutting without Ritual and Ritual without Cutting: Female 'Circumcision' and the Re-ritualization of Initiation in the Gambia," in Shell-Duncan and Hernlund, *Female "Circumcision" in Africa*, 235–52.

23. Gerry Mackie, "Female Genital Cutting: The Beginning of the End," in Shell-Duncan and Hernlund, *Female "Circumcision" in Africa*, 279–80, acknowledges the importance of overlapping marriage markets.

24. Cloward, *When Norms Collide*, 63, 205–25.

25. Bettina Shell-Duncan, Katherine Wander, Ylva Hernlund, and Amadou Moreau, "Legislating Change? Responses to Criminalizing Female Genital Cutting in Senegal," *Law and Society Review* 47, no. 4 (December 2013): 803–35.

26. Bettina Shell-Duncan, Katherine Wander, Ylva Hernlund, and Amadou Moreau, "Dynamics of Change in the Practice of Female Genital Cutting in Senegambia: Testing Predictions of Social Convention Theory," *Social Science and Medicine* 73, no. 8 (October 2011): 1275–83.

27. United Nations Children's Fund (UNICEF), *Female Genital Mutilation/Cutting: A Statistical Overview and Exploration* (New York: UNICEF, 2013), 58. A study focusing on exploring Gambian men's perceptions toward FGC found that only 8 percent of men took part in the decision to cut their daughters, and that 71.7 percent were unaware of its health consequences. And 51.6 percent thought men had a role to play in its prevention. A. Kaplan, M. Forbes, I. Bonhoure, M. Utzet, M. Martín, M. Manneh, and H. Ceesay, "Female Genital Mutilation/Cutting (FGM/C) in the Gambia: Long-Term Health Consequences and Complications during Delivery and for the Newborn," *International Journal of Women's Health* 5 (June 2013): 323–31, http://www.doi.org/10.2147/IJWH.S42064.

28. Bettina Shell-Duncan, A. Moreau, K. Wander, S. Smith, "The Role of Older Women in Contesting Norms Associated with Female Genital Mutilation/Cutting in Senegambia: A Factorial Focus Group Analysis," *PLoS ONE* 13, no. 7 (July 2018): 199–217, https://doi.org/10.1371/journal.pone.0199217.

29. Charles Tilly, *Contention and Democracy in Europe, 1650–2000* (New York: Cambridge University Press, 2004), 17–20, discussed in chapter 3 in this volume.

30. Michael Mousseau, "The End of War: How a Robust Marketplace and Liberal Hegemony Are Leading to Perpetual World Peace," *International Security* 44, no. 1 (Summer 2019): 160–96.

31. Hill Gates, "Footbinding and Handspinning in Sichuan," in *Constructing China: The Interaction of Culture and Economics*, ed. Kenneth Lieberthal, Shuen-fu Lin, and Ernest P. Young (Ann Arbor: Michigan Monographs in Chinese Studies, University of Michigan, 1997), 177–94.

32. Sheri Berman, *Democracy and Dictatorship: From the Ancien Régime to the Present Day* (New York: Oxford University Press, 2019), 2–3, 7, 376–98.

33. Shell-Duncan, Naik, and Feldman-Jacobs, *State-of-the-Art Synthesis*; Koustuv Dalal, Stephen Lawoko, and Bjarne Jansson, "Women's Attitudes towards Discontinuation of Female Genital Mutilation in Egypt," *Journal of Injury and Violence Research* 2, no. 1 (January 2010): 41–47, doi: 10.5249/jivr.v2i1.33.

34. Elizabeth H. Boyle, *Female Genital Cutting: Cultural Conflict in the Global Community* (Baltimore, MD: Johns Hopkins University Press, 2002), 44.

35. UNICEF, *Female Genital Mutilation/Cutting: A Statistical Exploration* (New York: UNICEF, 2005), 9–12.

36. Lori Leonard, "Adopting Female 'Circumcision' in Southern Chad: The Experience of Myabe," in Shell-Duncan and Hernlund, *Female "Circumcision" in Africa*, ch. 9.

37. Shell-Duncan, Naik, and Feldman-Jacobs, *State-of-the-Art Synthesis*, 20.

38. Cloward, *When Norms Collide*; Bettina Shell-Duncan, Gathara, and Moore, *Female Genital Mutilation/Cutting in Kenya*, 16–17.

39. G. Kidanu, "Prevalence and Associated Factors of Female Genital Cutting among Young-Adult Females in Jigjiga District, Eastern Ethiopia: A Cross-Sectional Mixed Study," in *Researching Female Genital Mutilation/Cutting*, ed. Els Leye and Gily Coene (Brussels: Academic and Scientific Publishers, 2017), papers presented at the Second International Academic Seminar: Female Genital Mutilation/Cutting, https://www.aspeditions.be/nl-be/book/researching -female-genital-mutilationcutting-e-book/15983.htm.

40. For the concepts behind this theory, see Martha Finnemore, *National Interest in International Society* (Ithaca, NY: Cornell University Press, 1996), and works by the sociologist John Meyer.

41. Boyle, *Female Genital Cutting*, 120, 132.

42. Janice Boddy, "The Normal and the Aberrant in Female Genital Cutting: Shifting Paradigms," *Journal of Ethnographic Theory* 6, no. 2 (Autumn 2016): 41–69, at 55–60.

43. Ylva Hernlund, "Gambia," in Shell-Duncan and Hernlund, *Female "Circumcision" in Africa*, 240.

44. Mackie, "Female Genital Cutting," 272–74; Claudie Gosselin, "Handing over the Knife: Numu Women and the Campaign against Excision in Mali," in Shell-Duncan and Hernlund, *Female "Circumcision" in Africa*, 193–214, at 193, 198, 201–4.

45. Gosselin, "Handing over the Knife," 204.

46. Susan Igras, author interview, Washington DC, August 20, 2008. See also Susan Igras (CARE-USA), Jacinta Muteshi, Asmelash WoldeMariam (CARE-Ethiopia) and Said Ali (CARE-Kenya), "Integrating Rights-Based Approaches into Community-Based Health Projects: Experiences from the Prevention of Female Genital Cutting Project in East Africa," August 2002, 6–7.

47. Cloward, *When Norms Collide*, 150.

48. Johnson, "Becoming a Muslim," 230, and Johnson, "Making Mandinga or Making Muslims?" in *Transcultural Bodies: Female Genital Cutting in Global Context*, ed. Ylva Hernlund and Bettina Shell-Duncan (New Brunswick: Rutgers, 2007), 202, 219. On cultural reasons for differences in the response to human rights advocacy in Christian and Muslim communities, see Elizabeth Boyle, Barbara McMorris, and Mayra Gómez, "Local Conformity to International Norms: The Case of Female Genital Cutting," *International Sociology* 17, no. 1 (March 2002): 5–33.

49. Shell-Duncan et al., "Role of Older Women," 199–217.

50. Boyle, *Female Genital Cutting*, 145. Elizabeth Boyle and Kristin Carbone-Lopez, "Movement Frames and African Women's Explanations for Opposing Female Genital Cutting," *International Journal of Comparative Sociology* 47, no. 6 (December 2006): 435–65.

51. Elizabeth Heger Boyle and Amelia Cotton Corl, "Law and Culture in a Global Context: Intervention to Eradicate Female Genital Cutting," *Annual Review of Law and Social Science* 6 (2010): 195–215.

52. Shell-Duncan, Gathara, and Moore, *Female Genital Mutilation/Cutting in Kenya*, 17.

53. Cloward, *When Norms Collide*, 243–44, 251.

54. Janice Boddy, "Womb as Oasis: The Symbolic Context of Pharaonic Circumcision in Rural Northern Sudan," *American Ethnologist* 9, no. 4 (November 1982): 682–98; Shell-Duncan and Hernlund, "Female 'Circumcision' in Africa," 21.

55. Boyle and Svec, "Success in Reducing Female Genital Cutting," 358.

56. Cloward, *When Norms Collide*, 190.

57. Cloward, *When Norms Collide*, 243; Shell-Duncan and Hernlund, *Female "Circumcision" in Africa*, 21.

58. Johnson, "Making Mandinga," 202–24.

59. Cloward, *When Norms Collide*, 245–46.

60. Sarah Bellows-Blakely, "Girlhood in Africa," *Oxford Research Encyclopedia of African History* (Oxford: Oxford University Press, 2020).

61. Jomo Kenyatta, *Facing Mount Kenya* (Heinemann Kenya, 1938; New York: AMS Press, 1978), 133; Shell-Duncan, Gathara, and Moore, *Female Genital Mutilation/Cutting in Kenya*, 8.

62. Shell-Duncan, Gathara, and Moore, *Female Genital Mutilation/Cutting in Kenya*, 8; Cloward, *When Norms Collide*, 104.

63. World Health Organization, "Female Genital Mutilation—Programmes to Date: What Works and What Doesn't" (Department of Reproductive Health and Research, original 1999, updated 2011), 17–18.

64. Emmanuel K. Bunei and Joseph K. Rono, "A Critical Understanding of Resistance to Criminalization of Female Genital Mutilation in Kenya," in *The Palgrave Handbook of Criminology and the Global South*, ed. Kerry Carrington, Russell Hogg, John Scott, and Maximo Sozzo (New York: Springer International, 2018), 901–12.

65. Janice Boddy, *Civilizing Women: British Crusades in Colonial Sudan* (Princeton, NJ: Princeton University Press, 2007).

66. Boddy, "Normal and the Aberrant," 54.

67. Boddy, "Normal and the Aberrant," 55.

68. Hernlund, "Cutting without Ritual."

69. Boyle and Svec, "Success in Reducing Female Genital Cutting," 353.

70. Elizabeth Syer, "The Status of the Crusade to Eradicate Female Genital Mutilation: A Comparative Analysis of Laws and Programs in the US and Egypt," *Penn State International Law Review* 22, no. 4 (Spring 2004): 843–62.

71. Shell-Duncan, *Female Genital Mutilation/Cutting in Kenya*.

72. Johnson, "Becoming a Muslim," 231.

73. Gosselin, "Handing over the Knife," 213.

74. Shell-Duncan et al., "Legislating Change?," 803–35, at 831.

75. Boyle and Svec, "Success in Reducing Female Genital Cutting," 357–58.

76. Daniel N. Posner, *Institutions and Ethnic Politics in Africa* (New York: Cambridge University Press, 2005); Lant Pritchett, Michael Woolcock, and Matt Andrews, "Looking Like a

State: Techniques of Persistent Failure in State Capability for Implementation," *Journal of Development Studies* 49, no. 1 (January 2013): 1–18.

77. For documents outlining transitional justice "best practices" according to the International Center for Transitional Justice, see "Policy Relations," ICTJ, accessed September 21, 2021, https://www.ictj.org/our-work/policy-relations.

78. Cloward, *When Norms Collide*, 250.

79. In addition to these participatory persuasion strategies, grassroots campaigns are usually run by local community members and conducted in the local dialect. In its first campaign, for instance, Tostan was run by Senegalese and conducted in Wolof rather than French.

80. World Health Organization, "Female Genital Mutilation," 35.

81. CARE, "Integrating Rights-Based Approaches," 10–11.

82. CARE, "Integrating Rights-Based Approaches," 20.

83. Anika Rahman and Nahid Toubia, eds., *Female Genital Mutilation: A Guide to Laws and Policies Worldwide* (New York: Zed Books in association with Center for Reproductive Law and Policy and Research, Action and Information Network for the Bodily Integrity of Women, 2000), 78–82.

84. Syer, "Status of the Crusade to Eradicate Female Genital Mutilation," 858.

85. CARE, "Integrating Rights-Based Approaches," 10.

86. Bettina Shell-Duncan, Carolyne Njue, and Zhuzhi Moore, "Trends in Medicalisation of Female Genital Mutilation/Cutting: What Do the Data Reveal? Updated October 2018," in *Evidence to End FGM/C: Research to Help Women Thrive* (New York: Population Council, 2018), 1–15.

87. Nina Van Eekert, Els Leye, and Sarah Van de Velde, "The Association between Women's Social Position and the Medicalization of Female Genital Cutting in Egypt," *International Perspectives on Sexual and Reproductive Health* 44, no. 3 (September 2018): 101–9.

88. Shell-Duncan, Njue, and Moore, "Trends in Medicalisation."

89. Author interview with senior public health research scholar at Al Azhar University in Cairo, 2012.

90. Shell-Duncan, Njue, and Moore, "Trends in Medicalisation," 14–15, 19–21.

91. Shell-Duncan, Njue, and Moore, "Trends in Medicalisation."

92. Boyle and Svec, "Success in Reducing Female Genital Cutting," 357.

93. L. Amede Obiora, "A Refuge from Tradition and the Refuge of Tradition: On Anticircumcision Paradigms," in Hernlund and Shell-Duncan, *Transcultural Bodies*, 81.

94. Annie Bunting, "Stages of Development: Marriage of Girls and Teens as an International Human Rights Issue," *Social and Legal Studies* 14, no. 1 (March 2005): 17–38. Fistula is an abnormal connection between different organs, such as between the bowel, bladder, or vagina.

95. Ruth Gaffney-Rhys, "International Law as an Instrument to Combat Child Marriage," *International Journal of Human Rights* 15, no. 3 (March 2011): 359–73, at 360.

96. Cloward, *When Norms Collide*, 248; Bunting, "Stages of Development."

97. Cloward, *When Norms Collide*, 119.

98. Cloward, *When Norms Collide*, 239.

99. Cloward, *When Norms Collide*, 193.

100. Sheetal Sekhri and Sisir Debnath, "Intergenerational Consequences of Early Age Marriages of Girls: Effect on Children's Human Capital," *Journal of Development Studies* 50, no. 12 (2014): 1670–86.

101. Zaki Wahhaj, "An Economic Model of Early Marriage," *Journal of Economic Behavior and Organization* 152 (September 2018): 147–76.

102. Susan B. Schaffnit, Mark Urassa, and David W. Lawson, "'Child Marriage' in Context: Exploring Local Attitudes towards Early Marriage in Rural Tanzania," *Sexual and Reproductive Health Matters* 27, no. 1 (2019): 93–105; Susan B. Schaffnit, Anushé Hassan, Mark Urassa, and David W. Lawson, "Parent–Offspring Conflict Unlikely to Explain 'Child Marriage' in Northwestern Tanzania," *Nature Human Behaviour* 3, no. 4 (2019): 346–53.

103. Sekhri and Debnath, "Intergenerational Consequences of Early Age Marriages of Girls," 1670–86.

104. Wahhaj, "Economic Model of Early Marriage."

105. Simon Haenni and Guilherme Lichand, "Harming to Signal: Child Marriage vs. Public Donations in Malawi," University of Zurich Department of Economics Working Paper no. 348, June 2020, https://SSRN.com/abstract=3633803.

106. Valerie Hudson and Hilary Matfess, "In Plain Sight: The Neglected Linkage between Brideprice and Violent Conflict," *International Security* 42, no. 1 (Summer 2017): 7–40; Scott Cook and Cameron Theis, "In Plain Sight? Reconsidering the Linkage between Brideprice and Violent Conflict," *Conflict Management and Peace Science* 38, no. 2 (2021): 129–46.

107. Nava Ashraf, Natalie Bau, Nathan Nunn, and Alessandra Voena, "Brideprice and Female Education," *Journal of Political Economy* 128, no. 2 (February 2020): 591–641.

108. Ashraf et al., "Brideprice and Female Education."

109. Wahhaj, "Economic Model of Early Marriage."

110. Cloward, *When Norms Collide*, 237–40.

111. Ragnhild L. Muriaas, Vibeke Wang, Lindsay J. Benstead, Boniface Dulani, and Lise Rakner, "Why Campaigns to Stop Child Marriage Can Backfire," Chr. Michelsen Institute, CMI Brief no. 2019:04, 2019.

112. Esther Duflo, P. Dupas, M. Kremer, and S. Sinei, "Education and HIV/AIDS Prevention: Evidence from a Randomized Evaluation in Western Kenya," World Bank Policy Research Working Paper 4024 (2006); Emmanuel Adu Boahen and Chikako Yamauchi, "The Effect of Female Education on Adolescent Fertility and Early Marriage: Evidence from Free Compulsory Universal Basic Education in Ghana," *Journal of African Economies* 27, no. 2 (2018): 227–48.

113. Lucia Corno, Nicole Hildebrandt, and Alessandra Voena, "Age of Marriage, Weather Shocks, and the Direction of Marriage Payments," *Econometrica* 88, no. 3 (May 2020): 879–915.

114. Cloward, *When Norms Collide*, 239; UNICEF, *Female Genital Mutilation/Cutting* (2013).

115. Cloward, *When Norms Collide*, 250–51. The program "Girls Not Brides" was established in 2011 by the Elders, Nelson Mandela's organization: "Girls Not Brides: Lessons Learned from Selected National Initiatives to End Child Marriage," July 2015, http://www.ungei.org/resources/files/Girls_Not_Brides.pdf; "A Theory of Change on Child Marriage—Girls Not Brides," Girls Not Brides, July 9, 2014, https://www.girlsnotbrides.org/theory-change-child-marriage-girls-brides/. Melinda Gates devoted one of six chapters of her book, *The Moment of Lift: How Empowering Women Changes the World* (New York: Flatiron Books, 2019), to the problem, advocating vernacularized persuasion and changes in local law.

116. Wahhaj, "Economic Model of Early Marriage," reports that "using data from 48 countries with at least two DHS/MICS surveys in the period 1986–2010, a UNFPA 2012 study finds little overall change in the practice in either rural or urban areas."

117. Dylan Groves's fieldwork, Columbia University.

118. UN Population Fund, *Marrying Too Young: End Child Marriage* (New York: UNFPA, 2012).

119. Kaushik Basu, "Child Labor: Cause, Consequence, and Cure, with Remarks on International Labor Standards," *Journal of Economic Literature* 37 (September 1999): 1083–1119.

120. "The End of Child Labour: Within Reach," Report of the Director-General, International Labour Conference, 95th Session, Report I(B), (2006), 10.

121. Carolyn M. Moehling, "State Child Labor Laws and the Decline of Child Labor," *Explorations in Economic History* 36, no. 1 (January 1999): 72–106.

122. Myron Weiner, *The Child and the State in India: Child Labour and Education Policy in Comparative Perspective* (Princeton, NJ: Princeton University Press, 1991).

123. Shareen Hertel, *Unexpected Power: Conflict and Change among Transnational Activists* (Ithaca, NY: Cornell University Press, 2006), ch. 3.

124. International Labour Organization, *Good Practices in Actions against Child Labour: A Synthesis Report of Seven Country Studies, 1997–98*, International Programme on the Elimination of Child Labour, December 1, 2001, 19–20. See also Hertel, *Unexpected Power*, 47–49.

125. International Labour Office, "A Future without Child Labour: Global Report under the Follow-up to the ILO Declaration on Fundamental Principles and Rights at Work," 90th session report I(B), 2002, 88–89.

126. International Labour Organization, UNICEF, and the World Bank, *Understanding Trends in Child Labor* (Rome: Understanding Children's Work Programme, November 2017); Ana C. Dammert, Jacobus de Hoop, Eric Mvukiyehe, and Furio C. Rosati, "The Effects of Public Policy on Child Labor," Policy Research Working Paper no. 7999, World Bank, March 2017.

127. Thanks to Dylan Groves for discussion on this point.

128. Robert Jervis, *System Effects* (Princeton, NJ: Princeton University Press, 1997).

129. Robert Jensen and Emily Oster, "The Power of TV: Cable Television and Women's Status in India," *Quarterly Journal of Economics* 124, no. 3 (2009): 1057–94.

130. Emma Riley, "Role Models in Movies: The Impact of Queen of Katwe on Students' Educational Attainment," CSAE Working Paper WPS/2017-13, July 14, 2018, https://www.csae.ox.ac.uk/materials/papers/csae-wps-2017-13.pdf.

Chapter 10. Human Rights at a Time of Global Stalemate

1. John Shattuck and Kathryn Sikkink, "Practice What You Preach: Global Human Rights Leadership Begins at Home," *Foreign Affairs* 100, no. 3 (May/June 2021), 150–60.

2. Jack Snyder, "The Broken Bargain: How Nationalism Came Back," *Foreign Affairs* 98, no. 2 (March/April 2019), 54–60; G. John Ikenberry, *A World Safe for Democracy* (New Haven, CT: Yale University Press, 2020).

3. John Mearsheimer, *The Great Delusion: Liberal Dreams and International Realities* (New Haven, CT: Yale University Press, 2018).

4. Robert A. Pape, "When Duty Calls: A Pragmatic Standard of Humanitarian Intervention," *International Security* 37, no. 1 (Summer 2012): 41–80.

5. James D. Fearon and Andrew Shaver, "Civil War Violence and Refugee Outflows," May 27, 2020, https://static1.squarespace.com/static/5a7d0ffaa9db09345b7ef6ba/t/5ed00cbe3eaad

50ebc203174/1590693059681/refprod_may_2020.pdf; Michael Clemens, "Does Development Reduce Migration?" Center for Global Development Working Paper No. 359, April 2014, https://www.cgdev.org/sites/default/files/does-development-reduce-migration_final_0.pdf.

6. Dale C. Copeland, *Economic Interdependence and War* (Princeton, NJ: Princeton University Press, 2014).

7. Henry Farrell and Abraham L. Newman, *Of Privacy and Power: The Transatlantic Struggle over Freedom and Security* (Princeton, NJ: Princeton University Press, 2019); Alexander Cooley and Daniel Nexon, *Exit from Hegemony: The Unraveling of the American Global Order* (New York: Oxford University Press, 2020), 196–200.

8. Carnegie Endowment for International Peace, "Global Protest Tracker," last updated September 3, 2021, https://carnegieendowment.org/publications/interactive/protest-tracker.

9. Daniel Byman, "Forever Enemies? The Manipulation of Ethnic Identities to End Ethnic Wars," *Security Studies* 9, no. 3 (Spring 2000): 149–90.

10. Elizabeth Sperber and Erin Hern, "Pentecostal Identity and Citizen Engagement in Sub-Saharan Africa: New Evidence from Zambia," *Politics and Religion* 11, no. 4 (June 2018): 1–33; Gwyneth McClendon and Rachel Beatty Riedl, *From Pews to Politics: Religious Sermons and Political Participation in Africa* (New York: Cambridge University Press, 2019).

11. Samuel P. Huntington, *The Third Wave: Democratization in the Late Twentieth Century* (Norman: University of Oklahoma Press, 1993).

12. Tenzin Dorjee, *The Tibetan Nonviolent Struggle*, ICNC Monograph (Washington, DC: International Center on Nonviolent Conflict, 2015), https://www.nonviolent-conflict.org/wp-content/uploads/2016/01/The-Tibetan-Nonviolent-Struggle.pdf.

13. Eric Foner, *The Fiery Trial: Abraham Lincoln and American Slavery* (New York: Norton, 2010), xviii–xix.

14. From a poem by Martin Niemöller.

15. Richard Youngs, "The New EU Global Human Rights Sanctions Regime: Breakthrough or Distraction?" Carnegie Europe, December 14, 2020, https://carnegieeurope.eu/2020/12/14/new-eu-global-human-rights-sanctions-regime-breakthrough-or-distraction-pub-83415.

16. Daniel Goldstein, *Outlawed: Between Security and Rights in a Bolivian City* (Durham, NC: Duke University Press, 2012); Rachel Wahl, *Just Violence: Torture and Human Rights in the Eyes of the Police* (Stanford, CA: Stanford University Press, 2017); Michael Barnett and Martha Finnemore, *Rules for the World: International Organizations in Global Politics* (Ithaca, NY: Cornell University Press, 2004), 73–120.

17. Ronald F. Inglehart, *Cultural Evolution: People's Motivations Are Changing, and Reshaping the World* (New York: Cambridge University Press, 2018).

INDEX

A NOTE ON THE TYPE

This book has been composed in Arno, an Old-style serif typeface in the classic Venetian tradition, designed by Robert Slimbach at Adobe.

Printed in the USA
CPSIA information can be obtained
at www.ICGtesting.com
JSHW021548121024
71500JS00002B/4

9 780691 231556